PRUDENCE LEITH founded Leith's Good Food, a City party-catering business which delivers all over London, in 1964; Leith's Restaurant, considered one of the top ten in London today, in 1969; and Leith's School of Food and Wine, Notting Hill Gate, in 1975.

Born in South Africa in 1940, she became addicted to cooking while in Paris, and trained at the Cordon Bleu school in London. She began her catering career from a bed-sitter in Earls Court, travelling about on the Tube with peach flans and cucumber soup. She has published three previous cookbooks and is cookery correspondent of the *Sunday Express*. Married to Rayne Kruger (writer and fellow-Director of the Leith's Group), she has two children and divides her time between her restaurant, school, catering business and Leith's Farm in Oxfordshire.

CAROLINE WALDEGRAVE, now Principal of Leith's School of Food and Wine, joined Leith's Good Food as a cook in 1971 after training at the Cordon Bleu school in London. She has studied food and cooking in America and is a qualified instructor in wine. She was born in 1952 and is married to William Waldegrave MP.

Leith's Cookery Course

Leith's Cookery Course consists of three books based, respectively, on the beginners', intermediate and advanced courses at Leith's School of Food and Wine.

Book 1 combines factual information about food and detailed instruction of kitchen techniques with step by step French and English recipes designed for the beginner.

Book 2 assumes basic knowledge and cooking experience on the part of the reader. The recipes build up to give the accomplished learner some mastery of French, English and many other *cuisines*.

Book 3 is for the dedicated amateur, or the professional cook: its recipes enable the reader to produce classic *haute cuisine* dishes with confidence.

Leith's Cookery Course 1

PRUDENCE LEITH
and
CAROLINE WALDEGRAVE

FONTANA PAPERBACKS

First published by Fontana Paperbacks 1979
Copyright © Leith's Farm Ltd 1979
Filmset in Monophoto Times by
Northumberland Press Ltd, Gateshead, Tyne and Wear
and printed in Great Britain by
Richard Clay (The Chaucer Press) Ltd, Bungay, Suffolk

ISBN 063 5271 05

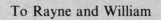

To Rayne and William

CONTENTS

ACKNOWLEDGEMENTS

We would like to thank, first and foremost, the staff and students of Leith's School of Food and Wine for testing, re-testing and perfecting the recipes, with special thanks to Sally Procter.

We also pay grateful tribute to most of the good cookery writers of today, especially to Rosemary Hume, Elizabeth David, Jane Grigson, Delia Smith, Katie Stewart, Robin Howe and Margaret Costa, whose recipes we have unashamedly pinched for use in the School, and used for inspiration and reference for this book.

For painstaking work in compiling the book, and for constant good temper, we would like to thank Polly Tyrer, Seemah Joshua, Margaret Cain and June Avis; and for recipe ideas and general helpfulness Jean Reynaud and Chef Max Markarian of Leith's Restaurant, and the staff of Leith's Good Food (Caterers).

In addition our thanks are due to Colin Cullimore, CBE, Managing Director of J. H. Dewhurst Ltd, for his help on the meat chapters, and to the White Fish Authority and the Herring Industry Board for helping on the fish chapters.

Finally, we would like to thank Myra Street for editing this book.

P.L.
C.W.

Note: Purists will complain about the hotch-potch of English and French culinary terms used in these books. We are unrepentant: French words are now so much part of the cook's vocabulary that they cannot be substituted. 'Sauté potatoes', for example, is precise and unambiguous. 'Fried potatoes' could mean chips, 'pommes sautées' could mean apples, and 'pommes de terre sautées' is too long and pompous. French words, we contend, are part of the international language of the kitchen.

P.L
C.W.

INTRODUCTION

LEITH'S COOKERY COURSE consists of three books. *Book 1* contains the chapter 'All about Cooking' which I hope answers every question that the cook, beginner or professional, is ever likely to ask – from how to grease a cake tin to how to carve smoked salmon, skin an eel or bone a turkey. The recipes in *Book 1* range from the very simple – poached eggs, rice pudding and macaroni cheese, for example – to the more complicated roast pheasant with sauerkraut or Chinese cabbage and apple salad; but all make use of the basic skills that are fundamental to good cooking.

Book 2 builds on those skills: the recipes become more advanced and there is special emphasis on yeast cookery, soufflé making, and *cuisines* other than French and British. It should, I think, provide a challenge to the interested cook and be a useful manual for the experienced one.

Book 3 is unashamedly written for the dedicated cook or enthusiastic amateur. It is not for the bachelor in a bed-sitter or the overworked Mum on a tight budget. It is, rather, for those who want to practise the art – as well as the science – of cooking, and who long occasionally to produce food as perfect as in the best restaurants.

Once the basic cooking methods have been mastered, advanced cookery is much like simple cookery: the techniques and ingredients are merely used in ever more interesting combinations. Someone who can make shortcrust pastry, custard, choux paste and caramel, and can whip cream, can also make that amazing pyramid of a French wedding cake, Gateau St Honoré. However, many keen enthusiasts, having realized this, start too soon to be 'creative', wrongly imagining that if one glass of sherry in a dish is good, four must be four times better; that if a recipe calls for a pinch of fresh thyme, two tablespoons of dried herbs must be an improvement.

My advice, especially to beginners, is to stick like a limpet to the recipe, and not hesitate to weigh and measure quantities. After a while you begin to tell by the look, texture or taste if the quantities are right; but I've been cooking all my grown-up life and I still weigh the beef to work out the roasting time, look up quantities for unfamiliar cakes, measure every ingredient for choux pastry.

When planning a menu, the rule is to keep it simple. If the main course needs last-minute work, choose a starter and pudding that can be done in advance. Try to balance the texture, colour and taste of the meal: avoid three white courses (vichyssoise, chicken with rice, and syllabub, for example); avoid cream or alcohol in all the courses; try to include something crisp and crunchy if the main part of the meal is soft and smooth. Serve vegetables that provide contrast in colour and texture – not cabbage with sprouts, for example.

The sight of food should make the mouth water, and induce feelings of positive greed and hunger. I think this is best achieved not by cutting radishes into roses or tomatoes into waterlilies, but by presenting food simply and freshly, with perhaps a sprig of watercress to set off the colour, or surrounded by simple fried croutons, or dusted with finely chopped herbs.

This does not mean that food should ever be sloppily served, or presented in a way which suggests anything other than care and calm organization. The cherished vision of great chefs gripped with rage and hurling knives is a myth. By and large, knife-hurlers make bad chefs, and the qualities required to earn a reputation for culinary genius are more mundane: a quiet temperament, a logical mind, a love of order – and of food. Another pre-requisite is clear information and a set of interesting, reliable recipes that whet the appetite and challenge the cook to attempt new dishes. I hope that this is what the three books in *Leith's Cookery Course* provide.

P.L.

1
All about Cooking

◆

CONVERSION TABLES

The tables below are approximate, and do not conform in all respects to the official conversions, but we have found them convenient for cooking.

WEIGHTS

Imperial	Metric
$\frac{1}{4}$oz	7$\frac{1}{2}$–8g
$\frac{1}{2}$oz	15g
$\frac{3}{4}$oz	20g
1oz	30g
2oz	55g
3oz	85g
4oz ($\frac{1}{4}$lb)	110g
5oz	140g
6oz	170g
7oz	200g
8oz ($\frac{1}{2}$lb)	225g
9oz	255g
10oz	285g
11oz	310g
12oz ($\frac{3}{4}$lb)	340g
13oz	370g
14oz	400g
15oz	425g
16oz (1lb)	450g

Imperial	Metric
1¼lb	560g
1½lb	675g
2lb	900g
3lb	1·35 kilos
4lb	1·8 kilos
5lb	2·3 kilos
6lb	2·7 kilos
7lb	3·2 kilos
8lb	3·4 kilos
9lb	4·0 kilos
10lb	4·5 kilos

LIQUID MEASURES

	ml	fl.oz
1¾ pints	1000 (1 litre)	35
1 pint	570	20
¾ pint	425	15
½ pint	290	10
⅓ pint	190	6·6
¼ pint (1 gill)	150	5
	56	2
2 scant tablespoons	28	1
1 teaspoon	5	

WINE QUANTITIES

	ml	fl.oz
Average wine bottle	730	25¾
1 glass wine	100	3½
1 glass port or sherry	70	2½
1 glass liqueur	45	1½

LENGTHS

Imperial	Metric
$\frac{1}{2}$in	1cm
1in	2$\frac{1}{2}$cm
2in	5cm
6in	15cm
12in	30cm

APPROXIMATE AMERICAN/EUROPEAN CONVERSIONS

Commodity	USA	Metric	Imperial
Flour	1 cup	140g	5oz
Caster and granulated sugar	1 cup	225g	8oz
Caster and granulated sugar	2 level tablespoons	30g	1oz
Brown sugar	1 cup	170g	6oz
Butter/margarine/lard	1 cup	225g	8oz
Sultanas/raisins	1 cup	200g	7oz
Currants	1 cup	140g	5oz
Ground almonds	1 cup	110g	4oz
Golden syrup	1 cup	340g	12oz
Uncooked rice	1 cup	200g	7oz

Note: In American recipes, when quantities are stated as spoons, 'level' spoons are meant. English recipes (and those in this book) call for rounded spoons except where stated otherwise. This means that 2 American tablespoons equal 1 English tablespoon.

USEFUL MEASUREMENTS

1 American cup	225ml/8 fl.oz
1 egg	56ml/2 fl.oz
1 egg white	28ml/1 fl.oz
1 rounded tablespoon flour	30g/1oz
1 rounded tablespoon cornflour	30g/1oz
1 rounded tablespoon sugar	30g/1oz
2 rounded tablespoons breadcrumbs	30g/1oz
2 level teaspoons gelatine	8g/$\frac{1}{4}$oz

30g/1oz granular (packet) aspic sets 570ml (1 pint) liquid. 15g/$\frac{1}{2}$oz powdered gelatine, or 4 leaves, will set 570ml (1 pint) liquid. (However, in hot weather, or if the liquid is very acid, like lemon juice, or if the jelly contains solid pieces of fruit or meat and is to be turned out of the dish or mould, 20g/$\frac{3}{4}$oz should be used.)

OVEN TEMPERATURES

C	F	Gas mark
70	150	$\frac{1}{4}$
80	175	$\frac{1}{4}$
100	200	$\frac{1}{2}$
110	225	$\frac{1}{2}$
130	250	1
140	275	1
150	300	2
170	325	3
180	350	4
190	375	5
200	400	6
220	425	7
230	450	8
240	475	8
250	500	9
270	525	9
290	550	9

GLOSSARY OF COOKING TERMS

Abats: French for offal (hearts, livers, brains, tripe etc.). Americans call them 'variety meats'.

Bain-marie: A baking tin half-filled with hot water in which terrines, custards etc. stand while cooking. The food is protected from direct fierce heat and cooks in a gentle, steamy atmosphere. Also a large container which will hold a number of pans standing in hot water, used to keep soups, sauces etc. hot without further cooking.

Bard: To tie bacon or pork fat over a joint of meat, game bird or poultry, to be roasted. This helps to prevent the flesh from drying out.

Baste: To spoon over liquid (sometimes stock, sometimes fat) during cooking to prevent drying out.

Beignets: Fritters.

Beurre manié: Butter and flour in equal quantities worked together to a soft paste, and used as a liaison or thickening for liquids. Small pieces are whisked into boiling liquid. As the butter melts it disperses the flour evenly through the liquid, so thickening it without causing lumps.

Beurre noisette: Browned butter – see *Noisette* (a).

Bisque: Shellfish soup, smooth and thickened.

Blanch: Originally, to whiten by boiling, e.g. briefly to boil sweetbreads or brains to remove traces of blood, or to boil almonds to make the brown skin easy to remove, leaving the nuts white. Now commonly used to mean parboiling (as in blanching vegetables when they are parboiled prior to freezing, or precooked so that they have only to be reheated before serving).

Bouchées: Small puff pastry cases like miniature vol-au-vents.

Bouillon: Broth or uncleared stock.

Bouquet garni: Parsley stalks, small bay leaf, fresh thyme, celery stalk, sometimes with a blade of mace, tied together with string and used to flavour stews etc. Removed before serving.

Braise: To bake or stew slowly on a bed of vegetables in a covered pan.

Canapé: A small bread or biscuit base, sometimes fried, spread or covered with savoury paste, egg etc., used for cocktail titbits or as an accompaniment to meat dishes. Sometimes used to denote the base only, as in *champignons sur canapé*.

Caramel: Sugar cooked to a toffee.

Chateaubriand: Roast fillet steak, for two people or more.

Clarified butter: Butter that has been separated from milk particles and other impurities which cause it to look cloudy when melted, and to burn easily when heated. It is usually clarified by first heating until foaming, then skimming; or (which is easier) straining through a double thickness of muslin, a coffee filter paper, or 2 J-cloths.

Court bouillon: Liquid used for cooking fish (see page 260).

Crêpes: Thin French pancakes.

Croquettes: Paste of mashed potato and possibly poultry, fish or meat, formed into small balls or patties, coated in egg and bread-crumbs and deep fried.

Croûte: Literally crust. Sometimes a pastry case, as in fillet of beef *en croûte*, sometimes toasted or fried bread, as in Scotch woodcock or scrambled eggs on toast.

Croutons: Small evenly sized cubes of fried bread used as a soup garnish, and occasionally in other dishes.

Dariole: Small castle-shaped mould used for moulding rice salads and sometimes for cooking cake mixtures.

Déglacer: To loosen and liquefy the fat, sediment and browned juices stuck at the bottom of a frying pan or saucepan by adding liquid (usually stock, water or wine) and stirring while boiling.

Deglaze: See *Déglacer.*

Dégorger: To extract the juices from meat, fish or vegetables, generally by salting then soaking or washing. Usually done to remove indigestible or strong-tasting juices.

Dépouiller: To skim off the scum from a sauce or stock: a splash of cold stock is added to the boiling liquid. This helps to bring scum and fat to the surface, which can then be more easily skimmed.

Dropping consistency: The consistency where a mixture will drop reluctantly from a spoon, neither pouring off nor obstinately adhering.

Duxelle: Finely chopped raw mushrooms, sometimes with chopped shallots or chopped ham, often used as a stuffing.

Eggwash: Beaten raw egg, sometimes with salt, used for glazing pastry to give it a shine when baked.

Entrecôte: Sirloin steak.

Entrée: Traditionally a dish served before the main course, but usually served as a main course today.

Entremets: Dessert or sweet course, excluding pastry sweets.

Escalope: A thin slice of meat, sometimes beaten out flat to make it thinner and larger.

Farce: Stuffing.

Fécule: Farinaceous thickening, usually arrowroot or cornflour.

Flamber: To set alcohol alight. Usually to burn off the alcohol, but frequently simply for dramatic effect. (Past tense flambé or flambée.) English: to flame.

Flame: See *Flamber.*

Fleurons: Crescents of puff pastry, generally used to garnish fish or poultry.

19

Fold: To mix with a gentle lifting motion, rather than to stir vigorously. The aim is to avoid beating out air while mixing.

Frappé: Iced, or set in a bed of crushed ice.

Fricassé: White stew made with cooked or raw poultry, meat or rabbit and a velouté sauce, sometimes thickened with cream and egg yolks.

Fumet: Strong flavoured liquor used for flavouring sauces. Usually the liquid in which fish has been poached, or the liquid that has run from fish during baking. Sometimes used of meat or truffle-flavoured liquors.

Glace de viande: Reduced brown stock, very strong in flavour, used for adding body and colour to sauces.

Glaze: To cover with a thin layer of shiny jellied meat juices (for roast turkey), melted jam (for fruit flans) or syrup (for rum baba).

God's gravy: Jus de viande or roasting juices, unthickened, served as sauce.

Gratiner: To brown under a grill after the surface of the dish has been sprinkled with breadcrumbs and butter and, sometimes, cheese. Dishes finished like this are sometimes called *gratinée* or *au gratin.*

Hard ball: Term used in sugar boiling. As *soft ball* (see below), but further heated and reduced until the sugar forms hard balls.

Hors d'oeuvre: Usually simply means the first course. Sometimes used to denote a variety or selection of many savoury titbits served with drinks, or as a mixed first course (*hors d'oeuvres variés*).

Infuse: To steep or heat gently to extract flavour, as when infusing milk with onion slices.

Julienne: Vegetables or citrus rind cut in thin matchstick shapes or very fine shreds.

Jus or *jus de viande:* God's gravy, i.e. juices that occur naturally in cooking, not a made-up sauce. Also juice.

Jus lié: Thickened gravy.

Knock down or *knock back:* To punch or knead out the air in risen dough so that it resumes its pre-risen bulk.

Knock up: To separate slightly the layers of raw puff pastry with the blade of a knife to facilitate rising during cooking.

Lard: To thread strips of bacon fat (or sometimes anchovy) through meat to give it flavour, and in the case of fat, to make up any deficiency in very lean meat.

Lardons: Small strips or cubes of pork fat or bacon generally used as a garnish.

Leavening or *leavening agent:* Ingredient used to make mixtures rise during cooking, e.g. yeast, baking powder, whisked egg whites.

Liaison: Ingredients for binding together and thickening sauce, soup or other liquid, e.g. roux, beurre manié, egg yolk and cream, blood.

Macedoine: Small diced mixed vegetables, usually containing some root vegetables. Sometimes used of fruit meaning a fruit salad.

Macerate: To soak food in a syrup or liquid to allow flavours to mix.

Mandolin: Frame of metal or wood with adjustable blades set in it for finely slicing cucumbers, potatoes etc.

Marinade (verb): To soak meat, fish or vegetables before cooking in acidulated liquid containing flavourings and herbs. This gives flavour and tenderizes the meat.

Marinade (noun): The liquid described above. Usually contains oil, onion, bay leaf and vinegar or wine.

Marmite: French word for a covered earthenware soup container in which the soup is both cooked and served.

Médallions: Small rounds of meat, evenly cut. Also small round biscuits. Occasionally used of vegetables if cut in flat round discs.

21

Mirepoix: The bed of braising vegetables described under Braise.

Moule-à-manqué: French cake tin with sloping sides. The resulting cake has a wider base than top, and is about 3cm/1½in high.

Napper: To coat, mask or cover, e.g. éclairs *nappées* with hot chocolate sauce.

Needleshreds: Fine, evenly cut shreds of citrus rind (French *julienne*) generally used as a garnish.

Noisette (a): Literally 'nut'. Usually means nut-brown as in beurre noisette, i.e. butter browned over heat to a nut colour. Also hazelnut.

Noisette (b): Boneless rack of lamb rolled and tied, cut into neat rounds.

Panade or *Panada:* Very thick mixture used as a base for soufflés or fish cakes etc., usually made from milk and flour.

Papillote: A wrapping of paper in which fish or meat is cooked to contain the aroma and flavour. The dish is brought to the table still wrapped up. Foil is sometimes used, but as it does not puff up dramatically, it is less satisfactory.

Parboil: To half-boil or partially soften by boiling.

Parisienne (usually *pommes Parisiennes*): Potato (sometimes with other ingredients) scooped into small balls with a melon baller and, usually, fried.

Pass: To strain or push through a sieve.

Pâte: The basic mixture or paste, often used of uncooked pastry, dough, uncooked meringue etc.

Pâté: A savoury paste or liver, pork, game etc.

Pâtisserie: Sweet cakes and pastries. Or cake shop.

Paupiette: Beef (or pork or veal) olive, i.e. a thin layer of meat, spread with a soft farce, rolled up, tied with string and cooked slowly.

Poussin: Baby chicken.

Praline: Almonds cooked in sugar until the mixture caramelizes, cooled and crushed to a powder. Used for flavouring desserts and ice cream.

Prove: To put dough or yeasted mixture to rise before baking.

Purée: Liquidized, sieved or finely mashed fruit or vegetables.

Quenelles: A fine minced fish or meat mixture formed into small portions and poached. Served in a sauce, or as a garnish to other dishes.

Ragout: A stew.

Rechauffée: A reheated dish made with previously cooked food.

Reduce: To reduce the amount of liquid by rapid boiling, causing evaporation and a consequent strengthening of flavour in the remaining liquid.

Refresh: To hold boiled green vegetables under a cold tap, or to dunk them immediately in cold water to prevent their further cooking in their own steam, and to set the colour.

Relax or *rest:* Of pastry: to set aside in a cool place to allow the gluten (which will have expanded during rolling) to contract. This lessens the danger of shrinking in the oven.
Of batters: to set aside to allow the starch cells to swell, giving a lighter result when cooked.

Roux: A basic liaison or thickening for a sauce or soup. Melted butter to which flour has been added.

Salamander: A hot oven or grill used for browning or glazing the tops of cooked dishes, or a hot iron or poker for branding the top with lines or a criss-cross pattern.

Salmis: A game stew sometimes made with cooked game, or partially roasted game.

Sauter: Method of frying in a deep-frying pan or sautoir. The food is continually tossed or shaken so that it browns quickly and evenly.

Sautoir: Deep-frying pan with a lid used for recipes that require fast frying and then slower cooking (with the lid on).

Scald: Of milk: to heat until on the point of boiling, when some movement can be seen at the edges of the pan but there is no over-all bubbling.
Of muslin, cloths etc.: to dunk in clean boiling water, generally to sterilize.

Seal or *seize:* To brown meat rapidly (usually in fat), forming a dryish skin to trap juices inside.

To season: Of food: to flavour, generally with salt and pepper.
Of iron frying pans, girdles etc.: to prepare new equipment for use by placing over high heat, generally coated with oil and sprinkled with salt. This prevents subsequent rusting and sticking.

Slake: To mix flour, arrowroot, cornflour or custard powder to a thin paste with a small quantity of cold water.

Soft Ball: The term used to describe sugar syrup reduced by boiling to sufficient thickness to form soft balls when dropped into cold water and rubbed between finger and thumb.

Suprême: Choice piece of poultry (usually from the breast).

Sweat: To cook gently (usually in butter or oil, but sometimes in the food's own juices) without frying or browning.

Tammy: A fine muslin cloth through which sauces are sometimes forced. After this treatment they look beautifully smooth and shiny. Tammy cloths have recently been replaced by blenders or liquidizers which give much the same effect.

Tammy strainer: A fine mesh strainer, conical in shape, used to produce the effect described under *Tammy*.

To the thread: Of sugar boiling. Term used to denote degree of thickness achieved when reducing syrup, i.e. the syrup will form threads if tested between finger and thumb. Short thread: about 1cm/½in; long thread: 5cm/2in or more.

Timbale: A dish which has been cooked in a castle-shaped mould, or a dish served piled up high.

Tournedos: Fillet steak. Usually refers to a one-portion piece of grilled fillet.

To turn vegetables: To shape carrots or turnips to a small olive shape. To cut mushrooms into a decorative spiral pattern.

To turn olives: To remove the olive stone with a spiral cutting movement.

Velouté: See under Sauces, pages 63 and 264.

Vol-au-vent: A large pastry case made from puff pastry with high raised sides and a deep hollow centre into which is put chicken, fish etc.

Well: A hollow or dip made in a pile or bowlful of flour, exposing the table top or bottom of the bowl, into which other ingredients are placed prior to mixing.

Zest: The thin coloured skin of an orange or lemon, used to give flavour. It is very thinly pared without any of the bitter white pith.

CLASSIC GARNISHES

Anglaise: Braised vegetables such as carrots, turnips and quartered celery hearts (used to garnish boiled salted beef).

Aurore: A flame-coloured sauce obtained by adding fresh tomato purée to a bechamel sauce; used for eggs, vegetables and fish. Means 'dawn'.

Bolognaise: A rich sauce made from chicken livers or minced beef flavoured with mushrooms and tomatoes. Usually served with pasta.

Bonne femme: To cook in a simple way. Usually, of chicken, sautéed and served with white wine gravy, bacon cubes, button onions and garnished with croquette potatoes. Of soup, simple purée of vegetables with stock. Of fish, white wine sauce, usually with mushrooms; and served with buttered mashed potatoes.

Boulangère: Potatoes and onions sliced and cooked in the oven in stock. Often served with mutton.

Bouquetière: Groups of very small carrots, turnips, French beans, cauliflower florets, button onions, asparagus tips etc. Sometimes served with a thin demi-glaçe or gravy. Usually accompanies beef or lamb entrées.

Bourgeoise: Fried diced bacon, glazed carrots and button onions. Sometimes red wine is used in the sauce. Used for beef and liver dishes.

Bourguignonne: Button mushrooms and small onions in a sauce made with red wine (Burgundy). Used for beef and egg dishes.

Bretonne: Haricot beans whole or in a purée. Sometimes a purée of root vegetables. Usually served with a gigot (leg) of lamb.

Chasseur: Sautéed mushrooms added to a sauté of chicken or veal.

Clamart: Garnish of artichoke hearts filled with buttered petits pois. Sometimes a purée of peas, or simply buttered peas.

Doria: A garnish of cucumber, usually fried in butter.

DuBarry: Denotes the use of cauliflower: potage DuBarry is cauliflower soup. Also, cooked cauliflower florets masked with Mornay sauce and browned under the grill, used for meat entrées.

Flamande: Red cabbage and glazed small onions used with pork and beef.

Florentine: Spinach in purée, or leaf spinach. Also a sixteenth-century name for a pie.

Indienne: Flavoured with curry.

Joinville: Slices of truffle, crayfish tails and mushrooms with a lobster sauce, used for fish dishes.

Lyonnaise: Denotes the use of onions as garnish – the onions are frequently sliced and fried.

Meunière: Of fish, lightly dusted with flour, then fried and served with beurre noisette and lemon juice; also frequently (but not classically) chopped parsley.

Milanese: With a tomato sauce, sometimes including shredded ham, tongue and mushrooms. Frequently served with pasta.

Minute: Food quickly cooked, either fried or grilled. Usually applied to a thin entrecôte steak.

Mornay: With a cheese sauce.

Nantua: With a lobster sauce.

Napolitana: A tomato sauce and Parmesan cheese (for pasta). May also mean a three-coloured ice cream.

Nicoise: Name given to many dishes consisting of ingredients common in the South of France, e.g. tomatoes, olives, garlic, fish, olive oil.

Normande: Garnish of mussels, shrimps, oysters and mushrooms. Or creamy sauce containing cider or calvados, and sometimes apples.

Parmentier: Denotes the use of potato as a base or garnish.

Paysanne: Literally, peasant. Usually denotes the use of carrots and turnips sliced across in rounds.

Portuguaise: Denotes the use of tomatoes or tomato purée.

Princesse: Denotes the use of asparagus (usually on breast of chicken).

Printanière: Early spring vegetables cooked and used as a garnish, usually in separate groups.

Provençale: Denotes the use of garlic, and sometimes tomatoes and/or olives.

St Germain: Denotes the use of peas, sometimes with pommes Parisienne. Also the name of a cream of pea soup.

Soubise: Onion purée, frequently mixed with a béchamel sauce.

Vichy: Garnish of small glazed carrots.

TRADITIONAL BRITISH ACCOMPANIMENTS

Roast lamb: Mint sauce or redcurrant jelly, onion sauce or gravy.

Roast beef: Horseradish, very thin gravy, Yorkshire pudding, mustard.

Roast chicken: Bacon rolls, sausages, bread sauce, gravy.

Roast turkey: Cranberry sauce, bread sauce, sausages, bacon, stuffings, gravy, sprouts or chestnuts.

Ham: Cumberland sauce or parsley sauce, mustard.

Game: Game chips, fried breadcrumbs, bread sauce, redcurrant jelly, unthickened 'God's gravy'.

Roast pork and goose: Apple sauce or gooseberry sauce, gravy.

METHODS OF COOKING

The tougher the food, or the larger its volume, the slower it must be cooked.

The quick methods of cooking – frying, deep frying (the quickest) and grilling – are suitable therefore for small pieces of tender meat, whereas the slower methods – braising, stewing etc. – are best for tough ones.

GRILLING

Brushing the grilling meat with butter or oil is done for two reasons – to stop it sticking to the pan or grill and to give flavour. The speed with which the food is cooked is the essential factor in keeping it moist. An outside cooked surface is quickly formed, which prevents the juices inside the meat running out. If the grill is not hot enough, the outer seal will not be formed and the inner juices will escape, giving a dried-up result. With practice it is possible to tell by pressure of the fingers if the food is cooked, but if you don't trust your 'feel' you will have to cut one piece open and look.

Heat

The grill must be really hot. Always pre-heat the grill well in advance.

Preparation of the food

The meat or fish should be brushed with oil or butter and seasoned with pepper. Never season foods for grilling with salt as this draws out the juices and renders the meat dry and tough.

Distance from the heat

The grill pan should be held at about 7·5cm/3in from the grill itself so that the meat can be 'sealed' immediately. The pan can be lowered for any further cooking that may be necessary. Thick pieces of meat are cooked further away from the heat for longer. Thin pieces are cooked close to the heat, faster.

Turning the food over

This should be done with a pair of tongs or with two spoons but not with a fork, which would pierce the meat and allow the juices to run out.

Serving

Grilled foods should be served at once. They dry out and toughen if kept hot.

FRYING

(*a*) SHALLOW FRYING

The principle of shallow frying is similar to that of grilling (see above). The essential difference is that whereas in grilling the fat drops off the meat, in frying it stays in the pan and can sometimes be served with the dish. Fat used for shallow frying should never be more than half the depth of the food.

Rules for shallow frying

1. Never add too many pieces of food to a frying pan at once as this reduces the temperature of the fat and the food will stew rather than fry.
2. Always fry first the side of the chop, steak, fish etc. which is to be uppermost; being fried in clean fat generally makes it look better.

(*b*) DEEP FRYING

Most foods to be deep fried are given a protective coating of beaten egg or a batter of egg and breadcrumbs. This is done for five reasons:

1. The frying fat is at an extremely high temperature (about 185 C/360 F), which would burn the outside of some foods before the middle was cooked. The insulating coating allows the food inside to cook evenly.

    Some foods, such as potato crisps, do not need any coating because they are in and out of the hot fat too fast to burn. All they have to do is brown and then they are done. Other unprotected foods (such as the larger potato chips) are generally given a first frying at a non-burning lower temperature to ensure that the insides are cooked before the foods are browned in the very hot fat.

2. The heat of the fat would make uncooked moist food (like fish fillets or pineapple rings) splutter and splash dangerously, and the hot fat would bubble over the edge of the pan, possibly causing a fire.

3. As the fat is to be used again it must be prevented from absorbing the taste and smell of foods, especially of fish. The neutral egg or egg and breadcrumb layer in contact with the fat is tasteless and odourless.

4. Many foods, such as cheese or cooking apple, become liquid on being cooked. The crisp batter then becomes a container for the runny inside.

5. The crisp coating provides a pleasing contrast with the moist food inside, which is the chief attraction of deep-fried food.

After use the fat should be strained through muslin to remove food particles. When it has become at all dark it should be replaced, rather than topped up.

Fats suitable for deep frying are almost-tasteless vegetable oils and lard as these can be heated without burning to the required 170–185 C/330–360 F. The lower temperature (which will produce a gentle fizzing if a piece of bread is dropped in) is suitable for the first frying of potato chips and for deep-fried choux pastry dishes such as beignets soufflés.

The higher temperature (when tested with a piece of bread the fat will fizz vigorously and the bread will begin to brown) is suitable for rissoles, croquettes, fruit fritters and the second frying of potatoes.

Deep-frying technique

When cooking a large amount of food in a fryer, fry only a small amount at a time – little enough not to lower the temperature of the fat significantly. If the fat has cooled too much, the batter or outer layer of the food will not instantly form an impervious crisp crust, but will become soggy and allow the fat to enter the food, producing a greasy unattractive dish. Once the food is cooked, lift it immediately out of the fat and drain it on absorbent paper. Crumpled brown paper, kitchen paper, or even dry-inked newspaper will do.

If you cannot serve the food immediately (which would be best) do not cover it with a lid. If you do, steam trapped inside will make the food soggy. Spread the cooked food in one layer only (if piled up the bottom pieces will become soggy) on a hot dish and put it in the warm oven, with the door ajar to allow free circulation of air.

Add a sprinkling of salt to the food (if savoury) or caster sugar (if sweet) just before serving.

Safety precautions when deep frying

Because of the great heat of the liquid fat the deep fryer is potentially the most dangerous object in the kitchen. The following points should be observed for safety's sake:

1. The fat or oil should not be too deep. When a basket of food is lowered into hot fat it will bubble up briefly, and if it should spill over (especially on to a naked gas flame beneath) fire could result.

2. Make sure that food is properly coated in batter or egg and breadcrumbs, or is really dry. Dry off potato chips in a tea-towel before frying. Wet food causes the fat to splash and splutter.

3. If the fat rises up dangerously, remove the food immediately and cool the fat slightly (or remove some of the food from the basket) before trying again.

4. Never go away and leave a heating fryer. Deep fat or oil does not boil; it simply explodes into flame. But if you are in the room, before it reaches that stage you will have seen and smelt it smoking.

5. Never attempt to move over-hot or burning fat. The danger is that you will spill it on your arm, or on to the flame beneath. Just turn off the source of heat and leave it where it is. Have the lid of the pan close at hand so that if the fat does catch fire, you can quench the flames calmly by shutting off their oxygen supply with the lid. Failing that, drop a thick woollen (not nylon) blanket or coat over the whole burning pot. Better a singed blanket than a burnt kitchen!

6. If the fat is obviously too hot, but not on fire, it will cool without danger if you turn off its source of heat. The cooling process can be hurried by putting a raw potato (dry) or a

large piece of bread into the fat. This will cool the fat as it
browns.

BROILING

Broiling is an American word usually used to mean grilling, but
sometimes roasting.

ROASTING

Roasting is the most satisfactory way of cooking large pieces of
fairly tender, or very tender, meat. The extremely fast frying,
grilling or deep frying would char the outside while the middle
is still raw. However the same principles apply, i.e. the meat is
first 'sealed' (the outer surface is cooked very fast either in a
frying pan or in a very hot oven) so that the juices of the meat
are locked in. The temperature is then lowered (or the meat is
put into a cooler oven) until the required degree of roasting has
been reached. With a small piece of meat it is not necessary to
lower the oven temperature as the cooking time will be short,
so the outside cannot over-cook.

The roasting meat is generally basted during cooking. Melted
fat (perhaps butter) and/or juices or stock are regularly ladled
over the roasting meat. This is done to add flavour and to keep
the outer skin from drying to a very hard and inedible layer.

When meat was roasted on a turning spit the dripping fat was
caught in a tray beneath the turning meat, and spooned back
over the top of it. Spit roasting is considered better than oven
roasting simply because as the meat turns, the fat runs automatically over the surface, even without the help of the additional
basting. With oven roasting, the top of the meat is bound to be
dryer than the bottom as the juices run down both inside and
outside the meat. For this reason it is a good idea to start roasting
a turkey or chicken upside down in the roasting pan to enable
some of the juices to run into the breast, before turning it right
side up to brown.

Roasting in a bag, in foil, or in a clay brick pot, are all attempts to keep the meat moist. They share the disadvantage that, because the meat is cooked in a closed steamy atmosphere, they do not have a crisp brown skin. But the oven is kept clean.

BAKING

Baking differs from modern roasting only in that with roasting, fat is generally basted over the food whereas baked food is left undisturbed. But they both entail putting food into a hot closed oven to cook. Baking, because of the perfectly controlled, all-over even heat, is most suitable for cakes and breads, where exact temperatures are vital. It is also an excellent method for the slow cooking of tough meats, which are usually baked in a closed container and therefore in a moist and steamy atmosphere. For breads, cakes etc. see pages 37–54.

STEAMING

There are two principal methods of steaming: for quickly cooked foods, such as fish, chicken or vegetables, the food is placed in the top of a two-tier steamer and cooked in the direct steam from the boiling water below. This method is frequently used for invalid cookery as no fat or sauce needs to be added to the food, and fatless food is easy to digest. It is a good method of cooking floury potatoes which might break up if boiled. Care should be taken not to overcook food as it may become tasteless with prolonged steaming. The steaming water should be saved for stock. If a two-tier steamer is not available one can be improvised by placing the food in a metal strainer (perhaps loosely lined with foil), and suspending this in a saucepan over boiling water. It may, however, be necessary to cover the saucepan and its lid with a layer of foil to prevent the steam from escaping under the lid which now will not fit properly on account of the strainer.

Foods that require prolonged gentle cooking, such as suet puddings and meat puddings, are steamed but the food itself does not come in contact with the moist steam. The pudding basin containing the food is placed in a large saucepan of boiling water, the water coming to within 5cm/2in of the rim of the pudding basin. The pudding must be carefully wrapped to prevent water getting into it and making it soggy. It is generally covered with a double layer of greaseproof paper which has a folded pleat down the centre, and tied firmly with string. The pleat is to allow the food inside to expand during cooking (even a Christmas pudding will rise slightly) without bursting through its coverings. The whole is then wrapped in foil. A folded cloth or double strip of foil laid under the basin but projecting up the sides of the saucepan will make lifting the pudding out of the boiling water easier. If the cloth used for this purpose is large it can be loosely tied over the top of the basin. It is vital that a well-fitting lid to the saucepan is used: if the steam is allowed to escape too freely the pudding will not cook in the specified time.

The water should be kept boiling vigorously throughout the process, and it is a good plan to have a kettle of steaming water handy to replenish the saucepan as and when necessary. The saucepan should be large enough for steam to surround the pudding easily.

Very large steamers with upper compartments large enough to take a pudding basin are available, but they are cumbersome items for the average kitchen, and a saucepan with a good lid works very well.

STEWING

Stewing is the perfect slow-cooking method for foods in a liquid. If there is any danger of the food breaking up with the agitation of the bubbling water or syrup (as with slices of apple) it is best to stew in the oven where the temperature can be fixed so low that it hardly moves the liquid. Stew pans are always covered to keep in the steam.

STEWING FRUIT

Fruit should never be boiled. It should be very gently poached in a sugar syrup (see page 350). The amount and thickness of the syrup depends on the fruit to be poached. Very juicy fruit (plums, cherries, raspberries, rhubarb) should be cooked in a small quantity of thick syrup while drier fruits (apples and pears) should be poached in a thinner syrup.

It is important to make a syrup rather than simply to put sugar, water and fruit together in a pan. The danger of the latter method is overcooking the fruit before the sugar is dissolved. Besides, heating undissolved sugar often leads to crystallized lumps.

When stewing whole fruits that are liable to discolour, there are several important rules to follow:

1. Peel the fruit with a stainless steel knife.
2. Dunk it, as soon as it is peeled, into the sugar syrup.
3. Allow the sugar syrup to boil once right up over the fruit, before turning down the heat to poach it gently.
4. Poach the fruit for at least 15 minutes in the syrup. This is to allow the sugar syrup (which will prevent discoloration) to penetrate the outer layer of fruit.

POT ROASTING

Pot roasting is not really roasting at all. But the resulting meat has the browned look of a roast. The meat is first browned by frying in the same deep pot that it will stew in. It is then covered and left to stew (in or out of the oven) in its own juice. This is done at a very low temperature. Great care must be taken not to allow the meat to catch at the bottom.

BRAISING

Braised foods (e.g. beef olives) are cooked on a bed of chopped-up root vegetables. Little or no liquid is added and the contents cook slowly in their own juices. The braising vegetables give flavour and moisture to the meat, but may be discarded before the meat is served, or used later in soup. Sometimes they are sieved and used for sauce.

BOILING

True boiling is a method of cooking rarely used except for the quick cooking of fresh vegetables, for rice and pasta, and for boiling puddings in a pudding bowl. It is also used for jam making, when a good rolling boil is essential.

Boiling often entails a considerable loss of nutritive value, as many nutrients are thrown away with the cooking water. The word 'boiled' is often incorrectly applied to dishes like boiled egg custard (which if it was really boiled would be curdled) and boiled salmon, which should be poached, not boiled.

POACHING

For food to be poached it must be submerged, or partly submerged, in a flavoured liquid (e.g. syrup for poached pears, or chicken stock for poached chicken), and it should be cooked so that the liquid barely moves. If it bubbles in only one part of the pan, it is simmering, and if it bubbles everywhere, it is boiling. Truly poached chicken or fish has a juiciness and tenderness not found in boiled food. If the food is cooled in the poaching liquid, so much the better. (Removing it allows it to dry out.) But the poaching pan should be stood in cold water so that the contents cool fast. This is to avoid the danger of food (kept too long in a warm steamy atmosphere) going bad.

BAKING BREADS, CAKES, PASTRIES ETC.

When wheat flour and water are mixed together and cooked, a primitive type of bread – a flat, hard biscuit – is produced.

Examples of this are the unleavened bread of the Israelites, the damper of the Australians and the flapjacks of prospectors and pioneers of America.

Wheat flour has a remarkable ingredient. This is the protein gluten, which, when wet, will stretch and expand, allowing the dough to be kneaded and pulled into a most elastic substance. The strands of dough can stretch without breaking even when expanding gas trapped inside caused the dough to puff up. This means that, provided we can get the dough to rise, the gluten will hold it in its puffed-up shape until it solidifies during baking. This makes a much lighter, less brittle bread and makes possible a hundred different recipes for breads, cakes and puddings which all depend on trapped gas for their lightness and open texture.

RAISING AGENTS

But how to get the gas into the mixture? And what gas will it be?

Air

There are several mechanical methods of incorporating air into a basic mixture, all of which depend on agitating the ingredients, rather like stirring up a bubble bath. These methods include sifting flour, creaming fat and sugar together until light and mousse-like, beating (as for batters) and whisking (as for egg whites). In all these, air is the raising agent.

Steam

Steam is also a raising agent. Some mixtures will rise, even though no effort has been made to beat air into them. These usually contain a high proportion of liquid, like Yorkshire pudding batter or choux pastry. What happens is that, because they are baked in a hot oven, the liquid ingredients quickly reach boiling point, and begin to convert to steam. As the steam rises it takes with it the dough or batter, and puffs it up, and while it is in this puffed-up state, the heat of the oven hardens the dry ingredients of the mixture and the dough becomes solidified with the steam trapped inside. The texture of such a mixture is generally very open and uneven, with large pockets of air.

Bicarbonate of soda

This is another effective raising agent. It is a substance which, when mixed with liquid and heated, will give off half its substance as the gas carbon dioxide (CO_2) which will puff up the mixture as it forms. But the residue of the 'bicarb' will remain in the cooked mixture as carbonate of soda. Unfortunately this carbonate of soda has an unpleasant taste and smell, and a yellow colour. This method of raising is therefore suitable for strong-tasting foods such as gingerbread, chocolate cake, and cakes flavoured with treacle, when the taste of the carbonate of soda will be masked.

The carbon dioxide trapped in the bread or cake will gradually escape and be replaced by air.

The addition of an acid substance (vinegar, sour milk, cream of tartar, tartaric acid, yoghurt, even marmalade or jam) speeds up the liberation of the carbon dioxide from the bicarbonate of soda, and is often included for this reason.

Bicarbonate of soda has a weakening effect on gluten, preventing it from forming a hard, bread-like crust. This makes it suitable for scones and cakes, when yeast (which does not so affect the gluten) would produce too crisp a crust.

A disadvantage of bicarbonate of soda is that it destroys many of the vitamins present in flour.

Baking powder

This is a mixture of bicarbonate of soda and acid powder – and also a filler to absorb any dampness in the air which might allow the two active ingredients to get going before they are thoroughly wet in a dough or cake mixture. A 'delayed reaction' baking powder is available in America which needs heat as well as moisture to start it off, but it is not widely known in Britain.

Self-raising flour

This is a flour (generally 'weak', i.e. low in gluten) already containing a raising agent (usually baking powder).

Yeast

Yeast, when activated, also produces carbon dioxide which will puff up the dough, but yeast cookery is complex enough to need a section of its own. See page 43.

CAKES

(See section on raising agents, page 38.)

THE FOUR BASIC METHODS

Rubbing-in method

The first stage of this method is similar to that for shortcrust pastry (see page 50): the fat is rubbed into the flour with the fingers. The remaining dry ingredients (sugar, peel etc.) are then added, and finally eggs and/or milk are added to give a sloppy 'dropping consistency' mixture.

This method is used in making rock buns and plain fruit cakes.

Melting method

The water, milk, syrup and the fat and any other liquid ingredients are heated together. They are then cooled and poured into a bowl containing all the sieved dry ingredients, usually including bicarbonate of soda and/or baking powder. The mixture is stirred, not beaten, until it resembles a thick batter.

This method produces very moist cakes, e.g. gingerbread.

Creaming method

The butter or margarine is creamed with a wooden spoon until it is smooth and very light in colour. The sugar is then added by degrees and beaten in the same way until the mixture is pale and fluffy. The eggs are then added, also by degrees, and finally the sifted flour is folded into the mixture, with as little mixing and stirring as possible. Adding the egg slowly, with much beating, and perhaps a spoonful of flour between each addition, is said to help prevent curdling.

This method is used for Victoria sandwich cakes, Dundee and Madeira cakes. Butter gives a better flavour, but margarine is easier to cream.

Whisking method

The simplest whisked cake is a fatless sponge. The sugar and eggs are whisked together until light and thick, and then the flour is folded in. A Genoise 'commune' has just-runny butter folded into it with the flour. The richer Genoise 'fine' cake has a greater proportion of butter to flour, and the eggs are separated. The yolks and sugar are whisked, the butter and flour folded in, and lastly the whisked egg whites.

But in all the whisked cakes the whisked-in air is the raising agent, and throughout the process, every effort is made to keep in as much air as possible.

The sugar and eggs (or yolks only) are whisked in a bowl set over a pan of near-simmering water. It is important that the base of the bowl does not touch the surface of the water as the heat at the bottom of the bowl would then be too great and the eggs would scramble. The gentle heat helps to melt the sugar and speeds up the whisking process. The mixture has been sufficiently whisked when it is very pale in colour, and leaves a ribbon-like trail on the surface when the whisk is lifted. When the flour is folded in, great care should be taken to fold rather than stir or beat, as the aim is to incorporate the flour without losing any of the beaten-in air. The correct movement is more of lifting the mixture and cutting into it, than stirring.

Butter, which should be just runny but not hot, should be poured round the edge of the bowl. If it is poured on top of the whisked cake mixture, it will push out some of the air. Folding in should be gentle and not over-done.

The cakes are cooked when the impression left by a finger on the surface of the cake will disappear. The sponge will be slightly springy. Cakes should be cooled for a few minutes in the tin, then turned out on to a cake rack.

Whisked sponges are used for many gateaux and composite cakes. They are sometimes simply filled with jam or cream, or eaten plain, perhaps dusted with icing sugar.

PREPARING A CAKE TIN

All tins should be greased before use. This is to prevent the cake mixture sticking or burning at the edges or bottom. Lard or oil are the most suitable fats. If using oil, always turn the tin upside down after greasing to allow any excess oil to drain away. Use a paint brush to get a thin layer.

Buns

The tins need no preparation other than greasing.

Cakes made by melting or creaming methods

Grease the tin, then line the base with greaseproof paper, cut exactly to size, and brush out with more melted lard or oil.

Cakes made by whisking method

As above, but dust with caster sugar and flour after lining and greasing.

Fruit cakes

Grease tin, then line sides and base with greaseproof paper as follows:-
1. Cut two pieces of greaseproof paper to fit the base of the cake tin.
2. Cut another piece long enough to go right round the sides of the tin and to overlap slightly. It should be 1cm/$\frac{1}{2}$in deeper than the height of the cake tin.
3. Fold one long edge of this strip over 1cm/$\frac{1}{2}$in all along its length.
4. Cut 1cm/$\frac{1}{2}$in snips at right angles to the edge and about 1cm/$\frac{1}{2}$in apart, all the way along the folded side. The snips should just reach the fold.
5. Grease the tin, place one of the paper bases in the bottom and grease again.
6. Fit the long strip inside the cake tin with the folded cut edge

on the bottom (the flanges will overlap slightly), and the main uncut part lining the sides of the tin. Press well into the corners.

7. Grease again and lay the second base on top of the first.
8. Brush out with more melted lard and dust with flour.

COOKING WITH YEAST

Yeast baking, one of the most addictive and satisfying forms of cookery, needs a book to itself. One of the best is *Beard on Bread* by James Beard. Another is Elizabeth David's *English Bread and Yeast Cookery*.

WHEAT FLOUR

Wheat flour (rather than cornflour, potato flour, rice flour, rye flour etc.) is most commonly used because of its high gluten content. Gluten is the protein that allows the dough to become elastic. The more gluten in the flour, the more it will be able to rise, the strands of dough stretching without breaking as the loaf fills with gas.

White flour

Made from ears of wheat that have had their outer casing of bran and inner centre of wheatgerm removed, white flour is very fine and can be bought bleached or unbleached. Obviously the more refining and processing that the flour goes through, the less flavour and vitamins it will have. For this reason white flours generally have some of the B vitamins returned to them before packaging.

Strong flour

This flour is made from hard wheat. The best hard wheat comes from North America and has an exceptionally high gluten content. This makes it highly suitable for use in bread-making, giving a well-risen light loaf. It is the flour most commonly used by professional bakers.

43

Plain household flour

This is a general all-purpose flour suitable for cakes and breads but more often used for the former as it does not have the high gluten content of strong flour. It is generally made from soft wheat of the kind grown in Europe. Bread produced with household flour will not have quite the lightness of that produced with strong flour.

Self-raising flour

Usually 'weak' i.e. made from soft wheat, this is flour to which a raising agent (generally baking powder) has been added. It is not used in yeast cookery.

Wholemeal flour (or wholewheat flour)

This is flour milled from the whole grain, including bran and wheatgerm. As most of the B vitamins in wheat reside in the wheatgerm, and bran provides roughage for the digestive system, bread made from wholewheat is much better for you. But it undoubtedly produces a heavier loaf, and because of the presence of wheatgerm, the bread does not keep as well as the white variety. A mixture of wholewheat and white flour is a good compromise.

Stoneground flour

Produced by the ancient method of milling between stone rollers, this flour is said to be a less 'messed about' and processed flour than that made by modern milling methods. It is certainly a slightly coarser, heavier flour, and, even in the white version, is heavier than factory milled flour. It needs more yeast to make it rise.

Brown flour

This is brown but not necessarily because of the inclusion of wheatgerm and bran. It may simply be dyed flour, so look for the word 'wholewheat' or 'wholemeal' on the packet. Dyed brown flour is lighter than wholewheat and usually sold as 'wheatmeal'.

Bran

Bran can be bought on its own in health food shops, to give a coarseness and colour to the bread, but provides neither flavour nor nutrition. It does provide roughage for the digestive system, however.

To conclude: strong, unbleached white flour is best for white loaves and a mixture of this and wholewheat flour is best for brown bread.

LEAVENING

Raising agents other than yeast have been discussed previously, but yeast is the most usual agent for bread.

Yeast is a one-celled plant of the fungus family. Its main advantage from a cook's point of view is that, given the right humid conditions, it can reproduce amazingly fast, giving off carbon dioxide (CO_2) gas as it does so. If yeast cells are incorporated into a mixture for baking, the carbon dioxide produced as the organisms grow will puff up the dough or batter, giving a light and aerated result. Yeast can be bought in two forms:

Compressed or fresh yeast

This is generally considered the most satisfactory kind of yeast, less likely to produce a loaf smelling and tasting beery or over-yeasty. But it is becoming very difficult to obtain, especially in small quantities. However, if you buy a pound at a time it can be frozen successfully. Freeze it in small pieces so that you can thaw them as you need them. Use as soon as the yeast has defrosted. Fresh yeast will keep in the refrigerator wrapped in plastic for a fortnight or so.

Dried yeast (often called 'active' dried yeast)

This is bought in granular form. You need half, or less than half, the weight specified for fresh yeast. It will keep fresh for six months in a cool dry place. To avoid the 'beery' taste referred to earlier, under- rather than over-estimate the amount of yeast needed, and allow rising and proving to take a good long time.

OTHER INGREDIENTS

Sugar (or molasses)

Generally included in a bread recipe to give the yeast something to feed on while busily multiplying. It does, of course, also add a touch of sweetness to the dough, but this is incidental.

Fat

Some breads call for fat, usually butter, which gives a richness to the bread, and a good flavour.

Liquid

Water is usually called for, but sometimes other liquids, such as beer or milk, are used. Milk gives a golden coloured crust.

MIXING AND SPONGING

The basic aim while preparing the dough for the oven is to create the right conditions for the yeast to grow, and the maximum elasticity in the bread to contain the gas released by the yeast. In the first stage – mixing and sponging – we are creating the incubating conditions for the yeast:

The ingredients and bowl should be warm: not so hot that the yeast cells will be killed, and not so cold that they will be discouraged from multiplying. The yeast is usually creamed with a little sugar (upon which it feeds) and mixed with a spoonful of warm (i.e. about 40°C/100°F) liquid. When the yeast looks frothy you know it is on its way. This is called 'sponging'. It is done to check that the yeast cells are alive before mixing in all the flour.

If nothing happens (although you have the yeast in a warm kitchen) in 15 minutes, the yeast is probably dead, and there is nothing for it but to begin again with fresh yeast.

Some recipes require the yeast mixture and all the liquid to be beaten to a batter with a small proportion of the flour, and then 'sponged'. The rest of the flour is then added, and the mixing completed.

KNEADING

Once the dough is mixed it should be kneaded. This is to distribute the yeast cells evenly and to promote the elasticity of the dough. The length of time for kneading varies according to the type of flour and the skill of the kneader, but 10 minutes should do it. The dough should be elastic and satiny-smooth.

Kneading techniques vary, the most common method being to push the lump of dough down and away with the heel of one hand, then to pull it back with the fingers, slap it on the tabletop and repeat the process, turning the dough slightly with each movement.

RISING

The dough is now formed into a ball and put into a warm, lightly oiled bowl. It is a good idea to roll the ball of dough over in the greasy bowl to coat it on all sides. This will prevent hardening and cracking. Cover the bowl with a piece of oiled polythene or a damp cloth. Put the bowl in a warm (about 32°C/90°F) draught-free place and leave it alone for at least one hour. The slower the dough rises the better. Over-risen bread has a coarse texture and beery smell. When it has doubled in bulk, remove it.

KNOCKING DOWN (or knocking back)

This is exactly what the name implies: the air is punched out of the risen dough and it is knocked back to its original size. Then it is kneaded again and shaped (into a round, oblong, plaited or what-have-you loaf) and put into the loaf tin or on to a baking sheet. Again, cover it with oiled polythene.

PROVING

This is the second rising of the dough. It is done when the loaf has doubled in bulk and looks the size and shape you hope the finished bread will be. This rising can be done in a slightly warmer place, for a shorter time – say at 40°C/100°F for 20 minutes. This is because as the dough has now had further kneading it is even more elastic and will rise more easily – rather as a balloon is easier to blow up the second time you do it.

BAKING

The bread will, inevitably, continue to rise for a short time when put in the oven. This is partly due to the rising steam, and partly to the continued growth of the yeast as more warmth is applied. But once the temperature of the dough reaches 60 C/140 F the yeast will be killed and the heat of the oven will cook the dough into a rigid shape. This final rising in the oven is called 'oven spring' and usually causes the top crust to be pushed up away from the body of the loaf, causing larger holes just under the crust. There is nothing wrong with it, but obviously too much oven-spring would have the crust separated entirely from the loaf. Some breads, such as rye bread (which develops a hard and un-yielding crust) is docked half way through baking. This means simply that the top crust is sliced off to allow the gases to escape, and a new crust forms.

To avoid too much oven-spring, bread is baked at a fairly high temperature so that yeast is killed as quickly as possible. Too cool an oven will not kill the yeast cells quickly and they will continue to grow, giving an over-risen, unevenly textured loaf.

The loaf is done when it sounds hollow when tapped. Tap the top first, and if satisfied that it sounds hollow, turn the loaf out (your hand covered with a cloth) and tap the underside. If it feels heavy and solid return it to the oven. Test again in six or seven minutes.

COOLING

Large breads should be cooled out of their tins to allow the steam to escape, thus further lightening the bread. After two hours a loaf will slice easily. If the bread is to be stored in a bread tin or plastic bag (in a refrigerator or freezer) it should be stone-cold before storing. A lukewarm loaf, put into an airtight place, will go soggy, if not mouldy.

GLAZING

Coating the top of the loaf, towards the end of cooking, will give different effects according to the glaze used:

Brushing with *water* ensures a crisp crust.
Milk gives a good pale gold colour and a crisp crust.
Egg yolks and cream produce a dark golden top.
Melted *butter* gives a softer crust.
Melted *apricot jam* gives a sweet sticky shine to sweeter breads.

PASTRIES

In almost all cases 'short' (i.e. crisp, crumbly, but neither brittle nor hard) pastry is the aim. The degree of shortness of pastry comes from the amount and type of fat incorporated in it, and the way in which the paste (uncooked pastry) is handled.

Fats

Butter gives a crisp and short crust, with very good flavour.
Margarine gives a result similar to butter, slightly less rich.
Lard gives a soft, very short but rather tasteless pastry.
Cooking fat gives a crisper crust than lard, also short, but also lacking in flavour.
Suet is only used in suet crust pastry. It produces a soft, rather heavy pastry. To combat this doughiness a raising agent is usually added to the flour.

Flours

Plain household flour is the flour most commonly used, but wholemeal flour and self-raising are used sometimes. Wholemeal flour produces a delicious nutty-flavoured crust, but is inclined to be heavy. For this reason it is sometimes used in conjunction (half and half) with white flour. Self-raising flour produces a thicker, softer, more cakey crust. It is sometimes used to lighten what might be a heavyish pastry (e.g. cheese pastry or suet crust).

Water

As a general rule, the less of this the better. Any child who has mixed flour and water to make a paste knows that the baked result is not unlike concrete. But some crispness and firmness is desirable and the inclusion of a little water ensures this.

Pastry is made in so many different ways that it is difficult to give general rules for success. So to take the broad categories one by one:

SHORTCRUST PASTRY

In this method of pastry-making fat is rubbed into the flour with the fingertips, and then any other ingredients (egg yolks, liquid etc.) are added.

Keep everything as cool as possible: if the fat is allowed to melt, the finished pastry may be tough. Cut the fat, which should be cool and firm rather than softened, into tiny pieces using a small knife and floured fingers (the flouring prevents the fat from sticking to your warm fingers and starting to melt). Add *chilled* water. Roll on a cold surface. Handle the pastry as little as possible.

When rubbing in the fat, handle it lightly so that it doesn't stick to your fingers. Keep your hands well floured to facilitate this. Pick up a few small pieces of fat, and plenty of flour between the fingertips and thumb of each hand. Hold your hands a good 23cm/9in above the bowl and gently and quickly rub the fat pieces into the flour, squashing the fat lightly as you do so. Then immediately drop the lot, from that height, into the bowl (dropping from a height both aerates and cools the mixture). Do not mash each lump of fat – the less thoroughly you do the rubbing in, the better. Keep shaking the bowl so that the big unrubbed pieces of fat come to the top. When the mixture looks like very coarse (by no means 'fine', as many recipes will say) breadcrumbs, stop.

Add only enough liquid to get the pastry to hold together. Rich pastries (with a high proportion of fat) need little if any water added. Although rather moist pastry is easier to handle and roll out, the resulting crust is tough and may well shrink out of shape as the water evaporates in the oven. The drier and more difficult-to-handle pastry will give a crisp 'short' crust.

Do not add too much flour during rolling as the proportion of flour to other ingredients will be altered and the pastry may become heavy.

Allow the pastry to 'relax' in a cool place before baking. This period (10 minutes will do) allows the gluten in the flour to contract, making the pastry less elastic. This will produce a lighter pastry, less likely to shrink.

Always wrap or cover pastry left to relax – especially if there is more rolling to come. The dry atmosphere of a refrigerator dries out the outside of pastry, causing it to crack and flake and making it difficult to handle.

SUET CRUST

The method for suet crust is similar to that for shortcrust, but the suet is generally chopped or shredded into the flour. As self-raising flour (or plain flour and baking powder) is used in order to produce a less doughy pastry, it is important to cook the pastry as soon as possible after making, so that the raising agent is working as the pastry cooks, rather than already spent before the pastry starts to cook. (The raising agent causes the dough to puff up and rise slightly and as the paste hardens during cooking the air will be trapped, and the pastry be light and slightly cakey.)

FLAKY PASTRY (and Puff Pastries)

The first stage in making these pastries is similar to the method used for shortcrust pastry, although the consistency is softer and less 'short'. After this more fat, either in a solid block or small pieces, is incorporated into the paste, which is then rolled, folded and re-rolled several times. This quickly creates layers of pastry which, when baked, will rise in light thin leaves. Pastry folded in three (and rolled out) six times will have 729 layers.

The whole aim at this stage is to create the layers without allowing the fat to melt. This requires quick short strokes with the rolling pin rather than steady long ones. The short strokes allow the bubbles of air in the pastry to move about without being forced out, while the fat is gradually and evenly incorporated in the paste. If there is any danger of the fat breaking through the pastry or becoming warm and sticky, wrap the paste and chill it, then proceed. It sounds a complicated business, but is a lot easier done than said.

Pastry rises evenly to a crisp crust in a damp atmosphere, and for this reason pastries like these, that are expected to rise in the oven, are generally baked at a high temperature in an oven with a roasting tin full of water at the bottom of it, or on a wet baking sheet.

PÂTE SUCRÉE, ALMOND PASTRY AND PÂTE A PÂTÉ

These pastries and others like them are made by working the egg yolks and fat, and sometimes sugar, together, using the fingertips, until soft and creamy, and then gradually incorporating the flour until a soft, very rich paste is achieved.

The butter and sugar should not be creamed together as for a cake, as this produces too spongy a result.

Use only the fingertips of one hand. Succumbing to the temptation to use both hands, or the whole hand, leads to sticky pastry. The warmth of the fingertips is important for softening the fat, but once that is done the mixing and kneading should be as light and quick as possible. Because of the high proportion of fat, no water is added. A buttery rich pastry results, rather like shortcake. If the pastry is sticky it may need chilling before rolling or pressing to shape. Very soft pastry can be more easily rolled between two sheets of greaseproof paper.

This pastry can be made in a machine, as can many pastries, but it is vital to under- rather than over-mix.

When the pastry is biscuit-coloured and cooked it will still be soft. Do not worry, it will crisp up as it cools. Slide it off the baking sheet (using a palette knife) when cool.

HOT WATER CRUST

For this pastry water and fat are heated together and mixed into the flour.

Because of the high proportion of water, this pastry is

inclined to be hard. Also, as the fat used is generally lard, it can be lacking in flavour, so add a good pinch of salt. Do not allow the water to boil before the fat has melted. If the water reduces by boiling, the proportion of water to flour will not be correct.

Mix the water and melted fat into the flour quickly and keep the pastry in a warm bowl, covered with a hot damp cloth. This prevents the fat becoming set and the pastry flaking and drying out so that it is unmanageable.

CHOUX PASTRY

This pastry, containing eggs and butter, is easy to make but strict adherence to the recipe (pages 372-3) is vital. The following points are particularly important:

1. Measure the ingredients exactly.
2. Do not allow the water to boil until the butter has melted, but when it has, bring it immediately to a full rolling boil.
3. Have the flour ready in a bowl so that the minute your rolling boil is achieved, you can tip the flour in, all in one go.
4. Do not over-beat. Once the mixture is leaving the sides of the pan, stop.
5. Cool before adding the egg – too much heat would scramble the eggs.
6. Do not beat in more egg than is necessary to achieve a dropping consistency. If the mixture is too stiff, the pastry will be stodgy. If it is too sloppy it will rise unevenly into shapeless lumps.
7. Bake on a wet baking sheet – the steam helps the paste to rise.
8. Bake until it is a good even brown, otherwise the inside of the pastry will be uncooked.
9. If the pastry is to be served cold, split the buns/rings, or poke holes in them with a skewer to allow the steam inside to escape. If the steam remains trapped the pastry will be soggy and a little heavy.
10. Serve the pastry on the day it is made, or store frozen. It will not keep well in a tin.

STRUDEL PASTRY

Unlike almost every other pastry, this one benefits from very heavy handling. It is in fact beaten and stretched, thumped and kneaded. This is all to allow the gluten to expand and promote elasticity in the dough. The paste is rolled and stretched on à cloth (the bigger the better) until it is so thin that you should be able to read fine print through it. Keep the paste covered and moist when not in use. When rolled out, brush with butter or oil to prevent cracking and drying.

SOUFFLÉS

Soufflé means 'puffed up', and that is what soufflés are. A true soufflé is hot and, because whisked egg white (containing a lot of air) is incorporated in the mixture, it is very light and puffs up as the air inside expands and rises. Cold soufflés, which are not true soufflés since they do not puff up, are so called because they have a texture similar to the true hot soufflé as they too contain whisked egg white (full of air). They are in fact light mousses. The setting agent (usually gelatine) traps the air in the mixture by firmly setting the solid ingredients. But the mixture does not rise at all. A hot soufflé, having no setting agent, will not stay indefinitely puffed up, but the ingredients of the soufflé will solidify somewhat in cooking, so trapping the risen air temporarily.

HOT SOUFFLÉS

General opinion, and myth fostered by cookery writers and teachers, is enough to make the inexperienced cook too nervous to attempt a hot soufflé. This is nonsense. Soufflés are extremely easy to make, seldom go wrong, can be very inexpensive, are quick to prepare and perfectly delicious. The base can be prepared well in advance, the whites being whisked and folded in whenever required.

In Leith's Restaurant we use a good trick, stolen from the Café Royal: the soufflé mixture is made, the egg whites folded in and the mixture turned into a soufflé dish. It is then immediately and very rapidly frozen. When a soufflé is ordered by a customer it is simply taken from the deep-freeze and immediately (without any thawing) baked. The baking time needed is generally one quarter as long again as the unfrozen soufflé requires. This takes the worry out of last-minute mixing and folding, and ensures that every soufflé is as it should be, having been carefully and exactly made in the peace of the morning.

The soufflé base for a savoury soufflé is generally a thick béchamel sauce (called a panade) mixed with the desired flavouring – grated cheese, flaked fish, purée of spinach or what have you. A sweet hot soufflé is often made with a white sauce panade (plus the puréed apricots, rhubarb etc.) but a crème pâtissière or a thick custard made with milk, arrowroot and butter may be used. The richest and most delicious sweet soufflé base is undoubtedly the crème pâtissière, but it is inclined to sink rather more quickly than the others.

All hot soufflés will finally sink, but if they are properly made they will not do so as soon as they are taken from the oven. Indeed, if the soufflé is not immediately required it can sit in a turned-off oven for ten minutes without coming to harm, and there will still be time to take it from the oven, dust it with icing sugar or grated Parmesan, wrap a napkin around it and carry it to the dining room at a leisurely pace, *and serve it*, before it looks any the worse for wear.

If you were to make a soufflé simply by mixing some sort of good tasting mixture with whisked egg whites, pouring it into a dish and baking it, you would probably get a perfectly good result. But having mastered such simple methods it is useful to know how the perfect, well and evenly risen, crisp-on-the-outside-and-moist-in-the-middle soufflé is achieved.

The following notes then are for the perfectionist, or for when something has gone wrong.

The base

When the base is made, and still warm, it should have a soft, not-quite-runny consistency. The too-solid base will not fold easily into the egg whites, and the too-runny one will not be held by the egg whites and will not rise as well. If the base has been made in advance and is cold, it should be gently warmed before the whites are added. Do not add more liquid to it as this will spoil the proportions.

The egg whites

Most recipes call for slightly more egg whites than egg yolks. This is because the aim is to achieve more bulk of whites than bulk of base. Obviously the more whites, the more the mixture will rise, but *too* many will make the rising too sudden and uneven, and the mixture will sink rapidly as there will not be enough solid ingredients to hold the risen mixture in place. It will also taste insipid. Too few whites will produce a poorly risen soufflé. The whites should be whisked at the last minute (they re-liquefy if left standing, and cannot be re-whisked satisfactorily). They should be whisked until the mixture, when the whisk is lifted, will stand in 'medium peaks' (i.e. the peaks will flop over slightly at the top, and not stay rigidly in place). If the whites are over-whisked and dry-looking they will be difficult to fold into the mixture. If they are underwhisked and still slightly runny they will not cause the soufflé to rise enough. In order to fold them in easily, it is a good idea first to mix in one table-spoon, which will loosen the base, then fold in the rest. The egg whites should be folded in to the base with a large metal spoon, held close to the bowl, not at the end of the handle. This makes it easier to lift and turn the mixture, getting the whites well distributed without bashing out all the carefully incorporated air. In order to dispel any large pockets of air that may be trapped in the mixture, cut through the mixture several times with a knife, once it is in the soufflé dish. Also give the dish a sharp crack on the table to 'settle' it evenly. Both these actions are to ensure even (as opposed to lop-sided) rising.

Note: It is true that whites steadily whisked by hand in a copper or metal bowl, with a balloon whisk, contain the most air at the end of the process, but machines are here to stay, and we have found machine-whisked whites perfectly satisfactory.

The soufflé dish

The ideal dish is a fine fireproof china one with straight sides up which the soufflé will easily rise. China is a good conductor of heat, and as it is thin the heat will penetrate quickly. But soufflés can be made in pie dishes or even bread or cake tins. The essential rule is to brush the sides lightly with melted butter so that the rising soufflé will not stick to the dry surface but will glide up smoothly. Another advantage of thin china is that it will not hold the heat like earthenware, and so the soufflé will not continue to cook once taken from the oven.

When preparing the soufflé dish a double band of greaseproof paper can be tied round the top of the dish to hold the rising soufflé in place. It is removed before serving and gives an evenly risen soufflé. But it is not necessary – unless the heat is uneven the soufflé will not fall over the edge. Too high a band of paper will prevent the heat from penetrating. About 2·5cm/1in is ideal. The inside of the paper, like the dish, must be brushed with butter.

The oven

It is vital that the oven be pre-heated completely. Uneven heat will produce a lop-sided result. Remove the shelves above the middle shelf so that the soufflé does not rise through them! To give the soufflé 'bottom heat' and extra 'lift', put a baking sheet into the oven on the middle shelf when heating it. Then the dish can be placed on this already hot surface. Do not open the oven door until the cooking time is up, or at least not until there is only five minutes to go – the blast of cold air could cause premature collapse. Obey the oven temperature instruction religiously. A moderately hot oven is ideal; too fierce a heat will cause a top crust to form before the soufflé has risen. The crust will then effectively prevent the mixture from rising. Too low a temperature will discourage rising and the soufflé will be stodgy and heavy.

To test if the soufflé is cooked

Open the door a crack and look at it. It should be well risen and a good brown. If it is not, shut the door carefully. The ideal soufflé is a little moist, not completely dry in the middle. With practice it is possible to tell if a soufflé is done by giving the dish a slight shove. If the mixture wobbles alarmingly it is still too raw, but if it only wobbles slightly and seems firm, it is done.

If there is a danger of the soufflé overcooking (perhaps because your lunch guests are notoriously unreliable about arriving on time) make a sauce (mornay sauce for a cheese soufflé, tomato sauce for a spinach soufflé etc.). Then if the soufflé is on the dry side, it won't matter.

COLD SOUFFLÉS

For these soufflés a band or collar of greaseproof paper (which should be lightly oiled, not buttered) is a good idea, as the resulting soufflé will then look even more like a hot one since the mixture will come above the rim of the dish. But it is not essential: the soufflé will taste as good without it.

Cold soufflés are a little trickier than hot ones as the timing of the actions and the temperature of the mixtures is very important.

The base

This is either made simply by beating egg yolks and sugar together, and adding the flavouring purée, melted chocolate or fruit juice; or it may be a thick custard; or a panade (thick white sauce); or it may consist of milk thickened with arrowroot. The base, if made in advance, should not be chilled, as too cold a mixture will cause the gelatine, when it is stirred in, to set in strings before it is thoroughly incorporated.

The cream

It should be fresh and half-whipped. Stiffly whipped cream will not easily be folded into the mixture; underwhipped cream makes the mixture too liquid, and less likely to set well.

The gelatine

This should be first soaked in liquid. Put the liquid (usually a few tablespoons) into a small saucepan and sprinkle on the gelatine powder. Leave undisturbed for at least 10 minutes to 'sponge': the gelatine will absorb the liquid and look solid and spongy. Then warm it over very gentle heat, resisting the temptation to stir, until the gelatine is clear and runny, but not very hot. If it boils it will go stringy and unusable. Weigh the gelatine or measure it accurately (7g/¼oz to ½ litre/¾ pint mixture). Too much and the soufflé will be rubbery, too little and it will be sloppy. The base must be briskly stirred when the gelatine is added, or it will set in strings or lumps.

Note: Gelatine leaves are very much easier to use than dry powder, but they are difficult to obtain. The above remarks assume powder is used. Gelatine leaves are simply melted in the liquid, the 'sponging' process being unnecessary.

Egg whites

As with hot soufflés the number of egg whites usually exceeds the yolks called for. They must be whisked just before folding in, until stiff but by no means dry. One spoonful may be thoroughly stirred in to loosen the base if the base is obviously stiffer than the whites, but it should not be necessary if the base is of the right consistency.

To sum up: the base, fruit purée (or melted chocolate etc.) and the egg whites should, as far as possible, have the same soft consistency. If there is an unavoidable difference in consistency add the thinner to the thicker one. The gelatine should be warm, clear and runny when added. The base should be at room temperature, not icy-cold or hot.

Once set, cold soufflés are usually decorated with whipped cream, nuts and/or fruit.

STOCKS

Good strong natural stocks are behind almost every good sauce or casserole. Stock-cubes are often over-salty and 'packet-flavoured', so should be used guardedly.

Brown stock is used in brown sauces and soups, and is of a stronger flavour than white stock. The secrets of a good brown stock are very thorough, even browning of the ingredients by frying, very slow cooking, and constant skimming.

Stocks should be simmered rather than boiled, and skimming off scum and fat is vital. A stock containing a lot of fat, boiled vigorously, will have an unattractive smell and a greasy, rather muddy taste, even if the fat is subsequently removed.

Salt should not be added to basic stocks as the stock may be used for cooking salted foods, which would then become over-salty. Add salt if necessary when using the stock.

Brown and white stock can be simmered with advantage for many hours, but fish bones become bitter with more than 30 minutes' cooking. Brown and white stocks can be kept on the go for weeks, as long as they are strained and religiously brought to the boil every day. The straining is to discard all the bones and vegetables that have given up their flavour. The boiling is to prevent fermenting – a disaster more likely to happen to chicken stocks than any other.

Stocks can be reduced by boiling to a very strong, almost thick consistency and frozen in small quantities (e.g. in an ice tray). They can then be used as needed with the addition of water to bring them back to the original strength.

Strong stocks should set like a jelly. Pigs' trotters or veal bones added to the stock will ensure setting.

Strong jellied stocks can be kept refrigerated for seven to ten days. If to be kept longer they should be reboiled.

SAVOURY SAUCES

Larousse defines a sauce as a 'liquid seasoning for food'. A sauce is normally thickened to prevent it running right off the food. There are four basic thickening agents:

Roux

Butter and flour are cooked together before the liquid is added. There are three degrees to which a roux can be cooked:

White: The butter and flour are merely mixed over a gentle heat without browning.
Blond: The roux is allowed to cook to a biscuit colour.
Brown: The roux is cooked until the butter and flour are distinctly brown.

These act as the base for three classic sauces mères (mother sauces) from which there are many derivatives or daughter sauces. See the sauce table.

Cornflour or arrowroot (fécule)

These are 'slaked' (mixed to a paste with cold water, stock or milk), added to hot liquid and allowed to boil for one or two minutes.

Beurre manié

Equal quantities of butter and flour are kneaded to a smooth paste and whisked into a boiling liquid. As the butter melts the flour is evenly distributed throughout the sauce, thickening the liquid without allowing lumps to form.

Egg yolks

These are used in two ways to thicken sauces. Oil or butter beaten into egg yolk will form an emulsion, as in mayonnaise and hollandaise sauces. Egg yolk can also be mixed with cream (or other liquid) to form a liaison. This is then added to a sauce or to milk, and the whole heated without boiling – enough to thicken the yolks without scrambling them. This is the method of thickening used in English custard and in blanquette de veau.

Most classic sauces are derived from basic mother sauces. The following table gives examples of classic daughter sauces and briefly explains how the mother sauce is made. After the table there follows a list of miscellaneous, but nonetheless classic, sauces that do not exactly fit into the mother/daughter pattern.

MOTHER	DAUGHTER	USES
WHITE SAUCE		
Seasoned milk thickened with a white roux.	*Anchovy:* with added anchovy essence.	Fish
Used for vegetables and as a binding for croquettes etc.	*Béchamel:* flavoured with bay leaf, onion, peppercorns.	Eggs, fish, chicken
	Cardinale: béchamel mixed with fish stock and flavoured with truffle essence, lobster butter, cayenne.	Fish
	Crème: with added cream.	Eggs, veal
	Egg: with added chopped, hardboiled eggs.	Fish
	Mornay: with added grated cheese.	Fish, eggs, cauliflower
	Soubise: with added cooked, chopped onion.	Mutton, eggs, fish, cauliflower

MOTHER	DAUGHTER	USES

BLOND SAUCE (Velouté)

White stock thickened with a blond roux.	*Aurore:* with added tomato purée.	Eggs, fish, meat, vegetables
Used for eggs, fish, vegetables and white meat.	*Poulette:* with added mushroom essence, lemon juice and chopped parsley.	Carrots, broad and French beans, boiled potatoes, calf's head, veal
	Suprême: made with chicken stock and cream, flavoured with mushroom peelings. Sometimes finished with an egg and cream liaison.	Chicken, vol-au-vents
	Mushroom: sauce suprême, with added mushrooms. Sometimes finished with an egg yolk and cream liaison.	Chicken, sweetbreads

BROWN SAUCES

Sauce espagnole
(also called easy demi-glace sauce)

A mirepoix of vegetables is cooked in fat until coloured. Flour is added and cooked until brown and sandy in texture. Brown stock is added with tomatoes and mushroom peelings.	*Chasseur:* espagnole with mushrooms, tomato and white wine, chopped parsley.	Grills, entrées, roasts, rabbit, chicken
Used for red meats and game.	*Robert:* chopped onions sweated in butter with added vinegar, white wine and pepper, reduced by half and added to espagnole. Flavoured with mustard.	Pork, kidneys, tongue, ham

MOTHER	DAUGHTER	USES

Sauce demi-glace

This is a more sophisticated brown sauce, made by simmering equal quantities of espagnole sauce with jellied bone stock. The sauce is then reduced by gentle boiling to half quantity, and is repeatedly skimmed. A good demi-glace looks like a rich syrupy gravy, when hot semi-clear in appearance and setting to a jelly when cold.

Used for red meats and game.

MOTHER	DAUGHTER	USES
	Madeira: espagnole or demi-glace with Madeira.	Veal, tongue
	Bordelaise: demi-glace with reduced wine, shallots and thyme.	Grilled steaks
	Poivrade: parsley stalks, thyme, crushed pepper corns and bay leaves cooked with a mirepoix which is then marinaded in wine or vinegar and reduced by half. Added to demi-glace and cooked 30 minutes, then strained.	Game
	Diane: poivrade with cream.	Grilled steaks
	Reforme: equal quantities of poivrade and demi-glace, garnished with julienne of egg whites, gherkins, truffles and tongue.	Lamb
	Perigueux: demi-glace with truffles or truffle essence.	Red meat, game

Note: All the brown daughter sauces can be made with either espagnole or demi-glace but the richer ones (madeira, bordelaise, poivrade, diane, reforme and perigueux) should classically by made with a proper demi-glace.

MOTHER	DAUGHTER	USES

BUTTER SAUCE
(Beurre à l'Anglaise)

White roux plus boiling water with added butter beaten in, flavoured with lemon juice.	*Bâtarde:* with added egg yolk.	Cauliflower, veal, eggs etc.
	Câpre (caper): with added capers.	Boiled turbot, cod, mutton
Used for vegetables and fish.	*Fennel:* with added blanched chopped Florence fennel.	Fish

EMULSIONS

Hollandaise sauce

This is an emulsion made with egg yolks and butter, flavoured with vinegar, peppercorns and salt.	*Béarnaise:* reduction of chopped shallots, pepper, tarragon, added to hollandaise, served with chopped tarragon and chervil.	Grilled steaks
Used for asparagus, broccoli, eggs etc.	*Choron:* béarnaise with added tomato purée.	Grills, fish and asparagus
	Mousselline: with added whipped cream.	Asparagus, sole, sea kale
	Moutarde: with added mustard.	Herrings, mackerel, poached fish

Mayonnaise

An emulsion of egg yolk and oil, seasoned with vinegar, pepper and salt.	*Aioli:* crushed garlic (and sometimes mashed potato) beaten into the emulsion of egg yolk and oil.	Soups, especially provençal fish soups
Served cold with cold salads and cold fish, poultry or meat.		Raw vegetables

65

MOTHER	DAUGHTER	USES
	Remoulade: with added mustard and sometimes capers, parsley, gherkins, chervil, tarragon and anchovy essence.	Celeriac, celery, salads and herrings
	Tartare: with added chopped hardboiled eggs, capers, gherkins and onions.	Fried fish and shellfish
	Andalouse: with added tomato purée and chopped sweet red peppers.	Salads, chicken and fish

MISCELLANEOUS

CRANBERRY

Cranberries, sugar and water, poached and sieved.

APPLE

Cooking apple, butter and sugar, cooked together to a thick purée and sieved.

BIGARADE

Duck gravy, orange juice and butter, thickened with arrowroot.

BREAD

Milk flavoured with bay leaf, onions and cloves and thickened with breadcrumbs. Seasoned with pepper and salt and enriched with added butter.

CUMBERLAND

Redcurrant jelly and port simmered together and flavoured with orange juice, lemon juice, mustard, cayenne, ginger and chopped cooked shallots. Served cold.

MINT

Vinegar, sugar, salt, pepper, chopped mint, sometimes mixed with small amount of boiling water.

TOMATO

Mirepoix, stock, tomato purée and fresh tomatoes, cooked for 30 minutes and sieved.

SOUPS

The word soup covers almost anything from a hefty peasant meal, thick with cereals or root vegetables, to a delicate clear consommé meant only to wake up the appetite for greater things to come.

BROTHS

Broths (or bouillons) are well-flavoured stocks which are served unthickened and unclarified. They are made from the liquor in which meat (and sometimes vegetables) has been cooked. Very little is done to the basic stock – it may be further seasoned with pepper and salt, or watered down if too strong, or reduced by rapid boiling if not strong enough. Broths are frequently garnished with a small handful of cooked rice, barley or small pasta such as vermicelli, or with small pieces of root vegetables cut into dice, or with chopped fresh parsley, or finely chopped leek.

CLEAR SOUPS

Clear soups (or consommés) are similar in taste to broths, but they have been cleared by the addition of egg whites and crushed egg shell to the stock, which is then filtered through the cooked egg-white mass, and through muslin. There is generally a good meat base (chicken, veal or beef) to a consommé, and if it is to be served chilled, a veal bone or extra gelatine is added to the stock to ensure a jelly-like set.

Many consommés take their names from their garnishes: julienne strips of vegetables (consommé Julienne), miniature choux pastry profiteroles (consommé aux profiteroles). Consommé is sometimes served with a dash of sherry in it – too often with too much sherry, to the ruin of an otherwise good soup. Cheese straws are frequently handed separately when consommé is served – a good idea as the crispness and tang of the cheese straws contrasts well with the silken, almost sticky, soup.

Chilled consommés form the base of many iced first courses, topped with sour cream and mock caviar for example, or with a curry-flavoured spoonful of cream cheese in each coup.

CREAM SOUPS

The word cream in this context does not necessarily mean that there is cream in the soup, only that the soup has been liquidized, beaten or mashed to a 'cream'. The simplest form of the cream soup is the vegetable purée, which is simply a liquidized mixture of vegetable and cooking stock. Cauliflower and parsnip soup, for example, may consist of a few roast parsnips left over from yesterday's lunch, the remains of a cauliflower in white sauce, a pint of chicken stock (perhaps made from a stock cube) and an onion, finely chopped and gently cooked in butter. All these ingredients liquidized together would give a delicious, though not grand, soup.

Cream soups are usually thickened with flour, however, or by the addition of some floury ingredient, such as potato. If potato or other starchy food (such as lentils or sweetcorn) is to provide the thickening, these are simply cooked in the soup, and the whole sieved or liquidized before serving. If flour is to be used, it is first mixed with butter (about 30g/1oz of each for 570ml/1 pint of liquid) and then dropped in small blobs into the hot soup, while it is stirred. The melting butter evenly distributes the flour, so preventing lumps forming. This flour-and-butter paste is called beurre manié (kneaded butter).

A similar, and more common way of thickening soups is the roux method. Here the butter is melted in the saucepan, the flour is then stirred into it, the liquid added, and the whole stirred until boiling. If the recipe calls for, say, onions to be gently 'sweated' in butter at the beginning of the process, this is done and the flour is then added to the onion/butter mixture before the liquid.

With both the beurre manié and the roux methods, it is essential that the soup be allowed to boil or simmer for at least 1 minute to thoroughly cook the flour, and to allow it to thicken the liquid.

The most difficult method of thickening soups and sauces is the egg and cream liaison, but it gives by far the richest and most velvety result. Egg yolks (usually two to 570ml/1 pint of soup) are mixed with half a cup or so of cream. Hot soup is then poured into the cup, mixed well, and the whole then poured back into the soup, while the soup is stirred. But on no account must the soup be allowed to approach boiling point, or the egg yolks will scramble into a curdled mess. Just enough heat is needed to thicken the yolks without cooking them completely.

Tapioca, sago, cornflour or arrowroot will thicken soup too, but give it a glassy, unattractive look.

BISQUES

There are soups made from shellfish, and, usually, fish stocks. The shells of the shellfish are boiled in the stock to give colour and flavour to the bisque. They are smooth cream soups, slightly thickened with an egg and cream liaison and often highly seasoned.

CHOWDERS

Chowders are thick soups, containing plenty of solid ingredients, which are not creamed to a smooth consistency. Clam chowder has whole clams in it; corn chowder, whole kernels of corn etc. The biblical 'mess of potage' would today be a chowder, a meal on its own.

GARNISHES FOR SOUP

In classic haute cuisine there are written rules about which garnish is permissible with what soup, but nowadays such pedantry seems irrelevant. The question to settle is, 'Will the garnish *do* anything for the soup?' If the answer is no, it is not worth the fiddling about. Just serve crisp hot toast.

Spicy garnishes, with a crisp texture (such as cayenne-flavoured croutons) are just right with a smooth bland soup. Very rich garnishes, such as cheese squares, are good with an acid, light soup, such as a thin tomato broth.

Some suggested garnishes:

For thin broths and clear soups

Tiny, deep-fried profiteroles made with cheese choux pastry.
Tiny, baked profiteroles sprinkled with cayenne before cooking.
Tiny, shell-shaped noodles or vermicelli.
Pulses – cooked rice or barley.
Cooked diced carrot, turnip and celery.
Squares (croutons) of fried bread or toast.
Squares of bread covered thickly with cheese and toasted.
Finely shredded raw lettuce leaf, spinach leaf or sprig of watercress (added at the last minute).
Finely shredded leek or cabbage (allowed to cook in the soup for one minute).
Cooked fine slices of Chinese dried mushroom.
Small slivers of peeled raw tomato.

For thick soups

Whole fresh small cooked peas in a pea soup.
Small squares of ham in a pulse (e.g. lentil or split pea) soup.
A thick paste of creamed cheese, flavoured with chopped fresh onion and curry paste, for cucumber soup, watercress soup, or chicken soup, especially if the soups are served chilled.
Small slices of fried apple for curry soup.
Sour cream for borscht (beetroot soup).
Slices of mushroom for chicken soup.

Chopped fresh basil and/or oregano for tomato soup.

Sour damsons or fresh plums cooked in red wine for potato soup.

Red caviar (salmon roe) or mock caviar (lumpfish roe) for fish soups.

Cucumber slices for all cold soups.

Swirl of cream on all thickened soups.

Liquor – dash of port in potato soup, sherry in tomato soup, brandy in seafood bisque.

VEGETABLES

Vegetables in Britain are served as an accompaniment to a main meat course. It is worth considering them, however, as first courses on their own, or as main courses if served in sufficient variety, or with, for example, a cheese sauce. For a salad or starter they may be served raw or cooked, with a dressing.

Bouquetière de légumes

A collection (or *bouquetière*) of freshly and simply cooked, well presented vegetables is a rare pleasure. Care should be taken, however, that each vegetable is carefully prepared and garnished with an appropriate herb and/or brushed with melted butter. Choose vegetables that are of contrasting flavour and colour, and arrange them on a heated platter so that, for example, green peas and green broccoli are separated by the red of tomatoes or carrots, and that white vegetables (like new potatoes and salsify) are not placed side by side. See the notes overleaf for cooking methods, and the following table for cooking times etc. for specific vegetables.

FRESH GREEN VEGETABLES

Blanching and refreshing

This method of cooking vegetables is commonly used in restaurants where some advance preparation is vital. It is worth doing when coping with a large selection of vegetables.

Boil the vegetables separately: bring the water to a good boil and drop in the vegetables. Use enough water only barely to cover them and add one teaspoon of salt for each pint of water. Do not cover the pan. Boil as rapidly as you dare (delicate vegetables like broccoli can break up if *too* rapidly boiled). As soon as they are tender, but not yet totally soft, drain them and rinse in cold water to prevent further cooking and to set the colour. This is called *refreshing*. Just before serving toss the vegetables separately in melted butter over a good heat.

Note I: As the cooking liquid contains much of the vitamins and minerals it should, if possible, be preserved and used for soups or sauces.

Note II: The word 'blanching' as used above is confusing since it used to mean to whiten (*blanche* = white in French) by rapid boiling, e.g. to blanch almonds would be to boil them to enable the cook to peel the brown skins off, leaving them white. Here, however, it simply means to boil until very nearly cooked. The cooking is finished in the re-heating process.

Boiling

Follow the same procedure as above. Drain the vegetables (without refreshing) and dish up. Brush with melted butter.

Sweating or half-steaming

There is no doubt that from a nutritional point of view this is a better way of cooking green vegetables as no minerals or vitamins are lost with the cooking water. This method, however, does not always produce a very attractive green colour, and cannot successfully be done in advance.

Put the prepared vegetables in a heavy saucepan with a table-spoon of butter or margarine (or, if preferred, water). Cover tightly with a lid. Cook very slowly. Shake the pan frequently until the vegetables are tender. Add salt and dish up.

Steaming

Steaming (in a proper steamer) is an excellent method of cooking root vegetables, but is less successful with green ones as their bright colour is sometimes lost. Nutritionally superior to boiling.

Stir frying

This cooking method (much beloved of Chinese cooks) is excellent for green vegetables. It preserves vitamins and minerals, and the vegetables remain bright in colour. The disadvantage is that you must stand over the cooking vegetables all the time.

Slice the vegetables as finely as you can, put in a large deep-sided frying pan (the Chinese wok is perfect) with a splash of oil. Toss the vegetables in the hot oil over a fierce heat. Shake the pan, and stir and turn the vegetables continually until they are just tender. Sprinkle with salt and serve.

FRESH NON-GREEN VEGETABLES

Boiling

Put the vegetables into cold salted water and bring slowly to the boil. Cook until completely tender. With the possible exception of carrots (which are good *al dente* or with a bit of bite to them), root vegetables should be cooked until soft right through. Drain and brush with melted butter. Unlike green vegetables, root vegetables are generally cooked in a covered saucepan, as their colour is unaffected by slower cooking in a closed pan, but they can be boiled rapidly as are green vegetables. Care should be taken to prevent potatoes breaking up.

Refreshing (see page 72)

This is sometimes advisable for carrots as this sets the bright colour, but is not necessary.

Sweating or half-steaming

Slice the vegetables fairly thickly. Cook them slowly in a covered saucepan with plenty of butter or oil. They will absorb more fat than green vegetables. Very good for mushrooms.

Steaming

Excellent for all root vegetables, particularly for large potatoes which might otherwise break up while boiling.

DRIED PULSES

Dried peas and beans (lentils, split peas, chick peas, green peas, black-eyed peas, haricot beans, lima beans, butter beans, brown beans, red kidney beans etc.) are generally cheaper than their fresh or tinned equivalents, are easy to cook and very nutritious. They should be bought from grocers with a good turnover, and as a rule small butter beans are better than large ones, small chick peas better than large etc.

Most pulses need soaking until softened and swollen before cooking. Soaking can take as much as 12 hours (e.g. butter beans) or as little as 20 minutes (e.g. lentils). Do not soak for more than 12 hours in case the beans start germinating or fermenting. If there is no time for preliminary soaking, unsoaked pulses may be cooked either in a pressure cooker or very slowly; but remember that enough water must be used to allow the beans first to swell and then to cook. Preliminary soaking is less hazardous.

To cook the pulses, simply cover them with fresh cold salted water, bring to the boil and simmer until tender. (Boiling the vegetables without salt is said to produce better results but we have not found this to be so.) Boiling times vary according to the age and size of the pulses (last season's pulses will cook faster than three-year-old ones). Small lentils may take as little as 15 minutes and large haricot beans or chick peas can take as long as 2 hours.

Vegetable	Preparation	Suggested method of cooking	Approx. cooking time	Suggested garnish
Artichoke, Jerusalem	Wash and peel.	Steam, sweat or boil.	30–40 min	Melted butter, black pepper and squeeze lemon juice.
Asparagus	Wash, remove hard ends and peel tough outer skin if necessary. Tie in bundles.	Steam or boil in unsalted water. Stems will cook slower than heads so stand bundles upright with heads above water level (where they will cook slowly in the steam while the stems cook fast in the boiling water).	10–15 min	Hollandaise sauce or melted butter (seasoned with salt, pepper and lemon juice) handed separately.
Beans, broad	Shell. (If very young they are good boiled whole.)	Boil in salted water. Remove outer skins after cooking if tough.	7–10 min	Melted butter and fried bacon bits, or white sauce, or fried chopped walnuts.
Beans, French	Wash, top and tail. String if necessary.	Boil in salted water.	8–12 min	Melted butter, fried almonds.
Beans, runner	String if necessary. Wash. Cut into 5cm/2in lengths.	Boil in salted water.	7–10 min	Melted butter, chopped fresh thyme.

Vegetable	Preparation	Suggested method of cooking	Approx. cooking time	Suggested garnish
Beetroot, young	Wash but do not peel.	Boil in salted water. Then peel.	1–2 hrs	White sauce. Or butter (melted) with raw onion, chopped.
Broccoli	Wash. Remove tough leaves or stalks.	Boil in salted water.	8–15 min	Melted butter or hollandaise sauce.
Broccoli, sprouting	Wash. Remove hard stalks.	Boil in salted water.	6–10 min	Melted butter or hollandaise sauce.
Brussels sprouts	Trim off outer tough leaves. Trim stalks. If large make a deep cup in base to promote quicker cooking.	Boil in salted water.	6–12 min	Melted butter, pinch nutmeg or caraway seeds.
Cabbage, Chinese	Wash. Slice coarsely.	Stir fry, sweat or boil very briefly.	4–6 min	Melted butter, squeeze of lemon. Black pepper.
Cabbage, red	Shred finely.	Stew gently (covered) in heavy pan with butter, chopped onions, chopped apples, sultanas, salt, pepper, sugar and a little vinegar. Turn frequently.	2–3 hrs or until very mushy	Serve as it is.

Cabbage, spring	Wash. Shred very finely.	Stir fry, or boil in salted water.	*Stir fry:* 10 min *Boil:* 5–7 min	Melted butter and caraway seeds.
Carrots	Peel and slice or cut into sticks.	Boil in salted water with pinch of sugar.	8–10 min	Melted butter, and chopped mint.
	Or peel and grate coarsely. Do not salt.	Stir fry in butter.	2 min	Salt, pepper, pinch of sugar.
Cauliflower	Wash. Break into florets. Remove large stalks.	Boil in salted water.	12 min	Browned butter (beurre noisette) *or* white sauce *or* mornay sauce.
Celery	Wash and cut in 5cm/2in pieces.	Boil in salted water.	15–20 min	White sauce *or* chopped dill and melted butter.
Courgettes	Peel strips of skin lengthwise from the courgette, leaving half the skin on. This looks pretty and stripey.	Boil in salted water, or sweat in butter.	*Boil:* 4–6 min *Sweat:* 5–10 min	Melted butter *or* Béchamel sauce.
	Or grate coarsely, including skin. Do not salt.	Stir fry in butter	35 sec	Salt and pepper

Vegetable	Preparation	Suggested method of cooking	Approx. cooking time	Suggested garnish
Endive	Wipe dry. Leave whole.	Steam, or bake in oven, covered, in water with lemon, chopped tarragon and thyme.	Steam: 20–30 min Bake: 1–1¼ hrs	Steamed: white sauce. Baked: melted butter, chopped parsley.
Kale, curly	Wash. Remove hard stalks.	Put in covered saucepan with no extra water. Shake over moderate heat. Drain very well.	6–10 min	Melted butter, pinch of nutmeg and squeeze of lemon.
Leeks	Wash. Remove outer leaves and tough dark green part. Split if large.	Boil in salted water in roasting tin or frying pan. Lift out with a fish slice.	10–15 min	Melted butter and black pepper or white sauce
Mange-tout	Wash, top and tail.	Stir fry, sweat or boil.	5–6 min	Melted butter only.
Marrow	Wash and peel if tough-skinned. Cut into 5cm/2in chunks.	Bake covered in moderate oven with a coating of melted butter. Or steam.	30 min	Browned butter (beurre noisette) and chopped parsley or white sauce.
Mushrooms	Do not peel unless very old and tough. Wipe and trim off any ragged stalks. Quarter if large.	Sweat in butter with squeeze of lemon juice. Or grill, brushed with butter.	4–8 min	Melted butter, black pepper and lemon juice. Or a little double cream or soured cream.

Onions	Peel.	Boil, steam or bake. If to be baked, peel after cooking.	*Boil:* 15–30 min *Steam:* 20–40 min *Bake:* 1–1½ hrs	*Boiled:* toss in butter plus pinch of sugar until pale brown. *Steamed:* white sauce. *Baked:* melted butter.
Parsnips	Peel, and cut up if large.	Boil in salted water. Or boil and mash. Or roast with butter.	*Boil:* 20–30 min *Roast:* 1–2 hrs	Melted butter, black pepper. Nothing if roasted.
Peas	Hull.	Boil in salted water with a good pinch of sugar and a sprig of mint.	5–20 min	Melted butter. Chopped mint.
Potatoes	Peel for steamed or boiled (except new). Scrub and rub with salt for baked. Blanch 5 min then scratch all over with fork for roast.	Steam, boil, sweat, bake or roast. See also deep-frying, potatoes (pages 31–3, 243–244, 228).	*Roast:* 1–1½ hrs *Other methods:* up to 30 min	Melted butter and chopped parsley *or* mint; *or* dill for boiled and steamed.
Pumpkin	Wash and peel. Cut into 5cm/2in chunks.	Roast: with butter and lemon juice. Steam or sweat: in butter.	*Steam or sweat:* 30 min *Roast:* 1–2 hrs	Melted butter and chopped parsley. Nothing if roasted.

Vegetable	Preparation	Suggested method of cooking	Approx. cooking time	Suggested garnish
Salsify (white-skinned)	Wash and cut into 5cm/2in lengths.	Boil. Peel after cooking.	15–20 min	Beurre noisette (browned butter).
Scorzonera (black-skinned salsify-like root)	Wash, peel and cut into 5cm/2in lengths.	Boil, steam or sweat.	15–20 min	Beurre noisette (browned butter).
Sea Kale	Wash and remove any tough stem.	Boil in salted water or steam.	10–20 min	Hollandaise sauce, or melted butter (seasoned with salt, pepper and lemon juice) handed separately.
Shallots	Peel.	Boil in salted water. Steam, sweat or roast with butter.	15–30 min More for roasting	*Steamed:* white sauce. *Boiled:* browned butter (beurre noisette).
Spinach	Wash well. Pull away stalks.	Put into covered saucepan *without any water*. Shake over moderate heat. Drain and squeeze dry.	4 min	Melted butter, grated nutmeg *or* crushed fried garlic.

Swedes	Peel thickly. Slice.	20–30 min	*Mashed:* plenty of butter, salt and pepper. *Whole:* melted butter *and/ or* chopped parsley.
Sweetcorn	Remove the outside leaves and thread-like fibres.	5–6 min (longer if old)	Melted butter and freshly ground black pepper.
Tomatoes	Wash. Split in half.	*Grill:* 5 min *Bake:* 12–15 min in moderate oven.	Chopped basil or parsley and black pepper.
	Grill or bake (boiled tomatoes are very dreary) sprinkled with butter and chopped onion and/or garlic.		
Turnips	Peel thickly. Slice thickly.	20–30 min	Melted butter and lemon juice.
	Sweat or steam. Mash if very wet and shake over heat to dry.		

HERBS AND SPICES

Many herbs (aromatic green plants used for flavouring) can be home-grown. Most spices have to be bought as they are the seeds, roots, berries or bark of plants grown in tropical climates.

Buying and storing

As far as possible always use fresh rather than dried herbs. They freeze well and taste infinitely better than their dried counterpart.

Dried herbs and spices lose flavour fairly rapidly and so it is essential to buy in small quantities to ensure as quick a turnover as possible. Always keep them in air-tight containers in a cool, dry place – not near the oven or sink.

Most fresh green herbs keep well for a few days in a plastic bag in the refrigerator.

FISH

The word 'fish' is used to include freshwater and sea fish, but not shellfish (see pages 104–11).

Freshwater fish are divided into coarse fish, fished mainly for sport with rod and line and generally thrown back live into the rivers, and game fish, which are caught both for sport and commercially. Recently, freshwater fish farms have been set up. Many freshwater fish, such as bass, sturgeon, sea trout and salmon spend most of their adult lives in the sea, swimming back up the rivers to spawn, but they are still classified as freshwater fish despite the fact that most of them are caught by trawl in the sea. Coarse river fish, such as roach, gudgeon and tench are not sold commercially and are seldom eaten except by anglers' families.

Most of our fish come from the sea. As the fishing industry

'modernizes' it is increasingly difficult to get locally caught fish, and in some villages and towns not ten miles from the sea the only fish available is in frozen packets – perhaps a choice of fish fingers, kipper fillets or cod steaks. For the cook this is sad. Fish is a valuable source of protein, vitamin D (in oily fish), calcium and phosphorus (especially found in the edible bones of whitebait, sardines etc.), iodine, fluorine and some of the B vitamins.

Fish contains very little fat. Even oily fish seldom has more than 20 per cent fat content. (A mutton chop will contain 50 per cent fat or more.) This means that fish is easily digestible, and contains fewer calories than its equivalent weight in meat. Fish flesh is so composed (with little connective tissue and little fat) that over-vigorous or over-long cooking will cause dryness and disintegration. For this reason fish is generally grilled or fried fast, or poached gently in barely moving liquid. It cooks a great deal quicker than meat.

Fish, unlike meat, does not improve on keeping. Some *aficionados* say that salmon is best eaten three days after catching, but we feel this is a rationalization of the fact that it used to take three days to bring a salmon down from Scotland to London. Likewise there are some fish chefs and restaurateurs who say that sole is better for a day or two in the chiller, as the flesh is then firmer. But what is undisputed is that any fish (including salmon or sole) eaten within a few hours of catching is remarkably good. Fish as fresh as that should be served as plainly as possible, perhaps with nothing but melted butter and a wedge of lemon.

Fish are either round when seen in section (like a salmon) or flat (like a sole), and are so described.

PREPARATION FOR COOKING

Removing the scales

Large fish have dry scales which should be removed before cooking. To do this, scrape a large knife the wrong way along the fish (from tail to head). This can be a messy business as the scales tend to fly about. But, unless you are buying fish from a wholesale market, the fishmonger will do it for you.

Gutting and cleaning

The fishmonger will probably clean the fish, but if you are to do it yourself you will need a very sharp knife. (Fish skin blunts knives faster than anything else.) If the fish is to be stuffed or filleted it does not matter how big a slit you make to remove the entrails. If it is to be left whole, the shorter the slit the better. Start just below the head and slit through the soft belly skin. After pulling out the innards wash the fish under cold water. If it is large, and of the round type, make sure all the dark blood along the spinal column is removed.

Now carefully cut away the gills. Take care not to cut off the head if you want to serve the fish whole. If you do not, cut off head and tail now. To remove the fins cut the skin round them, take a good grip (if you salt your fingers well it will stop them slipping) and yank sharply towards the head. This will pull the fin bones out with the fin.

Skinning and filleting flat fish

Fish skin is easier to remove after cooking when it comes away easily. But sometimes the fish must be skinned before cooking. Most whole fish are not skinned or filleted before grilling, but sole (and lemon sole, witch and plaice) are skinned on at least the dark side, and sometimes on both sides. To do this make a crosswise slit through the skin at the tail, and push a finger in. You will now be able to run the finger round the edge of the fish loosening the skin. When you have done this on both edges, take a firm grip of the skin at the tail end (salt your fingers to prevent slipping) with one hand, and with the other hold the fish down. Give a quick strong yank, peeling the skin back towards the head. If necessary, do the same to the other side.

Flat fish are generally filleted into four half-fillets. To do this, lay the fish on a board with the tail towards you. Cut through the flesh to the backbone along the length of the fish. Then, with a sharp pliable knife, cut the left-hand fillet away from the bone, keeping the blade almost flat against the bones of the fish. Then swivel the fish round so the head is towards you and cut away the second fillet in the same way. Turn the fish over and repeat the process on the other side. (If you are left-handed, tackle the right-hand fillet first.)

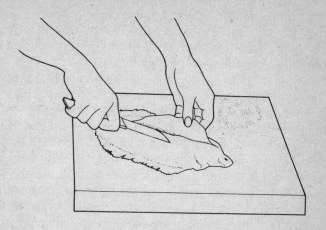

Filleting and skinning round fish

Round fish are filleted before skinning. If they are to be cooked whole, they are cooked with the skin, but this may be carefully peeled off after cooking (e.g. a whole poached salmon). To fillet a round fish lay it on a board and cut through the flesh down to the backbone from the head to the tail. Insert a sharp pliable knife between the flesh and the bones, and slice the fillet away

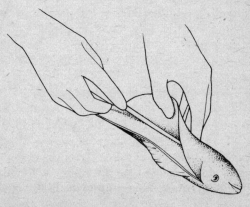

from the bones, working with short strokes from the backbone and from the head end. Remember to keep the knife as flat as possible, and to keep it against the bones. When the fillet is almost off the fish you will need to cut through the belly skin to detach it completely. Very large round fish can be filleted in four, following the flat fish method, or the whole side can be lifted as described here, and then split in two once off the fish.

To skin a fish fillet, put it skin side down on a board. Hold the tip down firmly, using a good pinch of salt to help get a firm grip. With a sharp, heavy, straight knife, cut through the flesh, close to the tip, taking care not to go right through the skin. Hold the knife at rightangles to the fish fillet, with the blade almost upright. With a gentle sawing motion work the flesh from the skin, *pushing* the fillet off rather than cutting it. The reason for keeping the knife almost upright is to lessen the danger of cutting through the skin, but with practice it is possible to flatten the knife slightly, so that the sharp edge is foremost, and simply slide it forward, without the sawing motion.

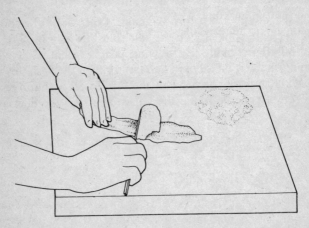

See also page 97 for boning herring and other small fish.

Skinning eel
Cut through the skin round the neck and slit the skin down the length of the body. Hang the eel up by its head – a stout hook

through the eyes is best. Using a cloth to get a good grip, pull hard to peel off the skin from neck to tail.

Stuffing fish

Round fish are more suitable for stuffing whole than flat fish, as there is more space in the body cavity after gutting. Stuffings usually contain breadcrumbs, which swell during cooking, so care should be taken not to overfill the fish. Fish fillets can be sandwiched with stuffing, or rolled up round the mixture. Well-flavoured expensive fish is less often stuffed than the more tasteless varieties, which need the additional flavour of an aromatic filling.

Slicing smoked salmon

Place the side of salmon, skin side down, on a board. Run the tips of the fingers of one hand over the surface of the flesh to locate the ends of the small bones. Pull the bones out with tweezers or pliers. Now slice the flesh in horizontal paper-thin slices, using a long, sharp ham knife. The slices should be long and wide. It is customary to remove the central narrow stripe of brownish flesh, but this is not strictly necessary – it tastes excellent.

If the whole side is not to be sliced, place a piece of plastic wrap on the cut surface of the remaining salmon to prevent drying out.

FRESHWATER FISH

Bass

Name given to many fish, both sea and freshwater. Freshwater bass is in season mid-June to mid-March. Can weigh up to 3·4 kilos/8lb, is sold whole, and has a pale pink, firm, delicately-flavoured flesh. Delicious cooked any way, but the plainer methods are probably best – poached, fried or grilled. Both black and white bass are available, though neither are abundant.

Bream

Sometimes a disappointing fish, lacking flavour and having rather too soft flesh. But good plainly cooked, if very freshly caught, or baked with a herby stuffing to give it bite. In season mid-June to mid-March. Weighs up to 4·5 kilos/10lb but smaller fish (1·35 kilos/3lb) are the norm.

Carp

Usually sold between 1·35 kilos/3lb and 3·4 kilos/8lb but can reach enormous size. Considered a festive fish in parts of Europe (rather like our Christmas Turkey), it is usually sold whole. Coarse texture, not very interesting taste, but good baked with stuffing, or fried in butter with plenty of lemon. In season mid-June to mid-March.

Char

A member of the salmon family, but small – 450g/1lb to 900g/2lb in weight. The flesh resembles that of trout, and recipes for trout will do well for char.

Eel

Usually caught weighing 225g/½lb–900g/2lb. The very small eels are unsatisfactory as they are too bony, and the very large ones (90cm/3ft long and more) have a coarse texture and taste. A 675g/1½lb–900g/2lb eel is best, traditionally eaten cold in a savoury eel jelly, or in pies. But eating habits change, and today they are more often sold smoked, or for use in fish soups or stews. Good coated in egg and breadcrumbs and fried. In season all the year round, best in autumn.

Grilse

This is young salmon which, having spent a year feeding at sea, returns to its native river to spawn. It is paler in colour, more delicate in flavour than older salmon and weighs up to 3·2 kilos/7lb or so.

Pike

Young pike (weighing up to 1·8 kilos/4lb) are best for flavour, but all pike make good quenelles, fish stocks and stews. This is because they contain a high proportion of gelatine. Pike is often added to salmon quenelle mixture to give tackiness and flavour. But they can be cooked in any other way, having good flavour and white flesh. In season mid-June to March.

Salmon

The king of fish, not only in flavour (which is superbly rich) but regrettably in price too. It has an oily, bright pinkish-red flesh ideal for plain poaching, grilling, steaming and frying. (See also under smoked fish.) Fish can reach 9 kilos/20lb or so, but are best at about 3·4 kilos/8lb. The first salmon of the season (which starts in February) are truly unsurpassed in flavour and delicacy. Towards the end of the season (October/November) the taste is sometimes slightly muddy. Canadian salmon sold in Britain is good, but not on a par with Scotch. Salmon steaks cut from the 'middle cut' are the most expensive to buy, but the tail steaks, though less uniform in shape, are even richer in taste. See also Grilse.

Sea trout

Often called salmon trout by fishmongers because of its similarity in looks and colour (pale pink to reddish when raw) to salmon. In fact salmon trout are simply river trout (brown trout, rainbow trout or speckled trout), but because they have spent a season or more in the sea, living on a diet largely composed of crustaceans, their flesh takes on a pink colour and fine flavour akin to that of salmon. It costs rather less than salmon, but is often more difficult to buy. The fish, when really fresh, are perhaps preferable even to salmon, being less rich and solid. They are smaller fish, seldom reaching more than 1·8 kilos/4lb. In season March to August and, like salmon, are best at the beginning of the season. Best cooked whole in the oven or poached. But they can be fried or grilled in fillets.

Smelt

Sometimes classed as a freshwater fish as it is caught in river estuaries as well as in coastal seas. (See under sea fish.)

Trout

Brown river trout and speckled trout are less widely available, and less popular, than Rainbow trout, but this is illogical as they are equally good. Both have firm, white-tending-to-pinkish flesh and are generally sold between 200g/7oz and 340g/¾lb in weight, but they may grow much larger. They are generally cooked whole, either fried or poached 'au bleu' (i.e. killed, gutted and dropped instantly into boiling liquid).

The fishing season is from March to September, but due to fish-farming and freezing rainbow trout are now available all the year round. However, it must be admitted that a line-caught trout, fresh from the river, is a finer thing than an artificially fattened one from a farm, unless the farmer goes to the trouble and expense of feeding his fish on the sort of diet they would find in rivers. Slightly pinkish flesh is common in line-caught fish and is usually an indication of fine flavour.

SEA FISH

FLAT WHITE FISH

(The term 'white' refers to the colour of the flesh, not the skin.)

Brill

An underrated fish, perhaps because its flesh is not as pure-white as some. But it has an excellent flavour. The texture is not as firm as that of turbot, which the fish resembles. Brill seldom grows larger than 3·4 kilos/8lb. It is served poached, grilled or fried, usually in flat pieces of fillet.

Dover sole

The undisputed king of white fish, it has a price to match. Very firm white flesh. The fish comes, not from Dover, but from the North Sea. It can weigh up to 900g/2lb, and is best grilled or fried on the bone, or in a delicate sauce. 170g/6oz soles are called slip soles. A 340g/¾lb sole is the usual weight for a main course. The skin on one side is brownish grey, on the other pearly white.

Lemon sole

So often considered the 'poor man's Dover sole' (it is less firm and flavoursome), it is a delicious fish in its own right. One side is white, the other lightish brown – paler and less grey than the Dover. It is also more rounded in shape, with a pointed nose. Weighs between 225g/½lb and 900g/2lb. The flesh is very white and delicate. Excellent grilled or fried. The fillets are good stuffed and baked in milk. Best in autumn or winter.

Plaice

Similar in shape (though often very much larger, reaching perhaps 2·3 kilos/5lb) to the lemon sole or witch. It has a brownish-grey side, spotted with orange. The other side is white. The flesh, delicious when very fresh, has the disadvantage of being soft rather than firm. Cooked in every possible way, plaice, next to cod, is Britain's most popular fish. It is best plainly grilled or fried. Or the fillets may be stuffed and baked, and served with a cheese sauce. At its best from June to January.

Turbot

An excellent, and expensive, fish of very firm texture and pure white flesh. One of the few fish large enough and firm enough to be cut into cubes and grilled on a skewer. The larger turbot (weighing up to 20 kilos/45lb) are cut across in steaks, the smaller ones (900g/2lb–1·35 kilos/3lb) cooked whole to serve two or three people. Any method of cooking is good. A fish popular with restaurant chefs due to their good size, flavour that does not disappear if the fish is kept for a day or two, and versatility. Best between July and March.

Witch

Used to be called Torbay sole, but this is now illegal. Very like lemon sole, though seldom larger than 675g/1½lb. Cooked similarly, and best in autumn or winter. The skin is pale grey on one side, white on the other.

ROUND WHITE FISH

Cod

Britain's most popular fish, most of it ending up in frozen packets or fish fingers and the like. Good firm white flesh, freezes almost perfectly. The flesh has large creamy flakes, and few bones, but not much taste. Its very non-fishiness may account for its popular appeal, and of course the fact that it is comparatively plentiful. Needs good seasoning, a cheesy sauce, or a crisp batter to counter-act slight dullness. Available all the year round.

Conger eel

The sea eel, stronger in flavour than the small freshwater one, can be up to 9 kilos/20lb in weight. In season from March to October. Used in pies or fish soups, or jellied with parsley. It has a strong and pervading taste, greatly liked by many people but detested by others. Baby eels caught in shoals and cooked like whitebait are excellent but rare.

Dabs

Small plaice-like fish, best served whole, plainly grilled.

Dogfish (flake, huss)

Once also called rock-salmon but this is outlawed now. Only good when very fresh – it develops an unattractive ammonia-like smell when stale. A cheapish fish, very common in fish-and-chip shops, it can be good if fresh and freshly cooked, but has a bad reputation from misuse. Deep frying in batter is best, as the rather soft and oily flesh needs the contrast of crisp batter. There are several varieties of dogfish, some spotted, and all long, round and looking slightly like baby sharks.

Grey mullet

Used to be a cheap and despised fish, but largely due to the Chinese restaurant trade wisely buying up all available stocks for baking whole, it is more popular, and consequently more difficult to buy today. It needs, more than most fish, to be really fresh to be good, quickly becoming dreary and tasteless if stale. Even when fresh it is helped by careful cooking such as baking whole, either stuffed, or sprinkled liberally with lemon, fennel or dill. The fish is generally sold weighing between 340g/¾lb and 1·35 kilos/3lb.

Haddock

Similar in shape to cod, but smaller. But haddock is an infinitely superior and unhappily more expensive fish, with a firmer, more flavoursome flesh. Good cooked almost any way, but a whole small haddock baked in the oven is one of life's big treats. Larger fish are sold in steaks for grilling or frying. Makes the best fish pie.

Hake

Similar in shape to cod and haddock, weighing up to 4·5 kilos/10lb. Can be rather dry if carelessly cooked, but has a good flavour. Cook as cod.

Halibut

A large flattish fish of excellent white firm flesh, and rich good flavour. Steaks are sold from the larger fish (they can weigh as much as 18 kilos/40lb) and the smaller halibut (known as chicken halibut) weighing as little as 900g/2lb are sold whole. Excellent grilled or fried plainly, baked, steamed, or poached. Needs no seasoning other than salt, pepper and a squeeze of lemon.

Huss – see Dogfish

John Dory

Sometimes called St Peter's fish, because like haddock (which is also known as St Peter's fish) it carries the 'finger-and-thumb' mark on each flank. Legend has it that when St Peter caught the fish, it groaned so loudly he tossed it back into the sea, leaving his imprint on it. It is also, confusingly, known as golden haddock. But there the resemblance ends. John Dory has such an ugly head fishmongers usually remove it before sale. It has a firm, almost lobster-like or nutty-flavoured flesh. Best grilled, fried or plainly baked. The fish can weigh up to 5·4 kilo/12lb but are frequently small enough for two portions. Unfortunately rare.

Ling (not to be confused with the freshwater grayling, which is a smaller game fish, rare and good to eat)

A large fish with almost nothing to recommend it, except perhaps for use in soups or stocks. The deceptively beautiful flesh (large, lean, almost boneless) becomes, even with the most careful of cooking, dry, shreddy, and totally tasteless. Too dry and lacking in gelatine for quenelles, too boring for grilling, too large for baking stuffed and whole, ling is best simply not bought.

Redfish (Norway haddock, ocean perch, soldier: sometimes incorrectly, and illegally, labelled 'bream' on the fish slab)

Has a not-too-tasty, firm pink flesh. Best when very fresh. 2·7 kilo/6lb fish are probably the best, and are excellent baked whole, perhaps with a lemony stuffing.

Sea bass (French *bar*). Also sometimes called *loup de mer* which is confusing as this correctly means catfish. The confusion deepens because some varieites of catfish are nicknamed dogfish, and there are many dogfish, some of them totally unrelated to each other, and so on almost indefinitely.

A scarce, totally delicious Mediterranean fish, usually weighing between 340g/¾lb and 1·35 kilos/3lb. Best baked or grilled whole with a sprig or two of fennel. It is shaped like a small salmon, with grey skin, and firm white delicate flesh.

Sea bream (French *daurade* or *dorade*)

Comes in many colours and sizes, the best being the golden dorade. One-portion size fish are good rolled in flour or cornmeal and fried in butter. The larger fish are good grilled or baked. Sea bream can be pink (like redfish, which, before the Trades Description Act, were often passed off as bream) but they are not as good as the golden. They are tastier than redfish, however. As usual freshness is all.

Skate

Now an expensive fish, skate used to be one of the cheapest available. The best skates are those weighing less than 1·35 kilos/ 3lb – larger ones tend to be tough and coarse-textured. The skin of skate is slimy when fresh and the flesh should be faintly pink. Best in the winter. Only the side pieces of the pectoral fins or wings are eaten. Sold in pieces, or (particularly in France) whole if small enough. The flesh (found between and over the cartilaginous ribs of the fin) is soft and of good flavour. Best served fried, with browned butter, or in a caper sauce.

Smelt

A curious small fish smelling, when just caught, of cucumber. They are cooked whole, having been gutted through the gills – to do this grip the gills and pull firmly, and the entrails will come out too. Wipe the fish with a damp cloth (do not wash) and grill or deep fry. Sometimes several smelts (enough for a portion) are grilled or fried on a wooden skewer. They are strung through the eye sockets, and served on the skewer.

Snapper or *schnapper*

Not often available in Britain but deserves a mention simply because it tastes so good. Cooks travelling in Australia or America should not miss the opportunity of at least eating, if not cooking it. There are various varieties, the most famous of which is the North American (eastern seaboard) red snapper. It is about 60cm/2ft long, and usually served as grilled steaks. The flesh is white, with large creamy flakes, sometimes compared to sea bass or lobster meat. The grey snapper is softer-fleshed but just as good. It grows slightly larger than the red.

Whiting

A small fish of the cod family, it is sold whole, and sometimes fried with its tail pulled through a hole made in its head, to look as though biting its tail. We have no idea why such a strange tradition should exist, but it is common in France as well as in Britain. Whiting has little flavour, and must be eaten very fresh if it is to have any taste at all. Because of its boniness (and subsequently gelatinous flesh) it is excellent for quenelles. Often used to bind less tacky fish in quenelle making – lobster quenelles would certainly be made with either whiting, pike, or similar 'sticky' fish added to the mixture.

OILY FISH

Although most fish contain very little oil (apart from in the liver), there are some varieties which contain more than most.

Anchovies

Tiny (10cm/4in–13cm/5in long), very strongly flavoured members of the herring family. Usually sold salted in tins. Used as flavouring or garnishing, and to make sauces or pastes.

Brisling

Baby sprats (see sprats) – even smaller and eaten whole like whitebait, or with mustard sauce.

Herrings

A very nutritious fish, particularly popular in the North, and once cheap and plentiful. Today it is more expensive, and less easily available fresh, a large proportion of the catch being sold for kippering. Average weight 170g/6oz. They should be shiny, feel fairly stiff, and not smell over-strong. The chief disadvantage of herrings is their boniness. But they can be boned, or almost boned, before cooking: split them open completely and lay, skin side up, on a board. With the heel of your hand press down firmly on the backbone of the fish. This will loosen it. Turn it over, cut through the backbone near the head and pull it out with, hopefully, all the side bones attached to it. (This is a good method of dealing with any small fish, such as trout, if it is to be baked stuffed.)

Herrings are used for pickling raw (rollmops), cooking in a mild pickle (soused herring), and for simple grilling, baking and frying.

Mackerel

A beautiful shiny fish with colourful green and black markings and a pearly white belly. Weighs 285g/10oz to 900g/2lb, and has a distinctive, delicious taste when fresh. Almost tasteless, and soggy in texture, if kept more than a day or two.

Generally fried or baked. Good with a mustard sauce, or a sharp one like gooseberry, to counteract the richness and slight oiliness. In season throughout the year, but availability is patchy, and the fish are not at their best during the late autumn or winter.

Pilchards

Pilchards are adult sardines and are delicious, though strong, when fresh. They are cooked like herring. Unfortunately they are generally canned, in sweetish tomato sauce, and are, in the opinion of the authors, perfectly disgusting.

Red mullet

Small, bony, rather dry and firm red-skinned fish of the Mediterranean. Wonderful flavour when fresh, and generally cooked with the liver left in the fish – giving it a strong distinctive flavour. Almost always grilled or fried, and served with plenty of melted butter. Often very expensive. Two red mullet are served per person if of average size (about 170g/6oz).

Sardines

Young pilchards, about 10cm/4in long, absolutely delicious when freshly caught and grilled. Available (and very good) frozen. Most frequently they are tinned in oil, which is good, but bears little resemblance to the fresh fish.

Sprats

Related to the herring, sprats are about 10cm/4in long. They are sometimes cooked ungutted, but they may be cleaned if preferred. Usually served deep-fried with a mustard sauce, or grilled and served with mustard butter. In season from October to March.

Tunny (tuna)

An enormous fish, seldom, unhappily, available fresh in Britain, but good packed in oil in cans. Its flavour is sometimes compared to chicken, and certainly it has a most un-fishy firm flesh. Pinkish in colour. When fresh it is delicious plainly grilled or fried; or braised on a bed of Mediterranean vegetables (tomatoes, peppers, aubergines and courgettes). Found in warm seas only.

Whitebait

These are baby herring or sprats, caught in shoals and eaten ungutted, and whole, head and tail included. They are delicious deep-fried after being dipped in milk and shaken in flour, or in a very light batter, 110g/¼lb of raw whitebait makes a good first course, served with brown bread and butter, half a lemon and salt, pepper and paprika.

SMOKED FISH

Most fish can be smoked. Small metal kits are available for smoking two or three small items – say a couple of trout or half a spring chicken. But most smoked fish is cured commercially, and sold ready to eat, or ready to cook.

Commercially smoked fish is first salted by immersion in brine. It is then hung up in the smoke of wood fires (originally simple pits were dug in the bottom of which smouldered a wood fire, and over which were suspended sides of fish, whole herring or what-have-you). The duration of the brining process and the length of time spent in the smoke determine the final colour and flavour of the fish. Refrigeration has meant that milder cures and less smoking are necessary. Smoking is now done for the flavour, where once it was a practical means of preserving fish.

Partly because the light smoking given today would produce a pallid-coloured fish, and partly because manufacturers regard bright colour as essential for 'plate appeal' for the housewife, many fish are coloured by immersion in food dye before smoking. There is also a chemical dipping process which simulates the flavour and colour of smoked fish, but it is illegal to sell fish as 'smoked' if it has not in fact been at least briefly hung in smoke. There is, however, a small 'connoisseur's market' for undyed smoked fish.

'Cold' smoking flavours but does not cook the fish, which is cooked before serving. 'Hot' smoked items are generally served without further cooking.

Bloaters

Made from longshore herring (or herring caught close enough to the shore to be landed while fresh: most herring destined for the kipper industry is salted on board the trawler). They are then only very lightly brined and cold-smoked. They do not keep well. Traditionally they are smoked ungutted, giving them a gamey flavour. Like kippers, bloaters are usually cooked before eating, though the fillets may be marinated and eaten raw.

Buckling

These are Baltic herring, imported already brined, and smoked in London. They, in contrast with the kipper or bloater, are hot-smoked at 100 C/212 F and can be eaten without further cooking. When fresh they are moist and delicious, milder in flavour than cold-smoked kipper, and make a good substitute for the more expensive smoked trout. Remove the tough skins before serving. They are bonier, and consequently more troublesome to eat, than trout.

Smoked cod

Cod fillet commercially available is dyed artificially, before light smoking. It lacks the flavour and firm texture of smoked haddock, being inclined to cook into dry shreds. It is used as a substitute for haddock.

Smoked eel

Both freshwater and sea eels are smoked, the commonest being the larger saltwater variety. They have a good rich taste, and are best eaten with a salad or bread, and plenty of lemon juice. Smaller eels are served in fillets, larger ones sometimes cut across in thick pieces.

Smoked haddock

Commonly sold by the pound, cut from large fillets. It is almost invariably dyed to a bright yellow hue. Today, with modern means of refrigeration, it is unnecessary to salt fish heavily to make it keep, and most smoked haddock is mild in flavour. Usually poached or grilled for breakfast or supper, or used in kedgeree. It makes good soup (in a creamy thickened fish stock) but few cooks realize this. The best smoked haddock are the famous Arbroath smokies, which once gutted and cleaned, are smoked closed; and those from Findon (known as finnan haddies) which are split and boned, and smoked opened out flat. Arbroath smokies' skin is almost black, finnans are pale translucent yellow. Sometimes Arbroath smokies are smoked ungutted, and occasionally whiting is used instead of young haddock.

Glasgow pales are small haddock, opened out and boned like finnans. All smoked haddock is cooked before eating.

Kippers

These are smoked herring. They are fairly strongly brined, and cold-smoked (at under 29°C/85°F). They are best poached in milk if very salty, or plainly grilled if not. The best kippers are from Craster in Northumberland and Loch Fyne in Scotland. Kipper fillets, sold packeted and frozen, are useful if boned flesh (for a pâté or mousse) is needed. Although kippers are generally cooked before serving, they can be marinated in oil and lemon juice for a few days, and served raw with toast or a salad.

Smoked mackerel

Mackerel can be either cold- or hot-smoked, the hot-smoked having a much more smoky flavour. Hot-smoked mackerel can be eaten without further cooking; cold-smoked mackerel is generally grilled and served with a mustard sauce. Smoked mackerel has very soft and moist flesh, and having bigger bones than many small fish it is easy to fillet for use in salads or pâtés. It does not keep well, and care should be taken to see it is absolutely fresh when bought. The skin should be dry to the touch and the smell light and pleasant.

Smoked salmon

Sides of smoked salmon are very lightly brined and smoked in coolish smoke for a maximum of 12 hours. Smoked salmon is eaten raw, with brown bread and butter. Less good smoked salmon (from Norway or Canada) has a rather reddish hue, and lacks the soft moistness and delicate pink colour of the best Scotch. But it is excellent for mousses or pâtés.

For carving, see page 87.

Smoked trout

Smoked trout are hot-smoked, and eaten without further cooking, usually served with brown bread and butter and horseradish sauce. The tough jacket of smoked skin is removed before serving, but the head and tail are usually left on. They make good, though expensive, pâté.

SALT FISH

All smoked fish are, to a greater or lesser degree, salted in brine before smoking. Indeed the cheaper varieties of 'smoked' fish may not be smoked at all, but simply brined and dyed. But some fish is dry-salted and sold without further treatment. The most common example is salt cod, beloved of the Portuguese, and once popular in Britain. But as salting is no longer necessary as a means of preservation, salt fish is becoming more difficult to find. Ling, a dreary fish when eaten fresh, profits from being salted, and there are few foods more delicious than Brandade de Morue made from salt cod. Salt fish needs 12 hours' soaking before cooking, if bought straight from the salt, but many fishmongers sell it ready-soaked.

FISH ROES

The roes of fish are very often a great delicacy. Some of them, such as cod roes, are sold boiled. They can be coated in egg and breadcrumbs and fried, served cold, or used in fish stuffings.

Caviar. Lightly salted sturgeon roes, of course, are the real thing, and the most famous varieties are Sevruga and Beluga. Beluga caviar is recognizable by its large, grey-black, translucent grains: Sevruga is smaller and darker. Both should be moist, oily and sweet-smelling. Once a jar is opened it should be kept refrigerated, and anyway eaten within two or three days.

Caviar is usually served (to the horror of connoisseurs who like it in large quantities on plain bread with no butter, lemon or anything else) with chopped egg yolk, chopped egg white, chopped parsley, finely chopped onion, pepper and lemon juice, the diner being offered all these condiments and hot toast and butter. It may be that all these bits and pieces 'stretch' the caviar, the most expensive food in the world, a little further. But, with or without the garnishes, caviar tastes wonderful. The cheaper, very salty pressed caviar is made from true sturgeon roes, but of damaged grains, or from less acclaimed fish than the Beluga or Sevruga.

Red caviar. Salmon roe, salted and sold in jars. Very good.

Mock caviar. Lump fish roe. Salty black small grains in jars. Adequate for cocktail party canapés.

Salted smoked soft roe of red mullet or cod is the main ingredient for taramasalata, and is sometimes eaten simply spread on bread or toast. Soft unsalted *herring roes*, sold canned or fresh, are delicious fried and served on toast as a first course or savoury.

Roes found in the fish you buy should not be discarded. Soft roes (the male fish's milt) are generally preferred by connoisseurs for their creamy soft texture, but the hard roe (female fish eggs) can be eaten too. Roes may be cooked and served with the fish, sieved and added to the sauce, or put in the stuffing. At the very least they should be frozen and kept for the next time you make fish stock.

COOKING TIMES FOR FISH

SMALL FISH

Small fish, or pieces of fish, are cooked according to their weight and thickness, but in any event the ultimate test of 'doneness' is how they look and feel. Whole small fish will have opaque eyes, the skin will peel easily, and the flesh will feel firm, and lift easily into flakes. A small brown trout, for example, dropped into hot poaching liquid, will take about six minutes; if fried it will need six minutes a side.

LARGE FISH

Large fish, poached or baked whole, are more difficult to test. The following is a rough guide of cooking times, after which the flesh should feel firm when pressed, and a skewer should glide easily into the thickest part of the flesh.

Poached

Eight minutes to the pound, timed from the minute the liquid reaches simmering point.

Baked

Assuming the oven is set at 180°C/350°F, gas mark 4, allow ten minutes for the fish to heat through (15 minutes if it is more than 2·3 kilos/5lb), then calculate 8 minutes to the pound. If it is stuffed weigh after stuffing.

SHELLFISH

The word *seafood* might be better than *shellfish* if we are categorizing those sea- or freshwater animals that are not scaled fish. However, the word seafood is unsatisfactory too, as fish are obviously food from the sea, and yet in culinary terms they are excluded when using the term.

To deal with real shellfish (i.e. those with shells) first: they fall into two broad categories – crustaceans and molluscs. The crustaceans all have legs, and move about, and some of them (like lobsters) have a jointed shell. Others (like crabs) do not, but they do get about on their legs.

Molluscs, on the other hand, do not usually move voluntarily. Indeed some bivalves (i.e. those with a hinged double shell, like oysters and mussels) stay on the same rock most of their lives. However, the bivalve cockles can leap short distances, and move with the tide in thousands. Most molluscs have an impenetrable protective shell, either of the hinged bivalve type, or a single conical shell like a limpet, or perhaps, for the slightly more mobile mollusc, a snail-like shell, such as found on the whelk or winkle. The exception to this general rule is the octopus family (which includes squid or ink-fish). They do not have a hard shell, and they swim, but nevertheless are molluscs. Oursins (those prickly black-brown molluscs beloved of the French who eat them raw, chilled like oysters) rely on their spines for protection. They are seldom available in Britain.

The clam (bivalve mollusc)

The most common clams in America are the soft shell (or long neck) clam, and the hard shell (or round) clam. Neither is frequently available in Britain, though the round clam is more often seen on the Continent. All clams are sandy and must be washed in several waters before cooking. After washing they are soaked in salty water to which a handful of oatmeal is added. (The clams ingest the oatmeal and excrete the dark matter from their intestines. This whitens them, improving their appearance. It is also said to cause the clam to open its shell, so allowing the sand to wash out.) They are then rinsed in fresh water and scrubbed well. Any that will not close tightly when tapped on the sink-edge must be discarded. Any that float or have damaged shells should be discarded too.

Long neck (or soft shell) clams are generally steamed in their shells – they will open during cooking – or are opened like oysters and eaten raw. To open a soft shell clam to eat raw run a sharp knife along the join of top and bottom shell, working over a basin so that none of the juices will be lost, and lift the top shell up. Cut the meat from the bottom shell, and slit the skin of the 'neck'. Pull the skin off and discard it. Serve with slices of lime or lemon and brown bread and butter.

The hard shell (or round) clams are generally steamed or used in chowders, or fried. The same washing, scrubbing and feeding with oatmeal procedure is necessary. If the clams have not been soaked in water with oatmeal, they must be opened before cooking (by cutting the muscle at the hinge with a short sharp knife and prising the shells apart) and the stomach opened up and cleaned.

Cockles (bivalve mollusc)

These are tiny shellfish with white fluted shells, similar in shape to a clam and found, like clams, on the beach, especially at low tide. Cockles are usually sold in Britain ready cooked, either plainly boiled or pickled. The old cockle stalls are disappearing fast, and cockles are proving uneconomic to harvest.

Crabs (crustacean)

Most crabs are edible but the small ones are too fiddly to bother with and the very large ones are sometimes almost hollow, coarse and dry in texture. The best are medium size (about 900g/2lb weight). They are brownish-pink before cooking, going bright orange when boiled. They are sold frozen cooked, freshly cooked and live. They undoubtedly have the best flavour if freshly cooked. The female or 'hen' crab is considered superior to the male crab because its roe imparts a distinctive 'crab flavour' to the flesh. Crabs are frequently plunged live into boiling water or court bouillon, where they die very quickly, but they may be killed by piercing the brain (found on the soft underside of the crab) before cooking. After cooking the legs are pulled off, the underside of the crab opened up, and the stomach sac, any green matter, and the lungs (spongy finger-like objects) are discarded. The soft brown meat is stronger in flavour and is generally mashed with lemon juice, or incorporated into a sauce, before serving. The meat in the claws and legs is very good, and the diner is generally served with these ready cracked to make extracting the flesh easier.

Crawfish (crustacean)

This is a saltwater crustacean, also known as the spiny lobster or rock lobster. It has no claws, but a very rough spiny back. Known as langouste in France, it is considered inferior to lobster, but of a good delicate flavour. They are available fresh or frozen in Britain, and are distinctly better if fresh. Generally between 225g/$\frac{1}{2}$lb and 1$\frac{1}{2}$ kilos/3lb in weight.

Crayfish (crustacean)

The crayfish is the most delicious and delicate of freshwater creatures. Generally weighing less than 450g/1lb they are rarely available live, except from tanks in smart restaurants. The tails containing most of the meat are available frozen raw, and are very good. Live crayfish are gutted by twisting off the middle tail fin, which takes the intestine with it, after which they are boiled in a court bouillon.

Lobster (crustacean)

Lobsters are blue-black when alive, turning bright red when boiled. They are best bought live, and will keep for a few hours in the warmest part of the refrigerator. If they are to be eaten cold, or in some sauce or pie, they are usually boiled. They can be dropped live into the boiling liquid (and contrary to legend they will *not* scream), or they can be killed first by being pierced through the clearly defined cross on the back of the head which indicates the nerve centre.

Many chefs claim that the tenderest and juiciest cold lobster is obtained by placing the lobster in cold court bouillon and bringing the liquid up to simmering point very slowly. This is inhumane if the lobster is dropped into fresh cold water, as it will live for a while until the heat overcomes it. But the method is not cruel provided the water or court bouillon has been previously well boiled, which eliminates the oxygen. The lobster is then put into the cold liquid, *and left for 30 minutes*. The lack of oxygen gently renders the lobster unconscious, and of course it then feels nothing when put over the heat.

For grilled lobster dishes, and for many other hot dishes such as lobster thermidor the animal is killed, then split in half down the back. The stomach sac, spongy gills and intestine – thread-like dark membrane running down the body – are removed and then the lobster is grilled or cooked in pan or oven. The meat of the lobster claws is much richer, more solid and of a different texture to the body meat, which is white (with a pinkish skin) when cooked. The claws must be cracked before serving to enable the diner to get at the flesh inside. The leg flesh is similar to that of the body. The flesh near the head (actually the liver) is often mistakenly thrown away by inexperienced cooks, as it has a soft grey-green look. But it is quite delicious and should be mixed with the sauce, or eaten as it is. The eggs (coral) of the 'hen' lobster are used, when available, to flavour sauces or lobster butter, and are perhaps the best-tasting part of a lobster.

Mussels (bivalve mollusc)

Mussels are seldom longer than a thumb and have blue-black shells. Like all seafood they must be bought absolutely fresh. Any that will not shut when tapped on the sink, or that float, or have damaged shells must be discarded. They are well washed in water, scrubbed hard, and their 'beards' (seaweed-like tentacles) are removed. They are generally cooked in a covered pan with very little liquid. They will open within a few minutes, and once open are cooked. The 'rubber band' of muscle surrounding the flesh may be gently pulled off and discarded.

Octopus (cephalopod mollusc)

The octopus (which can grow to 60cm/2ft long) consists of a large 'head' with two protruding eyes, and eight tentacles carrying suckers along their length. The body cavity contains a dark brown ink which the animal can squirt out to form a protective screen while it makes its escape from predators. It also has the ability to change colour like a chameleon.

To prepare the octopus for eating the ink and intestines are washed out, the outer membrane-like skin is peeled off and the eyes are removed. The flesh is then cut into strips and simmered until tender. It will be tender either if eaten after barely five minutes in the simmering liquid, or immediately after deep frying, or if it is left to cook slowly for a prolonged time (about 40 minutes) when it will have gone through the stages of initial tenderness, subsequent rubbery toughness, to tenderness again – rather like a steak which must be eaten quickly grilled, or after prolonged stewing, but not after 25 minutes cooking, when it would be very tough and dry.

Oysters (bivalve mollusc)

English oysters are said to be the best in the world; they are certainly extremely expensive. They are normally eaten raw, having simply been prised open with an oyster knife: to do this wrap a tea-towel around your left hand, place the oyster on your left palm, flat side up. Slip a short, strong, wide-bladed knife under the hinge and push it into the oyster. Holding the oyster pressed tightly with the left-hand fingers, jerk up the knife in your right hand, and prize the two shells apart. Pull the oyster from its shell, but put it back on one of them to serve. Serve the oysters lying in their shells on a bed of crushed ice, and hand salt, pepper, lemon juice and Tabasco sauce separately. Traditionally garnished with seaweed and served with champagne or Chablis.

Shrimps or *prawns* (crustacean)

Incorrectly called prawns, saltwater shrimps are also known as *crevettes* in France and as *gambaretti* in Italy. The commonest variety is greyish before cooking, orangy-pink and bright afterwards. The much-prized brown shrimp is pale brown when live, deep reddish-brown when boiled. It is used, cooked and packed in well-seasoned clarified butter for potted shrimps, as well as eaten plainly boiled. Prawns are bought either whole or shelled in the cooked state, and whole only (never shelled) when raw. If bought frozen they will almost certainly be cooked and shelled. They may be frozen in a solid block, or individually, when they are packed in a 'free flow' pack. As a general rule the free flow prawns are more expensive, but of better quality, than the solid packs. Cooked or raw unshelled prawns are sold by the pint as well as by weight.

To shell a cooked prawn the legs and roe (if any) under the body are pinched off, the head is broken off and the shell peeled away from the body. If the prawns are to be used whole for garnish, the legs and any roe are removed but the head and shell are left intact.

Prawn (*Dublin bay*) (crustacean)

This is similar to the small prawn, but much larger, rarer and more expensive. It can be bought fresh or frozen, both raw or cooked. Similar to the French *langoustine*, and the Italian *scampi*, it is best bought raw in its shell, but is acceptable raw, shelled and frozen. It has a very tender, juicy flesh, white when cooked, although the shell becomes bright pink. True Dublin Bays are not common today, and have been largely replaced by the boiled and frozen Pacific Prawn.

Scallops (bivalve mollusc)

Scallops are generally prepared for cooking by the fishmonger, who should be asked to supply the shells as well as the fish. The scallop (or Coquille St Jacques) has a shallow and deep shell and the deep one is used as a serving dish. Frozen scallops are sold without shells. The shells, if well scrubbed, can be used again and again. Scallops require extremely careful handling and cooking, as over-cooking, too high a heat, or too much delay before serving can make them dry and unappetizing. After cooking the tough muscle, found opposite the red roe (or coral), should be removed.

Squid (cephalopod mollusc)

The squid is much smaller than the octopus and has ten tentacles. It has a long sac-like body containing a transparent shell which must be removed when the animal is cleaned. In all other respects it is like the octopus, though considerably smaller (up to 25cm/10in long).

Whelks and *winkles* (molluscs with snail-like shells)

Both whelks and winkles are normally sold cooked. Whelks are the larger creature and are eaten much like snails, or served in vinegar, ready shelled. Winkles are smaller and a large winkle picker (or pin) is needed to remove the 'cap' or scale at the entrance to get at the winkle, which is then pulled out with the pin.

SEASONS FOR SEAFOOD

Clam	All year round, best in autumn.
Cockles	All year round, best September to April.
Crab	All year round, best May to October.
Crawfish	April to September.
Lobster	All year round, best April to August.
Mussels	September to March.

Octopus and Squid	All year round, but scarce.
Oysters	September to April.
Prawns	All year round.
Dublin Bay Prawns (scampi)	All year round, best May to November.
Scallops	September to March.
Shrimps	All year round.
Whelks	All year round, best September to February.
Winkles	All year round, best October to May.

MEAT

(For rabbit, hare and venison see also pages 159–62.)

The younger the animal, and the less exercise it has taken, the tenderer will be its meat; but its flavour will be less pronounced. A week-old calf will be tender as margarine, and about as flavourless. An ox that has pulled a cart all its long life will be quite the reverse – good on flavour, but tough as old boots. A relatively young, and therefore tender animal will have white or pale fat, rather than yellow, the meat will be less dark, and the bones more pliable than in an older, tougher animal. So rump steak with a bright red hue and white fat may well be tenderer than the dark flesh and yellow fat of older meat, but it will probably lose on flavour what it gains on texture.

Because tenderness is today rated highly, the most expensive cuts of meat are those from the parts of the animal's body that have had little or no exercise. For example, the leg, neck and shoulder cuts of beef are tougher (and therefore cheaper) than those from rump or loin.

But apart from the age of the animal, there are other factors that affect tenderness. Meat must not be cooked while the muscle fibres are taut due to *rigor mortis* which can last, depending on the temperature in which the carcass is stored, for a day or two. The state of the animal prior to slaughter can also affect the tenderness of the meat – if it is relaxed and peaceable the meat is likely to be more tender. Injections of certain enzymes (proteins that produce changes in the meat without themselves being changed) given to the animal before slaughter will produce the same result artificially.

But the most crucial factor affecting tenderness is the length of time it is stored before cooking. Meat hung in temperatures of 2 C/35 F will, due to enzyme activity, become increasingly tender. Temperatures should not be higher than this, because although the enzyme activity would be greater, the risk of spoilage due to bacterial action would become high. For beef 7 days is the minimum hanging time, 3 weeks or a month being desirable. However, with the commercial demands for quick turnover, the weight-loss during storage and the expense of storing, good hanging is rare these days.

Some enzyme activity continues if the meat is frozen, and the formation, and subsequent melting, of ice-crystals (which, in expanding, bruise the fibres of the meat) means that freezing meat can be said to tenderize it. However the inevitable loss of juices from the meat (and subsequent risk of dryness after cooking) is a disadvantage that outweighs the minimal tenderizing effect.

Hanging is most important in beef, as the animals are comparatively old, perhaps 2 or 3 years, when killed. It is less important for carcasses of young animals such as calves and lambs, as their meat is comparatively tender anyway.

Because, inevitably, some bacterial action (as well as enzyme action) must take place during hanging, the flavour of well-hung meat is stronger, or gamier, than that of under-hung meat. The colour will also deepen and become duller with hanging. But the prime reason for hanging meat is to tenderize it, rather than to increase or change its flavour. This is not so with game, including venison, which is hung as much to produce a gamey flavour as to tenderize the meat.

The last, and probably most important, factor that affects the ultimate tenderness of meat is the method of cooking. Half-cooked or rare meat will be tender simply because its fibres have not been changed by heat, and will still retain the softness of raw meat. But as the heat penetrates the whole piece of meat the fibres of meat set rigidly and the juices cease to run. Once the whole piece of meat is heated thoroughly, all the softness of raw meat is lost, and the meat is at its toughest. This explains the natural reluctance of chefs to serve well-done steaks – it is almost impossible to produce a *tender* well-done grilled steak.

But, paradoxically, further cooking (though not fast grilling or frying) will tenderize that tough steak. This is seen in cooking methods such as braising and stewing, when long slow cooking gradually softens the flesh. A joint from an older animal, which has done much muscular work during its lifetime, and is coarse-grained and fibrous, can be made particularly tender by prolonged gentle cooking. This is because much of the connective tissue present in such a joint, if subjected to a steady temperature of, say, 100°C/200°F, will convert to gelatine, producing a soft, almost sticky tenderness.

Joints with finer graining and little connective tissue, such as rump or sirloin, will never become gelatinous, and are consequently seldom cooked other than by roasting or grilling, when their inherent tenderness (from a life of inaction!) is relied on. But they will never be as tender as the slow-cooked shin or oxtail, which can be cut with a spoon.

It does not matter that few people have any idea which part of the animal their meat comes from. But it is useful to know, if not how to do the butcher's job, at least which cuts are likely to be tender, expensive, good for stewing, or not worth having, and what to look for in a piece of meat.

ROASTING MEAT

1. Weigh the joint and establish length of cooking time (see page 114).
2. Pre-heat the oven (electric ovens take much longer to heat up than gas ovens).
3. Prepare the joint for roasting (see page 125).
4. Heat some dripping in a roasting pan and if the meat is lean, brown the joint over direct heat so that it is well coloured. This helps to seal in the juices. Pork and lamb rarely need this but many cuts of beef do.

5. Place the joint in the pan, on a grid if you have one available, as this aids the circulation of hot air; roast for the time calculated.

6. Lean meat needs basting every 20–25 minutes, fatty meats need not be basted.

ROASTING TIMES

Obviously a long thin piece of meat weighing 2·3 kilos/5lb will take less time to cook than a fat round piece of the same weight, so that the times below are meant only as a guide. The essential point is that meat must reach an internal temperature of 60°C/ 140°F to be rare, 70°C/150°F to be medium pink and 80°C/170°F to be well done. A meat thermometer stuck into the thickest part of the meat, and left there during cooking, eliminates guesswork.

Beef

Beef is generally roasted in the hottest of ovens for 20 minutes to seal the meat (or it may be fried all over in fat before being transferred to the oven). Whatever the method, count the cooking time *after* the sealing has been done, and allow 15 minutes to the pound for rare meat, 20 minutes for medium and 25 for well done, roasting the meat in a pre-heated oven set at 190°C/375°F, gas mark 5.

Lamb

Put the lamb into the hottest of ovens, seal for 20 minutes, then allow 20 minutes to the pound at 190°C/375°F, gas mark 5. This will produce very slightly pink lamb. If lamb without a trace of pinkness is wanted allow an extra 20 minutes after the calculated time is up.

Pork

Pork must be well cooked. Allow 40 minutes to the pound at 170°C/325°F, gas mark 3. Sealing is not necessary. If crackling is required roast at 200°C/400°F, gasmark 6 for 25 minutes to the pound, plus 25 minutes over.

Veal

Seal in hot fat over direct heat. Or roast for 20 minutes at maximum temperature. Then allow 25 minutes to the pound at 180 C/350 F, gas mark 4.

BEEF

BEEF CUTS

For roasting: sirloin, wing rib, rump, fillet

For pot roasting: topside, silverside, brisket, thick flank

For stewing, braising and boiling, and for salting and boiling: chuck, shin, brisket, flank, neck, topside, silverside

For grilling and frying: fillet, rump and sirloin. But the names for steaks can be confusing:

Rump steaks (rumsteak or bifsteak in French)
These are thick (about 2cm/¾in) slices cut across the grain of the rump, and then, if for individual servings, cut into smaller neat pieces.

Fillet steak
It comes in various guises. Cut across into neat thick (2½cm/1in) slices it is a tournedos. A neat piece for two or three people, weighing perhaps 225g/½lb cut from the thick end (but with all the coarser meat trimmed from it) can be grilled, spitted or roasted as a chateaubriand. Medallions are thin neat slices cut across the fillet.

Sirloin steak
The name sirloin covers steak from the upper side of the true sirloin, wing rib and fore rib. The French *entrecôte* means only the true tender sirloin, which is cut in individual steaks or as T-bone steaks (on the rib, with the sirloin on one side of the

BEEF

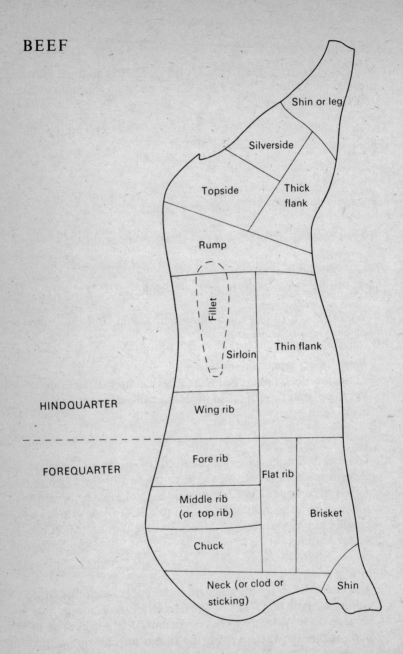

Shin or leg

Silverside

Topside

Thick flank

Rump

Fillet

Sirloin

Thin flank

HINDQUARTER

Wing rib

FOREQUARTER

Fore rib

Flat rib

Middle rib
(or top rib)

Brisket

Chuck

Neck (or clod or
sticking)

Shin

T and the fillet or undercut on the other). French *côte de boeuf* or our rib of beef are thick steaks on the rib bone, from the slightly less tender wing rib or fore rib. Porterhouse is a double-size T-bone, or double-size wing rib.

For pies: chuck, brisket, thick flank, shin (foreleg), shin or leg (hind leg)

Approximate times for cooking steaks

Steaks are grilled according to taste:

Blue	Dark on the outside but almost raw (hot but not cooked) in the middle.
Rare	Dark on the outside but red inside with plenty of red juices running freely.
Medium rare	As rare, but with very little free-flowing juices. Paler centre.
Medium	Pink in the centre but the juices set.
Well done	The centre pale beige but the steak still juicy.

	Total cooking time per side	
	Grilled	Fried
Fillet – 2½cm/1in thick		
Blue	2	1½
Rare	2½	2
Medium rare	3	2½
Medium	3½	3
Well done	5	4½
Sirloin – 2½cm/1in thick		
Blue	2½	2
Rare	3	2½
Medium rare	3½	3
Medium	4	3½
Well done	5½	4½

	Total cooking time per side	
	Grilled	Fried
Sirloin – 5cm/2in thick		
Blue	3	$2\frac{1}{2}$
Rare	$3\frac{1}{2}$	3
Medium rare	4	$3\frac{1}{2}$
Medium	5	4
Well done	7	6

Rump
As sirloin, but allow up to 50 per cent longer.

VEAL

The cuts of veal, and their names, more closely resemble those of a lamb or sheep than those of grown-up beef.

As veal is more tender than beef, more of the animal is suitable for quick cooking (roasting, frying). But as there is little fat on a calf, care must be taken to moisten the meat frequently during cooking to prevent dryness. Because of the absence of fat, veal is seldom grilled.

Dutch veal is milk-fed and expensive. It has a pale pink colour and the best cuts are exceptionally tender. But the taste is mild to the point of insipidity, and needs good seasoning, usually plenty of lemon, pepper or a good sauce. English veal is cheaper, has more flavour, and generally has a slightly more reddish hue. This is because the animals are killed older than their Dutch fellows, and are generally, though not always, grass-fed. But veal should never look bloody or really red.

VEAL CUTS

For roasting: leg, loin, best end, breast

For braising and stewing: leg, shoulder, neck end, scrag, breast,

For frying (and possibly grilling if frequently basted): cushion (fillet), loin chops, best end cutlets, rump, round (buttock)

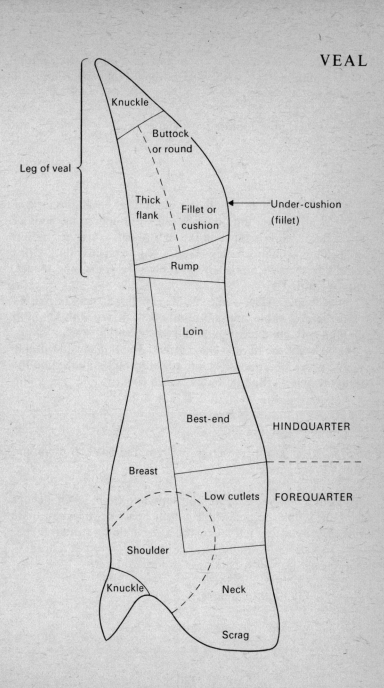

VEAL

Knuckle

Buttock
or round

Leg of veal

Thick
flank

Fillet or
cushion

Under-cushion
(fillet)

Rump

Loin

Best-end

HINDQUARTER

Breast

Low cutlets

FOREQUARTER

Shoulder

Knuckle

Neck

Scrag

Note: The more tender cuts from the forequarter, from a top-quality milk-fed calf, may also be boned out and sliced for escalopes.

For stock: knuckle, foot or scrag end of neck

PORK

Pork used to be eaten mainly in winter, or as bacon, because of the difficulty of keeping it fresh. But with modern methods of refrigeration pork is eaten all the year round.

The flesh should be pale pink, not red or bloody. Pork killed for the fresh meat market is generally very young and tender, carrying little fat.

Suckling pigs, killed while still being milk-fed, may be roasted or barbecued whole, and are traditionally served with the head on, and with an apple or an orange between the jaws.

Crackling is the roasted skin of pork. The skin must be deeply scored with a sharp knife before roasting. Salt is rubbed on the skin, making it crisp and bubbly when cooked.

PORK CUTS

For roasting: any part of the pig (bar the head, trotters and knuckle) are suitable.

For grilling and frying: spare rib chops, loin chops, chump chops from the saddle, best end cutlets, belly bones or American spare ribs (usually with a marinade), fillet (tenderloin), trotters

For boiling: leg, belly, hand and spring, trotters

For pies: any meat is suitable.

For sausages: any fatty piece, especially belly.

PORK

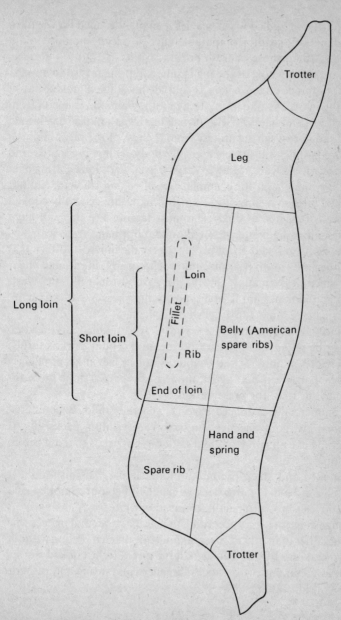

BACON

Bacon pigs are killed when heavier than pigs destined for the fresh pork market, so the comparable cuts of bacon should contain more fat than those of fresh pork.

Almost the whole of the pig is salted in brine for up to a week, then matured. Green bacon is sold at this stage. Smoked bacon is hung in cool smoke for up to a month. Gammon is bacon from a hind leg, and ham is bacon from a hind leg that has been brined or cured in dry salt separately from the rest of the pig. Gammon is cured while still attached to the body. Hams are salted and possibly smoked according to varying local traditions. Parma ham and Bayonne ham, for example, are salted and smoked, but not cooked further before eating. English hams are generally cooked before eating hot or cold. The most famous are the well-hung Braddenham ham and the sweet mild York ham. American Virginia hams are said to owe their sweet flavour to the fact that the hogs are fed on peanuts and peaches, cured in salt and sugar and smoked over apple and hickory wood for a month. Westphalian German ham is eaten raw in thin slices like Parma ham. Paris ham is similar to English York ham.

Since good refrigeration is now widely available, pork need no longer be salted as a preservative measure. Today pork is turned into bacon mainly for the flavour. Smoked bacon keeps slightly longer than green but, again, modern smoking is done more for the flavour than for preservation.

Commercially produced bacon is generally mild. Bacon cured at home, without chemical preservatives, vacuum packs etc., is likely to have more flavour and saltiness, but needs soaking before cooking.

Smoked and green bacon flesh look similarly reddish-pink. It should not be dry, hard, dark or patchy in colour. Smoked rind is yellowish-brown; green bacon rind is white.

English bacons vary according to manufacturer and price, some being saltier than others. So care should be taken if boiling without prior soaking. It is wise to soak large pieces to be cooked whole, such as gammons or forehocks. Smaller cuts, steaks and rashers, rarely need soaking.

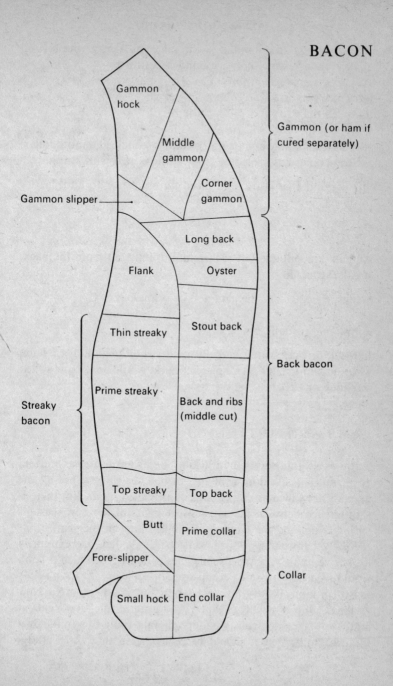

BACON

Gammon hock

Middle gammon

Corner gammon

Gammon slipper

Gammon (or ham if cured separately)

Long back

Flank

Oyster

Thin streaky

Stout back

Prime streaky

Back and ribs (middle cut)

Back bacon

Streaky bacon

Top streaky

Top back

Butt

Prime collar

Fore-slipper

Small hock

End collar

Collar

Danish pigs are all cured in the same manner, giving a good quality, mild-tasting, not-very-salty bacon.

BACON CUTS

For boiling or stewing

All cuts are suitable but the lean pieces (forehock, gammon, collar) are sometimes casseroled or stewed whole, tied with string.

Streaky and Flank are used diced for soups, or to add flavour to stews.

For frying or grilling

All cuts are suitable but rashers are usually cut from the back, streaky or collar.

Steaks are cut from the gammon or prime back.

For baking (usually boiled first)

Large lean pieces are generally used (whole gammon or ham, whole gammon hock, large piece of back, whole boned and rolled forehock or either of the collars).

LAMB AND MUTTON

Animals weighing more than 36 kilos/79·5lb are graded as mutton. Real mutton is seldom available in butcher shops since all the animals are killed young enough to be called lamb. But there is a difference between the small sweet joints of the new season's spring lamb, and the larger lambs killed later in the year.

Really baby lambs, killed while still milk fed, are extremely expensive, with very pale, tender flesh. A leg from such a lamb would feed only two or perhaps three people.

British lamb is very fine in flavour, but good imported New Zealand lamb is usually cheaper. As a general rule New Zealand lamb joints come from smaller animals than the full-grown English lambs, but it should be remembered that three grades of New Zealand lamb are imported into Britain, ranging from excellent to very tough. All New Zealand lamb comes into the country frozen, so it stands to reason that some lambs have been more recently killed than others. The best time to buy New Zealand lamb is from Christmas to the summer.

Lamb should be brownish-pink rather than grey in colour, but not bloody. Because the animal is killed young almost all the cuts are tender enough for grilling, frying or roasting, but the fattier, cheaper cuts are used for casseroles and stews too.

LAMB AND MUTTON CUTS

For roasting: Saddle or loin, best end of neck (rack of lamb), shoulder, leg, breast

For braising: chump chops, loin, leg

For grilling and frying: best end cutlets, loin chops, chump chops, steaks from fillet end of leg

For boiling and stewing: knuckle, scrag and middle neck, breast, leg

BUTCHERY

Most cuts of meat are available ready prepared from the shop or market. But it is useful to know how to bone and tie certain French and English cuts that a busy butcher may be unwilling to tackle.

Boning

Boning is easier than most people imagine. A short sharp knife is essential. Tunnel boning (where the bone, say from a leg, is extracted from the hole from which it protrudes, without opening out the meat) is more difficult than open boning, when the flesh is split along the bone, the bone worked out and the meat rolled up and tied or sewn. But, whether tunnel boning or open boning,

125

LAMB

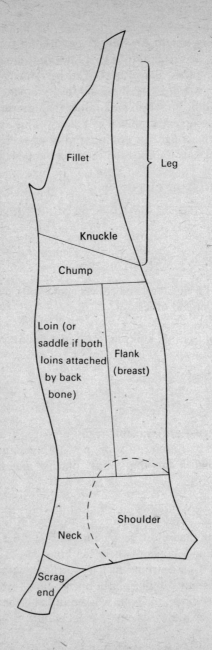

the essential is to work slowly and carefully, keeping the knife as close to the bones as possible, and scraping the meat off the bone rather than cutting it. Any meat extracted inadvertently with the bone can be scraped off and put back into the joint. With most bones it is possible, when tunnel boning, to work from both ends – for example, a leg of mutton can be worked on where the knuckle bone sticks out of the thin end, and the leg bone out of the fillet end.

But in most cases it is simpler to cut neatly through the flesh, along the length of the bone, from the side nearest to the bone, and work the bone out all along its length. After all, some sewing or tying is necessary at the ends of the joints even if tunnel boned, and it is simpler to sew up the length of the joint.

For safety reasons trainee butchers are taught to use the knife in such a way that should it slip it will not hurt them. This means never pulling the knife directly towards the body. In addition the knife is held firmly like a dagger when working, with the point of the knife down (see drawing). But the safest precaution that cooks can take is to see that their knives are sharp. Blunt knives need more pressure to wield, and are therefore more inclined to slip.

Rolling and tying

Once a joint, such as a loin, is boned, remove most of the fat and lay it, meat side up, on the board. Season it or spread sparingly with stuffing. Roll it up from the thick end and use short pieces of thin cotton (not nylon) string to tie round the meat at 3cm/1½in intervals. These can easily be cut off when serving, or the carver can slice between them when cutting the meat into thick slices.

Sewing up whole joints after stuffing

Use a larding needle or large darning or upholstery needle. Some of these are curved slightly which makes the job easier. Use thin old-fashioned white string, not nylon which will melt under heat. Leave a good few inches of string at the beginning and end, but do not tie elaborate knots which are difficult to undo when dishing the meat. Not-too-tight simple largish stitches are best – the whole length of string can be pulled out in one movement when dishing.

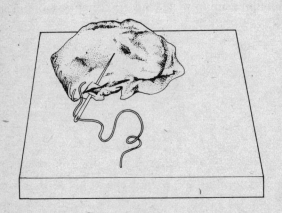

Larding

Some very lean or potentially tough meat is larded before roasting. This promotes tenderness and adds flavour. Most commonly used for slow-roasted dishes like boeuf à la mode or roast veal. A special larding needle is used.

To lard a joint: cut the larding fat (usually rindless back pork fat) into thin strips and put one of them into the tunnel of the needle, clamping down the hinge to hold it in place. The fat should extend a few inches out of the needle. Thread through the meat, twisting the needle gently to prevent the fat pulling off. Once threaded through the meat, release the clamp, and trim the two ends of fat close to the meat. Repeat this all over the lean meat at 2½cm/1in intervals.

BEEF

Steaks for grilling or frying

Cut across the grain of the meat, if possible into thickish slices. Trim neatly, and cut rump slices into two or three individual steaks.

Minute steaks

Cut large thin steaks. Put them between two sheets of paper or polythene and bat gently with a cook's mallet or rolling pin to flatten the meat.

Tournedos steaks

Cut 2cm/1in slices across the trimmed fillet.

For stewing

Remove the gristle, but not *all* the fat (it will add moisture and flavour). Cut into 2½cm/1in cubes, or larger. Too-small pieces are difficult to seal, and may become shreddy and dry during cooking.

For stroganoff

Cut into small strips across the grain of the meat – about the thickness of a pencil.

For roasting

If the meat has no fat on it, tie a piece of pork fat, or fatty bacon, round it. Tie up as described on page 128.

LAMB

Saddle

This consists of both loins of the lamb, left attached at the back-bone, in the same way as a baron of beef.

First remove the skin: with a small sharp knife lift a corner of the skin, hold this firmly with a tea-towel (to get a good grip) and tug sharply to peel off. Trim off any very large pieces of fat from the edges of the saddle, but leave the back fat. Tuck the flaps under the saddle. Cut out the kidneys but keep them (they can be brushed with butter and attached to the end of the saddle with wooden skewers 30 minutes before the end of the roasting time). Using a sharp knife score the back fat all over in a fine criss-cross pattern.

The pelvic or aitch bone, protruding slightly from one end of the saddle, can be removed, or left in place and covered with a ham frill when the saddle is served.

French trimmed best end cutlets (and how to chine)

Skin the best end: lift a corner of the skin from the neck end with a small knife, hold it firmly (using a cloth to get a good grip) and peel it off.

Chine if the butcher has not already done so. This means to saw carefully through the chine bone (or spine) just where it meets the rib bones. Take care not to saw right through into the eye of the meat. Now remove the chine bone completely. Chop off the cutlet bones so that the length of the remaining bones is not more than twice the length of the eye of the meat. Remove the half-moon shaped piece of flexible cartilege found buried between the layers of fat and meat at the thinner end of the best end. This is the tip of the shoulder blade. It is simple to work out with a knife and your fingers.

If thin small cutlets are required cut between each bone as evenly as possible, splitting the rack into six or seven small cutlets. If fatter cutlets are required carefully ease out every other rib bone. Then cut between the remaining bones into thick cutlets. Now trim the fat from the thick end of each cutlet, and scrape the rib bones free of any flesh or skin.

Noisettes

These are boneless cutlets, tied into a neat round shape with string. They are made from the loin or best end. Skin the meat: lift a corner of the skin with a small knife, holding it firmly (using a cloth to get a good grip), and pull it off.

Chine the meat (see page 130). Now remove first the chine bone and then all the rib bones, easing them out with a short sharp knife.

Trim off any excess fat from the meat and roll it up tightly, starting at the meaty thick side and working towards the thin flap. Tie the roll neatly with separate pieces of string placed at 3cm/1½in intervals. Trim the ragged ends of the roll to neaten them. Now slice the roll into pieces, cutting accurately between each string. The average English best end will give four good noisettes. The string from each noisette is removed after cooking.

Crown roast

Two racks (best ends) are needed. For a larger roast use three. The rack is prepared similarly to one destined for cutlets (see above) but the rib bones are left slightly longer, and the rack is not split into cutlets. But it is skinned, chined, the shoulder cartilege is removed, excess fat is cut off and the top inch of the bones are scraped in the same way.

Bend each best end into a semi-circle, with the fatty side of the ribs inside. To facilitate this it may be necessary to cut through the sinew between each cutlet, from the thick end for about 2cm/1in. But take care not to cut into the fleshy eye of the meat. Sew the ends of the racks together to make a circle, with the meaty part forming the base of the crown. Tie a piece of string round the 'waist' of the crown. Traditionally, stuffed; but this can result in undercooked inside fat.

Guard of honour

Prepare two best end racks exactly as for the crown roast. Score the fat in a criss-cross pattern. Hold the two best ends, one in each hand, facing each other with the meaty part of the racks on the board, and the fatty sides on the outside. Jiggle them so the rib bones interlock and cross at the top. Sew or tie the bases together at intervals. Stuff the arch if required.

To score crackling

It is vital that crackling should be scored evenly and thoroughly, each cut (which should penetrate the skin and a little of the fat below it) being even and complete. Unscored crackling is tough and difficult to carve. Make the cuts not more than 1cm/½in apart all over the skin. Score the crackling after boning but before rolling and tying the joint.

PORK AND BACON

Chops

Chops are trimmed of rind, and the fat snipped or cut across (from the outside towards the meat). This is because as the fat shrinks during cooking it tends to curl the chops out of shape.

Gammon steaks or bacon chops

Snip the surrounding fat as described above. Bacon chops (really thick rashers from the prime back) are sometimes cooked with the rind left on. But the snipping is still essential to prevent curling.

American or Chinese spare ribs

These are made from belly of pork (not English spare rib). They can be cut before or after cooking. Simply cut between each belly bone, splitting the meat into long bones.

CARVING MEAT

The most important factor in good carving is a really sharp knife, a fork with a safety guard, and a board or flat plate unencumbered by vegetables and garnishes. Common sense usually dictates how joints are to be tackled. Meat off the bone is simple – just cut in slices of whatever thickness you prefer, *across the grain* of the meat. Pork, beef and veal are traditionally carved in thinner slices than lamb.

Legs

The legs of pork, lamb, bacon (gammon, or ham), veal and venison are carved similarly. Put the leg meaty side up on the board or plate and grasp the knuckle bone with one hand, or pierce the joint firmly with a carving fork. Cut a small shallow V or scoop out of the middle of the top of the meat. Carve slices of meat from both sides of the V. Then turn the leg over and take long horizontal slices from the other side.

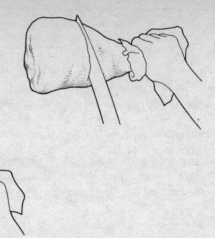

Legs can also be cut in diagonal slices from the knuckle end. This is more common with hams, but both methods are used for all legs.

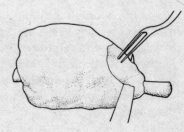

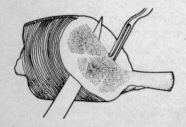

Loins

Loins and best ends of pork, veal and lamb are cut straight down between the bones if the joint is simply chined but not boned. If boned, the meat is cut similarly, but in thinner slices (about ¾cm/¼in thick). Beef strip loin (boned sirloin) is cut in the same way, thinly in Britain, thickly in America.

Sirloin of beef on the bone is tackled from the top and bottom, the slices cut as thinly as possible on the top, the undercut or fillet slices being carved more thickly. Each diner should be given a slice or two from both top and bottom.

Saddle of lamb

The chump end of the saddle is cut in thin slices across the grain of the meat, at rightangles to the backbone. But the main part of the saddle, lying each side of the backbone is cut in thin strips or narrow slices down the length of the saddle.

Under the rib cage, close to the backbone is found the tender thin mignon fillet. It is awkward to turn the saddle over and carve this, but it is the most delicious meat and should not be wasted.

Crown roast and guard of honour

Remove string and split into cutlets.

OFFAL AND ODDMENTS

Although in the West we are tucking into more and more meat, we have become squeamish about offal. In America the very word offal is thought so unattractive that it is called 'variety meats'. But such things as liver and kidney, and even intestines (for chitterlings) and blood (for black pudding) used to be part of our everyday diet. Most offal is highly nutritious, and some of it is comparatively cheap. It must be eaten very fresh.

LIVER

Liver should not have a strong smell when fresh, and should not be dry and wrinkled or discoloured. It may however be bloody.

The fine outer membrane should be peeled off before slicing for cooking, and any tubes or sinews removed.

Calves' liver

Should be pale milky brown in colour. It has a fine even texture and excellent delicate flavour. It is expensive. Dutch liver is considered better than English. Usually grilled or fried.

Lambs' liver

Is the next most expensive of the livers. It is reddish-brown, darker than calves'. It has a good flavour, is tender, and is generally fried.

Pigs' liver

Cheaper than lambs' liver. Dark brown and close textured, it is rather strong in flavour. It can be fried, but is usually made into pâtés or terrines.

Ox liver

Dark bluish-brown in colour, very strong in flavour, and tough. The cheapest of the livers. Needs soaking or blanching to reduce the flavour. Used, with other ingredients, for stews. Can be braised.

KIDNEY

Kidneys are sold either in their suet or loose. They keep, if they must be kept, better in the suet than out. They should smell mild and pleasant, be smooth and clean-looking, not have discoloured dark patches on them, and feel soft to the touch. The fine membrane enclosing them should, if possible, be removed, especially from lambs' or pigs' kidney. The core of sinew and gristle is removed before cooking.

Veal (calves') kidneys

These are the most expensive kidneys. They are pale milky brown, with creamy white suet, and are shaped rather like a bunch of grapes. They are very tender and delicate in flavour. Usually sautéed, fried or grilled but may be barded with fat and roasted, or left in their suet and roasted. Also used for puddings, pies and stews. Generally in very short supply.

Lambs' kidneys

These are medium brown, sometimes faintly bluish, firm-textured and egg-shaped. Usually split in half, cored, and used for grilling, frying or in sauté dishes. Good taste, neither too strong nor insipid.

Pigs' kidneys

Pale brown, similar in texture to lambs', but slightly longer. Not sold in suet. Stronger flavour than lambs', used for stews and casseroles, and sometimes for frying or grilling.

Ox kidneys

The largest kidney, shaped as veal kidney, but much darker, almost bluish-red in colour. Strong flavour, tough in texture, suitable only for long slow cooking, e.g. in pies and puddings.

TONGUE

Pigs' tongues are sold in the head, and calves' tongues are very rarely available. Ox and lambs' tongues can be bought, however.

Ox tongue

Should feel soft to the touch, though it might have a rough and pigmented skin. It is sold whole, fresh or salted. It is usually boiled, skinned and served either hot or cold. Tongue is sometimes pressed while hot into a mould to give it a round shape when cold. The thicker, fattier part of the tongue is very soft, the tip leaner and tougher.

Lambs' tongues

Small and generally sold by the pound. They are usually pale pink in colour, but the roughish skin may be pigmented light or dark grey. Usually skinned after cooking. Lambs' tongues are very delicate in flavour, and extremely tender. Sometimes pressed and served cold in their jelly, or used for hot sauté dishes.

HEADS AND BRAINS

Calves' heads

Sometimes available if specially ordered. They are used mainly for boiling and serving hot. Salted, they are used for brawn.

Calves' brains

The most delicate and expensive. They are soaked and blanched to remove all traces of blood before cooking, and skinned of membrane and sinew after blanching. Excellent fried plainly or in a crumb coating. Almost creamy texture when cooked.

Pigs' heads

Used for brawn, fresh or salted, and can be used for sausages. The cheeks of certain long-faced breeds of pig are lightly salted, and sold as Bath Chaps. They are rather fatty, but of good flavour, usually eaten crumbed and fried, or cold like ham. A pig's head is sometimes used on banqueting tables as a stand-in for the now unavailable boar's head. Pigs' brains are sold in the heads.

Sheep's heads

Can be boiled or stewed for use in broths and pie fillings, but are seldom available, and involve a lot of labour for very little meat.

Sheep's brains

Less fine and delicate than calves', but more readily available. Treated in exactly the same way.

Ox cheek

Sold for brawns and stews.

SWEETBREADS

Each animal has a pair of thymus glands in the throat, and another pair (called heartbreads) in the body. The heartbreads are considered the best. Pigs' sweetbreads are not sold.

Calves' sweetbreads

The most expensive and delicate, but hard to come by. They have a soft texture, not as creamy as brains, but good. They are treated like brains, or sautéed and used in savoury mixtures.

Ox breads

Less tender than calves' but have an excellent flavour. They are sometimes available in provincial and country butcher shops, and are usually cheap.

Lambs' sweetbreads

The next best thing to calves', but they lack the extreme delicacy of taste and texture.

HEART

Heart is highly nutritious, but needs slow cooking to tenderize it. It is also very lean, and needs a sauce or plenty of basting to keep it moist. Hearts must be cleaned of all sinew and the tubes removed before cooking.

Ox heart

Large, very tough, strong-flavoured, coarse and muscular and bluish-red. It is generally used with other ingredients chopped or minced – perhaps for a filling or pie.

Lambs' hearts

The smallest and most tender of the hearts. But stuffing to add flavour, slow cooking and careful basting are still necessary to moisten and tenderize the naturally lean and tough flesh.

PLUCK

The pluck is the name given to the lights (lungs), liver, pancreas and spleen. Lights are today generally sold for pet food. The liver is sold separately. Sheep's pluck is minced for haggis.

FEET AND TROTTERS

Calves' feet

Seldom sold to the public. Good for stock and calf's foot jelly due to the high concentration of gelatine present in it.

Pigs' trotters are high in gelatine, good for setting stocks, and brawn. Can be boned, stuffed, braised, served hot with mustard sauce, or hot or cold with vinaigrette.

Sheep's trotters and ox feet are not sold.

Cow heel is treated before sale, and looks and tastes, similar to tripe. It consists of the whole foot and heel of the animal.

TRIPE

Tripe can come from all cud-chewing animals, being the first and second stomachs, but in practice only ox tripe is sold. The first stomach (blanket tripe) is smooth, the second honeycombed. Tripe is sold parboiled, but needs further long boiling to tenderize it. It is wise to ask the butcher how much more boiling it will need.

Grey, slimy, flabby, strong-smelling tripe should be avoided. It should be thick, firm and very white. Tripe can be stewed, boiled or deep fried. A very specialist taste, with its addicts and its detesters.

OXTAIL

Sold skinned and, usually, jointed. Choose fat large tails with plenty of meat on them. Cow tails, which are skinny and rather tasteless, are sometimes passed off as oxtail. The meat should be dark and lean, the fat creamy white and firm.

Oxtail is high in gelatine content, so cooks to a tender, almost sticky stew. Good for soups. Very rich in flavour.

MARROW BONES

Marrow bones are from the thigh and shoulder bones of beef. They are sawn across in short cylinders by the butcher. They are boiled whole and served in a napkin, the diner extracting the soft rich marrow and eating it on toast. Marrow is also used as a flavouring in other dishes, such as entrecôte à la bordelaise, where it moistens and flavours the steak.

BLOOD

Pigs' blood is used in the making of black pudding. It is mixed with fat, and stuffed into intestines like a sausage.

POULTRY AND GAME BIRDS

Domesticated birds lead an unenergetic but well-fed life. The resulting flesh from such creatures is naturally very tender (they get less exercise than their wild cousins and are almost always killed young) but it lacks the pronounced taste of wild birds feeding in woods and on moors. Bone meal or broilers' pellets can hardly be expected to produce the flavour of wild heather and grasses.

If a bird has not been plucked, and still has its head, it is easy to tell whether it is young or old. Young birds, be they chickens, ducks, pheasants or turkeys will have pliable beaks and smooth legs, the scales not coarse, and barely overlapping. The spurs of the male birds will be little more than knobs, and the breastbone, when pushed down with the heel of the hand will 'give' a bit. In addition, the webbing on ducks, geese and waterfowl will tear easily. If the bird has been freshly killed the eyes will be clear, there will be no loss of feathers, and the quill feathers will come out comparatively easily when pulled.

HANGING

Hanging of birds (i.e. suspending them in cool fresh air out of the reach of flies – usually in a larder) is done for three reasons: *a.* to allow the toughening effects of *rigor mortis* to disappear; *b.* to allow enzyme activity to tenderize the meat; and *c.* to improve the flavour.

No bird *need* be hung longer than 24 hours, when it will still be extremely fresh, but game birds are often hung for up to two weeks, by which time they have a markedly high gamey flavour, beloved of some, hated by others. Recently the trend has been to eat game birds hung for between four days and a week. Chickens are usually hung for 24 hours, ducks for one or two days, turkeys for three or four.

Traditionally small birds, such as pheasant and grouse, are hung by a piece of string round their necks, and large birds, such as geese and turkeys, by their feet. In fact all birds can be suspended by the feet, the only reason for hanging game birds by the neck being to increase their gameyness by preventing the bleeding from the beak that results if birds are hung head-down. Some sportsmen do not consider their game sufficiently high until the neck parts and the bird falls. Birds hung overlong of course will finally go bad – a bluish-green tinge will be seen on the skin when the feathers are plucked and the smell will be very unpleasant.

Hanging is always done before the bird is eviscerated. Once gutted, birds must be cooked and eaten. Birds that are to hang for more than a day or two are not plucked when freshly killed. This is because if the bird is to hang for any length of time the exposed skin of a plucked bird would dry out. But they may be hung plucked for short periods.

PLUCKING

Some birds are easier to pluck than others, ducks being notoriously tedious. All birds are easier to pluck if still warm when tackled. Work away from draughts, as the feathers fly about, and pluck straight into a dustbin. Tug the feathers, working from the tail to the head, pulling against the way the feathers grow. If the bird is very young indeed, pull downwards towards the tail to avoid tearing the flesh.

Once plucked, the bird should be singed. This can be done with a burning taper, or directly over a gas flame, but care should be taken to singe only the down and small feathers, and not to blacken the flesh. The bird should then be rubbed in a clean tea-towel to remove any remaining stubble. It is now ready for drawing.

CLEANING AND DRAWING

Surprisingly, birds keep better, when hanging, with their insides intact. Once eviscerated they must be cooked within a day or two. So when you are ready to cook the bird, take it down, and proceed as follows.

1. Pluck it if you have not already done so.
2. Cut round the feet, at the drumstick joint, but do not cut right through the tendons. Pull the legs off the bird, drawing the tendons out with them. (If the bird is small this is easy enough – just bend the foot back until it snaps, and pull, perhaps over the edge of a table. Turkeys are more difficult: snap the feet at the drumstick joint by bending them over the end of the table, then hang the bird up by the feet from a stout hook, and pull on the bird. The feet, plus tendons will be left on the hook, the turkey in your arms.) All too often birds are sold with the tendons in the legs, making the drumsticks tough when cooked.
3. Now the head and neck. Lay the bird, breast side down, on a board. Make a slit through the neck skin from the body to the head. Cut off the head and throw it away. Pull back the split neck skin, leaving it attached to the body of the bird (it will come in useful to close the gap if you are stuffing the bird). Cut the neck off as close to the body as you can.
4. Put a finger into the neck hole, to the side of the stump of neck left in the bird, and move the finger right round, loosening the innards from the neck. If you do not do this

you will find them difficult to pull out from the other end.

5. With a sharp knife slit the bird open from the vent to the parson's (or pope's) nose, making a hole large enough to get your hand in. Put your hand in, working it so the back of your hand is up against the arch of the breastbone, and carefully loosen the entrails from the sides of the body cavity, all the way round. Pull them out, taking care not to break the gall bladder, the contents of which would embitter any flesh they touch. The first time you do this it is unlikely that you will get everything out in one motion, so check that the lungs and kidneys come too. Have another go if necessary. Once the bird is empty, wipe any traces of blood off with a damp clean cloth. (Covering the gutting hand with a cloth helps extract the intestines intact.)

GIBLETS ETC.

The neck and feet go into the stockpot. So can the heart and the cleaned gizzard. To clean the gizzard, carefully cut the outside wall along the natural seam so that you can peel it away from the inner bag of grit. Throw the grit bag away, with the intestines, and the gall bladder (be careful not to pierce or break this).

Do not put the liver in the stockpot. It may make the stock bitter. It may be fried and served with the dish, or fried, chopped and added to the sauce, or kept frozen until enough poultry liver has been collected to make pâté. But if the liver is to be used, carefully cut away the discoloured portion of it where it lay against the gall bladder (it will be bitter) and trim off any membranes.

TRUSSING

Trussing is done to keep the bird in a compact neat shape. To truss the bird (usually done after stuffing) sew it up as shown in the following drawings. We feel, however, that trussing large birds is largely unnecessary as the bird is to be carved up anyway, and trussing serves to prevent the inside thigh being cooked by the time the breast is ready. Small birds, especially game birds where underdone thighs are desirable, are trussed, but their feet are left on. Their feet may simply be tied together for neatness sake, and the pinions skewered under the bird. Or they may be trussed in any number of ways, one of which is described below. This is also suitable for large birds such as turkeys and chickens.

Arrange the bird so that the neck flap is folded over the neck hole, and the pinions turned under and tucked in tight. They will, if folded correctly, hold the neck flap in place, but if the bird is well stuffed the neck flap may have to be skewered or sewn in place. Press the legs down and into the bird to force the breast into a plumped up position.

Thread a long trussing needle with thin string and push it through the wing joint, right through the body and out of the other wing joint. Then push it through the body again, this time

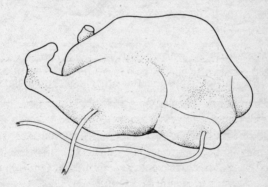

through the thighs. You should now be back on the side you started. Tie the two ends together in a bow to make later removal quick. Then thread a shorter piece of string through the thin end of the two drumsticks, and tie them together, winding the string round the parson's nose at the same time to close the vent. (Sometimes a small slit is cut in the skin just below the end of the breastbone, and the parson's nose is pushed through it.)

JOINTING

Small birds such as quail are invariably cooked whole, perhaps stuffed, and perhaps boned (see boning, pages 148–9). But medium-sized ones, like chickens and guinea fowl, are often cut into two, four, six or eight pieces.

To split a bird in half simply use a sharp knife to cut right through flesh and bone, just on one side of the breastbone, open

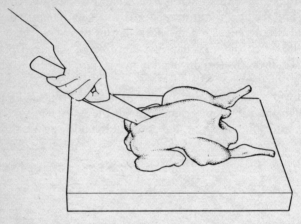

out the bird and cut through the other side, immediately next to the backbone. Then cut the backbone away from the half to which it remains attached.

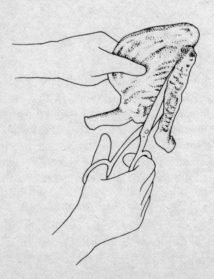

The knobbly end of the drumsticks, and the fleshless tips to the pinions can be cut off before or after cooking. In birds brought whole to the table they are left on.

To joint a bird into four, first pull out any trussing strings, then pull the leg away from the body. With a sharp knife cut through the skin joining the leg to the body, pull the leg away further and cut through more skin to free the leg. Bend the leg outwards and back, forcing the bone to come out of its socket close to the body. Turn the bird over, feel along the backbone to find the oyster (a soft pocket of flesh at the side of the backbone, near the middle). With the tip of the knife, cut this away from the carcass at the side nearest the backbone and farthest

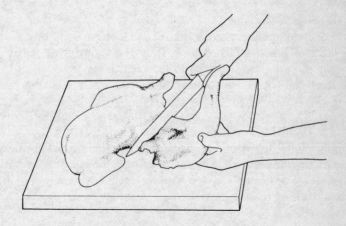

from the leg. Then turn the bird over again, and cut through the flesh (the knife going between the end of the thigh bone and the carcass) to take off the leg, bringing the oyster with it.

Then, using poultry shears or a heavy knife, split the carcass along the breastbone (see page 148). Then cut through the ribs on each side, to take off the fleshy portion of the breast, and with it the wing. Trim the joints neatly to remove scraps of untidy skin.

For six joints, proceed as above but split the legs into thigh portions and drumsticks. The exact join of the bones can be easily felt with a finger if the leg is laid on the board, skin side down.

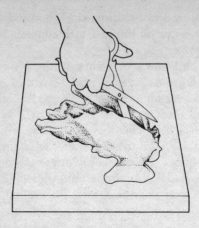

Cut between the bones.

For eight joints, proceed as above and then cut each wing, with a piece of breast attached to it, from the main breast portion. Make the cut almost parallel to the breastbone.

Keep the scraps, backbone, pinions etc. for the stockpot.

BARDING

Poultry liable to dry out during cooking is often barded: lay fatty bacon or rindless back pork fat strips over the body of the bird, and secure or tie in place. The barding is removed during cooking to allow the breast to brown.

BONING AND STUFFING

A short flexible knife is essential. The main point to remember is to keep the boning knife as close to the bone as possible, scraping and easing the flesh away carefully.

Turn the bird breast side down and cut through the skin, along the backbone, from the parson's nose to the neck. Work the skin and flesh away from the bones, peeling back the flesh as you go, gradually exposing the rib cage. When you get to the legs and wings, cut through the tendons close against the carcass at the joints. This will mean the wings and legs stay attached to the skin – not to the carcass. Continue working round the bird, taking special care when boning the breast where the skin and bone are very close.

If the wings and legs are to be boned too, chop off the wing pinions and the knuckle-end of the drumsticks. Working from the thicker end of the joints ease the bones out, scraping the flesh from them carefully. It may be necessary, especially with big birds, to work from the drumstick or the wing tip ends as well, but most of the work should be done from the body side.

Cut off any excess fat, especially from near the parson's nose. When all the bones are out scrape off any flesh still adhering to them and add it to the stuffing.

When stuffing the bird the stuffing is laid down the middle and the sides brought up to enclose it. The bird must then be sewn up if it is to be roasted, and sewn up and/or wrapped in muslin if it is to be poached.

CHICKEN AND BOILING FOWL

A chicken that has run about a bit, pecked at the ground, and perhaps been fed some corn and scraps, will have more flavour than a deep-litter broiler. In addition, if the commercially-reared broiler is frozen as soon as it is killed, it will have had little or no time to 'hang' or mature, and the taste will be delicate in the extreme. But worse can happen. If the bird is fed on fish-meal right up to the day of its death, the smell and taste of the flesh can be distinctly fishy.

Unfortunately, intensively reared chickens are all most of us can obtain. Our only hope is to buy, if we can get them, fresh rather than frozen chickens, and buy them from a reputable dealer who ensures that his poultry has been taken off fish-meal at least a week or so before slaughter, and fed a bit of corn.

Boiling fowls are rare today. The long slow cooking they require has made them almost unsaleable. But they can be had, especially from kosher butchers who sell them for their high proportion of fat (used extensively where the non-kosher cook would use butter), and their good strong taste for that Jewish culinary corner-stone, chicken noodle soup.

Butchers sell their chickens plucked and drawn and they are almost certain to be tender. The skin should feel dry to the touch, but soft, and there should be no strong unpleasant odour.

Most chickens in Britain are white-skinned, but they can be yellow. Boiling fowls will be larger and have plenty of fat around the vent.

Capons

These are de-sexed cockerels who, losing interest in sex, eat voraciously, and are very plump and tender. They have pale livers. They weigh between 2·7 kilos/6lb and 4·6 kilos/10lb, and can be cooked in all ways used for chicken or turkey.

DUCK

Most ducks sold today are really ducklings – seven to nine weeks old. A 1·8 kilos/4lb duck will feed only two people, in spite of its size. This is because there is little meat on the carcass, a great proportion of the weight coming from the fat, which runs from it during cooking. Because of its fattiness duck is roasted without additional fat, and indeed 290ml/½ pint of liquid fat can be extracted from an average duck.

Old ducks can be very tough. For this reason it is not wise to buy duckling frozen, unless from a reputable supplier, because it is impossible to tell, in a rigidly frozen duck, whether its backbone is pliable, and of course it has no telltale feet or bill.

The skin of a fresh duck should be dry, soft and smooth. It should not be slimy, and there should be no strong smell. The flesh is dark, very fine and rich in flavour, and more tender on the breast than leg.

GOOSE

A 4·6 kilos/10lb goose will feed five or six people. It is less fatty than the duck, and should be basted during cooking. Fresh young goose has a clean white skin, soft and dry to the touch.

Geese are large and have very short legs, which makes trussing them difficult, but as they are very compact, nicely shaped birds, trussing is even more unnecessary than usual.

Goose can be tough. Buy only from a good dealer, specifying a young tender bird. The flesh is rich, and a little heavy. Excellent for casseroles, cassoulet (hot-pot of haricot beans, salt pork and goose or mutton), and preserved or potted goose (French *confit d'oie*).

TURKEY

Turkeys used to have a reputation for being tough, dry and tasteless but today's turkeys are fattened fast and killed young, so are generally moist and tender. Hens are considered better than turkey-cocks, having plumper breasts, and less weight of bone.

The breast flesh is very white, inclined to be dry if over-cooked and the legs are dark meat, of good flavour but marginally tougher.

Fresh turkeys, as opposed to frozen ones, cost more but generally repay the expense with more pronounced flavour. Frozen turkeys, though perhaps lacking something in flavour, are seldom tough as only young birds are frozen.

Fresh turkeys should have a snow-white firm flesh, dry soft skin and a thin layer of fat over the back. They can weigh anything from 4·6 kilos/10lb to 9·9 kilos/22lb, and are usually served roasted whole and carved at table. Left-over meat is good in fricassées. Turkey breasts can now be bought separately, and they are cooked in any way suitable for chicken or veal.

Many cooks, tackling a fresh turkey for the first time are dismayed at the bloodiness, and comparatively 'high' smell of the neck and giblets. This is nothing to worry about. When the giblets and neck are removed (to be used for stock) and the bird well wiped inside and out with a damp clean cloth, the bird will be found to have a distinct, but by no means bad, smell. Of course if the smell makes you reel with digust, a second opinion should be sought – it is possible, though unlikely, that decomposition has begun.

GUINEA FOWL

Classed as a game bird, but in fact reared commercially, the guinea fowl is about the size of a chicken, and has beautiful grey feathers, spotted with white. The flesh is tender, with a taste somewhere between pheasant and chicken. Being rather dry if roasted in the English way, it is usually covered with a piece of fat or streaky bacon. A smallish fowl is usually served for two people.

QUAIL

Quail are small birds and for a good-sized portion two are served. One will do if it is a fat one, and has been boned and stuffed with a veal or poultry forcemeat. Most of today's quail come from farms, and are almost always plump and tender. They have the most delicate soft flesh, more flavour than a chicken, but less gameyness than their cousins the partridge.

Quail are often considered a fiddle to eat but, as long as finger-bowls are provided, this is not so. The flesh is so tender it comes off the breast easily, and the legs can be tackled in the fingers. Quails, like most white-fleshed birds, are served cooked through – not rare. When quails are boned the legs are usually left intact, so that the object still resembles a bird – without its legs such a small thing might look like a dumpling.

Quails must be eaten really fresh – preferably 24 hours after being killed. They are almost always bought plucked and cleaned, but should you need to pluck them yourself, do it as soon as they are killed.

GROUSE

In season 12 August to 10 December. Best early in season.

The prince of game birds. The best grouse is shot in Scotland, and has russet feathers. The hen is considered superior to the cock. It can be hung as long as a fortnight, when the gamey flavour and pronounced smell will be almost overpowering – but beloved of some *cognoscenti*. Today more grouse are eaten fresh and indeed to eat one on the evening of 13 August, 24 hours after the opening of the gaming season on the Glorious Twelfth is many a gourmet's aim. Indeed many are sold in London on the Twelfth, having been shot at dawn.

A fat hen grouse may serve two people, but grouse lovers prefer to have the bird to themselves. The flesh of a young bird is pink and tender on the breast, browner, and slightly tougher, on the legs. It is roasted, like steak, to the diner's preference, some liking it rare, some well-done. It has a full but not fatty flavour when fresh, tasting strong and gamey if well-hung.

Usually bought in brace (i.e. a pair, one cock, one hen) but can of course be bought singly. Older birds are casseroled, stewed, or used in pies.

Capercaillie and ptarmigan are species of grouse.

PHEASANT

In season 1 October to 1 February. Best from November to January.

The cock pheasant is a glorious bird, with brilliant green neck and long speckled tail feathers. The body, like the hen all-over, is mottled brown, but varies considerably from variety to variety. But the hen is plumper, tenderer and tastes better.

Pheasants may be eaten fresh (but benefit from at least three days' hanging, lest they taste as insipid as chicken) or really well hung. They are served underdone if required. The breast flesh is pale brown, the leg flesh darker.

Slightly larger than the grouse, a pheasant is served for two people, and if large and casseroled may serve three. Older birds are generally casseroled or used in pies, the young ones roasted in much the same way as grouse, the breast kept moist by a covering of pork fat.

Cock pheasant tail feathers are traditionally used to adorn a platter of roast birds.

PARTRIDGE

In season 1 September to 1 February. Best in October.

Smaller than grouse or pheasant, larger than quail, the common grey British partridge is thought by some to be finer in texture and taste than the much-marketed French red-leg. But the red-legged partridge is found in parts of Britain anyway, and most game-dealers make no distinction.

In feather, the partridge is small, round, and orangey in colour. Young birds of six months and under are *Perdreau* on a French menu, older birds *Perdrix*. Plucked young birds should have pale skin and fat breasts. They weigh up to 400g/14oz. They are roasted much as grouse or pheasant, but are not often served very under-done, though they may be. They may be fresh or well hung. In general young birds for plain roasting are less high than older birds, which may weigh 450g/1lb or more, for casseroling or pies.

A partridge is too small to serve two, and a hearty eater may indeed eat two by himself.

WILD DUCK, TEAL AND WIDGEON

Seasons vary according to variety, starting in August, ending in March.

The variety of wild duck is legion, ranging from largish mallard to the tiny teal. All are truly delicious, with rich well-flavoured flesh, even when eaten very fresh – which they should anyway be.

Wild duck are tricky to pluck. Sometimes they are painted with, or dipped in, melted paraffin wax which, when it dries and hardens, can be removed, bringing the feathers with it.

Unlike the domestic duck wild duck does not carry very much fat and needs to be barded and basted frequently if roasted. The flesh may have a distinctly fishy flavour and this can be par-ticularly, but never completely camouflaged by filling the cavity with sliced orange, by marinating in wine, or by parboiling in salty water before roasting. Some duck, notably widgeon, develop from their marshy feeding grounds a faintly muddy taste.

Although the French sometimes eat wild duck, and indeed domestic duck, underdone, this is not common in Britain.

PIGEON AND SQUAB

In season all the year as they are a real pest to farmers, and are classified vermin. They are generally much cheaper than other birds. But there is little flesh on them, and the best plan is to strip the breast of feathers, ease it away from the carcass, and discard the rest.

Squab (or fledgling pigeons) are killed at about four weeks old, and are fat and tender. In France they are farmed, but this is rare in England.

Pigeon breasts consist of dark lean flavoursome meat, which can, according to the age of the bird from which they were taken, be fried, grilled on a skewer, or casseroled. Whole squabs can also be cooked on a skewer. The average diner would need three pigeon breasts, or two whole squabs. Pigeon is a good cheap addition to game pie.

As mature pigeons are amazingly tough, care should be taken in ascertaining from the supplier that the pigeons in question are young. It is difficult to tell by the look of them.

SNIPE

In season August to January.

A small bird with a long bill which is sometimes pushed into the body of the bird, like a skewer, drawing the head through the legs, before roasting. Traditionally hung four days, then roasted ungutted, and served on a crouton. Can be served, two or three at a time, drawn and grilled on a skewer.

WOODCOCK

In season October to January, but best in November and December.

Resembles the snipe but is slightly larger. It is also roasted undrawn, and then served split in two, on toast as a savoury or starter.

CARVING POULTRY

Most small birds are served whole, the diner doing the best he can with his table knife and fork, and perhaps fingers if a finger-bowl is supplied.

But the breast of larger birds may be carved in slices, and some of both the breast meat, and of the dark leg meat or perhaps the whole drumstick, thigh or wing joint being offered. Large birds are carved as shown in the diagrams. Duck breast, however, is usually carved in long thin fillets, more or less parallel with the backbone.

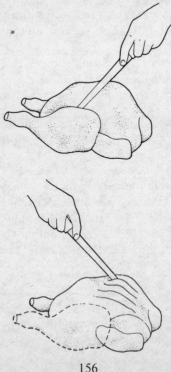

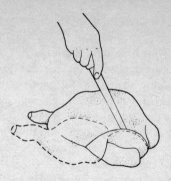

ROASTING TIMES

FOR POULTRY

White poultry, which is cooked through, not left pink, is done when the leg joint will wobble freely, not lifting the whole bird with it, and when the juices run clear, not pink, when the thigh is pierced with a skewer. To calculate cooking times, weigh after stuffing.

Chicken

With the oven set to 220 C/425 F, gas mark 7, allow 15 minutes to the pound. If the juices still run out pink when the flesh is pierced allow a further 15 minutes.

Turkey

Large turkeys should be slow-roasted but smaller birds (under 5·4 kilos/12lb) may be cooked at a higher temperature. Allow 10 minutes to the pound for small birds at 200 C/400 F, gas mark 6.

For larger turkeys use a cooler oven (180 C/350 F, gas mark 4) and allow 15 minutes to the pound, or an even cooler one (170 C/ 325 F, gas mark 3) and allow 25 minutes to the pound. Keep the breast covered to prevent burning, removing the covering (bacon, foil or what have you) for the last 45 minutes.

Thawing and cooking times for turkeys

Although the thawing time in this table can be relied on absolutely, the cooking times are dependent on an accurate oven. For safety's sake, plan the timing so that, if all goes right, the bird will be ready 1 hour before dinner. This will give you leeway if necessary. When the bird is cooked, open the oven door to cool the oven, then put the turkey on a serving dish and put it back in the oven to keep warm.

Thawing in a warm room (over 18 C/65 F) or under warm water is not recommended, as warmth will encourage the growth of micro-organisms, which might result in food poisoning.

Weight of bird when ready for the oven, regardless of whether it is boned stuffed or empty	Thawing time at room temperature 18 C/65 F	Thawing time in refrigerator 5 C/40 F	Cooking time at 180 C/ 350 F, gas mark 4	Cooking time at 170 C/ 325 F, gas mark 3
	hours	hours	hours	hours
4– 5 kilos/ 8–10lb	20	65	$2\frac{1}{4}$–$2\frac{3}{4}$	4 –$4\frac{1}{2}$
5– 6 kilos/11–13lb	24	70	3 –$3\frac{1}{2}$	5 –$5\frac{1}{2}$
6– 7 kilos/14–16lb	30	75	$3\frac{3}{4}$–$4\frac{1}{4}$	$5\frac{3}{4}$–$6\frac{1}{4}$
8– 9 kilos/17–20lb	40	80	$4\frac{3}{4}$–$5\frac{1}{4}$	$6\frac{1}{2}$–$7\frac{1}{2}$
9–11 kilos/21–24lb	48	96	$5\frac{1}{2}$–$6\frac{1}{2}$	8 –9

FOR GAME BIRDS

	C	F	Gas mark	Minutes
Pigeon	200	400	6	25–35
Grouse	190	375	5	25–35
Partridge	190	375	5	20–25
Pheasant	190	375	5	45–60
Snipe	190	375	5	10–12
Wild Duck	200	400	6	30–35
Woodcock	190	375	5	20–30
Quail	180	350	4	20
Teal	210	425	7	20

OTHER GAME
(VENISON, RABBIT, HARE)

In France wild boar is still occasionally sold. The famous banquet showpiece, boar's head, today is a pig's head, cooked and covered in a heavy dark aspic. (The true wild boar has a long snout and cheeks with something to eat on them but the decorated centre-piece of the Mayor's banquet table today is not eaten – which is perhaps just as well.) But we are concerned only with the game easily available to the British non-sportsman – rabbit, hare and venison.

RABBIT

In season all year.

Most rabbits on the butcher's slab have been reared in farms. They are almost certain to be young and tender with pale delicate flesh very like chicken. Wild rabbits come tough, tender, tasty and inedible, depending on their age and what they have been eating. A rabbit from a cornfield is bound to be good, one from the garlic farm revolting.

Young rabbits have smooth sharp claws, older beasts rough hard ones. Young rabbits have small even white teeth, older rabbits look like Peter Rabbit. Young ones have delicate soft ears, easy to tear, older animals dry tough ones.

Wild rabbits are smaller than tame ones, and carry less fat. Rabbits must be eaten fresh. They are paunched (gutted) as soon as they are brought in, and hung for 24 hours by the legs. The skin is left on to keep the flesh moist.

To paunch a rabbit simply split the skin of the abdomen the length of the belly. The stomach and entrails practically fall out, and are easily removed. Look at the liver – if it is blotchy and unhealthy looking, throw away the rabbit. Make sure the inside of the rabbit is quite clean, taking extra care near the tail and head, and wipe with a clean damp cloth.

To skin the rabbit first cut off the head and the feet. Work the skin off the body. With practice it will come off like a vest. Traditionally the head was left on but the eyes and ears removed. But the sight of a rabbit's head is more than squeamish townees, if not countryfolk, can take. Indeed, if the tastes of the people for whom the rabbit is intended are not known it is wise to joint (or 'unlace' as it once was called) the rabbit before taking it to table.

Rabbits are cooked in any way suitable for chicken – roasted, casseroled, grilled with mustard etc. They are jointed in the same way as hare, see below.

HARE

In season all year.

Much of what is written above about rabbits is true of hares: the age or otherwise of the animal is told the same way. In addition, young hares (or leverets) have a hardly noticeable hare-lip – this becoming deeper and more pronounced the older the animal. The paunching and skinning instructions apply. But there are major differences.

Hare has a much more pronounced and gamey flavour than rabbit, and this tendency is traditionally accentuated by five or six days hanging head down, *unpaunched*. The blood dripping from the mouth is caught and used as a liaison to thicken the sauce of, say, a jugged hare.

Only young hare is suitable for roasting and, because of a tendency to dry flesh, must be covered in a layer of pork fat and well basted. The saddle is the prime cut, the saddle and hind-quarters being used for roasts, the legs and belly for stews etc. The whole hare, in pieces, goes into a jugged hare.

JOINTING RABBITS AND HARES

Put the animal belly down on a board with the hind legs towards you. Cut round each hind leg in a curve, turn over and ease the legs out and away from the body to expose the ball and socket joint. Cut through the ligaments and remove the legs.

Twist the pelvis off the body and discard it (it is said to give too strong a flavour). Run the knife round under the shoulder blades and take them off, with the front legs. Now cut the back and saddle across in three or four even-sized pieces. With a large rabbit or hare, split the back piece or pieces in two along the backbones if they are over-large.

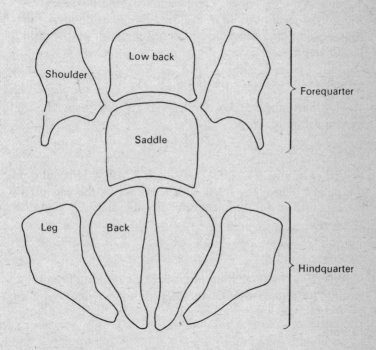

VENISON

Bucks are in season from June to September, does from October to December.

Venison (deer meat) is available frozen all the year round, and fresh only in the open season. The prime cuts for roasting are haunch, loin and saddle. The other, less tender, cuts are used for stewing or pies. Small collops or slices from the fillet can be treated as steaks, or fried à la crème.

Because venison is lean, and inclined to dryness, it is barded with fat, perhaps larded too, and basted well when roasted. It is frequently marinaded in wine and oil, both to tenderize it and to accentuate the flavour. Fresh venison has very little game flavour, tasting more like beef, but the longer it is hung, or marinaded, the more pronounced will be the taste.

When trimming a piece of venison for cooking, all the fat (there will not be much) should be removed, because although it may have a slight tenderizing and moisturising effect on the dish, it has an unpleasant taste.

ROASTING TIMES FOR GAME

Rabbit, hare and venison are lean meats and should be well barded before roasting.

Rabbit

Set the oven at 220 C/425 F, gas mark 7. Allow 15 minutes to the pound. Pierce the thigh with a skewer at the end of the cooking time, and if the juices run pink, not clear, give it another 15 minutes.

Hare

Seal the meat by fast frying in fat over direct heat. Then roast, basting, for a total of 45–50 minutes for a young hare.

Venison

Seal in the hottest oven for 20 minutes, then roast at 170 C/325 F, gas mark 3, for 15 minutes to the pound for rare meat, 20 minutes for barely pink.

ICE CREAM

Note: On freezing, ice cream will lose a little colour, sweetness and taste, so this must be compensated for during preparation.

METHODS OF MAKING

HAND-OPERATED CHURN

This is a wooden or heavy plastic bucket with a tightly covered metal container which fits inside. There are paddles reaching into the centre of the container. These are churned by a handle at the side of the bucket. The space between the churn and the bucket is packed with freezing salt and ice. Do not let any of the salt get into the ice cream as this will ruin the taste.

1. Put the churn into the bucket.
2. Surround the metal container with chopped ice and rock salt (1 part salt to 3 parts ice) and pack it in tightly. (The salt first melts some of the ice, resulting in chips of ice suspended in a saline solution. This prevents the ice settling into a solid igloo round the churn. Then, paradoxically, this saline solution is cooled by the remaining ice to *below* water-freezing point, brine having a lower freezing point than water. Now the ice-chips, surrounded by the below $-0\,°C$ solution, cannot readily melt and the mixture, thus stabilized, rapidly freezes the ice cream.)
3. Pour in the ice cream mixture taking care not to fill the container more than three-quarters full.
4. Insert the paddles and cover the metal churn with a piece of greaseproof paper. Fix the lid on over the paper. Assemble the rest of the machine.

5. Churn steadily, refilling the bucket with ice as it melts.
6. When the handle becomes difficult to turn the ice cream is set.
7. Remove the lid, scrape the paddles clean and replace the lid.
8. If the ice cream is for the day it is made, it should be kept in the refrigerator for one hour before serving.
9. If the ice cream is for a later date, pile it into a suitable container and keep it in the deep freeze until 1 hour before serving, when it should be put into the refrigerator to 'ripen'.

ELECTRIC ICE CREAM BUCKET

Pack the machine as for a hand churn and then set it in operation. When the hum of the motor becomes a high-pitched whine the ice cream is set.

ELECTRIC TRAY FREEZER (or sorbetière)

This is a rectangular aluminium box with plastic paddles. It fits into the freezer compartment of a refrigerator. Set the freezer at its lowest temperature, i.e. the highest setting. Pour the mixture into the sorbetière, place on the lid and put into the freezer. Turn on the machine; when the hum of the motor becomes a high-pitched whine the ice cream is set. Turn off the machine, scrape down and remove the paddles, cover the ice cream and leave to 'ripen' in the refrigerator for 1 hour.

REFRIGERATOR-FREEZER

This method does not rely on an ice cream machine of any sort but on everyday kitchen equipment.

Make sure that the fork, rotary beater, spoon, bowl and ice tray to be used are well chilled and that the freezer is set to the highest setting (lowest temperature). Pour the mixture into a chilled tray, and put into the freezer. Whisk with a fork every 20 minutes until the mixture is half frozen, then tip into a chilled bowl and whisk with a rotary beater. Return to the freezer in the bowl and whisk again at 20-minute intervals until the ice cream has become completely frozen. If the ice cream is to be eaten at a later date, allow 40–60 minutes in the refrigerator before serving, to soften slightly.

Exceptions

If the ice cream mixture already contains a high proportion of trapped air (for example, if it is made with a meringue base) the occasional whisk during the freezing process is not necessary. In addition, if a good processor such as a Magimix is available the ice cream can be completely frozen without whisking, then broken up and whisked in the machine to a creamy airy consistency. It must then be returned to the freezer.

WATER ICES

Water ices are better made in an ice cream machine, because the absence of any fat means that large ice crystals form very easily. The addition of whipped egg whites or gelatine helps to prevent this. A *granita* is a water ice made without egg whites or gelatine, having a rather icy and grainy, not creamy, texture.

BOMBES

Bombes are iced desserts frozen in a special bombe mould or in a pudding basin and turned out before serving. They generally consist of an outside layer of ice cream or sorbet and a filling of a contrasting ice cream, sorbet or a cream mousse or meringue mixture. When cut into segments the slices have a pretty stripey appearance. The traditional bombe mould was completely round, but modern ones are often shaped like jelly moulds. A pudding basin works perfectly well.

Making bombes

1. To line a bombe mould with ice cream:
    (i) Chill the mould in the freezer.
   (ii) Soften the ice cream so that it can be spread.
  (iii) Line the bottom and sides of the mould with ice cream.
   (iv) Freeze until firm.

2. For the filling:
  (i) Chill the filling well.
  (ii) Pour or spoon into the mould.
3. Cover and freeze until firm, preferably overnight.
4. Place in the ordinary refrigerator one hour before serving.
5. To unmould:
  (i) Remove lid. Prick the mixture to release any vacuum.
  (ii) Invert a plate over the mould and turn mould and plate over together.
  (iii) Cover with a cloth wrung out in hot water and hold it there. When the cloth becomes cold, wring it out again in hot water and replace it over the bombe.
  (iv) Remove the cloth. The bombe case should now lift off easily.
  (v) If the ice cream has melted slightly, return the bombe to the freezer until firm.
6. Decorate with fruit, nuts or whipped cream, as appropriate.

Easy bombe filling

Flavour whipped cream as you like (e.g. with a liqueur or with finely chopped fruit or with ginger). Mix it with an equal quantity of broken meringues.

FREEZING

Freezing is a method of preserving food – not indefinitely, but for some weeks or months. Bacterial action, which causes spoilage, is prevented by keeping the food at extremely low temperatures. Some deterioration in the taste, texture and colour of the food will take place if food is kept frozen for longer than the recommended times.

Providing the simple instructions for freezing are followed religiously, some food can be successfully stored without loss of nutritional value or quality.

RAPID FREEZING

The quicker the freezing process the smaller will be the ice-crystals formed in the food. Large ice-crystals, resulting from slow freezing, damage the cell walls of the food, and when that food is thawed liquid will be lost, including some soluble nutrients. Meat, particularly, will lose moisture on thawing if too slowly frozen, and will be dry when cooked.

PACKING THE FREEZER

In order to facilitate rapid freezing, only small amounts of unfrozen food should be put into the freezer at one time. Large quantities of room-temperature food would raise the temperature in the freezer, and the freezing process would inevitably be slower. For the same reason food should not be packed in large parcels, and the parcels should be separated in the freezing compartment, allowing the air to circulate round them. Once they are frozen, however, they can be – and indeed should be for economy's sake – packed tightly together with as little space between them as possible. A full freezer costs less to run than a half-empty one. Most freezers contain a fast-freeze compartment for the actual freezing, and larger compartments for storage. The freezer should be set to its coldest setting at least 12 hours before the food to be frozen is put into it. This is essential for meats, less important for vegetables, but advisable anyway.

WRAPPING THE FOOD

Because the cold atmosphere of a freezer is very drying, and direct contact with the icy air causes 'freezer burn' (dry discoloured patches) on some foods, most foods need careful wrapping before freezing. Heavyweight polythene bags are the cheapest and best wrappers, because it is possible to see through them, and they take various shapes of food without too many air-spaces. But any air-tight container will do. Foil is sometimes used, as are rigid plastic containers, old yoghurt cartons, bowls with lids etc. Whatever the container it must be robust enough to withstand a bit of bashing about in the freezer, and it must be possible to label it clearly. Freezer labels, or polythene bags with white labels on which it is possible to write with a Chinagraph pen or 'freezer pencil' are best. Once the food is packed into the container, as closely wrapped as possible, it should be labelled with the contents and the date, and frozen immediately.

Liquids can be poured into a polythene bag set in square containers and frozen. Once solid, the bag is lifted out of the outer container and stored thus. This means fewer kitchen containers are out of use because they are in the freezer, and liquids can be stored in space-saving rectangular shapes.

Liquids in plastic tubs or containers should be frozen with a $2\frac{1}{2}$cm/1 in gap between bowl and lid to allow for expansion.

Food should be used up in the right order – peas frozen last week should not be eaten before the batch frozen 2 months ago. To facilitate this a record or inventory of what is in the freezer should be kept on it, in it or near it, with additions and subtractions made each time food is put in or taken out.

OPEN FREEZING

Fruits and vegetables, if frozen in a mass, will emerge from the freezer in a solid block. This can be inconvenient for thawing in a hurry, or if only a small quantity of the food is needed. For this reason many foods are frozen on open trays so that each raspberry, pea, broad bean or sprig of cauliflower is individually frozen before packing into bags. The frozen produce will then be free-flowing and separate. Use this method for sausages, hamburgers, breadcrumbs, bread rolls etc. as well as for fruit and vegetables. Decorated cakes and puddings can be open-frozen then packed once the decoration is hard enough to withstand the tight wrapping around it.

MASS FREEZING

If the food to be frozen is not the type suitable for open freezing, make sure that the block is not too thick. This will make cooking and thawing easier and quicker. For example, meatballs in tomato sauce should be laid one deep in a plastic box, not piled one on top of each other; spinach should be in a flattish pack so it can be cooked from frozen (a thick block would mean overcooked outside leaves when the middle was still frozen).

Air should be excluded as far as possible. This is especially important with casseroles, where the chicken or meat should be completely coated or covered by the sauce. Otherwise the meat may become dry and shreddy.

THAWING

Thawing, if it is necessary before cooking, reheating or eating, should be as slow as possible. Rapid thawing leads to loss of moisture and subsequent dryness or tastelessness of the food. However it is sometimes imperative to thaw food in a hurry. To do this put it into an air-tight polythene bag and dunk it in cold, not hot, water. Hot water tends to cook the outside of the food, and anyway encourages bacterial activity which would cause the food to go bad if not immediately completely cooked.

Meat should be completely thawed, and should be at room temperature before it is cooked. Half frozen or very cold meat becomes tough on cooking. This does not apply to meatballs or sausages where the meat is minced. For thawing turkeys, see the table on page 158.

RE-FREEZING FROZEN FOOD

Freezing does not kill bacteria present in food, it simply inhibits growth. So when food is out of the freezer the bacteria in it will multiply normally. When put back, the now considerably increased population of bacteria will cease breeding, to start afresh when the food is brought back into the warmth. For this reason frozen food manufacturers caution purchasers not to re-freeze the product once thawed. They are justly nervous that if the food is in and out of the freezer, the food could contain germs in dangerous concentrations, and the cook will still regard the product as perfectly fresh, because it has just emerged from the freezer. The foods most likely to cause illness are commercial ice cream and seafood, as both deteriorate rapidly. But this is not to say that no food should *ever* be re-frozen. It is a matter of common sense. Say, for example, a loaf of bread is freshly made, then frozen: a week later it is thawed. Similarly liver pâté is freshly made, frozen, then thawed in the same way. Sandwiches are then made using the bread and the pâté, and frozen. The total time that either bread or pâté would have had to deteriorate would have been the time they remained unfrozen – perhaps a few hours; so they would be perfectly good to eat when next thawed. But if that pâté had been in the refrigerator for a week before being frozen, then at room temperature for a day before being used for sandwiches, then out in a sunny garden for half a morning before being eaten, the bacteria present would have had plenty of breeding time to do their dirty work.

The main thing to remember is to keep food as cold as you can between freezings, and put it back as quickly as possible. For example if stuffing a frozen turkey for Christmas two weeks before the day the following procedure should be followed:

1. Thaw the turkey in the refrigerator or cool larder, not at room temperature.
2. Get the freshly made stuffing well chilled before tackling the turkey.
3. Bone and stuff the turkey in a cool place, working as rapidly as possible.
4. Freeze it again immediately.
5. Thaw again in the refrigerator, not in the room.
6. Roast in a hottish oven (this will kill any bacteria present, whereas a cool oven would encourage breeding, spoiling the food before the increased heat killed the organisms).

To sum up, it is vital to know how fresh the food in your freezer is. It will come out as fresh, or as stale or as bad as it went in.

FOODS THAT CANNOT BE FROZEN SUCCESSFULLY

Although most food will be prevented from going bad if kept at freezing point, some foods cannot be successfully frozen as the texture is ruined by freezing. This is particularly true of foods with a high water content. However, some of these may be frozen if wanted for soups or purées, in which case they should normally be frozen in purée form. Examples are *bananas*, *cucumbers*, *lettuce* and *watercress*.

Emulsions such as *mayonnaise* or *hollandaise* sauce do not freeze successfully as they separate when thawed.

Yoghurt, milk and cream can be frozen but will not be totally smooth when thawed. Double cream freezes better if whipped first. Storage time: 4 months.

Eggs cannot be frozen in the shell, but both whites and yolks freeze well, either lightly beaten together or separated. Storage time: 9 months.

Jelly, both savoury and sweet, loses its texture if frozen, and would have to be reboiled and allowed to set again after thawing if required jellied.

Strawberries keep their colour and flavour well, but become soft on thawing.

Melon is too watery to remain crisp when thawed. Best frozen in balls in syrup. But even this is not totally satisfactory.

Tomatoes emerge mushy when thawed, but are good for soups and sauces. One bonus of freezing tomatoes whole is that they peel well if run, still frozen, under the hot tap. They can, of course, be frozen as purée or juice.

Fats, or foods with a high fat content, as a rule freeze less successfully than those without. They have a tendency to develop a slightly rancid flavour if stored for more than three months.

FOODS THAT FREEZE SUCCESSFULLY

Most foods freeze well if some care is taken with wrapping etc. But some foods freeze so well that no-one would know that they had been frozen. Baked or raw *pastries*, *breads*, *bread or biscuit doughs*, *cakes* and *sandwiches* containing not-too-wet fillings, are good examples.

As a general rule raw food (or briefly blanched food, see vegetables, pages 173–4) keeps better and longer than cooked food. But cooked food, especially if well covered in a sauce, or under a potato or pastry crust, keeps well. There is a snag: soups and sauces thickened with flour sometimes thaw to a too-thin consistency. This can be overcome by using special thickening agents designed for frozen food, but as the liquid will usually re-thicken on heating anyway it does not seem worth it.

Vegetables freeze well if they are to be eaten cooked. They cannot be frozen if intended to be eaten raw. In order to prevent enzyme activity green vegetables are briefly boiled, then rapidly cooled, before freezing. They may be frozen without this 'blanching' but their storage time would be much less, and it is foolish to lose food through lazy freezing. Only the best vegetables, very fresh, should be used. They should be washed, or picked over, or otherwise prepared as if for immediate cooking. A large saucepan of water is brought to a rapid boil, and the vegetables (not more than a pound or so at a time) lowered into it. Accurate timing of the blanching process is important. The minutes are counted from the time the water reboils. As soon as the time is up, the vegetables are lifted out, and *immediately* cooled in a sink full of cold water, if possible. Once stone cold, the vegetables are lifted out, drained well, patted dry if necessary, and frozen. The same blanching water can be used for several batches of vegetables. Some vegetables (onions, mushrooms, potatoes) may be cooked completely in butter or blanched in oil instead of water. They are allowed to cool normally before freezing.

VEGETABLES

Where a choice of times is given the shorter time is for smaller vegetables, longer time for larger ones.

Vegetable		Blanching time in minutes	Storage time in months
Asparagus	Do not tie in bunches.	3–4	12
Artichoke (globe)	Remove stalks and outer tough leaves.	7	6
Artichoke (Jerusalem)	Freeze cooked into a purée.	—	6
Beans, broad	Sort by size.	3	12
Beans, French or runner	French: trim ends.	2–3	12
	Runner: slice thickly.	1½–2	6
Beetroot	Freeze completely cooked and skinned. Slice if large.	—	6
Broccoli	Trim stalks.	2½–4	12
Brussels sprouts	Choose small, firm sprouts. Remove outer leaves.	4–6	12
Cabbage	Shred. (As cabbage is available all year freezing is not usual.)	1½	6
Carrots	Choose small young ones with good colour. Scrape. Freeze whole.	5–6	12
Cauliflower	Break heads into sprigs.	3–4	6
Celery	Will be soft when thawed, but good for soups and stews.	3	
Corn on the cob	Remove husks and silks.	6–10	9
Courgettes	Use only very small ones. Do not peel.	1	12
Kale	Remove stalks.	1	6

Vegetable		Blanching time in minutes	Storage time in minutes
Leeks	Finely slice, chop in chunks or leave whole.	1–3	12
Mushrooms	Do not peel. Freeze unblanched for up to 1 month. For longer storage, cook in butter.	—	4
Onions	Store unblanched onions, sliced or chopped, for up to 3 months. Sliced or chopped onions can be blanched in water or oil. Button onions can be blanched whole.	1–3	5
Peas	Choose young, very fresh peas.	1–2	12
Potatoes	Chips – blanch in oil. Boiled or mashed: freeze cooked and cooled.	4	6
Root vegetables	Cut into chunks and blanch or cook completely.	3	12
Spinach	Move about in water to separate leaves.	1	12
Tomatoes	Do not blanch. Freeze whole, in slices or as juice or purée, cooked or raw.		

FRUITS (Storage time: 9 months)

Only freeze fruit in prime condition. Unripe, overripe or blemished fruit gives poor results. There are three methods used to freeze raw fruit. (Cooked fruit may also be frozen, whole or puréed.)

Open freezing

Suitable for most soft fruit such as raspberries and currants. Spread the fruit out on a baking sheet or tray and place in freezer uncovered. When hard pack into polythene bags or rigid container, with or without adding sugar.

Purée

Suitable for any fruits. Stew the fruit and mash, liquidize or sieve. Allow the purée to cool. Pack into containers, leaving head space, cover, label and freeze. Raw purée freezes well, too.

Dry sugar pack

Suitable for most fruit to be used in cooked puddings. Prepare the fruit, toss it in sugar and freeze, with any juices that may have run from it during preparation. Care should be taken to exclude air, which may cause discoloration of the fruit.

HERBS (Storage time: 3 months)

Herbs should be frozen dry in small polythene bags or packets, or chopped finely, put into ice-trays and just covered with water. The frozen cubes can be transferred to labelled bags.

MEAT AND FISH (Storage time: raw meat, 9 months; cooked meat, 4 months; raw fish, 5 months; cooked fish, 3 months)

Special care should be taken in wrapping to prevent freezer burn.

CAKES AND BREADS (Storage time: 12 months)
Both raw and cooked doughs and pastries freeze well.

DEFROSTING THE FREEZER

A tedious but necessary job. Follow the manufacturer's instructions to the letter. Keep the frozen food wrapped in newspaper or a blanket so it will not thaw, and transfer rapid-thawing foods like ice cream to the refrigerator, while you work. Work as fast as possible, melting the ice in the freezer by standing trays or bowls of hot water in it, scraping the ice carefully with a *blunt* instrument that will not damage the freezer. Use the opportunity to have a sort-out, and re-label foods if necessary.

Most freezers need defrosting once a year, and late spring, before the garden vegetables come flooding in, is a good time to do it.

CATERING QUANTITIES

Few people accurately weigh or measure quantities as a control-conscious chef must do. But when catering for large numbers it is useful to know the minimum quantities required to provide well without great waste.

As a general rule, the more people you are catering for the less food *per head* you need to provide, e.g. 250g/½lb of stewing beef per head is essential for 4 people, but 180g/6oz per head would feed 60 people.

POULTRY

Chicken and turkey: 450g/1lb weight per person, weighed when plucked and drawn

Duck: 3 kilos/6½lb bird for 3–4 people; 2 kilos/4½lb bird for 2 people

Goose: 3·4 kilos/8lb for 4 people; 6·9 kilos/15lb for 7 people

GAME

Pheasant: 1 bird for 2 people (roast); 1 bird for 3 people (casseroled)

Pigeon: 1 bird per person

Grouse: 1 young grouse per person (roast); 2 birds for 3 people (casseroled)

Quail: 2 small birds per person, *or* 1 large boned stuffed bird (served on a crouton)

Partridge: 1 bird per person

Venison: 170g/6oz lean meat per person (casseroled); 2 kilos/4½lb cut of haunch weighed on the bone, for 8–9 people (braised or roast); weighed off the bone, 170g/6oz per person (braised or roast)

Steaks: 170g/6oz per person

MEAT

Lamb or mutton

Casseroled: 275g/½lb per person (boneless, with fat trimmed away)
Roast leg: 1·35 kilos/3lb for 3–4 people; 2 kilos/4½lb for 4–5 people; 3 kilos/6½lb for 7–8 people
Roast shoulder: 2 kilos/4½lb shoulder for 5–6 people; 3 kilos/6½lb shoulder for 7–9 people

Roast breast: 450g/1lb breast for 2 people

(British lamb joints are frequently larger than New Zealand joints.)

Grilled best end cutlets: 3–4 per person
Grilled loin chops: 2 per person

Beef

Stewed: 225/½lb boneless trimmed meat per person
Roast (off the bone): if serving men only, 225g/½lb per person; if serving men and women, 200g/7oz per person
Roast (on the bone): 340g/¾lb per person
Roast whole fillet: 2 kilos/4½lb piece for 10 people
Grilled steaks: 200–225g/7–8oz per person depending on appetite

Pork

Casseroled: 170g/6oz per person
Roast leg or loin (off the bone): 200g/7oz per person
Roast leg or loin (on the bone): 340g/¾lb per person
(2 average fillets will feed 3–4 people)
Grilled: one 170g/6oz chop or cutlet per person

Veal

Stews or pies: 225g/½lb pie veal per person
Fried: one 170g/6oz escalope per person

Minced meat

170g/6oz per person for shepherd's pie, hamburgers etc.
110g/¼lb per person for steak tartare
85g/3oz per person for lasagne, canneloni etc.
110g/¼lb per person for moussaka
55g/2oz per person for spaghetti

FISH

Whole large fish (e.g. sea bass, salmon, whole haddock), weighed uncleaned, with head on: 340–450g/¾lb per person

Cutlets and steaks: 170g/6oz per person

Fillets (e.g. sole, lemon sole, plaice): 3 small fillets per person (total weight about 170g/6oz)

Whole small fish (e.g. trout, slip soles, small plaice, small mackerel, herring): 225–340g/½–¾lb weighed with heads for main course; 170g/6oz for starter

Fish off the bone (in fish pie, with sauce etc.): 170g/6oz per person

Shellfish

Prawns: 55–85g/2–3oz per person as a starter; 140g/5oz per person as a main course

Mixed shellfish: 55–85g/2–3oz per person as a starter; 140g/5oz per person as a main course

VEGETABLES

Weighed before preparation and cooking, and assuming three vegetables, including potatoes, served with a main course: 110g/4oz per person, except (per person):

French beans: 85g/3oz

Peas: 85g/3oz

Spinach: 340g/¾lb

Potatoes: 3 small (roast); 170g/½lb (mashed); 10–15 (Parisienne); 5 (chateau); 1 large or 2 small (baked), 110g/¼lb (new)

Rice

Plain, boiled or fried: 55g/2oz (weighed before cooking) *or* 1 breakfast cup (measured after cooking)

In risotto or pilaf: 1oz per person (weighed before cooking) for starter; 55g/2oz per person for main course

Note: As a general rule men eat more potatoes and less 'greens' than women!

MISCELLANEOUS

Brown bread and butter: 1–1½ slices (3 triangular pieces) per person

French bread: 1 large loaf for 15 people; 1 small loaf for 10 people

Cheese

After a meal if serving one blue-veined, one hard and one cream cheese: 225g/½lb piece of each for 8 people if serving one variety of cheese only: 85g/3oz per person up to 8 people; 55g/2oz per person for up to 20 people; 30g/1oz per person for over 20 people.

At a wine and cheese party: 110g/¼lb per person for up to 8 people; 85g/3oz per person for up to 20 people; 55g/2oz per person for over 20 people.

Inevitably, if catering for small numbers, there will be cheese left over but this is unavoidable if the host is not to look mean.

Biscuits

3 each for up to 10 people
2 each for up to 30 people
1 each for over 30 people

Butter

30g/1oz per person if bread is served with the meal
45g/1½oz per person if cheese is served as well

Cream

20ml/¾oz per person for coffee
50ml/1½oz per person for pudding or dessert

Milk

¼ litre/1 pint for 18–20 cups of tea

SALADS

Obviously, the more salads served, the less guests will eat of any one salad. Allow 1½ large portions of salad, in total, per head – e.g. if *only* one salad is served make sure there is enough for 1½ helpings each. Conversely if 100 guests are to choose from five different salads, allow a total of 150 portions – i.e. 30 portions of each salad.

Tomato salad

450g/1lb tomatoes, sliced, serves 5 people

Cole slaw

1 small cabbage, finely shredded, serves 10–12 people

Grated carrot salad

450g/1lb carrots, grated, serves 6 people

Potato salad

450g/1lb potatoes (weighed before cooking) serves 5 people

Green salad

Allow a loose handful of leaves for each person (i.e. a large Cos lettuce will serve 8, a large Webb's will serve 10, a Dutch hot-house 'butterhead' will serve 4)

COCKTAIL PARTIES

Allow 10 cocktail mouthfuls per head if served at a 'cocktail party'
14 cocktail mouthfuls per head if served at lunchtime when guests are unlikely to go on to a meal
4–5 cocktail mouthfuls with pre-lunch or pre-dinner drinks
8 cocktail mouthfuls, plus 4 miniature sweet cakes or pastries, per head for a wedding reception

Sliced bread

A large loaf, thinly sliced, generally has 18–20 slices

Butter

30g/1oz soft butter will cover 8 large bread slices

Sausages

450g/1lb = 32 cocktail sausages

COFFEE-MAKING

Machines and devices for making coffee are legion. But delicious coffee can be made, like tea, in a pot or jug.

5 heaped tablespoons coffee to each litre/1¾ pints water (more or less according to taste)

1. Heat the coffee pot and a large jug. Spoon the coffee into the jug.
2. Boil the water, remove it from the heat and pour on to the coffee. (It should not be actually bubbling as it is poured. Just a fraction cooler than for tea.)
3. Give one brisk stir and allow to stand for 5 minutes.
4. Strain into the coffee pot.

For white coffee
Serve with cream or hot (but not boiled) milk

If reheating coffee: Take care not to allow coffee to boil as it will become grey, bitter and oily.
Storing: The flavour of coffee is volatile and quickly lost if left open to the air. It is best to buy no more than 1 week's supply

at a time; or to buy it vacuum packed. Always store coffee in an air-tight container. It will not keep well beyond 5 weeks once opened, even if re-sealed. But coffee freezes perfectly: freeze the beans or the freshly milled coffee in an air-tight plastic bag. If using a percolator there is no need to thaw the grounds, but frozen coffee grounds make the coffee too cool if using the jug method described above.

2
Soups, Starters
and Light Meals

◆———

SOUPS

Gazpacho

Gazpacho was made long before liquidizers were invented, but we feel that the laborious chopping and sieving involved is not justified. This recipe therefore assumes that the cook has a blender or liquidizer.

900g/2lb fresh, very ripe
   tomatoes, peeled
450g/1lb tin Italian peeled
   tomatoes
1 large mild-tasting Spanish
   onion
2 red peppers
1 small cucumber
1 thick slice white bread, the
   crust cut off
1 egg yolk

2 large cloves garlic
6 tablespoons olive oil
1 tablespoon tarragon vinegar
1 tablespoon tomato purée
Freshly ground black pepper
Plenty of salt (preferably sea
   salt)

To serve:
1 large bowl croutons

1. Chop or dice finely a small amount of the tomato, onion, red pepper, and cucumber and put in separate small bowls for garnish.
2. Put the bread, egg yolk and garlic into the liquidizer. Turn it on and add the oil in a thin steady stream while the

machine is running. You should end up with a thick mayonnaise-like emulsion.

3. Add the vinegar and then gradually add all the soup ingredients (roughly chopped if necessary) a little at a time and blend until smooth. It will be necessary to remove the contents when the liquidizer is about half full, to prevent the machine from clogging.
4. Sieve the soup to remove the tomato seeds and check that you have included the tomato purée and sufficient pepper and salt.

Note: Gazpacho should be served icy-cold with the small bowls of chopped vegetables and fried croutons handed separately. Sometimes crushed ice is added to the soup at the last minute.

If the soup is preferred thinner dilute it with iced water or tomato juice.

Serves 6

Lebanese Cucumber and Yoghurt Soup

1 large cucumber, peeled	2 tablespoons tarragon vinegar
290ml/½ pint single cream	1 tablespoon chopped mint
150g/5 fl.oz carton yoghurt	Salt and pepper

1. Wash and grate the cucumber coarsely.
2. Stir in the rest of the ingredients and season to taste.
3. Chill for 2 hours before serving.

Note: This soup may be garnished with cold croutons; chopped chives; a spoonful of soured cream added just before serving; chopped gherkins; a few pink shrimps. It is also good flavoured with garlic.

Serves 4

Quick Fish Soup

Two 140g/5oz cod fillets
Can of V8 juice *or* other
 vegetable and tomato juice
1 garlic clove, crushed

150ml/¼ pint chicken stock
 (made from a bouillon cube
 if necessary)
Salt and freshly ground black
 pepper
Chopped fresh parsley

1. Cut the cod into 1cm/½in cubes.
2. Heat the V8 with the garlic and chicken stock.
3. When the V8 and stock is boiling add the fish and reduce the heat.
4. Season well with salt and pepper.
5. Cook slowly for 15 minutes or until the fish is tender.
6. Serve with chopped parsley sprinkled over the top.

Serves 2–3

Spicy Tomato Soup

15g/½oz butter
½ onion, finely chopped
15g/½oz flour
200g/7oz can tomatoes
425ml/¾ pint chicken stock
1 bay leaf
Pinch of nutmeg

Salt and freshly ground black
 pepper
½ teaspoon paprika
1 clove
½ teaspoon sugar
Squeeze of lemon
110g/¼lb fresh tomatoes
1½ tablespoons port

1. Melt the butter. Add the chopped onion and cook gently until pale yellow and transparent.
2. Stir in the flour, cook for 1 minute, then add the canned tomatoes and stock. Stir until the mixture boils.
3. Add the bay leaf, nutmeg, a pinch of salt, about ½ teaspoon pepper, the paprika, clove, sugar and squeeze of lemon.

4. Simmer, stirring occasionally, for 30 minutes.
5. Skin and chop the fresh tomatoes.
6. Push the soup through a sieve and return it to the saucepan.
7. Add the port and fresh tomatoes. Reheat and adjust seasoning.

Serves 4

Creamy Vegetable Soup

225g/½lb leeks, well washed
30g/1oz butter
225g/½lb onions, very finely sliced
1 small head celery, finely sliced
1 large potato, peeled and finely sliced

1 tablespoon flour
570ml/1 pint chicken stock
290ml/½ pint creamy milk
Salt, pepper and nutmeg
1½ tablespoons thin cream
1½ tablespoons port (optional, but very good)

1. Finely slice the leeks, both white and green parts, discarding any tough outside leaves.
2. Melt the butter in a very large pan and gently cook the sliced onions, leeks, celery, and potatoes in it, stirring occasionally, until the whole mass is soft and cooked (about 20 minutes). The vegetables should not be allowed to brown at all. Do this 'sweating' of vegetables with the saucepan lid on, as the juices run more easily in a steamy atmosphere and they are less likely to fry brown.
3. Stir in the flour, then add the stock.
4. Bring to the boil stirring, and boil for 1 minute.
5. Add the salt, pepper and nutmeg to taste.
6. Simmer gently for 20 minutes.
7. Liquidize the soup in an electric blender or pass through a vegetable mill.
8. Add the milk, reheat, and add the cream and port. Use white port if you would prefer the soup not to go faintly pink.

Serves 4

Iced Vichyssoise

55g/2oz butter
1 medium onion, chopped
The white part of 3 large *or* 5
  small leeks, washed and
  chopped
110g/¼lb potatoes, peeled and
  sliced

Salt and pepper
860ml/1½ pints chicken stock
290ml/½ pint creamy milk
2 tablespoons cream
Chopped chives

1. Melt the butter in a heavy-bottomed pan and add the chopped onion and leek.
2. 'Sweat' the vegetables for 15 minutes or so, i.e. cook very slowly with a tightly-fitting lid or covered with a piece of greaseproof paper. The vegetables must soften without crisping or browning. It is possible to 'sweat' vegetables without a covering, but much more difficult as the steam escapes and they are inclined to fry.
3. When they are transparent and soft, add the potatoes, salt and pepper and the stock. Simmer until the potatoes are soft.
4. Liquidize the soup or push it through a vegetable mill.
5. Add the milk and cream.
6. Check the seasoning. Chill.
7. Add the chives just before serving, and perhaps a swirl more cream.

Note: The soup is good hot, too. Reheat without boiling.

Serves 4

Corn Chowder

1 large potato
3 sticks celery
1 large onion
110g/¼lb streaky bacon,
  rindless
1 large green pepper
30g/1oz butter

1 bay leaf
30g/1oz flour
570ml/1 pint milk
4 ears corn on the cob
Salt and pepper
Chopped fresh parsley

1. Wash and peel the potato.
2. Cut it, and the celery, onion and streaky bacon into dice.
3. Remove the seeds from the pepper and dice the flesh.
4. Fry the bacon in the butter. When brown but not brittle add the diced vegetables and the bay leaf. Turn down the heat and cook slowly until the onion looks soft and transparent.
5. Draw the pan from the heat; mix in the flour and then the milk.
6. Return the pan to the heat and stir steadily until boiling.
7. Scrape the kernels from the cobs and add them to the soup. Scrape the cobs with a sharp knife to extract all the juice and add this too. Season with salt and pepper to taste. Simmer for 5 minutes or until the vegetables are soft but not broken.
8. Serve sprinkled with chopped parsley.

Serves 4

Scotch Broth

450g/1lb leg of mutton *or* lamb,
  cut into 4 pieces
1 mutton *or* lamb knuckle bone
1·5 litres/2½ pints water
Salt and freshly ground black
  pepper
45g/1½oz split dried peas
1 turnip, diced

2 small carrots, diced
1 small onion, sliced
The white part of a small leek
45g/1½oz barley
85g/3oz hard white cabbage
1 tablespoon chopped fresh
  parsley

1. Put the meat and bone in a pan with the water and bring to the boil. Skim off any fat or scum.
2. Add salt and pepper, cover and simmer gently for 1 hour.
3. Add the peas, turnip, carrots, onion, leek and barley. Cover and simmer for 30 minutes.
4. Put in the shredded cabbage and continue simmering for 10 more minutes.
5. Taste and add salt and pepper if needed. Serve sprinkled with chopped parsley.

Serves 4

Lentil Soup

340g/¾lb lentils
1 litre/2 pints ham stock, saved from a bacon joint; *or* if not available use 1 small bacon bone and water
1 bay leaf
55g/2oz onion

1 stock cube
1 parsley stalk
3–4 tablespoons cream
Chopped fresh mint
Croutons
Water

1. Wash the lentils and drain them. Boil, covered with the ham stock, for about 30 minutes. If no ham stock is available use cold water and add the bacon bone, bay leaf, sliced onion, stock cube and parsley stalk.
2. When the lentils are soft remove the bone etc. Liquidize or sieve the soup.
3. Return the soup to the pan with the cream and heat up. Serve with a little chopped mint and the hot croutons.

Note: The addition of cream gives a richer texture and a blander taste.

Serves 4

Chilled Cream Cheese Soup

340g/12oz can jellied
  consommé
170g/6oz mild cream cheese

1 teaspoon curry powder
Squeeze of lemon juice

1. Reserve 1 cupful of consommé for the top.
2. Liquidize the remaining consommé with the cheese, curry powder and a squeeze of lemon juice. Pour into cocotte dishes.
3. Chill until set.
4. Spoon over the remaining consommé (which should be cool, on the point of setting) and chill again until ready to serve.

Note: Some tinned consommé will not set. Test it by chilling for an hour. If the soup is still liquid, melt a teaspoon of powdered gelatine in the consommé and allow to cool. Consommé with 'serve hot' on the label is generally non-setting.

Serves 4

STARTERS WITH EGGS

Scrambled Eggs on Anchovy Toast

1 slice of crustless buttered
  toast, spread with anchovy
  paste
2 eggs

1 tablespoon cream *or* creamy
  milk
Salt and freshly ground black
  pepper
1 teaspoon butter

1. Get the toast ready first. Put on a heated plate and keep warm.
2. In a bowl mix together the eggs, cream or milk, salt and pepper.

191

3. Melt the butter in a frying pan. Tip in the egg mixture and, using a fish slice, keep it constantly moving until thickened and creamy but still fairly wet.
4. Pile on to the prepared toast and serve immediately.

Note: This method makes scrambled eggs of a creamy texture, with large egg pieces. If you want the smoother scrambled eggs with small egg pieces, use a saucepan and a wooden spoon instead of the pan and fish slice. Go very slowly and be careful not to overcook the eggs or they will become grainy and watery.

Serves 1

Plain French Omelette
(using a 15cm/6in pan)

3 eggs	1 tablespoon cold water
Salt and fresh ground black pepper	15g/½oz butter
Pinch of grated Parmesan cheese (optional)	

1. Break the eggs into a bowl and with a fork mix in the seasoning, Parmesan and water.
2. Melt the butter in a heavy frying pan and swirl it around so that the bottom and sides are coated. When foaming pour in the egg mixture.
3. Hold the frying pan handle in your left hand and move it gently back and forth over the heat. At the same time, with a wooden spoon, move the mixture slowly, scraping up large creamy flakes of egg mixture. As you do this some of the liquid egg from the middle of the omelette will run to the sides of the pan. Tilt the pan to help this process. Leave over the heat until the bottom has set and the top is creamy. Remove from the heat.
4. With a fork or palette knife fold the nearside edge of the omelette over to the centre and then flick the whole omelette over on to a warmed plate with the folded edges on the

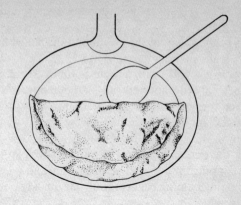

underside. Alternatively, fold the omelette in two and slide on to the plate.

Note: Grated cheese, fresh chopped herbs, fried mushrooms or other flavourings can be added to the basic omelette mixture.

Serves 1

Arnold Bennett Omelette

1 slice of onion
1–2 slices carrot
1 bay leaf
4 peppercorns
150ml/¼ pint milk
110g/¼lb smoked haddock

55g/2oz butter
15g/½oz flour
3 tablespoons cream
3 eggs, separated
1 tablespoon grated Parmesan
  cheese
Pepper

1. Put the onion, carrot, bay leaf, peppercorns and milk in a saucepan and heat slowly.
2. When the milk is well flavoured, add the haddock and poach gently for 10 minutes or until the fish is just cooked.
3. Take out the fish and flake it.
4. Melt half the butter in a small pan, add the flour and stir over heat for 1 minute.

5. Add 110ml/$\frac{1}{4}$ pint of the strained cooking milk. Stir until boiling.
6. Add 1 tablespoon of the cream and the flaked haddock. Set aside while making the omelette.
7. Beat the egg yolks with a tablespoon of cream. Season with pepper only (do not add salt as the haddock is salty).
8. Whisk the egg whites and fold into the yolks with the haddock and half the grated cheese.
9. Turn on the grill to a high heat.
10. Melt the remaining butter in an omelette pan over a good heat, tipping the pan so that the bottom and sides are coated. When the foaming begins to subside quickly pour in the egg mixture.
11. When the omelette is fairly firm, sprinkle on the remaining cheese, pour over the remaining tablespoon of cream and brown quickly under the pre-heated grill.
12. Slide on to a hot dish.

Serves 4

Tortilla

450g/1lb floury potatoes, peeled and finely sliced
1 small onion, finely sliced

Salt and freshly ground black pepper
4 eggs, beaten
Oil for frying

1. Heat about 1cm/$\frac{1}{2}$in of oil in a frying pan, add the potatoes and onions, season with salt and pepper and fry slowly until soft, but not coloured. Leave to cool and then add them to the beaten egg.
2. Tip all the oil, but for a thin film, out of the pan and pour in the egg mixture.
3. Cook the omelette over a moderate heat until it is set and then slip on to a plate. Turn it over and put it back into the frying pan with the uncooked side down.
4. Cook for a further minute and then turn out on to a serving plate – serve warm or cold, cut into wedges.

Note: Frying the potatoes from raw is the usual Spanish method. But if the potatoes are small and waxy a better result would be had by boiling them first, then slicing and frying. Unboiled potatoes can give a rather tough and bendable omelette rather than a light, soft one. Old floury potatoes need not be pre-boiled, however.

Serves 4

Piperade

For the filling:
15g/½oz butter
½ onion, finely chopped
½ green pepper, finely sliced
1 cap pimento *or* ½ fresh
   red pepper
1 tomato, skinned, seeded and
   roughly chopped
1 teaspoon chopped fresh
   parsley

For the omelette:
3 eggs
Salt and freshly ground black
   pepper
1 teaspoon cold water
15g/½oz butter

1. First prepare the filling. Melt the butter and add the onion and green pepper. When soft but not coloured add the pimento, tomato and parsley and cook for a further ½ minute. Season well and keep warm.
2. Break the eggs into a bowl and with a fork stir in the seasoning and water.
3. Melt the butter in a frying pan and swirl it around so that the bottom and sides are coated. When foaming pour in the egg mixture. Hold the frying pan handle in your left hand and move it back and forth over the heat. At the same time with a wooden spoon stir the mixture, scraping up large creamy flakes of egg. As you do this some of the liquid from the middle of the omelette will run to the sides of the pan. Tilt the pan to help this process. Leave over the heat until the bottom has set and the top is creamy.

4. Remove from the heat. Spread the warm filling over half the omelette. Fold it in half and turn it on to a warmed plate. Serve immediately.

Serves 2

Anchovy Eggs

10 anchovy fillets
A little milk
10 hardboiled eggs
30g/1oz butter

3 teaspoons mayonnaise
  (page 266)
Anchovy essence
Freshly ground black pepper

1. Soak the anchovy fillets for half an hour in milk to remove some of the salt. Drain them.
2. Split the eggs lengthwise and remove the yolks.
3. Mash or sieve the yolks.
4. Beat the butter until very soft and stir in the mayonnaise and egg yolks. Season to taste with anchovy essence and pepper.
5. Using a teaspoon or forcing bag fitted with a fluted nozzle fill the egg-white hollows with this mixture.
6. Split the anchovy fillets in half lengthwise and lay each one diagonally across an egg.

Makes 20

Mimosa Eggs

Hardboiled eggs ($1\frac{1}{2}$ per
  person)
Mayonnaise (page 266)
Anchovy essence

Pepper
Milk
Olives (preferably black)

1. Split the eggs lengthwise and scoop out the yolks.
2. Push the yolks through a sieve.
3. Put a quarter of the sieved yolks aside for decoration and

mix the rest with sufficient mayonnaise to bind into a thick paste. Add anchovy essence and pepper to taste. Fill the hollows in the egg whites with this mixture and place the filled eggs stuffed side down on a serving dish.

4. Thin the mayonnaise to a coating consistency with milk (it should just flow off the spoon reluctantly, but voluntarily – not needing a shake). Cover the eggs with a layer of mayonnaise.

5. On each alternate egg place a sliver of olive, and on the remaining eggs put a sprinkling of the 'mimosa' or sieved egg yolk.

Tarragon Eggs

4 medium-sized eggs,
  preferably at room
  temperature
Salt and pepper

8 leaves fresh tarragon
4 teaspoons single cream
15g/$\frac{1}{2}$oz butter

1. Heat up 4 cocotte dishes and brush out with butter. Stand them in a pan or roasting tin of hot water (a bain-marie).

2. Break an egg carefully into each dish and season with salt and pepper. Place two tarragon leaves on each egg and spoon over a little cream. Place a knob of butter on top.

3. Simmer gently on top of the cooker for 7–9 minutes with the bain-marie covered with a lid or foil. The whites should be set and the yolks runny.

Note: The eggs will continue cooking for a short time after removing from the heat so be very careful not to overcook. These eggs can also be baked in a moderate oven (180 C/350 F, gas mark 4), where they will take 12 minutes. They do not need to be covered if cooked this way, but it is still advisable to stand them in a bain-marie to prevent the edges drying out.

Serves 4

Portuguese Eggs

4 hardboiled eggs
45g/1½oz butter
1 tablespoon, chopped fresh
  parsley
Salt and pepper
4 ripe tomatoes
1 clove, crushed garlic

290ml/½ pint coating
  consistency Béchamel sauce
  (page 261)
45g/1½oz strong Cheddar *or*
  Gruyère, grated
1 tablespoon dried crumbs

1. Set the oven to 200 C/400 F, gas mark 6. Light the grill.
2. Cut the eggs in half lengthwise and sieve or mash the yolks.
3. Cream half the butter well and beat in the yolks, parsley and seasoning. Taste.
4. Pile this mixture back into the egg whites and press together until they resemble hardboiled eggs.
5. Plunge the tomatoes into a pan of boiling water for 5 seconds. Skin and slice them, cutting across horizontally.
6. Fry the tomato slices briefly in a frying pan with the crushed garlic and remaining butter. When barely cooked lay them in a heat-proof dish.
7. Place the eggs on top of the tomatoes and coat with the Béchamel sauce. Dust with grated cheese and crumbs.
8. Bake in the oven for 10 minutes and then place under the grill to brown.

Serves 4

Oeufs Florentine

450g/1lb leaf spinach
15g/½oz melted butter
Salt and freshly ground black
  pepper
Good pinch of nutmeg

4 eggs, chilled
290ml/½ pint mornay sauce
  (page 262)
A little extra grated cheese
Browned crumbs

1. Remove the stalks of the spinach and wash thoroughly. Put into a pan *without water*. Add a sprinkling of salt, cover and cook gently, shaking the pan, for 5–7 minutes. It will reduce in quantity by about two-thirds. Drain very thoroughly by squeezing between two plates.
2. Chop finely and turn in the melted butter. Season with salt, pepper and nutmeg. Place in the bottom of a fireproof dish.
3. Set the oven to 220 C/425 F, gas mark 7, and heat the grill.
4. Poach the eggs: three-quarters fill a large shallow pan with water, adding a tablespoon of vinegar for each pint of water. Bring to the boil, then lower the temperature to a fast simmer. Break an egg into a cup and slip it into the water. Immediately raise the temperature slightly so that the bubbles help to draw the white round the yolk. Poach for about 3 minutes, lift out with a perforated spoon.
5. Trim the whites neatly with a pair of scissors or a stainless steel knife and drain thoroughly on absorbent paper or a clean cloth.
6. Arrange the eggs on top of the spinach and coat with the cheese sauce. Sprinkle over the grated cheese and browned crumbs.
7. Brown the top under a hot grill.

Serves 4

Scotch Eggs

340g/¾lb sausage-meat	Seasoned flour
Salt and pepper	Beaten egg
4 hardboiled eggs, shelled	2 tablespoons dried
Flour	breadcrumbs
Oil for frying	

1. Season the sausage-meat with salt and pepper. Divide it into four.
2. Roll the eggs in flour. Dip your hands in a little flour and mould the sausage-meat around each egg making sure they are completely and evenly covered.

3. Place at least 3·5cm/1½in of oil in a fryer and begin to heat it up slowly.
4. Dip the eggs in seasoned flour, brush with beaten egg and coat with breadcrumbs.
5. Place the prepared eggs into the wire basket from the fryer and when the oil is hot enough to fizzle gently when a breadcrumb is added to it put in the eggs and fry for about 12 minutes.
6. Remove the basket and increase the temperature of the oil until a crumb will sizzle vigorously in it.
7. Return the eggs to the fryer and cook until the crumbs are golden brown (about 4–5 minutes). Drain well.

Note: Scotch eggs are cooked in two stages because the sausage-meat must cook completely. If fried in the cooler oil, the meat would be cooked, but the breadcrumbs soggy. If cooked in only the hotter oil, by the time the sausage-meat was cooked the breadcrumbs would be too dark.

Serves 4

Danish Egg Mayonnaise

2 eggs
1 tablespoon cream *or* creamy milk
Salt and freshly ground black pepper

1 teaspoon butter
1 tablespoon mayonnaise (page 266) thinned with a little cream
Paprika

1. Mix the eggs, cream, salt and pepper in a bowl.
2. Melt the butter in a frying pan and when foaming pour in the egg mixture.
3. Lower the heat and allow the egg mixture to set a little.
4. Stir the eggs once or twice until they are just cooked.
5. Turn into a shallow ovenproof dish.
6. When cold spoon over the mayonnaise and dust with a little paprika.
7. Serve with brown bread and butter.

Serves 2

STARTERS WITH VEGETABLES

Ratatouille with Eggs

2 small aubergines
2 courgettes
Olive oil
1 large onion, sliced
1 garlic clove, crushed
1 medium green pepper, sliced
1 small red pepper, sliced

4 tomatoes, peeled, quartered
   and seeded
Salt and freshly ground black
   pepper
Crushed coriander
4 eggs

1. Set the oven to 190 C/375 F, gas mark 5.
2. Wipe the aubergines and courgettes and cut into bite-sized chunks. Degorge (sprinkle with salt and leave to drain for about an hour). Rinse away the salt and dry well.
3. Melt the oil in a pan and add the onion and garlic. When soft but not brown add the aubergine and courgette and a little extra oil if necessary. Add the peppers and cook gently for 25 minutes.
4. Add the tomatoes, salt (if necessary), pepper and crushed coriander. Cook covered for about 10 minutes.
5. Turn into a shallow ovenproof dish.
6. Break 4 eggs over the top, season lightly and bake until the whites are set but the yolks still runny – about 7–8 minutes.

Serves 4

Stuffed Courgettes

170g/6oz frozen prawns
Lemon juice
Salt and pepper
4 medium courgettes
1 small onion
2 tomatoes
30g/1oz butter

1 teaspoon finely chopped fresh
  parsley
290ml/½ pint cheese (mornay)
  sauce (page 262)
A little grated cheese
A handful of browned crumbs

1. Defrost the prawns, preferably overnight, and season with lemon juice and salt.
2. Wash the courgettes and cut off the ends. Place them whole in a pan of boiling salted water and boil until barely tender. Cool in a colander under running cold water.
3. Split the courgettes lengthwise and, using a melon baller or spoon remove a 'channel' of flesh down the middle of each half courgette. Reserve the scooped-out flesh.
4. Drain the shells very well – otherwise the whole dish will become watery.
5. Heat the oven to 200 C/400 F, gas mark 6.
6. Chop the onion very finely.
7. Dip the tomatoes in boiling water for 5 seconds. Peel them, chop the flesh and discard the seeds.
8. Roughly chop the reserved courgette flesh.
9. Melt the butter in a frying pan and add the onion. Fry gently for 2 minutes. Add the tomatoes and courgette flesh and continue to cook without colouring until the ingredients are soft, allow to cool slightly.
10. Stir in the parsley and prawns and season well.
11. Place a spoonful of this mixture in each courgette shell and lay in a buttered ovenproof dish. Coat each courgette with a spoonful of cheese sauce and sprinkle over a little grated cheese and browned crumbs.
12. Heat up the grill.
13. Put the dish in the pre-heated oven for 15 minutes and then under the grill until delicately browned.

Serves 4

Stuffed Cream Cheese Tomatoes

4 tomatoes
110g/¼lb good cream cheese *or* sieved cheese
1 tablespoon chopped fresh mint
Squeeze of lemon
¼ garlic clove, crushed
Salt and freshly ground black pepper
1 tablespoon chopped fresh parsley
French dressing (page 268)
Sprigs of watercress

1. Dip the tomatoes in boiling water for 5 seconds. Peel them.
2. Slice a quarter of each tomato off at the rounded end. Scoop out the flesh and seeds. Discard the seeds and coarsely chop the flesh.
3. Mix a little of the flesh with the cream cheese, mint, lemon, garlic and the salt and pepper.
4. Fill the hollow tomatoes with this mixture and stick the tops back at a jaunty angle. Arrange on a plate.
5. Add the parsley to the dressing and shake or mix well. Spoon this over the tomatoes, and garnish with the well-washed watercress.
6. Serve with brown bread and butter.

Serves 2

Stuffed Mushrooms

8 large flat mushrooms
1 shallot
1 garlic clove
55g/2oz butter
2 rashers of streaky rindless bacon, finely diced
85g/3oz chicken livers
1 tomato, skinned and finely chopped
½ teaspoon chopped fresh parsley
Dried white breadcrumbs
Salt and pepper
Oil for shallow frying
8 slices French bread
Chopped fresh parsley to garnish

1. Wipe the mushrooms and remove the stalks.
2. Chop the shallot and the mushroom stalks finely and crush the garlic.
3. Trim away and discard any discoloured parts of the livers and dice them finely.
4. Heat up the grill.
5. In a saucepan, melt half the butter and when foaming add the bacon and shallot. Fry gently until the shallot is soft.
6. Add the livers, increase the temperature, and fry rapidly until the livers start to brown.
7. Add the mushroom stalks and garlic. Cook for 1–2 minutes.
8. Add the tomato and parsley. Season.
9. Place the mushroom tops, smooth side down, on the grill pan, brush with the rest of the butter, and grill for 1 minute, turn over and grill for a further minute.
10. Fill the mushrooms with the stuffing and sprinkle over the breadcrumbs.
11. Heat the oil in a frying pan and fry the bread slices until a golden brown on each side. Drain well.
12. As the bread fries place the mushrooms back under the grill for a minue to reheat them.
13. Place the mushrooms on the rounds of fried bread and sprinkle with chopped parsley.

Serves 4

Avocado Mousse

15g/½oz gelatine
2 rashers rindless back bacon
About 10 walnut halves
2 ripe avocado pears
150ml/¼ pint mayonnaise (page 266)
Lemon juice

1 teaspoon Worcestershire sauce
Salt and pepper
1 teaspoon onion juice
150ml/¼ pint double cream, whipped

1. In a small saucepan soak the gelatine in 3 tablespoons of cold water.

2. Grill the bacon until crisp but not brittle. Drain well and when cold chop finely. Chop the walnuts.
3. Peel the avocados and mash until smooth. Add the mayonnaise, lemon juice, Worcestershire sauce, salt and pepper, onion juice, walnuts and bacon.
4. Melt the gelatine over gentle heat and when dissolved stir into the avocado mixture. With a metal spoon fold in the cream.
5. Pour into an oiled mould and refrigerate until set.
6. Just before serving turn out on to a serving dish.

Note I: If the mousse is to be eaten from the dish in which it is set oiling is not necessary.

Note II: Avocado mixtures are inclined to discolour. This can be prevented by covering the mousse with a thin coating of seasoned cream cheese, soured cream or mayonnaise.

Serves 4

PÂTÉS

Sardine and Lemon Pâté

110g/¼lb butter
225g/½lb canned sardines
110g/¼lb cream cheese
½ teaspoon French mustard
Juice of ½ lemon

Salt and freshly ground black pepper
1 egg white (optional)
6 black olives, stoned

1. Beat the butter until soft and creamy.
2. Add the sardines with their oil and beat.
3. Add the cream cheese, mustard, lemon, salt and plenty of pepper and mix well. (Alternatively all the above ingredients can be beaten together in an electric machine.)
4. Whisk the egg white stiffly and fold into the mixture.

5. Pile onto a dish and garnish with black olives. Serve with hot toast.

Note: This pâté looks very festive and pretty served in scooped-out lemon halves with a sprig of mint decorating each stuffed lemon.

Serves 8

Kipper Pâté

340g/¾lb kipper fillets
85g/3 oz softened butter
85g/3oz cream cheese
Freshly ground black pepper

Lemon juice
4 black olives *or* 4 slices
  lemon

1. Skin and mince the kipper fillets.
2. Beat the butter until very creamy (but do not melt it) and stir in the kippers and cream cheese.
3. Beat until completely incorporated.
4. Season well with black pepper and lemon juice.
5. Pile into a dish and garnish with slivers of black olive or slices of lemon.

Note: For a party this pâté can look very good spooned into scooped-out lemon halves and garnished with bay leaves.

Serves 6

Chicken Liver Pâté

285g/10oz butter
1 large onion, very finely
  chopped
1 large garlic clove, crushed
450g/1lb chicken livers *or*
  225g/½lb duck livers and
  225g/½lb chicken livers

Salt and freshly ground black
  pepper
85g/3oz clarified butter (if the
  pâté is to be stored)

1. Melt half the butter in a large thick frying pan and gently fry the onion in it until soft and transparent.
2. Add the crushed garlic and continue cooking for a further minute.
3. Discard all the discoloured bits from the livers as they are very bitter.
4. Add the livers to the pan and cook, turning them to brown on all sides, for 8 minutes or so, when they should be firm and cooked.
5. Add salt and plenty of pepper.
6. Mince the mixture or liquidize it in an electric blender with the rest of the butter. Put it into an earthenware dish or pot.
7. If the pâté is to be kept for more than three days cover the top with a layer of clarified butter.

Serves 6

Potted Turkey

225g/½lb smoked turkey   Pepper
110g/¼lb butter, clarified, but
  cold

1. Mince the turkey and pound it with three-quarters of the butter. Season with pepper.
2. Press the mixture tightly into small pots, making sure that there are no air spaces.
3. Melt the remaining butter, allow to cool until on the point of setting and pour over the pots. Leave to set. Store in a cool place. It will keep for two weeks, or more in a cold refrigerator.

Note: To clarify butter, heat until foaming, then strain through a piece of muslin or a J-cloth.

Serves 4

FRUIT STARTERS

Grape and Grapefruit Cocktail

2 grapefruit
110g/¼lb white grapes
1 teaspoon sugar
1 tablespoon oil

3 teaspoons chopped fresh mint
Salt and freshly ground black
  pepper
30g/1oz flaked almonds

1. Halve the grapefruit and, using a grapefruit knife, remove all the segments, leaving the membranes attached to the shell. Put the segments, with the juice, in a bowl.
2. Dip the grapes for 4 seconds in boiling water and peel them. Cut them in half lengthwise and discard the pips. Add the grapes to the grapefruit with the sugar, oil, mint, salt and pepper. Leave for at least 30 minutes.
3. Pull the membrane from the grapefruit shells and fill the shells with mixture.
4. Scatter almonds on top. Serve with brown bread and butter.

Note: If the grapes are soft-skinned and nice-looking do not bother to peel them.

Serves 4

Melon and Prawn Cocktail

1 small honeydew melon
450g/1lb cooked peeled prawns
150ml/$\frac{1}{4}$ pint thick mayonnaise
2 tablespoons cream
3 teaspoons tomato ketchup
1 teaspoon lemon juice
1 drop Tabasco *or* a pinch of
cayenne

2 tarragon leaves, finely
chopped
1 large whole cooked prawn
per person
1 small green pepper, finely
chopped

1. Cut the melon flesh into balls and divide between six goblets.
2. Mix together the mayonnaise, cream, ketchup, Tabasco, lemon juice and chopped tarragon. Add the peeled prawns.
3. Taste, and add salt and pepper if necessary.
4. Divide this mixture between the glasses.
5. Sprinkle the chopped green pepper on the top.
6. Remove the legs and roe (if any) from the whole prawns, and tuck one into the side of each glass.

Note: This starter looks particularly good served in scooped-out small melon shells.

Serves 6

PASTRY AND YEAST STARTERS

Bacon Pasties

285g/10oz plain flour
Pinch of salt
70g/2½oz butter
70g/2½oz lard
225g/½lb uncooked gammon
  steak *or* lean bacon (soaked
  overnight)

1 very small onion
1 very small potato
Pinch of thyme
Freshly ground black pepper
Milk

1. Sift the flour and salt into a bowl. Rub in the fats and when
    the mixture resembles breadcrumbs mix in enough water to
    make a firm dough.
2. Set the oven to 200 C/400 F, gas mark 6.
3. Roll out the pastry on a floured board. Using a pastry cutter
    cut out six 15cm/6in circles. Place in the refrigerator to relax
    while you prepare the filling.
4. Cut off the rind of the gammon and dice the flesh. Chop
    the onion and dice the potato. Mix together and season with
    the thyme and pepper. Divide the mixture between the pastry
    rounds.
5. Brush the edges with cold water and bring them together over
    the filling so that the pasties look like closed purses. Using
    floured fingers and thumb crimp the edges to make a
    decorative pattern. Brush all over with a little milk.
6. Place on a baking sheet and bake for 45–50 minutes.

Serves 6

Quiche Lorraine

110g/¼lb flour–quantity rich shortcrust pastry (page 369)

For the filling:

½ small onion
55g/2oz bacon
7·5g/¼oz butter
5 tablespoons milk
5 tablespoons single cream

1 egg
1 egg yolk
30g/1oz grated cheese (strong
    Cheddar *or* Gruyère)
Salt and pepper

1. Roll out the pastry and line a flan ring about 15cm/6in in diameter. Leave in the fridge for about 45 minutes to relax – this prevents shrinkage during cooking.
2. Set the oven to 190 C/375 F, gas mark 5.
3. Chop the onion finely and dice the bacon. Fry both gently in the butter. When cooked but not coloured, drain well.
4. Mix together the milk, cream and eggs. Add the onion, bacon and half the cheese. Season carefully with salt and pepper (the bacon and cheese are both salty, so be careful not to overseason).
5. Pour the mixture into the prepared flan ring and sprinkle over the remaining cheese. Place the flan in the middle of the heated oven and bake for about 20 minutes. Then turn down the oven to 150 C/300 F, gas mark 2 and cook for a further 15 minutes.
6. Remove the flan ring to allow the sides of the pastry to cook and take colour. Bake for a further 5 minutes until the filling is browned and set.
7. Serve hot or cold.

Note: If using a flan dish instead of a flan ring, the pastry case should be baked blind, i.e. before filling: line the raw pastry case with a piece of foil or a double sheet of greaseproof paper and fill it with dried lentils, beans, rice or even pebbles or pennies. This is to prevent the pastry bubbling up during cooking. When the pastry is half cooked (about 15 minutes) the 'blind beans' can be removed and the empty pastry case further dried out in the oven.

The beans can be re-used indefinitely.

Serves 4

Spinach Flan

110g/¼lb flour–quantity rich shortcrust pastry (page 369)

For the filling:

340g/¾lb spinach	1 egg
½ onion, finely chopped	1 egg yolk
15g/½oz butter	Salt and pepper
5 tablespoons milk	30g/1oz grated cheese (strong
5 tablespoons single cream	Cheddar *or* Gruyère)

1. Roll out the pastry and line a flan ring about 15cm/6in in diameter. Leave in the refrigerator for about 45 minutes to relax – this prevents shrinkage during cooking.
2. Set the oven to 200 C/400 F, gas mark 6.
3. Bake the pastry case blind for 10–15 minutes and remove from oven.
4. Reduce the heat to 170 C/325 F, gas mark 3.
5. Remove the stalks of the spinach, wash thoroughly and put into a pan *without water*. Add a sprinkling of salt. Cover and cook gently, shaking the pan, for 5–7 minutes. The spinach will reduce by about two-thirds. Drain very thoroughly by squeezing between two plates. Turn on to a board.
6. Chop the onion finely. Fry it gently in the butter. When cooked but not coloured drain well.
7. Mix together the milk, cream and eggs. Add the fried onion, spinach and half the cheese. Season carefully with salt and pepper (the cheese is salty, so be careful not to overseason).
8. Pour the mixture into the prepared flan case and sprinkle over the remaining cheese.
9. Place the flan in the middle of the prepared oven and bake for about 30–40 minutes.

10. Remove the flan ring to allow the sides of the pastry to cook evenly and colour. Bake for a further 5 minutes until the filling is brown and set.
11. Serve hot or cold.

Note: For baking blind, see page 211, *note.*

Serves 4

Creamy Asparagus Flan

170g/6oz flour-quantity shortcrust pastry (page 369)

For the filling:

110g/¼lb asparagus	Salt, pepper and nutmeg
290ml/½ pint milk	1 egg yolk
30g/1oz butter	15g/½oz grated cheese (Gruyère
30g/1oz flour	*or* strong Cheddar)

1. Set the oven to 200°C/400°F, gas mark 6.
2. Line a 20cm/8in flan ring with pastry and bake blind.
3. Reduce the oven to 180°C/350°F, gas mark 4.
4. Trim the asparagus so that they are all the same length, cutting off the very toughest part of the stalk. Using a sharp knife or peeler peel away the tough skin from the ends.
5. Tie the asparagus in a bundle. Cook upright in a deep pan of boiling salted water, leaving the tips exposed (the tips will cook in the steam). Simmer for 12–15 minutes or until the stalks are tender. Remove from the pan and drain well.
6. Chop the asparagus and liquidize in a blender with the milk, or push through a sieve.
7. Melt the butter, add the flour and cook for half a minute.
8. Draw the pan off the heat and add the asparagus and milk mixture. Stir well and return to the heat. Bring slowly to the boil, stirring all the time until the sauce is thick and shiny. Season with salt, pepper and nutmeg and simmer for 2 minutes.
9. Remove from the heat, cover with a piece of wet greaseproof

paper (this prevents a skin forming) and set aside to cool slightly.

10. Beat in the egg yolk and pour the mixture into the flan case. Sprinkle on the grated cheese.

11. Bake for about 35 minutes. The mixture should be firm and golden brown.

Note I: This flan is a *flamiche* which, as opposed to a quiche, does not depend entirely on eggs to thicken the filling. It has a white sauce base rather than a custard one. For a more soufflé-like filling the egg white can be used as well as the yolk: whisk until stiff and fold into the mixture before pouring into the flan case.

Note II: For baking blind, see page 211, *note.*

Serves 4

Blinis

225g/½lb buckwheat flour
45g/1½oz fresh yeast
2 teaspoons sugar
720ml/1¼ pints warm milk
225g/½lb plain flour

Salt
3 eggs
1 tablespoon melted butter
Lard for frying

1. Put the buckwheat flour into a warm dry mixing bowl.
2. Cream the yeast with the sugar and add half the milk. Mix well.
3. Pour the yeasty milk into the buckwheat flour and mix to a paste.
4. Cover the bowl with a sheet of greased polythene or a cloth and leave in a warm place to rise.
5. Sift the plain flour with a good pinch of salt into another basin. Make a hollow (or 'well') in the centre and drop in the 2 whole eggs and 1 egg yolk, reserving 1 egg white.
6. Gradually mix to a batter, bringing in the surrounding flour, and adding the melted butter and the rest of the milk. Beat well.

7. Beat this batter into the yeasty one, cover again with the greased polythene or cloth and leave in a warm place for 2 hours.
8. Just before cooking whip the remaining egg white and fold it in to the mixture.
9. Grease a girdle iron or heavy frying pan lightly with lard. Heat it gently over steady heat.
10. When the girdle is hot pour enough of the batter on to the surface to make a blini the size of a saucer. When bubbles rise, turn over and cook the other side to a light brown.
11. Keep the blinis warm in a cool oven.

To serve
Caviar: Butter the hot blini, place a spoonful of caviar (or Danish lumpfish roe) on top and surround with sour cream. Serve at once.
Smoked salmon: Butter the hot blini, spread liberally with sour cream and place a roll of smoked salmon on top. Serve at once.
Pickled herring: Mix herring fillets with sour cream. Butter the blini and top with the herring and sour cream mixture. Serve at once.

Note: If using dried yeast use half the amount called for, mix it with 3 tablespoons of the liquid (warmed to blood temperature) and a teaspoon of sugar. Leave until frothy, about 15 minutes, then proceed. If the yeast does not go frothy it is dead and unusable.

Serves 4

FISH STARTERS

Marinated Kipper Fillets

8 kipper fillets
1 medium onion, sliced
2 bay leaves
Freshly ground black pepper

1 teaspoon mustard powder
150ml/$\frac{1}{4}$ pint olive oil
1 teaspoon brown sugar
2 tablespoons lemon juice

To serve:
Lettuce
Lemon wedges

Onion rings
Brown bread and butter

1. Skin the kipper fillets.
2. In a small dish layer the fillets with the onion and bay leaves, grinding black pepper between the layers.
3. Place the mustard, olive oil, sugar and lemon juice in a jar with a lid and shake vigorously.
4. Pour over the fillets.
5. Cover the dish well with a lid or plastic film and leave refrigerated for at least two days, preferably a week.
6. Drain off most of the oil and discard the onion and bay leaves.
7. Serve on lettuce with lemon wedges and fresh onion rings. Hand brown bread and butter separately.

Serves 4

Soused Herring Salad

8 herring fillets

For the court bouillon:

425ml/¾ pint water
150ml/¼ pint vinegar
4 bay leaves
6 peppercorns
2 cloves

4 allspice berries
Blade of mace *or* pinch of
  nutmeg
1 teaspoon salt

For the salad:

1 tablespoon grated onion
1 tablespoon chopped pickled
  cucumber

1 tablespoon chopped fresh
  parsley
2 tablespoons French
  dressing (page 268)

1. Heat the oven to 170 C/325 F, gas mark 3.
2. Place the herring fillets skin side up in a fireproof dish. Cover with the water and vinegar. Add the bay leaves, peppercorns, spices and salt.
3. Cover the dish and bake for 30 minutes. Allow to get completely cold in their liquid.
4. Lift out, drain well and arrange on a dish.
5. Mix the onion, cucumber and parsley with the French dressing and spoon over the fish.

Serves 4

Savoury Stuffed Pancakes

12 pancakes (page 384)
450g/1lb smoked haddock
290ml/½ pint milk
1 bay leaf
1 slice of onion
3–4 peppercorns
1 parsley stalk
Salt and pepper
20g/¾oz butter

20g/¾oz flour
55g/2oz grated Cheddar cheese
Pinch of mustard
Pinch of cayenne
1 teaspoon chopped fresh *or*
  ½ teaspoon dried tarragon
30g/1oz melted butter
1 tablespoon grated Parmesan

1. Heat the oven to 190 C/375 F, gas mark 5.
2. Place the smoked haddock in a fireproof dish with the milk, bay leaf, onion, peppercorns, parsley stalk, salt and pepper.
3. Cover the dish and cook for 15 minutes or until the fish will flake easily with a fork.
4. Strain off the liquor and flake the fish, taking care to remove any bones or skin.
5. Melt the butter, add the flour and cook for 1 minute. Draw the pan aside, pour on the liquor and bring to the boil, stirring continuously.
6. Remove the sauce from the heat, stir in the grated cheese and season with salt, pepper, mustard, cayenne and tarragon.
7. Stir in the fish.
8. Heat the grill.
9. Place a good spoonful of the fish mixture on each pancake and roll up.
10. Lay the pancakes side by side in a buttered fireproof dish. Brush with melted butter. Sprinkle with Parmesan cheese.
11. Place under the hot grill until well browned.

Serves 4

Tuna Fish Mousse

2 teaspoons gelatine
285g/10oz tinned tuna fish
150ml/¼ pint mayonnaise
  (page 266)
Salt and freshly ground black
  pepper
1 garlic clove, crushed

Lemon juice
1 tablespoon fresh chopped
  parsley
150ml/¼ pint double cream,
  whipped
Oil for greasing

For the garnish:
Slices of cucumber   Stoned black olives

1. In a small saucepan, soak the gelatine in 2 tablespoons water.
2. Oil a mould for the mousse and leave it to drain upside down.
3. Pour off the oil from the tuna fish and flake the fish with a fork. Mix to a pulp. Stir in the mayonnaise, seasoning, garlic, lemon juice and parsley.
4. Melt the gelatine over a gentle heat and when clear and runny stir into the mixture.
5. Fold in the cream. Pour into the mould. Refrigerate until set.
6. To turn out, invert a serving dish over the mould and then turn both the dish and the mould over together. Give both a sharp shake, and remove the mould.
7. Decorate with slices of cucumber and stoned black olives.

Note: If the mousse is to stand for more than an hour after decorating, the cucumber slices should be *degorgé*, i.e. salted, allowed to stand for 30 minutes, rinsed well and patted dry. If this is not done the salt in the mousse draws out the moisture in the cucumber and the result looks wet and messy.

Serves 4

3
Vegetables, Rice and Salads

BOILED

Boiled Rice

55g/2oz long-grain white rice
  for each person

Slice of lemon
1 tablespoon oil

1. Take a large saucepan and fill it with salted water (1 cup of rice will need at least 6 cups of water, but the exact quantities do not matter as long as there is plenty of water). Bring to a rolling boil.
2. Tip in the rice and stir until the water re-boils. Add the lemon slice and oil.
3. Boil for exactly 10 minutes and then test: the rice should be neither hard nor mushy, but firm to the bite (*al dente*). It may need 1 more minute.
4. Drain the rice in a colander or sieve, and swish plenty of hot water through it.
5. Stand the colander on the draining board. With the handle of a wooden spoon, make a few draining holes through the pile of rice to help the water and steam escape. Alternatively, every few minutes turn the mass of rice over with a spoon.

Note I: Rice may be rinsed, if for a salad, in cold water after cooking, but it will need longer to drain dry – if the water is hot it steams dry faster.

Note II: Natural brown rice takes about 40 minutes to cook.

Cabbage with Caraway

450g/1lb white cabbage, finely sliced
30g/1oz butter
2 onions, sliced
1 level teaspoon caraway seeds
1 teaspoon vinegar *or* lemon juice
Salt and freshly ground black pepper

1. Put the cabbage into a pan of boiling water. Simmer until tender (about 5 minutes) and drain well.
2. While the cabbage cooks, melt the butter in a frying pan and add the sliced onion. Cook over a gentle heat until soft but not coloured.
3. Add the caraway seeds and lemon or vinegar and cook gently for 1 more minute.
4. Stir this into the drained cabbage and season well with salt and pepper.

Serves 4

French Beans with Almonds

450g/1lb whole French beans
Salt and freshly ground black pepper
20g/¾oz butter
30g/1oz flaked almonds
Squeeze of lemon juice

1. Wash and top and tail the beans.
2. Place in a pan of boiling salted water and cook until just tender.
3. Meanwhile melt half the butter and when foaming add the almonds. Fry until golden brown, then add the lemon juice.
4. Drain the beans well and mix with the buttery almonds. Sprinkle with pepper.

Serves 4

Brussels Sprouts and Chestnuts

450g/1lb very small Brussels
  sprouts
225g/½lb fresh chestnuts

45g/1½oz butter
Salt, freshly ground black
  pepper and nutmeg

1. Wash and trim the sprouts, paring the stalk and removing the outside leaves if necessary.
2. Make a slit in the skin of each chestnut and put them into a pan of cold water. Bring to the boil and then take off the heat. Remove one or two nuts at a time and peel. The water must not boil again but can be reheated – the skins come off easily if the chestnuts are hot, but not too cooked.
3. Melt the butter in a frying pan, and slowly fry the chestnuts (which will break up a little) until brown.
4. Bring a large pan of salted water to the boil, and tip in the sprouts. Boil fairly fast until they are just cooked, but not soggy: the flavour changes disastrously if boiled too long. Drain them well.
5. Mix the sprouts and chestnuts together gently, adding the butter from the frying pan. Season with salt, pepper and nutmeg.

Serves 4

Leeks with Tomato

4 large tomatoes
340g/¾lb young leeks
15g/½oz butter

Salt and freshly ground black
  pepper

1. Plunge the tomatoes in boiling water for 5 seconds. Peel them and slice thickly.
2. Wash the leeks and cut each one into rings about 2cm/¾in wide. Plunge then into a pan of boiling salted water for 5 minutes, or until they are just tender but still green.

3. Melt the butter in a frying pan and when foaming add the tomatoes. Cook for about 30 seconds. Mix the tomatoes with the leeks. Season with salt and pepper.

Note: A little crushed garlic fried with the tomato is a good addition.

Serves 4

Vichy Carrots

560g/1¼lb carrots
150ml/¼ pint water
2 teaspoons butter
½ teaspoon salt

1 teaspoon sugar
Freshly ground black pepper
2 teaspoons chopped mint and
    parsley, mixed

1. Peel the carrots and cut them into slices or even-sized barrel shapes; or if they are very young leave them whole.
2. Put everything except the pepper and herbs into a saucepan, and boil rapidly until the water has almost evaporated. Then turn down the heat and allow the carrots to brown slightly in the remaining butter and sugar.
4. Season with pepper and mix in the herbs.

Note I: It is important not to oversalt the water. When the water has evaporated the entire quantity of salt will remain with the carrots.

Note II: Vichy carrots, made classically, need careful watching lest they boil dry and burn. Ordinary boiled carrots may be tossed over the heat in butter and sugar until browned.

Serves 4

ROAST

Roast Potatoes

900g/2lb potatoes
4 tablespoons dripping

1. Peel the potatoes and, if they are large, cut them into 5cm/2in pieces.
2. Bring them to the boil in salted water. Boil for 5 minutes.
3. Drain them and, while still hot, scratch all over with a fork to roughen and slightly crumble the surface of each potato. (This produces deliciously crunchy potatoes that can be kept warm for up to two hours without coming to any harm. Potatoes roasted without this preliminary boiling and scratching tend to become tough and hard if not eaten straight away.)
4. Melt the fat in a roasting pan and add the potatoes, turning them so that they are coated all over.
5. Roast, basting occasionally, and turning the potatoes over at half-time. See note below.

Note: Potatoes can be roasted at almost any temperature, usually taking 1 hour in a hot oven, or $1\frac{1}{2}$ hours in a medium one. They should be basted and turned over once or twice during cooking, and they are done when a skewer glides easily into them. Potatoes roasted in the same pan as the meat have the best flavour, but this is not always possible if the joint or bird is very large, or if liquid has been added to the pan.

Serves 4

Fantail Potatoes

4 large potatoes   30g/1oz grated cheese
30g/1oz butter

1.   Heat the oven to 190 C/375 F, gas mark 5.
2.   Peel the potatoes.
3.   Shave off a piece from the underside of each potato to prevent them rolling over.
4.   Cut them as if you were slicing them, but without cutting right through. Spread with the butter.
5.   Roast for 1–1½ hours, basting occasionally.
6.   After 45 minutes or when the potatoes are almost cooked, sprinkle them with cheese, taking care not to let cheese fall into the dish – it must stay on the potatoes or it will stick to the bottom of the pan and burn. Take them out when they are soft inside.

Serves 4

Glazed Vegetables

450g/1lb large potatoes
450g/1lb carrots
450g/1lb turnips
12 button onions
1 tablespoon bacon *or* pork dripping
½ teaspoon sugar
Salt and freshly ground black pepper
110g/¼lb button mushrooms
55g/2oz butter
Juice of ½ lemon
1 tablespoon chopped fresh parsley

1.   Wash and peel the potatoes, carrots and turnips. Using a melon scoop, scoop the flesh of the potato into balls. Dry them in a clean cloth. Trim the carrots and turnips into small barrel shapes.
2.   Peel the onions. (Dipping them into boiling water for 10 seconds makes this easier.)

3. Heat the oven to 200 C/400 F, gas mark 6.
4. Put the prepared vegetables in a roasting pan and baste with the dripping. Roast, shaking the pan occasionally and turning the vegetables over, for 25 minutes.
5. When the vegetables are tender, put the roasting pan over direct heat, add the sugar and shake the pan until browned to a good even colour. Season with salt and pepper. Keep warm.
6. Trim the mushroom stalks. Melt the butter over a good heat and toss the mushrooms into it. Shake the pan to make sure that every mushroom is coated with butter. When they are beginning to turn brown add the lemon juice and allow this to sizzle and evaporate a little. Add salt and pepper and the chopped parsley.
7. Serve the vegetables mixed together on a heated dish.

Note I: If these vegetables are to accompany a roast meat dish, the root vegetables can be cooked in the meat roasting tin. Add them about half an hour before the meat is due to come out.

Note II: The root vegetables can be 'pot roasted' instead of cooked in the oven. (This is a good idea if nothing else is being baked or roasted at the time, when it would be wasteful to heat the oven just for this dish.) In a heavy casserole or pan toss the vegetables in the fat. Cover with a lid, and turn the heat down low. Cook like this for 20 minutes or until the vegetables are tender, giving the pan a shake every now and then to prevent sticking. When they are cooked, brown them with the sugar, and fry the mushrooms etc. as described above.

Serves 6–8

Roast Parsnips with Honey

675g/1½lb parsnips
30g/1oz butter
2 teaspoons runny honey

Salt and freshly ground black
pepper

226

1. Heat the oven to 200 C/400 F, gas mark 6.
2. Wash and peel the parsnips. Cut in half lengthwise.
3. Boil in salted water for 5 minutes. Drain well.
4. Melt the butter in a roasting pan and add the honey. Roll the parsnips in the mixture until well-coated and add salt and pepper.
5. Roast, basting and turning frequently, until brown (about 15 minutes).

Note I: Parsnips can be roasted without boiling first: allow 1½ hours if about 2·5cm/1in thick, only adding the honey for the last 15–20 minutes of cooking time.

Note II: The honey may be omitted if preferred.

Serves 4

Chateau Potatoes

675g/1½lb small even-sized potatoes
Oil *or* beef dripping

Salt and freshly ground black pepper

1. Wash and peel the potatoes. Trim each one into a barrel shape about 3·5cm/1½in long and 2cm/¾in wide.
2. Set the oven to 190 C/375 F, gas mark 5.
3. Heat a few spoons of oil or dripping in a sauté pan. Add the potatoes and brown gently on all sides (shaking the pan constantly) until they are just brown. Season with salt and pepper.
4. Cover the pan and place in the oven for about 45 minutes or until the potatoes are tender. (Alternatively, they can be cooked on the hob, but care must be taken so they do not burn: shake the pan frequently. Do not remove the lid as this allows the steam to escape, and the potatoes will fry rather than cook gently.)

Serves 4

MASHED

Mashed Potatoes

Potatoes | Milk
Salt and ground white pepper | Butter

1. Peel the potatoes and cook until soft in boiling salted water.
2. Drain them and return to the empty saucepan.
3. Mash them over a medium heat, allowing them to dry out while you do so, but taking care that the potato does not stick to the bottom of the pan and burn. (If mashing a large quantity of potato it is simpler to mince them or put them through a mouli and then return them to the pan to dry out.)
4. Push the mound of mashed potato to one side of the saucepan and pour a little milk into the exposed side of the pan. Put this side over direct heat and get the milk boiling. Now beat it into the potato.
5. Add a good lump of butter and beat that in too. Add pepper and salt.
6. Add more milk in the same way as before, and more butter, salt and pepper if necessary. You should have a well-seasoned, absolutely smooth, fluffy but not sloppy mixture.

Bashed Neeps

675g/1½lb swedes
30–55g/1–2oz butter
Pinch of sugar

Salt and freshly ground black pepper
Water

1. Peel and thinly slice the swedes.
2. Put the slices, with a good ounce of butter, in a thick-bottomed saucepan that has a good lid. Add a sprinkle of sugar, salt and pepper.
3. Pour in about 1cm/½in of water and put on the lid. Simmer *very gently* until the vegetable is soft right through (about 40 minutes), adding more water only if the pan is in danger of boiling dry.
4. Remove the lid and rapidly boil off the rest of the water, but do not let the swedes catch on the bottom.
5. Mash them patiently over a gentle heat until they look really smooth, dry and fluffy. Taste, adding extra butter, salt and pepper if necessary

Note: The Scots call a swede a neep (or turnip). Very confusing.

Serves 4

Pommes Duchesse

675g/1½lb potatoes   Salt and pepper
About 3 tablespoons milk   1 egg yolk, beaten
30g/1oz butter

1. Heat the oven to 200 C/400 F, gas mark 6. Grease two baking sheets.
2. Peel, boil and drain the potatoes.
3. Mash the potato flesh in a large saucepan until free of lumps (alternatively pass through a sieve or mincer) and return to the pan.
4. Push the potato mixture to one side of the pan and pour the milk into the other side. Put this over direct heat and get the milk boiling. Then beat it into the potato. The mixture should be fluffy but on no account sloppy in texture; if it is too dry, heat up a little more milk and beat it in in the same way. Add half the butter and season with salt and pepper. Allow to cool slightly.
5. Beat in the yolk.

6. Place the purée in a forcing bag fitted with a fluted nozzle.
7. Pipe rosettes of the mixture on to the greased baking sheets.
8. Melt the remaining butter and use to lightly brush the duchesse potatoes.
9. Bake in the oven until a golden brown (about 15 minutes).

Serves 4

BAKED

Baked Potato with Chives and Soured Cream

1 large potato, well scrubbed
Salt and pepper
2 tablespoons soured cream

2 walnuts, chopped
1 teaspoon chopped chives

1. Prick the potatoes with a fork to eliminate any risk of their bursting in the oven.
2. Bake in a fairly hot oven (200 C/400 F, gas mark 6) for 1 hour or until a skewer glides easily through the largest potato.
3. Mix the remaining ingredients together and season with salt and pepper.
4. Split the potatoes without cutting them quite in half and fill with the soured cream mixture.
5. Serve immediately and hand the extra soured cream separately.

Note: There is some controversy about preparing potatoes for baking: oiling and wrapping them in foil gives a soft shiny skin, wetting them, with water, and sprinkling them with salt gives a dull very crisp skin.

Serves 1

Baked Tomatoes

4 tomatoes
Butter

Salt and freshly ground black
pepper

1. Heat the oven to 190 C/375 F, gas mark 5.
2. Remove the stalk from the tomatoes. With a sharp knife cut a shallow cross in the rounded end of each tomato.
3. Brush with a little melted butter and season with salt and pepper.
4. Put the tomatoes in a roasting dish and bake for about 10 minutes, until soft but not out of shape.

Serves 4

Boulangère Potatoes

675g/1½lb potatoes, thinly
   sliced
55g/2oz butter
1 onion, thinly sliced

Salt and freshly ground black
   pepper
290ml/½ pint chicken stock

1. Heat the oven at 190 C/375 F, gas mark 5.
2. Butter a pie dish and arrange the potatoes in layers with the onion, adding a little salt and pepper as you go.
3. Arrange the top layer of potatoes in overlapping slices.
4. Dot with the rest of the butter and pour in the stock.
5. Bake in the oven for about 1 hour or until the potatoes are tender and the top browned.

Serves 4

Provençale Tomatoes

4 medium tomatoes
55g/2oz butter
1 onion, finely chopped
½ garlic clove, crushed
4 tablespoons stale white
  breadcrumbs

Salt and freshly ground black
  pepper
Pinch of nutmeg
2 teaspoons chopped fresh
  parsley
1 teaspoon chopped tarragon
Chopped parsley to garnish

1. Heat the oven to 200 C/400 F, gas mark 6.
2. Cut the tomatoes in half horizontally.
3. Melt half the butter and gently cook the onion in it until soft. Add the garlic and cook for 1 more minute.
4. Mix the breadcrumbs, seasoning, nutmeg, herbs, and onion mixture together with a fork.
5. Pile the breadcrumb mixture on to the tomatoes and place a knob of the remaining butter on each.
6. Put the tomatoes in an ovenproof dish and bake in the oven for about 20 minutes or until the breadcrumbs are golden.
7. Sprinkle with chopped parsley.

Serves 4

Potatoes Baked with Cheese

450g/1lb potatoes
Butter
Salt and freshly ground black
  pepper
85g/3oz grated Gruyère *or*
  strong Cheddar cheese

1 tablespoon grated Parmesan
  cheese
150ml/¼ pint double cream
1 egg, beaten

1. Peel and cut the potatoes into slices about the thickness of a two-pence piece. Soak in a bowl of cold water for 15 minutes (this removes some of the starch and prevents the slices sticking together).

2. Heat the oven to 180 C/350 F, gas mark 4. Butter an oven-proof pie dish.
3. Drain and dry the potatoes and place a layer in the bottom of the pie dish. Sprinkle with salt, pepper and cheese. Continue to layer potatoes, seasoning and cheese, reserving a little cheese for the end, until the dish is nearly full.
4. Mix the cream with the beaten egg, season with salt and pepper and pour over the potatoes.
5. Sprinkle the remaining grated cheese and place a few knobs of butter on top.
6. Bake in the oven until the potatoes are tender and the top brown and crisp. This will take 1–1½ hours. Test with a skewer.

Serves 4

Pommes Anna

675g/1½lb potatoes   Salt and pepper
55g/2oz butter, clarified   Nutmeg

1. Heat the oven to 190 C/375 F, gas mark 5. Brush a small heavy frying pan with the butter.
2. Wash, peel and slice the potatoes very finely.
3. Arrange a neat layer of overlapping slices on the bottom of the frying pan. Brush the potatoes with the melted butter and season well with salt, pepper and nutmeg.
4. Continue to layer the potatoes, butter and seasoning until all the potatoes have been used. Finish with butter and seasoning.
5. Hold the pan over direct medium heat for two minutes to brown the bottom layer of potatoes.
6. Take off and cover with greased paper and a lid (or foil). Bake in the oven for about 45 minutes.
7. When the potatoes are tender, invert a serving plate over the pan and turn the potatoes out so that the neat first layer is now on top.

Serves 4

Piedmont Beans

900g/2lb French beans
Salt and freshly ground black
   pepper
45g/1½oz butter
1 garlic clove

1 egg
55g/2oz grated Edam *or*
   Gruyère cheese
Parmesan cheese
Dry white crumbs

1. Heat the oven to 180 C/350 F, gas mark 4. Butter an oven-proof serving dish.
2. Wash, top and tail the beans. Place in a pan of boiling salted water and cook until just tender.
3. Drain well and mince or push through a vegetable mill, or chop finely.
4. Melt the butter and when frothing add the beans and garlic. Shake over the heat for 1 minute. Tip into the mixing bowl.
5. Separate the egg and beat the yolk and cheese into the bean mixture. Taste and season with salt and pepper. Be careful not to overseason as cheese is salty.
6. Whisk the egg white until stiff but not dry. Using a large metal spoon fold into the beans.
7. Turn the mixture into an overproof dish and sprinkle with Parmesan and breadcrumbs.
8. Bake for 40 minutes.

Serves 4

BRAISED

Petits Pois à la Française

225g/½lb peas, shelled (use
  frozen peas if fresh are not
  available)
1 large mild onion, finely
  sliced
1 small lettuce, shredded
150ml/¼ pint water

30g/1oz butter
Handful each of fresh mint and
  parsley
½ garlic clove, crushed
  (optional)
Salt, freshly ground black
  pepper
1 teaspoon sugar

1. Mix the peas, onion and lettuce in a heavy casserole. Add
   the water, butter, mint, parsley, garlic (if used), salt and
   pepper and sugar.
2. Cover tightly (a double seal of greaseproof paper put over
   the pan before the lid is pushed down makes a good seal).
3. Cook on a very gentle heat until the peas are tender, almost
   mushy (about 50 minutes), or, better still, bake in a slow oven
   170 C/325 F, gas mark 3 for 1½–2 hours.

Note: The liquid may be thickened by the addition of beurre
manié (see page 61) if preferred, but care should be taken not
to mash the peas while stirring.

Serves 4

Red Cabbage

1 small red cabbage
1 onion, sliced
30g/1oz butter
1 cooking apple, peeled and
  sliced
1 dessert apple, peeled and
  sliced

2 teaspoons brown sugar
2 teaspoons vinegar
Pinch of ground cloves
Salt and freshly ground black
  pepper

1. Shred the cabbage and discard the hard stalks. Rinse well.
2. Using a large pot, fry the onion in the butter until it begins to soften.
3. Add the drained but still wet cabbage, apples, sugar, vinegar and cloves, and season with salt and pepper.
4. Cover tightly and cook very slowly, mixing well and stirring every 15 minutes or so. Cook for 2 hours, or until the whole mass is soft and reduced in bulk. (During the cooking it may be necessary to add a little water.)
5. Taste and add more salt, pepper or sugar if necessary.

Serves 6

Baked Fennel

675g/1½lb Florence fennel
  (vegetable, not herb)
30g/1oz butter
1 tablespoon chopped fresh
  mint

1 tablespoon chopped fresh
  parsley
Juice of 1 lemon

1. Discard any discoloured outside leaves and quarter the heads of fennel neatly.
2. Lay the pieces in a roasting pan or ovenproof dish. Melt the butter and add the chopped herbs and lemon juice. Brush this over the fennel.

3. Cover tightly with a lid or foil and bake in the oven for about 1½ hours at 180°C/350°F, gas mark 4 until the fennel is quite tender.

Serves 4

Braised Celery

1 head celery	1 bay leaf
15g/½oz butter	Salt and freshly ground black
1 small onion, chopped	pepper
1 carrot, finely chopped	15g/½oz butter
290ml/½ pint chicken stock	15g/½oz flour

1. Heat the oven to 180°C/350°F, gas mark 4.
2. Wash and cut the celery into even-sized pieces, about 8cm/3in long. Remove any tough strings.
3. Melt the butter in a heavy roasting pan and cook the onions and carrots in it until soft but not coloured.
4. Add the celery, stock, bay leaf, salt and pepper and bring to the boil.
5. Cover with a lid or foil and bake in the oven until tender (about 1½ hours).
6. Mix the butter and the flour together to a smooth paste.
7. When the celery is tender place the roasting tin over direct heat. When the liquid boils stir in a little of the flour paste (beurre manié) to thicken the sauce. Do not add too much at a time. Stir until boiling.
8. Simmer for 2 minutes to cook the flour. Taste and adjust the seasoning if necessary.
9. Remove the bay leaf. Transfer celery and liquid to a warmed serving dish.

Serves 4

Vegetable Mornay

1 small cauliflower	450g/1lb carrots
Salt	3 tomatoes
225g/½lb shelled peas *or* 1 small packet frozen peas	570ml/1 pint mornay sauce (page 262)

1. Break the cauliflower into sprigs and cook them in boiling salted water until just tender, but not soft.
2. Boil the peas.
3. Peel and slice the carrots and boil in salted water until just tender.
4. Skin the tomatoes (plunge then into boiling water for 5 seconds to loosen the skins) and cut them in half.
5. Put all the vegetables into an ovenproof dish.
6. Heat the mornay sauce and pour it over the vegetables.
7. Heat the oven to 230 C/450 F, gas mark 8. Bake the vegetables until bubbling and brown on top.

Serves 6

Salsify (*or Scorzonera*) in Mornay Sauce

Salsify and scorzonera are classified as different vegetables but they taste very alike and are treated similarly, the only practical difference being that salsify is peeled before cooking and scorzonera afterwards. In fact both may be peeled before cooking but the flavour of scorzonera boiled in its skin is said to be superior.

8 roots salsify *or* scorzonera	Grated cheese
Lemon juice (for salsify only)	Dried breadcrumbs
290ml/½ pint mornay sauce (page 262)	

If using salsify (which is white):
1. Wash, peel and cut each root into 3–4 pieces.
2. Place in a pan with a cupful of salted water with a little lemon juice and simmer, with a tightly closed lid, for 12–20 minutes. or until tender, topping up with water if necessary.
3. Drain well and arrange in a serving dish.
4. Coat with the hot mornay sauce, sprinkle with grated cheese and breadcrumbs and brown under the grill.

If using scorzonera (blackish in colour):
1. Wash and cut each root into 3–4 pieces.
2. Place unpeeled into a pan of boiling salted water and simmer until tender; about 15–20 minutes.
3. Drain well and peel off the skin.
4. Proceed as for salsify.

Serves 4

Beetroot in White Sauce with Spring Onions

2 cooked beetroots, sliced	290ml/½ pint milk
6 spring onions	Freshly ground black pepper
30g/1oz butter	Pinch of sugar
20g/¾oz flour	1 teaspoon wine vinegar

1. Put the beetroot in an ovenproof dish, cover and put in a warm oven to heat up.
2. Cut the spring onions into 2·5cm/1in sticks. Melt the butter, add the onions and cook till soft but not coloured.
3. Stir in the flour. Cook for 1 minute.
4. Draw the pan off the heat and add the milk.
5. Return to the heat and bring the sauce slowly to the boil, stirring continuously.

6. Add the seasonings, sugar and vinegar, and simmer for 2–3 minutes.
7. Pour over the beetroot and serve.

Serves 4

Cauliflower with Green Sauce

1 large cauliflower
425ml/$\frac{3}{4}$ pint green sauce
  (page 264)

1. Cut away and discard the outer leaves and very thick stalk of the cauliflower.
2. Break into florets. Drop these into boiling salted water and cook for 8 minutes or until the stalks are just tender.
3. Drain and put into a serving dish.
4. Cover with a creamy green sauce.

FRIED

Cooked Cucumber with Dill

2 cucumbers
Salt and pepper
30g/1oz butter

2 teaspoons chopped fresh dill
Squeeze of lemon juice

1. Peel the cucumbers and cut into 1cm/$\frac{1}{2}$ in cubes.
2. Drop them into boiling salted water and cook for 3 minutes.
3. Rinse under running cold water and drain well.
4. Melt the butter in a frying pan and when foaming add the cucumber and dill.

5. When the cucumber is beginning to turn a delicate brown season with pepper and lemon juice and shake over the heat.

Note: If cucumbers are cheap and plentiful it is worth shaping them into balls with a melon baller – wasteful but very pretty.

Serves 4

Rosti Potatoes

1 Spanish onion, finely chopped	675g/1½lb large potatoes, peeled and parboiled
55g/2oz streaky bacon, finely chopped	Salt and freshly ground black pepper
Oil	Butter

1. Take a 23cm/9in frying pan and put into it the onion and bacon and a tablespoon of oil.
2. Cook slowly over gentle heat until the onion is transparent and soft but not coloured. Remove from heat.
3. Coarsely grate the potatoes. Season with salt and pepper. Fork in the onion and bacon.
4. Heat up a tablespoon of mixed butter and oil in the frying pan. Add the potato mixture. Pat it lightly into a flat cake with straight sides.
5. Fry gently until the underside is crusty and golden brown (about 15 minutes). Shake the pan every so often to ensure that the cake does not stick.
6. Place a plate larger than the frying pan over the pan and turn both plate and pan over to tip the rosti out on to the plate.
7. Slip it immediately back into the pan to cook the other side for 5 minutes.
8. Place in a warm oven for 15 minutes.
9. Serve on a large flat dish, cut into wedges like a cake.

Note: Finely grated raw carrots are sometimes added to the mixture. The potato-cake can be baked in the oven rather than fried (190 C/375 F, gas mark 5) for about 30 minutes.

Note II: Very old large floury potatoes need not be parboiled before grating. The boiling is to remove some of the sticky starch which is present in small young waxy potatoes.

Serves 4

Sweetcorn Fritters

2 eggs
Salt and freshly ground black
  pepper
225g/½lb cooked sweetcorn

1 teaspoon baking powder
15g/½oz fresh breadcrumbs
Oil for shallow frying

1. Separate the eggs. Mix the yolks with the seasoning and the sweetcorn.
2. Whisk the whites until stiff but not dry and fold them into the mixture.
3. Stir in the baking powder and add the breadcrumbs. Taste and add more salt and pepper if necessary.
4. Heat the oil in a frying pan and when hot add the batter in spoonfuls. Fry to a golden brown on both sides. Drain well.

Serves 4

Fried Rice

Salt and pepper
8 tablespoons polished rice
Oil

55g/2oz pine kernels
  (optional)
2 spring onions

1. Bring a large saucepan full of salted water to the boil and tip in the rice. Stir, bring back to the boil, and cook for 10 minutes or until the rice is just tender.
2. Rinse plenty of hot water through the rice to remove the

242

excess starch and drain well. While it is draining, occasionally turn it over with a spoon to allow trapped steam to escape.

3. Pour 3 tablespoons of oil into a frying pan and heat it. Put in the rice, now quite dry. Fry, turning all the time to brown evenly.
4. Add plenty of pepper, salt if necessary, and the pine kernels.
5. Chop the spring onions finely and stir them in.

Note: 'Easy cook' or polished rice is much easier to fry evenly.

Serves 4

DEEP FRIED

Chips

675g/1½lb potatoes
Oil for frying
Salt

1. Peel and, as far as possible, cut the potatoes into 5cm × 1cm/ 2in × ½in sticks. Keep them in a bowl of cold water until ready for cooking. This will prevent any discoloration and remove excess starch which tends to stick the chips together.
2. Heat the oil to a medium temperature (when a crouton of bread is dropped in it should fizzle gently).
3. Dry the potatoes carefully and place a few at a time in the chip basket (too many will stick together).
4. Fry for 7–8 minutes until soft. Remove from the fat.
5. Heat the oil until a crouton of bread will frizzle and brown in 30 seconds.
6. Repeat the frying process in the hotter oil until the chips are well browned and crisp.
7. Drain the chips on absorbent paper. Sprinkle with salt.

8. Serve immediately. Do not cover the chips or they will lose their crispness.

Note: Chips are cooked in two stages because if the fat is hot enough to crisp and brown the chips, the process is so quick that the middle of the potato will not be cooked. On the other hand, if the oil is cooler, although the chip will cook through, it will be soggy. The second frying, to create the crisp brown outside, should be done just before serving.

Serves 4

Game Chips

450g/1lb large potatoes
Oil for frying
Salt

1. Wash and peel the potatoes. If you want even-sized chips trim each potato into a cylinder shape.
2. Slice them very finely, preferably on a mandolin. Soak in cold water to remove the excess starch (this will prevent them from discoloring or sticking together).
3. Heat the oil until a crumb will sizzle vigorously in it.
4. Dry the chips very thoroughly on a tea towel.
5. Lower a basket of chips into the hot fat. They are cooked when they rise to the surface and are golden brown.
6. Drain on absorbent paper, sprinkle with salt and serve immediately.

Note: Commercial potato crisps, providing they are the plain variety and not 'cheese and bacon' or some such, will do very well as game chips. Simply heat them, uncovered, in a moderate oven.

Serves 4

SIMPLE SALADS

Everything Green Salad

1 lettuce (any kind)   French dressing (page 268)

Choice of the following:

Green pepper   Watercress
Cucumber   Green beans
Fennel   Peas
Celery   1 teaspoon chopped fresh
Chicory   mint, parsley *or* chives
Spring onions

1. Prepare the salad ingredients:
    Lettuce: Wash, drain and shake to allow to drip dry. Do not
    twist or wring the leaves together, which bruises them, but
    break each lettuce leaf individually and place in a salad bowl.
    Green pepper: Wash, cut off the top and remove the seeds.
    Slice finely.
    Cucumber: Peel or not, as desired. Slice finely.
    Fennel: Wash and shave into thin slices.
    Celery: Wash and chop together with a few young leaves.
    Chicory: Wipe with a damp cloth. Remove the tough core
    with a sharp knife and cut each head at an angle into 3 or
    4 pieces.
    Spring onions: Wash and peel. Chop half the green stalks
    finely. Keep the white part with the rest of the salad.
    Watercress: Wash and pick over, discarding the thick stalks
    and any yellow leaves.
    Beans and peas: Cook in boiling salted water until just

tender and cool under running cold water. Drain well and pat dry in a tea-towel.

2. Add the chopped herbs and the chopped spring onion tops (if used) to the dressing.

3. Mix the salad ingredients together and just before serving toss them in French dressing.

Caesar Salad

2 large garlic cloves
4 tablespoons olive oil
2 finely chopped anchovy
    fillets
2 tablespoons lemon juice
Dry English mustard

Freshly ground black pepper
1 egg
2 slices bread
1 cos lettuce
4 tablespoons Parmesan cheese

1. Crush the garlic and mix with the olive oil.
2. Strain off three-quarters of the olive oil (now flavoured with garlic) to make the dressing.
3. Add it to the anchovy fillets, lemon juice, mustard, pepper and raw egg and whisk well or blend in liquidizer.
4. Cut the crusts off the bread and cut the rest into small dice.
5. Pour the remaining oil and the garlic into a frying pan.
6. Heat slowly. When the garlic shreds begin to sizzle add the diced bread and fry, turning frequently with a fish slice or spoon, until the croutons are crisp and brown. With a perforated spoon lift out the croutons and drain and cool them on absorbent paper.
7. Toss the lettuce in the dressing.
8. Sprinkle over the croutons and cheese.

Serves 4

Tomato, Mushroom and Spring Onion Salad

450g/1lb tomatoes
110g/¼lb mushrooms

Small bunch of spring onions
Vinaigrette dressing (page 268)

1. Plunge the tomatoes into boiling water for 5 seconds and then skin them.
2. Cut them into slices *across* rather than down.
3. Wipe but do not peel the mushrooms. Slice them very thinly.
4. Peel the spring onions and chop them finely. Mix them with vinaigrette dressing.
5. Combine all the ingredients and mix together carefully.
6. Tip into a clean bowl and leave for 2 or more hours before serving.

Serves 4

Tomato, Onion and Pimento Salad

900g/2lb tomatoes
1 Spanish onion
Small can of red pimento caps

1 teaspoon sugar
French dressing (page 268)

1. Plunge the tomatoes into boiling water for 5 seconds. Skin them and cut into quarters.
2. Slice the onion into thin rings.
3. Drain the water from the can of pimentos and reserve it.
4. Mix the sugar, French dressing and pimento liquid together.
5. Slice the pimentos.
6. Put the tomatoes, onions and pimentos into a bowl and pour over the dressing.

Serves 8

Tomato and Basil Salad

6 tomatoes   French dressing (page 268)
8–10 leaves of fresh basil

1. Dip the tomatoes in boiling water for 5 seconds and then skin them.
2. Chop the basil coarsely.
3. Slice the tomatoes horizontally and arrange them on a plate.
4. Mix the dressing and basil together and spoon over the tomatoes.
5. Chill for 1–2 hours before serving.

Serves 4

MORE COMPLICATED SALADS

Coleslaw with Raisins and Walnuts

225g/½lb hard white cabbage   1 teaspoon sugar
3 small carrots   Salt and pepper
Mayonnaise (page 266)   1 tablespoon raisins
1 teaspoon French mustard   1 tablespoon chopped walnuts

1. Shred the cabbage as finely as possible.
2. Peel the carrots and grate them coarsely.
3. Mix the mayonnaise with all the remaining ingredients and, using your hands, combine it with the cabbage and carrots.

Note: Mayonnaise for coleslaw is delicious made with cider vinegar.

Serves 4

Cabbage with Lemon Cream Sauce

450g/1lb hard white cabbage   Lemon cream sauce
                                (page 271)

1. Shred the cabbage as finely as you can.
2. Mix the sauce well into the cabbage using your hands.
3. Allow to stand for 2 hours before serving.

Serves 4

Chinese Cabbage and Apple Salad

450g/1lb Chinese cabbage   2 dessert apples
  (Chinese leaves)   Chopped parsley

For the dressing:
3 tablespoons oil   3 tablespoons chopped fresh
1 tablespoon vinegar   mint
                                2 tablespoons soured cream

1. Mix all the ingredients for the dressing together in a screw-top
   jar and shake until well emulsified.
2. Shred the cabbage finely and slice the apples but do not peel
   them.
3. Toss the cabbage and apple in the dressing.
4. Tip into a wooden salad bowl and sprinkle with plenty of
   chopped parsley.

Serves 4

Spinach Salad with Bacon and Yoghurt

450g/1lb fresh young spinach
6 rashers streaky rindless bacon

For the dressing:

2–3 tablespoons plain yoghurt
2 tablespoons oil
2 teaspoons vinegar

1 teaspoon French mustard
½ garlic clove, crushed
Salt, pepper and sugar

1. Heat the grill.
2. Wash the spinach and remove the stalks. Drain well and shred finely.
3. Grill the bacon for about 2 minutes on each side until brown and crispy. Cool, then chop up.
4. Mix all the ingredients for the dressing together.
5. Toss the spinach and bacon in the dressing just before serving.

Serves 4

Chicory and Watercress Salad

2 chicory heads, plump, white
   and tight closed (the ones
   with green tips are too bitter)

Bunch of watercress
French dressing (page 268)

1. Wipe the chicory heads with a clean damp cloth, remove any outside leaves that are discoloured at the edges and break the leaves apart. Discard the bitter core.
2. Wash and drain the watercress. Cut away any very tough stalks.
3. Toss the chicory and watercress together in French dressing.

Note: If the chicory is prepared in advance leave it in a bowl of acidulated water (water with a squeeze of lemon added) to prevent discoloration. Dry well before using.

Serves 4

Pineapple, Almond and Celery Salad

3 tablespoons salad oil (not olive oil)
2 teaspoons lemon juice
½ teaspoon salt
½ teaspoon pepper

1 small pineapple *or* 1 small can drained pineapple chunks
8 sticks celery
30g/1oz flaked almonds

1. Mix the oil, lemon juice, salt and pepper together to make the dressing.
2. Cut the top and bottom off the pineapple leaving a cylinder of fruit. With a sharp knife cut off the skin. Cut the pineapple in quarters lengthwise, discard the woody core and cut the flesh into small chunks.
3. Wash the celery and chop it very finely.
4. Mix the pineapple with the celery and almonds and toss in the dressing.

Serves 8

Orange and Watercress Salad

6 oranges

For the dressing:
3 tablespoons oil
1 tablespoon wine vinegar
1 tablespoon finely chopped fresh mint

Large bunch of watercress

Salt and freshly ground black pepper
Pinch of sugar

1. Mix all the ingredients for the dressing together in a screw-top jar and shake until well emulsified.
2. Peel the oranges with a knife as you would an apple, making sure that all the pith is removed.
3. Cut horizontally into thin slices.
4. Wash and drain the watercress. Remove the tough stalks and discard them.

5. Lay the slices of orange in a glass bowl. Pour over some of the dressing.
6. Dip sprigs of watercress into the rest of the dressing and place on top of the sliced oranges.

Serves 4

Avocado, Apple and Lettuce Salad

1 eating apple
French dressing (page 268)

1 ripe avocado pear
1 small cos *or* round lettuce

1. Cut the apple into thin slices, unpeeled.
2. Put straight into the French dressing.
3. Peel and cut the avocado into cubes and turn carefully with the apple in the French dressing until they are completely coated.
4. Use only the best lettuce leaves and pull them into small pieces.
5. Toss the lettuce with the avocado and apple.

Serves 4

Cauliflower and Ham Salad

1 small cauliflower
2 slices ham, cut into thin strips
3 hardboiled eggs

For the dressing:

1 level tablespoon chopped
   fresh mint
1 level tablespoon chopped
   fresh chives
1 teaspoon chopped fresh
   tarragon

3 tablespoons salad oil
1 tablespoon wine vinegar
1 small garlic clove, crushed
Salt and freshly-ground black
   pepper

252

1. Break the cauliflower into sprigs and boil in salted water until barely cooked. Drain well.
2. While still hot, put into a bowl and pour over the combined dressing ingredients.
3. When the cauliflower is quite cold arrange on a dish with the strips of ham mixed among the sprigs.
4. Surround with the hardboiled eggs, cut into quarters lengthwise, and pour any remaining dressing over the eggs.

Serves 4

RICE, PASTA AND CEREAL SALADS

Rice Salad

Almost any vegetables can be added to cold cooked rice to make a salad, but it is important to have approximately equal quantities of rice and vegetables, or the result may be lifeless and stodgy. The dressing should moisten, not soak, the dish.

225g/½lb long-grain rice
110g/¼lb frozen peas
½ green pepper, seeded and chopped
½ red pepper, seeded and chopped

Small stick of celery
¼ cucumber peeled
2 tomatoes
Few black olives
Finely chopped fresh parsley, mint, chives *or* dill

For the dressing:
4 tablespoons salad oil
1 tablespoon vinegar

1 medium onion, finely chopped
Salt and pepper

1. Boil the rice in plenty of water until just tender (about 10 minutes).
2. Rinse under the cold tap and leave to drain well.
3. Cook the peas.
4. Chop the peppers (discarding the seeds), celery and cucumber.
5. Plunge the tomatoes into boiling water for 5 seconds so that they will peel easily. Peel them and cut into quarters.
6. Stone the olives.
7. Put the dressing ingredients into a screw-top jar and shake well.
8. Mix everything together and add salt and pepper if necessary.

Note: Rice salad looks pretty when turned out of a ring mould, jelly mould, or even a mixing bowl. Push it down firmly in the oiled mould, then invert it on to a dish. If simply served in a bowl or on a dish keep back a few olives and tomato pieces for the top.

Serves 8

Curried Rice Salad

2 tablespoons oil
1 large onion, finely chopped
1 stick celery, finely chopped
½ teaspoon ground coriander
½ teaspoon turmeric
225g/½lb cooked rice, cold
½ green *or* tart eating apple, peeled, cored and chopped
Salt and freshly ground pepper

Handful of currants, sultanas, raisins
A few chunks of pineapple
30g/1oz pine nuts *or* blanched almonds
1 tablespoon mixture of fresh chopped herbs, e.g. mint, parsley, thyme
French dressing (page 268)

1. Heat the oil and soften the onion and celery in it until half-cooked.
2. Add the coriander and turmeric and continue to cook gently for 2-3 minutes.

254

3. Put the rice into a bowl and using a fork mix in the apple, salt and pepper, dried fruit, pineapple, nuts, herbs and the onion-celery mixture.
4. Moisten with French dressing just before serving.

Serves 6

Barley and Beetroot Salad

1 large beetroot, cooked
1 small onion
½ green apple

French dressing (page 268)
30g/1oz barley
110g/¼lb shredded lettuce *or* white cabbage

1. Boil the barley in plenty of salted water for about 1 hour, until tender. Drain well.
2. Chop the beetroot, onion and apple (unskinned).
3. Toss these in French dressing with the barley.
4. Serve on a bed of shredded lettuce.

Serves 4

Italian Tuna Salad

1 onion, finely sliced
225g/½lb haricots blancs – dried if possible; canned may be used but they are expensive
198g/7oz can tuna fish
110g/¼lb shell-shaped pasta

Salt and freshly ground pepper
French dressing (page 268)
1 teaspoon chopped fresh basil
1 box mustard cress
6 black olives, stoned

1. Soak the haricot beans (if dried) in cold water for 6 hours.
2. Rinse them and put in a pan of cold salted water. Bring slowly to the boil, cover and simmer until tender (45–60 minutes). Cool under running cold water and drain well. If using canned beans rinse them well.

3. Cook the pasta in boiling salted oiled water until just tender (about 15 minutes). Rinse under running water and drain well.
4. Gently mix the onion, beans, tuna fish, pasta and basil in just enough French dressing to moisten. Care should be taken not to overmix or an unattractive soggy salad will result.
5. Sprinkle over the snipped cress and black olives.

Serves 8

4
Stocks and Savoury Sauces

◆———

STOCKS

Good strong natural stocks are behind almost every good sauce or casserole. Stock-cubes are often over-salty and 'packet-flavoured', so should be used with caution. See page 60 for detailed notes on stock-making.

White Stock

Onion   Fresh parsley
Celery   Fresh thyme
Carrot   Bay leaf
Chicken *or* veal bones, skin Peppercorns
  or flesh

1. Peel the onion. Slice it and the celery and carrot roughly.
2. Put all the ingredients into a saucepan. Cover generously with water and bring to the boil slowly. Skim off any fat, and/or scum.
3. Simmer for 2–3 hours, skimming frequently and topping up the water level if necessary. The liquid should reduce to half the original quantity.
4. Strain, cool and lift off all the fat.

Brown Stock

Onion
Turnip
Carrot
Celery
Marrow bones (*or* beef bones,
    veal bones, duck carcass,
    bacon – green *or* smoked
    – *or* pieces of raw meat, but
    not mutton, lamb or pork)

Dripping
Fresh parsley stalks
Bay leaf
Pinch of fresh thyme
Black peppercorns

1. Peel the onion but keep the skin.
2. Peel the turnip, wash the carrot and the celery.
3. Chop all the vegetables into small dice.
4. Chop the meat or bacon up into small pieces.
5. Heat the fat in a large heavy-bottomed pan and brown the meat and vegetables really well all over, scraping the bottom of the pan frequently.
6. Add the herbs, onion skin and pepper (but not salt).
7. Cover with water and bring very slowly to the boil, skimming off any scum as it rises to the top.
8. When clear of scum, simmer gently for at least 2 hours, preferably all day, skimming off the fat as necessary, and topping up with water if the level gets dangerously low. The longer it simmers, and the more the liquid reduces by evaporation, the stronger the stock will be.
9. Strain, cool and lift off any remaining fat.

Note: Cooked bones are less satisfactory than raw bones as they have lost a good deal of their flavour.

Fish Stock

Onion	Fresh parsley stalks
Carrot	Bay leaf
Celery	Pinch of fresh thyme
Fish bones, skins, fins, heads	Pepper
or tails, crustacean shells	
(e.g. prawn shells, mussel	
shells etc.)	

1. Slice the peeled onion, the carrot and the celery.
2. Put everything together in a pan, with water to cover, and bring to the boil. Turn down to simmer and skim off any scum.
3. Simmer for 20 minutes if the fish bones are small, 30 minutes if large. Strain.

Note: Care should be taken not to overcook fish stock, as the flavour is impaired if the bones are cooked too long. Once strained, however, fish stock may be strengthened by further boiling and reducing.

Fond Brun

1½ kilos/3lb beef and veal bones, broken	3 bay leaves
A little bacon rind	Pinch of fresh thyme
110g/¼lb onion, peeled and chopped roughly	2 fresh parsley stalks
110g/¼lb carrot, chopped roughly	4 peppercorns
	1 litre/2 pints water

1. Set the oven to 200°C/400°F, gas mark 6.
2. Place the broken bones in a large, deep-sided roasting pan.

259

3. Roast until very brown, about 2 hours, turning the bones occasionally. Add the vegetables and bacon rind and continue roasting for a further 45 minutes.
4. Transfer everything to a heavy saucepan. Add the herbs, peppercorns and water. Simmer slowly, covered, for 2–3 hours.
5. Strain and leave to get cold.
6. Skim off all the fat.

Glace de Viande

570ml/1 pint fond brun as
 above, absolutely free of fat

1. In a heavy-bottomed saucepan reduce the fond brun by boiling over a steady heat until thick, clear and syrupy.
2. Pour into small pots. When cold cover with polythene or jam covers and tie down.
3. Keep in the refrigerator until ready for use.

Note: Glace de viande keeps for several weeks and is very useful for enriching sauces.

Court Bouillon

1 litre/2 pints water
$\frac{1}{4}$ litre/scant $\frac{1}{2}$ pint vinegar
1 carrot, sliced
1 onion, sliced

1 stick celery
12 peppercorns
2 bay leaves
2 tablespoons salad oil
Salt

Bring all the ingredients to the boil and simmer for 20 minutes.
 Ideally the liquid should now be allowed to cool and the fish, meat or vegetables should be placed in the cool liquid, and then brought slowly to simmering point.

WHITE SAUCES

White Sauce
(coating consistency)

20g/¾oz butter
20g/¾oz flour
Pinch of dry mustard

290ml/½ pint creamy milk
Salt and white pepper

1. Melt the butter in a thick saucepan.
2. Add the flour and the mustard and stir over the heat for 1 minute. Draw the pan off the heat, pour in the milk and mix well.
3. Return the sauce to the heat and stir continually until boiling.
4. Simmer for 2–3 minutes and season with salt and pepper.

Béchamel Sauce
(coating consistency)

290ml/½ pint creamy milk
Slice of onion
Blade of mace
Few fresh parsley stalks
4 peppercorns

1 bay leaf
20g/¾oz butter
20g/¾oz flour
Salt and white pepper

1. Place the milk with the onion, mace, parsley, peppercorns and bay leaf in a saucepan and slowly bring to simmering point.
2. Lower the temperature and allow the flavour to infuse for about 8–10 minutes.

3. Melt the butter in a thick saucepan, stir in the flour and stir over heat for 1 minute.
4. Remove from the heat. Strain in the infused milk and mix well.
5. Return the sauce to the heat and stir or whisk continuously until boiling.
6. Simmer for 2–3 minutes.
7. Taste and season.

Mornay Sauce (*Cheese Sauce*)

45g/1½oz butter
45g/1½oz flour
570ml/1 pint milk
85g/3oz grated Gruyère *or* strong Cheddar cheese

30g/1oz grated Parmesan cheese
Salt and pepper

1. Melt the butter and stir in the flour. Cook, stirring, for 1 minute. Draw the pan off the heat. Add the milk slowly, beating out the lumps as you go.
2. Return the pan to the heat and stir until boiling. Simmer for 2 minutes.
3. Add all the cheese and mix well, but do not re-boil.
4. Season with salt and pepper as necessary.

Parsley Sauce

290ml/½ pint creamy milk
Slice of onion
Good handful of fresh parsley
4 peppercorns

1 bay leaf
20g/¾oz butter
20g/¾oz flour
Salt and pepper

1. Put the milk, onion, parsley stalks (but not leaves), peppercorns and bay leaf in a saucepan and slowly bring to simmering point.

2. Lower the temperature and allow the flavour to infuse for about 10 minutes.
3. Melt the butter in a thick saucepan, stir in the flour and cook, stirring, for 1 minute.
4. Remove from the heat. Strain in the infused milk and mix well.
5. Return the sauce to the heat and stir continuously until boiling, then simmer for 2–3 minutes. Taste and season.
6. Chop the parsley leaves very finely and stir into the hot sauce.

Soubise Sauce

For the béchamel sauce:

20g/¾oz butter	20g/¾oz flour
Bay leaf	290ml/½ pint milk

For the soubise:

30g/1oz butter	225g/½lb onions, very finely chopped
4 tablespoons water	3–4 tablespoons cream

1. First prepare the béchamel: melt the butter, add the bay leaf and flour and cook, stirring, for 1 minute. Draw off the heat, and stir in the milk. Return to the heat and bring slowly to the boil, stirring continuously. Simmer for 2 minutes. Remove the bay leaf.
2. To make the soubise, melt the butter in a heavy pan. Add the water and the finely chopped onions and cook very slowly, preferably covered with a lid to create a steamy atmosphere. The onions should become very soft and transparent, but on no account brown. Add the cream, and mix with the béchamel.

Note: This sauce can be liquidized in a blender or pushed through a sieve if a smooth texture is desired.

Green Sauce

(for cauliflower, pasta, fish)

45g/1½oz butter
30g/1oz flour
425ml/¾ pint milk

Salt and pepper
Bunch of watercress

1. Melt the butter and stir in the flour.
2. Cook, stirring, for 1 minute. Stirring briskly as you go, pour in the milk and continue stirring until the sauce boils. Simmer for 2 minutes. Season to taste.
3. Wash the watercress, removing stalks.
4. Cook the leaves briefly (30 seconds) in boiling water. Drain and rinse under the cold tap to stop further cooking and to 'set' the green colour.
5. Press all the moisture out of the watercress and add to the sauce.
6. Liquidize the sauce, or push through a sieve.
7. Reheat briefly – long cooking will spoil the colour.

Note: A handful of spinach may be used instead of watercress.

BLOND SAUCE

Velouté Sauce

20g/¾oz butter
20g/¾oz flour
290ml/½ pint white stock,
   strained and well skimmed
   (page 257)

Salt, pepper and a few drops of
   lemon juice

1. Melt the butter, add the flour and cook, stirring, over a gentle heat until pale brown. Remove from the heat.
2. Add the stock. Bring to the boil, stirring, and simmer until slightly syrupy and semi-clear. Taste and add seasoning and lemon juice.

BROWN SAUCES

Demi-Glace
(short method)

2 tablespoons oil
1 small carrot, finely chopped
½ onion, finely chopped
½ stick celery, finely chopped
½ tablespoon flour
290ml/½ pint stock

½ teaspoon tomato purée
A few mushroom stalks
Bouquet garni of 2 parsley
  stalks, bay leaves, blade of
  mace

1. Heat the oil in a heavy saucepan, add the vegetables and fry until brown.
2. Stir in the flour and continue to cook slowly, stirring occasionally with a metal spoon, scraping the bottom of the pan to loosen the sediment. Cook to a good russet brown.
3. Draw aside, add three-quarters of the stock, the tomato purée mushroom peelings and the bouquet garni.
4. Return to the heat, bring to the boil, half cover and simmer for 30 minutes.
5. Depouille twice to remove scum. Strain.

Depouille: To depouiller, add a splash of cold stock to the boiling liquid to help bring scum and fat to the surface. Tilting the pan slightly, skim the surface with a large metal spoon. Repeat as necessary.

Demi-Glace
(long method)

290ml/½ pint short-method demi-glace (page 265)

290ml/½ pint fond brun (page 259)

1. Combine the demi-glace with the fond brun.
2. Simmer over gentle heat, skimming repeatedly until reduced by half.

Note: A good demi-glace looks like a rich syrupy gravy when hot, setting to a jelly when cold.

EMULSION SAUCES

Mayonnaise

2 egg yolks
1 teaspoon pale mustard
290ml/½ pint olive oil *or*
   150ml/¼ pint each olive and
   salad oil

Squeeze of lemon juice
1 tablespoon wine vinegar
Salt and pepper

1. Put the yolks into a bowl with the mustard and beat well with a wooden spoon.
2. Add the oil, literally drop by drop, beating all the time. The mixture should be very thick by the time half the oil is added.
3. Beat in the lemon juice.
4. Resume pouring in the oil, going rather more confidently

now, but alternating the dribbles of oil with small quantities of vinegar.

5. Add salt and pepper to taste.

Note: If the mixture curdles, another egg yolk should be beaten in a separate bowl, and the curdled mixture beaten drop by drop into it.

Elizabeth Sauce

This sauce was invented by the staff at the Cordon Bleu School for the Coronation in 1953 and has become a classic.

1 small onion, chopped	Salt and pepper
2 teaspoons oil	2 teaspoons apricot jam
2 teaspoons curry powder	1 slice lemon
$\frac{1}{2}$ teaspoon tomato purée	1 teaspoon lemon juice
3 tablespoons water	290ml/$\frac{1}{2}$ pint mayonnaise
1 small bay leaf	(page 266)
$\frac{1}{2}$ wineglass red wine	2 tablespoons double cream

1. Cook the onion gently for 4 minutes in the oil.
2. Add the curry powder and fry gently for 1 minute.
3. Add the tomato purée, water, bay leaf, wine, salt, pepper, jam, lemon slice and juice and simmer for 8 minutes.
4. Strain the mixture, pushing as much as possible through the sieve.
5. Use this sauce to flavour the mayonnaise to the desired strength.
6. Half-whip the cream and stir into the sauce.

Green Mayonnaise

Bunch of watercress
290ml/½ pint mayonnaise

1. Pick over the watercress to remove stalks and yellowed leaves. Wash well.
2. Chop roughly.
3. Add to the mayonnaise and blend in a liquidizer to a smooth sauce.

Note: Cooked and very well drained spinach can be used instead of watercress.

French Dressing (*Vinaigrette*)

3 tablespoons salad oil
1 tablespoon wine vinegar
Salt and pepper

Put all the ingredients into a screw-top jar. Before using shake until well emulsified.

Note I: This dressing can be flavoured with crushed garlic, mustard, a pinch of sugar, chopped fresh herbs etc., as desired.

Note II: If kept refrigerated the dressing will more easily form an emulsion when whisked or shaken, and has a slightly thicker consistency.

MISCELLANEOUS SAUCES

Apple Sauce

450g/1lb cooking apples
Finely grated rind of ¼ lemon
3 tablespoons water

1 teaspoon sugar
15g/½oz butter
Pinch of cinnamon

1. Peel, quarter, core and slice the apples.
2. Place in a heavy saucepan with the lemon rind, water and sugar. Cover with a lid and cook very slowly until the apples are soft.
3. Beat in the butter and cinnamon. Serve hot or cold.

Horseradish Cream

1–1½ heaped tablespoons
   grated fresh horseradish
2 teaspoons wine vinegar
½ teaspoon made English
   mustard

Salt and pepper
Sugar to taste
150ml/¼ pint double cream

Mix all the ingredients together.

Note: If a fluffy non-runny sauce is required whip the cream until stiff, mix in the other ingredients and then fold in one whipped egg white.

Mint Sáuce

Large handful of fresh mint
2 tablespoons caster sugar

2 tablespoons hot water
2 tablespoons vinegar

1. Wash the mint and shake it dry.
2. Remove the stalks, and chop the leaves finely. Place in a bowl with the sugar.
3. Pour in the hot water and leave for 5 minutes to dissolve the sugar.
4. Add the vinegar and leave to soak for 1–2 hours.

Note: When mint is plentiful it is a good idea to chop a quantity of it and mix it with golden syrup. This base can then be used for instant mint sauce, vinegar and boiling water being added when the sauce is required.

Bread Sauce

1 large peeled onion
6 cloves
290ml/$\frac{1}{2}$ pint milk
1 bay leaf
10 peppercorns *or* 1 pinch of white pepper

Pinch of nutmeg
Salt
55g/2oz fresh white breadcrumbs
55g/2oz butter
2 tablespoons cream (optional)

1. Cut the onion in half. Stick the cloves into the onion pieces and put with the milk and bay leaf into a saucepan.
2. Add the peppercorns, a pinch of nutmeg, and a good pinch of salt. Leave to stand for 30 minutes or more if you can. If not, bring very slowly to the boil, and then simmer for 10 minutes. If you have had time to let the milk infuse (stand with its flavourings) you will not need to simmer it. But bring it to the boil very slowly just the same.
3. Strain the hot milk on to the breadcrumbs. Add the butter and cream. Mix and return to the saucepan.

4. Reheat the sauce carefully without reboiling.
5. If it has become too thick by the time it is needed, beat in more hot milk. It should be creamy.

Tomato Sauce

396g/14oz tin peeled plum tomatoes
1 small onion, chopped
1 carrot, chopped
1 stick celery, chopped
$\frac{1}{2}$ garlic clove, crushed
1 bay leaf
Fresh parsley stalks

Salt and pepper
Juice of $\frac{1}{2}$ lemon
Dash of Worcestershire sauce
1 teaspoon sugar
1 teaspoon chopped fresh *or* 1 pinch of dried basil *or* thyme

1. Put all the ingredients together in a thick-bottomed pan and simmer over medium heat for 30 minutes.
2. Sieve the sauce and return it to the pan.
3. If it is too thin reduce by boiling rapidly. Check the seasoning, adding more salt or sugar if necessary.

Lemon Cream Sauce

1 tablespoon lemon juice
1 tablespoon olive oil
Grated rind of $\frac{1}{2}$ lemon

Salt and freshly ground black pepper
$\frac{1}{2}$ teaspoon sugar
3 tablespoons single cream

Mix all the ingredients together, adding the cream last.

5
Main Dishes

◆

FISH

Cold Trout with Green Mayonnaise

4 medium-sized trout

For the poaching liquid (*court bouillon*):

1·14 litres/2 pints water	12 peppercorns
1 teacup vinegar	2 bay leaves
1 sliced carrot	2 tablespoons salad oil
1 sliced onion	Salt
1 stick celery	

Green mayonnaise (page 268)
Watercress

1. Clean the trout (by splitting down the belly and washing out the insides under the cold tap) and snip off the body fins, but leave on the head and tail.
2. Bring the court bouillon ingredients to the boil and simmer for 20 minutes or so. Ideally the liquid should now be allowed to cool and the fish placed in the cool liquid, then brought slowly to simmering point. If this is done the fish will take about 4 minutes (depending on size) from the time the water has reached boiling point. As soon as boiling point is reached, it is vital that the heat is lowered so that the trout *poach* (this means that no bubbles at all rise to the surface, but the water simmers very slightly – it is cooler than simmering). If there is not time to cool the court

272

bouillon before adding the fish, make sure the liquid is below simmering heat and gently drop the trout into it. They will take about 8 minutes if done this way.

3. As soon as the fish are cooked (the skin will be easy to remove, and the eyes look very white and prominent), stand the pan in a basin of cold water to cool it. This will prevent further cooking. The fish should cool in the liquid as they will steam dry if exposed to the air while still hot.

4. When the fish are quite cold carefully lift them out, and skin them without removing heads or tails.

5. Arrange them on a serving dish and coat with the green mayonnaise (thinned if necessary with milk), leaving the heads and tails exposed. Garnish with washed watercress.

Serves 4

Scallops in Velouté Sauce

16 scallops, frozen *or* fresh
1 small onion, chopped
Sprig of fresh thyme
1 bay leaf
1 parsley stalk
4–5 tablespoons white wine
1 slice lemon

Salt and freshly ground black pepper
290ml/½ pint good fish stock (page 259)
20g/¾oz butter
20g/¾oz flour
2 tablespoons cream
4–5 tablespoons water

1. Place the scallops in a pan with the onion, thyme, bay leaf, parsley stalk, wine and lemon.

2. Add a little water (if necessary) so that the scallops are half covered with liquid. Season with salt and pepper.

3. Bring slowly to simmering point and poach very gently for 3–4 minutes. Lift out the scallops with a perforated spoon.

4. Sometimes there is a greyish, tough piece of muscle opposite the roe: this should be removed. Cut the scallops in half.

5. Strain the fish liquid, add the stock. Boil rapidly until reduced to 290ml/½ pint.

6. Melt the butter and add the flour. Cook over a gentle heat for 1–2 minutes. Take off the heat and beat in the fish stock.

Return to the heat and bring slowly to the boil, stirring continuously until you have a creamy sauce. Check the seasoning.

7. Add the scallops and stir in the cream just before serving.

Note: Never boil or overcook scallops. They lose their succulence and become tough and tasteless.

Serves 4

Mackerel with Gooseberry Sauce

Four 225g/½lb mackerel

For the court bouillon:

570ml/1 pint water
2 tablespoons wine *or* wine
   vinegar
1 bay leaf

1 slice lemon
6 peppercorns
1 parsley stalk

For the gooseberry sauce:

340g/¾lb young gooseberries
30g/1oz sugar

30g/1oz butter
Pinch of ground ginger

For the garnish:
Lemon wedges

1. First prepare the court bouillon: place all the ingredients in a saucepan and simmer for 35 minutes. Strain and allow to cool slightly.
2. Set the oven to 200°C/400°F, gas mark 6.
3. Clean the fish, cut off the fins and with a pair of scissors cut a 'V' shape out of the tail of each fish. Place the fish in a fireproof dish.
4. Pour on the court bouillon. Bake, covered, in the oven for 15–20 minutes or until the fish is quite firm to the touch.
5. Meanwhile prepare the gooseberry sauce. Top and tail the berries and place them in a pan with a little water and the sugar. Simmer until tender.

6. Push the berries through a nylon or stainless steel sieve. Beat in the butter and ginger and taste for sweetness.
7. Arrange the mackerel on a serving dish. Garnish with lemon wedges. Hand the sauce separately.

Note: The same gooseberry sauce is good with grilled mackerel.

Serves 4

Haddock with English Egg Sauce

1·5 kilos/3lb haddock
570ml/1 pint milk

1 onion, sliced

A bouquet garni of:
  Bunch of parsley
  1 stick celery
  1 bay leaf
  Sprig of thyme

Salt and pepper
570ml/1 pint English egg sauce
  (page 276)

1. Set the oven at 170 C/325 F, gas mark 3.
2. Wash the fish, scrape off any scales and lay in a roasting tin.
3. Pour in the milk and add the onion, bouquet garni and seasoning.
4. Cover the dish with greased paper or a lid and bake in the slowish oven until the fish is tender to the touch of a skewer (40–45 minutes).
5. Take out the fish and dish it on an ovenproof platter.
6. Cover again with the paper and keep warm while you make the sauce.
7. Before serving skin the fish and pour over the sauce.

Serves 4

English Egg Sauce

3 hardboiled eggs
45g/1½oz butter
45g/1½oz flour
570ml/1 pint fish *or* chicken
  stock

3 tablespoons cream
4 tablespoons chopped fresh
  parsley

1. Using a stainless steel knife chop the eggs roughly.
2. Melt the butter in a saucepan. Stir in the flour and cook for 30 seconds.
3. Add the liquid and stir until boiling. Add the other ingredients and check for seasoning.

Note: The liquid in which fish or chicken is cooked is suitable as stock. Chicken stock will do for veal, fish or chicken dishes, but fish stock is only good for fish, of course.

Easy Salmon Koulibiaca

110g/¼lb long-grain rice
170g/6oz flour-quantity
  rough-puff pastry
  (page 371)
285g/10oz cooked fresh salmon
55g/2oz butter
1 onion, finely diced
30g/1oz mushrooms, chopped
1 tablespoon chopped fresh
  parsley

2 hardboiled eggs, coarsely
  chopped
Salt and freshly ground black
  pepper
Juice of ½ lemon
1 egg, beaten with a pinch of
  salt

1. Set the oven to 200°C/400°F, gas mark 6. Wet a baking sheet.
2. Place the rice in a large pan of boiling water and cook for 10–12 minutes. Drain in a colander or sieve and swish plenty of hot water through it. Stand the colander on a draining board. With the handle of a wooden spoon make a

few draining holes through the pile of rice to help the water and steam escape. Leave for 30 minutes.

3. Roll a third of the pastry into a rectangle 15cm × 5cm (6in × 2½in). Leave to relax for 10 minutes in the refrigerator.

4. Place on the prepared baking sheet, prick lightly with a fork and bake until a golden brown, about 15 minutes. Leave on a wire rack to cool. Do not turn the oven off. Rinse the baking tray under cold water until cool.

5. Bone, skin and flake the salmon.

6. Melt the butter over moderate heat, and add the onion. When nearly cooked add the mushrooms and cook gently for 1 minute.

7. Put the rice in a bowl and fork in the onion, mushroom, parsley, salmon, eggs, plenty of seasoning and lemon juice.

8. Place the cool pastry base on the wet baking sheet and pile on the rice mixture.

9. Shape it with your hands into a neat mound, making sure that it completely covers the base.

10. Roll the remaining pastry into a 'blanket' large enough to cover the mixture with an excess 1·5cm/¾in all the way round.

11. With a sharp knife cut the corners off the blanket at right angles to the cooked base. Working carefully with a palette knife, lift the base and tuck the pastry blanket underneath it.

12. Repeat with the other three sides. Refrigerate for 10 minutes.

13. Meanwhile shape each of the discarded corners of pastry into a diamond shape. They should resemble leaves so draw in the vein and stems with the back of a knife.

14. Brush with egg, decorate with the pastry leaves and brush again.

15. Bake in the oven for 30 minutes, until the pastry is a golden brown. Serve hot or cold.

Note: If a sauce is required serve plain soured cream, seasoned with salt and pepper.

Serves 4

Stuffed Mullet

900g/2lb grey mullet
1 small can salmon
1 tablespoon fresh chopped
    parsley
Lemon juice
1 level tablespoon fresh white
    crumbs
1 tablespoon cream

1 tablespoon beaten egg
Salt and freshly ground black
    pepper
Oil (preferably olive)
2 bay leaves
Cucumber slices *or* watercress
    to garnish

1. Wash the fish and scrape off the scales. Split down the belly and remove first the entrails and then, opening the fish out more, the backbone and bones: to do this lay the opened fish, skin side up, on a board and press firmly with the heel of your hand. Snip the backbone at tail and head and ease it out, along with its bones.
2. Set the oven to 180°C/350°F, gas mark 4.
3. Skin and bone the salmon and break up the flesh with a fork. Put into a bowl.
4. Add the parsley, lemon juice, breadcrumbs and cream. Add enough beaten egg to hold the stuffing together. Season with salt and pepper.
5. Stuff this mixture into the fish and sew it up with fine string.
6. Brush the fish with oil, season with salt, pepper and lemon juice. Put the bay leaves on top of the fish. Wrap up in oiled foil.
7. Bake until tender – about 35 minutes.
8. Remove the foil and the string. Serve hot or cold, garnished with watercress or cucumber slices.

Note I: Grey mullet is a delicious fish, but not very pretty to look at. Opening the foil at the top to allow the fish to brown while cooking produces a better-looking dish. Alternatively the fish can be coated with sauce just before serving hot, or skinned and coated with creamy mayonnaise when cold. Or a good handful of chopped fresh herbs scattered generously over the fish will greatly improve its appearance.

Note II: A large very fresh mackerel makes a good substitute for grey mullet. Sea bass, though expensive, is the best of all.

Serves 2

Fish Pie

1 kilo/2lb fillet of haddock, whiting, cod *or* a mixture of any of them
425ml/¾ pint milk
½ onion, sliced
6 peppercorns
1 bay leaf
Salt and pepper
5 hardboiled eggs

1 tablespoon chopped fresh parsley
30g/1oz butter
30g/1oz flour
2 tablespoons cream
340g/¾lb mashed potatoes made with 675g/1½lb potatoes (page 228)
Butter

1. Set the oven to 180°C/350°F, gas mark 4.
2. Lay the fish fillets in a roasting pan.
3. Heat the milk with the sliced onion, the peppercorns, bay leaf and a pinch of salt.
4. Pour over the fish and cook in the oven until the fish is firm and creamy-looking (about 25 minutes).
5. Strain off the milk, reserving it for the sauce.
6. Flake the fish into a pie dish.
7. Halve the hardboiled eggs and add them to the fish.
8. Sprinkle over the chopped parsley.
9. Heat the butter in a saucepan, stir in the flour and cook for 30 seconds. Draw off the heat and add the milk.
10. Return to the heat and stir while bringing slowly to the boil. Taste and add salt and pepper as needed. Stir in the cream and pour over the fish, mixing it with a palette knife or spoon.
11. Spread a layer of mashed potatoes on the top and mark with a fork in a criss-cross pattern. Dot a little butter over the surface.

12. Brown in a hot oven (230°C/450°F, gas mark 8) for about 10 minutes.

Serves 6

Fish in Batter

Oil for deep frying
2 teaspoons oil
55g/2oz plain flour
Pinch of salt
1 egg yolk

3 tablespoons warm water
4 cutlets *or* steaks of any
    white fish
Lemon wedges

1. Heat the frying oil until a crumb will sizzle gently in it.
2. Mix the oil with the flour and add the salt, egg yolk and water.
3. Dip the fish into this batter, hold it with tongs and lower it into the hot fat. Increase the temperature of the oil.
4. Cook for 4–10 minutes depending on the thickness of the fish pieces.
5. Drain well on absorbent paper and sprinkle lightly with salt. Serve with wedges of lemon.

Serves 4

Lemon Sole Doria

Three 675g/1½lb lemon soles
1 large cucumber
Seasoned flour

55g/2oz butter
Salt and pepper
Lemon juice

1. Skin and fillet the soles.
2. Peel the cucumber and, using a melon-baller, scoop the flesh into balls. Place these in a pan of boiling salted water for 4–5 minutes. Drain and dry well.
3. Dip the fillets in seasoned flour. Lay them on a plate but do not allow them to touch each other – they will become soggy and will not fry so well.

4. Heat half the butter in a frying pan. When foaming, put in the fillets – not too many at a time. Turn them over when a golden brown; allow about 3 minutes on each side. Dish on to a shallow platter and keep warm.
5. Melt the remaining butter in the pan. Add the cucumber balls and fry quite briskly until a delicate brown. Add salt, pepper and lemon juice. Boil up and tip over the fish. Serve at once.

Serves 4

Salmon Fish Cakes

225g/½lb flaked cooked salmon *or* tinned salmon
225g/½lb cooked mashed potato
Salt and freshly ground black pepper
25g/1oz melted butter
1 level tablespoon chopped fresh parsley
1 egg, beaten
Dry white breadcrumbs
Oil for frying
Parsley sauce (page 262)

1. Mix the fish and potato together. Season well with salt and pepper.
2. Add the melted butter, parsley and enough beaten egg to bind the mixture until soft but not sloppy. Allow to cool.
3. Flour your hands and shape the mixture into 8 flat cakes about 2cm/1in thick. Brush with beaten egg and dip into breadcrumbs.
4. Heat 6 tablespoons of oil in a frying pan and fry until the fish cakes are brown on both sides.
5. Serve with parsley sauce.

Serves 4

Poached Fish, Hot or Cold

Use salmon, haddock etc., either whole or in a large piece. If the fish, or piece of fish, weighs over 1·5 kilos/3lb, double the court bouillon quantities.

The fish

For the court bouillon:

About 1·25 litres/2 pints water
1 teaspoon salt
150ml/¼ pint wine vinegar
1 medium onion, sliced

Bunch of fresh parsley
Sprig of fresh thyme
1 bay leaf
6 peppercorns

For hot fish:
Lemon wedges
Boiled potatoes
Melted butter

For cold fish:
Watercress
Cucumber slices
Mayonnaise

1. Simmer together all the court bouillon ingredients, except the peppercorns, for 50 minutes.
2. Add the peppercorns and simmer for 10 minutes. Strain and allow to cool.
3. Put the fish in the cold court bouillon and heat gently, bringing up to poaching temperature. Do not allow the water to simmer or boil – it should barely move.
4. If the fish is to be served cold, turn the heat off now and leave the fish to cool. It will finish cooking as it does so. If the fish is to be served hot, poach it for 4 minutes to the pound, then carefully lift it out.
5. If the fish is to be served hot skin it carefully if necessary, garnish with lemon wedges, surround with hot potatoes and pass the melted butter separately.

   If to be served cold garnish the skinned fish with watercress and cucumber and hand the mayonnaise separately.

Note: Starting with a cooled court bouillon is considered to produce moister flesh, but it is not always practicable. If the fish has to be put into a hot court bouillon allow 6 minutes to the pound and remove at once.

Grilled Fish Cutlets

This recipe is suitable for brill, cod, halibut, haddock, turbot or salmon cutlets. The pieces of fish should, if possible, be cut to a uniform thickness.

Four 170g/6oz fish cutlets   Freshly ground black pepper
Melted butter   Juice of $\frac{1}{2}$ lemon

For the garnish:
Tender young fresh parsley sprigs *or* watercress
Lemon wedges

1. Heat the grill. Brush the cutlets and the bottom of the grill pan with melted butter. Season the cutlets with pepper and lemon juice. Lay them in the grill tray (not on the wire tray where they might stick).
2. Grill them until pale brown. Turn over and brush with more melted butter. Season again with pepper and lemon juice and grill for a further 3 minutes or until cooked. They will feel firm to the touch, and the flesh will flake easily.
3. Serve on a heated dish with the pan juices poured over, garnished with parsley or watercress and lemon wedges.

Serves 4

POULTRY

Chicken Elizabeth

The Cordon Bleu School devised this dish for the Coronation celebrations in 1953.

1·5 kilos/3lb roasting chicken, washed and dried
Chicken stock *or* water with:
    1 bay leaf, 6 peppercorns,
    2 parsley stalks, 1 slice lemon
    and 2 teaspoons fresh thyme

225ml/8fl.oz Elizabeth sauce (page 267)

To serve:
Rice salad (page *000*)
Bunch of watercress

1. Place the chicken, untrussed, in a saucepan of simmering chicken stock or in a pan of water with flavourings.
2. Cover the pan and cook gently for about 1¼–1½ hours until the chicken is tender and the drumsticks feel loose and wobbly. Remove from the stock and set aside to cool.
3. Take the flesh from the chicken bones, and when it is quite cold mix with the sauce, keeping a little back.
4. Pile the chicken into the middle of a serving dish and coat with the reserved sauce. Surround with the rice salad and garnish with watercress.

Note I: The chicken is removed from the stock to cool, first to prevent further cooking, and secondly to eliminate any possibility of the chicken going bad – a real risk if food is kept at a lukewarm temperature for long periods.

    But there is no question that food cooled in the cooking liquid (providing it is not overcooked) is juicier. The best solution perhaps is to cool the chicken in the stock – but as rapidly as possible: stand the saucepan in a plastic washing-up bowl on the drainer or in the sink and fill the bowl with cold water. Allow the cold tap to trickle steadily into the water making it slowly over-flow and consequently keeping the water renewed and cool. As soon as the stock in the pan and the chicken are cold remove both to the refrigerator until needed.

Note II: It is easier to strip chicken flesh from the bones if this is done while the bird is still lukewarm. But on no account should the sauce be added to the flesh until the chicken is stone cold.

Serves 4

Poached Chicken with Parsley Sauce

2 kilos/4lb chicken, cleaned but not trussed

For the court bouillon:
1 onion, sliced	6 peppercorns
2 carrots	2 sticks celery
2 parsley stalks	2 bay leaves

For the parsley sauce:
30g/1oz butter	2 tablespoons single cream
30g/1oz flour	(optional)
150ml/$\frac{1}{4}$ pint milk	2 tablespoons chopped
About 150 ml/$\frac{1}{4}$ pint chicken	fresh parsley
stock taken from the cooking	Salt and freshly ground
liquid	black pepper

1. Put the chicken into a large suacepan with the onion, carrots, parsley stalks, peppercorns, celery and bay leaves. Half-submerge the bird with water and put on a well-fitting lid.
2. Bring to the boil, reduce the heat and simmer gently for 1$\frac{1}{2}$ hours or until the chicken is cooked. (The legs will feel loose and wobbly when it is.)
3. Remove the chicken from the pan and strain the stock. Cover the chicken to prevent it drying out.

4. Carefully skim the stock of all the fat: when you have spooned off as much grease as possible, lay successive sheets of absorbent paper on the surface of the liquid to remove the rest.

5. Now start the parsley sauce. Melt the butter, add the flour and cook for 1 minute. Remove from the heat.

6. Gradually add the milk and chicken stock, stirring continuously while bringing to the boil.

7. Simmer for 2 minutes, then add the cream (if using) and set aside, covered tightly.

8. Skin the chicken and remove the bones, leaving the flesh in large pieces.

9. Reheat the sauce and add the parsley. Season if necessary with salt or pepper. Add more stock if the sauce is too thick. Add the chicken to the sauce, turn gently, and tip into a serving dish.

Note: Do not add the parsley to the sauce in advance as it will lose its colour.

Serves 4

Chicken Sauté Normande

1·5 kilos/3½lb roasting chicken
45g/1½oz butter
1 shallot, chopped
1 tablespoon Calvados
2 teaspoons flour
225ml/8fl.oz dry cider

150ml/¼ pint chicken stock
Bouquet garni (bay leaf, parsley stalks and 4 sprigs of thyme, tied together with string)
2 tablespoons cream

For the garnish:
2 dessert apples
15g/½oz butter

Chopped fresh parsley

1. Joint the chicken and brown the pieces in the butter.
2. Add the shallot and sauté for 2–3 minutes.
3. Add the Calvados, light it with a match and shake the pan until the flames die down. Remove the chicken joints.

4. Stir in the flour. Add the cider. Blend well and add the stock, bringing slowly to the boil, stirring continuously. Season and add the bouquet of herbs.
5. Replace the chicken, cover and simmer gently for about 40–50 minutes until tender.
6. Meanwhile prepare the garnish by frying slices of peeled apple in the butter until a good brown on each side. Keep warm.
7. When the chicken is tender lift it out and trim the joints neatly. Dish on an ovenproof platter and keep warm.
8. Add the cream to the sauce. Adjust the seasoning and reheat. Spoon over the chicken joints.
9. Garnish with apple slices and sprinkle with chopped parsley.

Serves 4

Coq au Vin

55g/2oz butter
110g/¼lb lean bacon, finely diced
8 button onions
12 button mushrooms
1·5 kilos/3lb roasting chicken, jointed into 8 pieces
290ml/½ pint red wine

Chicken stock
1 small garlic clove, crushed
Bouquet garni (1 bay leaf, 1 sprig each of thyme and parsley and 1 stick of celery, tied together with string)
Salt and pepper
20g/¾oz flour

To serve:
Buttered rice (page 220)
12 small triangular croutons

1 tablespoon chopped fresh parsley

1. Drop the bacon into a pan of boiling water for 30 seconds. Drain and dry well.
2. Put half the butter in a large heavy saucepan and slowly brown the bacon in it.
3. Add the onions, shaking the pan to brown them evenly all over.

4. Add the mushrooms (do not bother to peel them unless the skins are very tough). Fry fast for a further 2 minutes, then lift out all the fried food. Do not wash the pan.

5. Add the remaining butter to the juices in the pan and brown the chicken pieces slowly and well on all sides.

6. Return the vegetables and bacon pieces to the pan, and add the wine and enough stock to nearly cover the chicken pieces.

7. Add the crushed garlic, bouquet of herbs and salt and pepper.

8. With a wooden spoon move the pieces about and stir the sauce until it has come to the boil. Cover with a well-fitting lid and simmer slowly until the onions and chicken are tender (about 1 hour).

9. Remove the bouquet garni. Lift out all the solid ingredients and put them on to a serving dish. Keep them warm while you make the sauce.

10. Skim all the fat from the cooking liquid, putting a table-spoonful of fat into a cup. Measure the liquid and make it up to 290ml/$\frac{1}{2}$ pint with more chicken stock or water. (If there is more than 290ml/$\frac{1}{2}$ pint boil the liquid rapidly to reduce it.)

11. Mix the flour with the fat in the cup, stir well and add a little of the hot cooking liquid to this paste. Return this mixture to the pan and bring gradually to the boil stirring continuously. Simmer for 2 minutes until the sauce is smooth and shiny.

12. Dish the joints on a deep platter, surround with the rice and spoon the sauce over the chicken. Garnish with the croutons and chopped parsley.

Note I: If there is time, marinade the chicken joints in the wine and bouquet garni for a few hours or overnight – this will improve the taste and colour. Dry the joints well before frying, or browning them will be difficult.

Note II: Coq au vin used to be made with a sauce thickened with the blood of the cockerel – rather like jugged hare. But today a freshly-killed chicken with the blood in a jug is very rare. However, if this method is to be followed, omit the flour from the recipe.

When the chicken is cooked stir some of the hot liquid into the blood, then return this 'liaison' to the sauce and stir without boiling. Overheating will cause curdling.

Serves 4

Curried Chicken and Ham Pie

45g/1½oz butter
1 onion, chopped
1 teaspoon curry powder
½ teaspoon turmeric
55g/2oz flour
290ml/½ pint stock reserved after cooking the chicken
150ml/¼ pint creamy milk
1 teaspoon chopped fresh parsley
1 teaspoon chopped fresh mint
Pinch of crushed cardamon seeds
Pinch of dry English mustard

Squeeze of lemon juice
Salt and freshly ground black pepper
2 hardboiled eggs, chopped
110g/¼lb ham, cut into 1cm/½in dice
1·5 kilos/3lb chicken, poached, boned and cut into large chunks
225g/½lb flour-quantity wholemeal pastry (page 370)
1 beaten egg mixed with 1 pinch of salt and 1 teaspoon water (eggwash)

1. Set the oven to 200°C/400°F, gas mark 6.
2. Melt the butter and add the onion. Cook gently until soft but not coloured.
3. Stir in the curry powder and turmeric and cook for 2 minutes.
4. Add the flour and cook over a gentle heat for 2 minutes. Draw the pan off the heat. Add the chicken stock and stir well. Return to the heat. Bring slowly up to the boil, stirring continuously, until you have a thick shiny sauce.
5. Add the milk and stir again until the sauce returns to the boil.
6. Add the parsley, mint, mustard, cardamon seeds and seasoning. Simmer for 2–3 minutes.
7. Taste, adding more salt if necessary, and the lemon juice. Allow to cool.

8. Stir in the hardboiled eggs, the ham and the chicken. Pour the mixture into a pie dish.
9. Roll the pastry on a floured board into a rectangle about ·5cm/¼in thick.
10. Cut a band of pastry slightly wider than the edge of the pie dish. Brush the rim of the dish with water and press on the band of paste. Brush with a little beaten egg or water and lay the pastry lid over the pie. Cut away surplus pastry from the sides with a knife.
11. Press the pie edges together and mark a pattern with a point of a small knife, or pinch with the fingers into a raised border. Shape the pastry trimmings into leaves for decoration.
12. Brush the pastry with beaten egg and decorate with the pastry leaves. Brush again with egg.
13. Bake for 30–35 minutes.

Note: If the pie is not to be baked as soon as it has been assembled it is essential that the curry sauce and the chicken are both completely cold before they are combined. Keep the pie refrigerated or frozen until baking. If frozen thaw in the refrigerator before cooking.

Serves 4

Chicken Croquettes

45g/1½oz butter
1 small onion, chopped
30g/1oz mushrooms, chopped
45g/1½oz flour
290ml/½ pint milk *or* milk and chicken stock mixed
Salt and pepper
1 teaspoon chopped fresh parsley

Oil for deep frying
1 egg yolk
Lemon juice
285g/10oz cooked chicken, diced finely *or* minced
Seasoned flour
1 egg, beaten
Dry white breadcrumbs

1. Melt the butter and add the onion. When the onion is soft but not coloured add the mushrooms and cook for 1 minute.
2. Add the flour and cook, stirring, for 1 minute. Draw the pan off the heat and stir in the milk. Return to the heat and bring slowly up to the boil, stirring continuously. Simmer for 2–3 minutes, season and add the chopped parsley. Remove from the heat and allow to get completely cold.
3. Meanwhile heat the oil until a crumb will sizzle in it.
4. When the sauce is cold beat in the egg yolk, add a squeeze of lemon juice and stir in the chicken flesh.
5. Using floured hands, shape the mixture into cylinders about 3·5cm/1½in long.
6. Coat with beaten egg and dip into breadcrumbs.
7. Deep fry the croquettes until golden brown. Drain well and serve at once.

Serves 4

Lemon Chicken

85g/3oz butter	2 teaspoons sugar
Juice of 2 lemons	Paprika
Three 2-portion spring chickens *or* two 1·5 kilo/3lb roasting chickens	Salt and freshly ground black pepper
	Watercress

1. Melt the butter in a large saucepan (or two if necessary) and add the lemon juice.
2. Lay the chickens in whole and cover with the lid.
3. Cook on a gentle heat for 30 minutes, turning the chickens to brown slightly on all sides. They should now be partially cooked, and the butter and lemon juice in the pan should be brown but not burnt.
4. Take out the birds and split them in two or joint them if large.
5. Heat the grill. Lay the portions of chicken cut-side up on the grill tray. Brush them with some of the lemon juice and

butter from the saucepan(s). Sprinkle with half the sugar and plenty of paprika and pepper. Grill slowly for about 15 minutes or until a really good brown.

6. Turn the joints over and again brush with lemon juice and butter, and sprinkle with sugar, paprika and pepper. Grill for a further 15 minutes until cooked through and very dark – almost, but not quite, charred. Sprinkle with salt.

7. Arrange on a heated dish, pour over the juices from the grill pan and garnish with sprigs of watercress.

Serves 6

Mustard and Paprika Grilled Chicken

4 teaspoons butter
2 tablespoon French mustard
2 kilos/4½lb chicken, cut into
   8 joints
Juice of 1 lemon

1 teaspoon sugar
1 teaspoon paprika
Salt and pepper
Few sprigs watercress

1. Combine the butter and mustard into a paste.
2. Heat the grill to maximum temperature.
3. Spread each chicken joint on the underside (i.e. the non-skin side) with the mustard mixture.
4. Put into the grill pan (without the wire rack). Sprinkle with half the lemon juice, sugar and paprika. Season with salt and pepper.
5. Grill for 15 minutes.
6. Turn the joints over and spread again with the mustard mixture. Sprinkle with the rest of the paprika, lemon juice and sugar. Season with salt and pepper.
7. Return to the grill for 15 minutes until the chicken is cooked and the surface dark and crisp.
8. Arrange the joints neatly on a flat serving dish, pour over the juices from the grill pan and garnish with watercress.

Serves 4

French Roast Chicken

Butter
2 kilos/4½lb roasting chicken
  with giblets
Pepper and salt

Slice of onion
Bay leaf
Few parsley stalks

For the gravy:
About 2 teaspoons flour
200ml/⅓ pint chicken stock *or*
  vegetable water

1. Set the oven to 200°C/400°F, gas mark 6.
2. Smear a little butter all over the chicken. Season inside and out with pepper only (no salt). Put the bird *breast-side-down* in the roasting tin.
3. Put all the giblets (except the liver) and the neck into the pan with the chicken. Add the onion, bay leaf and parsley stalks. Pour in a cup of water. Roast the bird for 30 minutes.
4. Take out, season all over with salt, turn the bird right side up and baste it with the fat and juices from the pan. Return to the oven.
5. Check how the chicken is doing periodically. It will take 60–80 minutes. It is done when the leg bones wobble loosely and independently from the body. Baste occasionally as it cooks, and cover with foil or greaseproof paper if it is browning too much. When the chicken is done remove it to a serving dish, and keep warm while making the gravy.
6. Place the pan with its juices on a low heat on top of the cooker. Skim off most of the fat.
7. Whisk in enough flour to absorb the remaining fat.
8. Add the chicken stock or vegetable water and stir until the sauce boils. Strain into a gravy boat.

Note: If liked the chicken liver can be fried in a little butter, chopped and added to the gravy.

Serves 4

English Roast Chicken

2 kilos/4½lb roasting chicken
Slice of lemon

15g/½oz butter
Freshly ground black pepper

For the stuffing:
30g/1oz butter
1 small onion, finely chopped
55g/2oz fresh breadcrumbs
30g/1oz chopped nuts
1 small cooking apple, grated

2 teaspoons chopped mixed
  fresh herbs
Grated rind ½ lemon
Beaten egg
Salt and pepper

For the garnish:
4 chipolata sausages

4 rashers streaky bacon

For the gravy:
2 teaspoons flour
290ml/½ pint chicken stock
  (made from the neck and
  giblets, see page 285)

To accompany:
Bread sauce (page 270)

1. Set the oven to 200°C/400°F, gas mark 6.
2. Rub the chicken all over with the lemon slice.
3. Start the stuffing by melting the butter and frying the onion until soft but not coloured.
4. Put the breadcrumbs, nuts, cooking apple, herbs and lemon rind together in a mixing bowl.
5. Add the softened onion and enough beaten egg to bind the mixture together. Do not make it too wet. Season to taste.
6. Stuff the chicken from the neck end, making sure the breast is well plumped. Draw the neck skin flap down to cover the stuffing. Secure with a skewer if necessary.
7. Smear a little butter all over the chicken and season with pepper only – salt draws out the juices and will make the bird less moist. Roast for about 1½ hours or until the juices run clear when the thigh is pierced with a skewer.
8. Meanwhile make each chipolata sausage into two cocktail-sized ones by twisting gently in the middle. Take the rind

off the bacon and cut each rasher into two short lengths. Roll them up.

9. When the chicken has had 45 minutes in the oven put the sausages and bacon rolls in the same pan, wedging the bacon rolls so that they cannot come undone.

10. Baste occasionally and check that the sausages and bacon are not sticking to the side of the tin and getting burnt.

11. When the chicken is cooked lift it on to a warm serving dish, surround with the bacon rolls and sausages and keep warm while you make the gravy.

12. Slowly pour off all but a tablespoon of fat from the roasting pan, taking care to keep any juices. Add the flour and stir over heat for 30 seconds. Add the chicken stock and stir until the sauce boils. Simmer for 2 minutes. Taste and add more pepper and salt if necessary. Strain into a gravy boat.

13. Serve the chicken with bread sauce and gravy handed separately.

Note I: English chicken is usually stuffed from the neck end or breast but the stuffing may be put into the body cavity if preferred.

Note II: The chicken looks neater if it is trussed after stuffing, but it is more difficult to get the thighs cooked without the breast drying out if this is done.

Serves 4

Roast Turkey

A large square of fine muslin (butter-muslin) is needed for this recipe.

5·35 kilos/12lb turkey

For the oatmeal stuffing:
1 large onion, finely chopped
340g/¾lb medium oatmeal
1 teaspoon rubbed dried sage
  or 4 leaves fresh sage,
  chopped

170g/6oz shredded beef suet
Salt and freshly ground black
  pepper

For the sausage-meat and chestnut stuffing:
450g/1lb sausage-meat
450g/1lb unsweetened
  chestnut purée
110g/¼lb fresh breadcrumbs

1 large egg
Salt and freshly ground black
  pepper

To prepare the turkey for the oven:
170g/6oz butter
Freshly ground black pepper
Giblets
½ onion

2 bay leaves
Few parsley stalks
290ml/½ pint water

For the garnish:
1 chipolata sausage per person
1 streaky bacon rasher per
  person

For the gravy:
1 tablespoon flour

Stock *or* vegetable water

1. Weigh the turkey. Calculate the cooking time with the help of the chart on page 158.
2. Make the oatmeal stuffing: mix together the onion, oatmeal, sage, and shredded suet. Add enough water just to bind the mixture together, taste and season as required. Stuff into the cavity of the turkey.

3. Make the sausage-meat and chestnut stuffing: mix together the sausage-meat, chestnut purée, breadcrumbs and beaten egg. Taste and season as required. Stuff this into the neck end of the turkey, making sure that the breast is well-plumped. Draw the skin flap down to cover the stuffing. Skewer in place.

4. Set the oven to 180 C/350 F, gas mark 4.

5. Melt the butter and in it soak a very large piece of butter-muslin (about four times the size of the turkey) until all the butter has been completely absorbed.

6. Season the turkey well with pepper only – salt draws out the juices and will make the bird less moist. Put it into a large roasting tin with the giblets (except the liver) and neck, add the onion, bay leaf and parsley stalks and pour in the water. Completely cover the bird with the doubled butter-muslin and roast in the prepared oven for the time calculated (a 5·3 kilo/12lb turkey should take 3–3½ hours).

7. Meanwhile prepare the garnishes: make each chipolata sausage into two cocktail-sized ones by twisting gently in the middle. Take the rind off the bacon. Stretch each rasher slightly with the back of a knife, cut into two and roll up. Put the sausages and bacon rolls into a second roasting pan, with the bacon rolls wedged in so that they cannot unravel. Half an hour before the turkey is done put the sausages and bacon in the oven.

8. When the turkey is cooked – the juices that run out of the thigh when pierced with a skewer should be clear – remove the muslin and lift on to a serving dish. Surround with the bacon and sausages and keep warm while making the gravy.

9. Lift the pan with its juices on to the top of the cooker and skim off the fat. Whisk in the flour and add enough chicken stock or vegetable water to make up to about 425ml/¾ pint. Stir until boiling, then simmer for a few minutes. Taste and add salt and pepper if necessary. Strain into a warm gravy boat.

Serves 12

GAME

Pigeon Pie

3 plump young pigeons
½ carrot, chopped
½ onion, chopped
Pinch of dried marjoram
Pinch of dried thyme
225g/½lb rump steak
Seasoned flour
1 onion, finely chopped
1 tablespoon chopped fresh
  parsley

A little grated lemon rind
55g/2oz button mushrooms
A little nutmeg
Salt and freshly ground black
  pepper
225g/½lb flour-quantity
  rough-puff pastry (page 371)
A little beaten egg mixed with
  1 pinch of salt and 1
  teaspoon of water (eggwash)

1. Set the oven to 200°C/400°F, gas mark 6.
2. Separate the breasts from pigeons with a small, very sharp knife by running the knife along the length of the breast bone and carefully scraping downwards against the rib cage, removing each breast separately.
3. Treat the legs in the same way, using quick strokes of the knife along the bones. Cube the pigeon flesh.
4. Place the bones and carcass in a small saucepan with the carrot, onion and herbs. Cover with water and bring to the boil. Skim and simmer for 30 minutes to make a good strong stock.
5. Cut the rump steak into very small cubes and toss them in seasoned flour.
6. Slice the mushrooms.
7. Mix the steak, onion, pigeons and mushrooms with the lemon rind and parsley and season with nutmeg, salt and pepper.
8. Turn the mixture into the pie dish and add enough stock to come three-quarters of the way up the dish.

9. Roll out the pastry to about the thickness of a penny. Cover the pie dish with pastry and brush with eggwash.

10. Place the pie in the pre-heated oven and cook for 20–25 minutes (this will cook the pastry).

11. Lower the heat to 140°C/275°F, gas mark 1, to cook the meat very slowly for 1½ hours.

12. After 30 minutes place a piece of wet greaseproof paper over the pastry to prevent burning. Serve hot.

Serves 4

Venison Casserole

675g/1½lb venison

For the marinade:

1 onion, sliced	Slice of lemon
1 carrot, sliced	1 bay leaf
Stick of celery, sliced	290ml/½ pint red wine
1 garlic clove	2 tablespoons wine vinegar
6 juniper berries	6 peppercorns

For the casserole:

1 tablespoon oil	1 tablespoon cranberry jam
30g/1oz butter	Salt and freshly ground black
110g/¼lb onions, peeled	pepper
110g/¼lb button mushrooms	110g/¼lb cooked whole
30g/1oz flour	chestnuts
150ml/¼ pint beef stock	Chopped fresh parsley
1 garlic clove, crushed	

1. Cut the venison into 5cm/2in cubes, trimming away any tough membrane or sinew.

2. Mix the ingredients for the marinade together and add the meat. Mix well, cover and leave in a cool place or in the refrigerator overnight.

3. Set the oven to 170°C/325°F, gas mark 3.
4. Lift out the venison cubes and pat dry with absorbent paper. Strain the marinade, reserving the liquid for cooking.
5. Heat half the oil in a heavy saucepan and in it brown the cubes of meat well, frying a few at a time. Lay them in a casserole. If the bottom of the pan becomes brown or too dry, pour in a little of the strained marinade, swish it about, scraping off the sediment stuck to the bottom, and pour over the cubes of meat. Then heat a little more oil and continue browning the meat.
6. When all the meat has been browned, repeat the déglaçage (boiling up with a little marinade and scraping the bottom of the pan).
7. Now melt the butter and fry the onions until they are pale brown all over. Add the mushrooms and continue cooking for 2 minutes.
8. Stir in the flour, add the rest of the marinade and the beef stock and stir until boiling, again scraping the bottom of the pan. When boiling, pour over the venison.
9. Add the crushed garlic and the cranberry jam. Season with salt and pepper.
10. Cover the casserole and place in the heated oven for about 1½ hours or until the meat is really tender.
11. Lift the venison pieces, mushrooms and onions with a perforated spoon into a serving dish.
12. Boil the sauce fast until reduced to a shiny, almost syrupy, consistency. Add the chestnuts and simmer gently for 5 minutes.
13. Pour the sauce over the venison and serve garnished with chopped parsley.

Serves 4

Peppered Venison Steak

Four 140g/5oz venison collops
  (steaks) cut from the fillet
2 tablespoons whole
  peppercorns
30g/1oz unsalted butter

1 tablespoon oil
  (preferably olive)
2 tablespoons brandy
2 tablespoons double cream
Salt

1. Wipe the steaks and trim off any gristle.
2. Crush the peppercorns coarsely in a mortar or under a rolling pin and press them into the surface of the meat on both sides.
3. Cover the steaks and leave them for 2 hours at room temperature for the flavour to penetrate the meat.
4. Heat the oil in a heavy-based pan, add the butter and when it is foaming fry the steaks as fast as you dare. Get them to the degree you like them (generally they need about 2 minutes per side for blue, 3 minutes for rare, 3½ minutes for medium and 4 minutes for well done).
5. Pour in the brandy and set it alight. Add the cream and a pinch of salt. Mix the contents of the pan around a bit, scraping up any sediment stuck to the bottom.
6. Place the steaks on a heated platter.
7. Boil up the sauce again and pour over the meat. Serve at once.

Note I: If the venison is very fresh and you want a gamier taste, marinate it for two days in red wine and oil (equal quantities), flavoured with sliced onion, six juniper berries and a bay leaf. Dry well before frying.

Serves 4

Roast Woodcock

4 woodcock
4 rashers bacon
Salt and freshly ground black
  pepper
4 rounds white bread 13cm/5in
  in diameter, toasted on one
  side (croutes, page 303)

1 teaspoon flour
150ml/¼ pint stock
Squeeze lemon juice
Watercress to garnish

1. Pluck the woodcock. Remove the heads and draw the gizzards through the neck openings, but do not draw entrails. Truss neatly.
2. Set the oven to 180°C/350°F, gas mark 4.
3. Cover the birds with rashers of bacon and season well. Place in a roasting pan and roast for about 25 minutes, removing the bacon after 20 minutes to allow the breasts to brown thoroughly.
4. Spread the entrails on the untoasted side of the bread and place a bird on top of each. Keep warm while you prepare the gravy.
5. Tip off all except a scant tablespoon of the fat from the roasting pan.
6. Add the flour and cook for 1 minute until a russet brown.
7. Pour in the stock and bring up to the boil, stirring continuously with a spoon, scraping the bottom of the pan to loosen the sediment as it comes to the boil.
8. Season with salt, pepper and lemon juice. Strain the gravy into a warmed boat.
9. Place the woodcock on a serving dish and garnish with watercress.

Serves 4

Croutes for Roast Game Birds

When roasting small game birds such as snipe or woodcock, the 'trail' or entrails is left inside and only the gizzard removed. After roasting, the liver, juices etc. are spread on the uncooked side of a slice of bread which has been fried or toasted on one side only. The roasted bird is served on this croute.

Larger birds like pheasant and grouse are drawn before roasting, but the liver may be returned to the body cavity to cook with the bird. This, plus any other scrapings from the inside of the bird, is spread on the uncooked side of the croute, which is then cut diagonally in half and served as a garnish to the whole roast bird.

Fried Crumbs
(for serving with roast game birds)

55g/2oz butter
4 tablespoons dry white
    breadcrumbs

Melt the butter and very slowly fry the crumbs in it until they have absorbed most of the butter, and are golden in colour and crisp. Serve in a warm bowl, handed to the diners with the sauce or sauces.

Note: Fresh white crumbs can be used, but rather more butter will be needed as they are very absorbent, and great care should be taken to fry slowly so that the crumbs become crisp before they turn brown.

Roast Pheasant with Sauerkraut

2 medium pheasants
Salt and pepper
Butter

2 strips of pork fat
6 juniper berries
225g/½lb sauerkraut

For the gravy:
2 teaspoons flour
1 tablespoon ruby port

1 teaspoon redcurrant jelly

1. Wipe the birds and remove any remaining feathers.
2. Set the oven to 220°C/425°F, gas mark 7.
3. Season the birds inside and put a knob of butter in the body cavity.
4. Tie slices of pork fat over the breasts (this is called barding and is to prevent drying out during cooking).
5. Spread a little butter over the rest of the birds and season with salt, pepper and crushed juniper berries.
6. Place in a roasting tin, pour 0·5cm/¼in water into the bottom of the tin and cook for about 50–60 minutes, basting frequently.
7. Drain the sauerkraut. Heat it with a good 30g/1oz of butter over gentle heat.
8. When cooked lift the pheasants out of the tin and keep warm while you make the gravy.
9. Sprinkle the flour into the roasting juices and add the port and the redcurrant jelly.
10. Place the roasting pan over heat and stir and scrape the bottom until the liquid boils.
11. Add a little more water or stock if it is too thick. Boil for 2 minutes, then season well and strain into a warmed gravy boat.
12. Serve the pheasants surrounded with sauerkraut. Hand the gravy separately.

Serves 4–5

BEEF

Meat Loaf

340g/¾lb minced beef
340g/¾lb sausage meat
225g/½lb lamb's liver
1 medium onion, finely
  chopped
1 small egg, beaten
3 tablespoons fresh white
  breadcrumbs

1 tablespoon chopped fresh
  parsley
Small pinch of thyme
Small glass red wine
½ teaspoon chopped fresh basil
Salt and pepper
3 hardboiled eggs

1. Grease a large pudding basin or cake tin.
2. Mix all the ingredients except the hardboiled eggs together
   with your hand.
3. Season with salt and pepper.
4. Pile half the mixture into the pudding basin, lay on the hardboiled eggs and fill with the remaining mixture.
5. Cover with greaseproof paper and tin foil. Tie down with
   string.
6. Cook in a steamer or covered saucepan half-filled with water
   for 1½–2 hours, topping up the boiling water with more
   as and when necessary.
7. Serve hot or cold.

Note: If baking is preferred the mixture may be cooked in a bread
tin, well covered with foil. The tin should stand in a roasting pan
half-filled with boiling water and cook for 1½ hours at 180°C/
350°F, gas mark 4.

Serves 4

Steak and Kidney Pudding

675/1½lb chuck steak
225g/½lb ox kidney
Flour
Salt and pepper
340g/¾lb flour-quantity suet
  pastry (page 370)

2 teaspoons chopped onions
2 teaspoons chopped fresh
  parsley

1. Cut the steak into cubes about 1·5cm/¾in square.
2. Chop the kidney, discarding any sinew.
3. Place both steak and kidney in a large sieve. Pour over flour and shake until the meat is lightly coated.
4. On a floured surface, roll out two-thirds of the suet pastry into a round about 1cm/½in thick. Flour the surface lightly to stop it sticking together when folded. Fold the pastry over to form a half-moon shape. Place the pastry with the straight side away from you and roll it lightly so that the straight side becomes curved and the whole rounded again. Now separate the layers, and you should have a bag, roughly the shape of a 1 kilo/2lb pudding basin. Use it to line the basin, easing the pastry where necessary to fit, and trimming off the top so that 1cm/½in sticks up over the edge.
5. Fill the lined basin with the meat, sprinkling plenty of seasoning, chopped onion and parsley in between the layers.
6. Add water to come three-quarters of the way up the meat.
7. Roll the remaining third of suet pastry 0·5cm/¼in thick, and large enough to just cover the pudding filling. Put in place, wet the edges and press them together securely.
8. Cover the pudding with a double piece of greaseproof paper, pleated down the centre (this is to allow room for the pastry to expand), and a similarly pleated piece of foil. Tie down with string.
9. Place in a saucepan of boiling water with tightly closed lid, or in a steamer, for 4 hours, taking care to top up with boiling water occasionally.
10. Remove the paper and tin foil and serve the pudding from the bowl.

Note I: Traditionally, steak and kidney puddings served from the bowl are presented wrapped in a white linen napkin.

Note II: As the filling of the pudding may, with long cooking, dry out somewhat, it is worth having a gravy boat of hot beef stock handy to moisten the meat when serving.

Serves 4

Steak and Kidney Pie (*I*)
(with pastry and filling cooked together)

675g/1½lb chuck steak	Chopped fresh parsley
225g/½lb ox kidney	225g/½lb flour-quantity
Flour	rough-puff pastry (page 371)
Salt and pepper	Beaten egg
1 onion, finely chopped	150ml/¼ pint beef stock

1. Preheat the oven to 220°C/425°F, gas mark 7.
2. Trim away the excess fat from the steak and cut the meat into cubes about 2·5cm/1in square.
3. Slice the kidneys very finely, discarding any sinew.
4. Place the meat in a large sieve and pour a small cup of flour over it. Shake thoroughly so that the meat is lightly coated.
5. Pack the meat and onions into a pie dish, adding salt, pepper and parsley as you go. Pour in enough water to come half-way up the pie dish.
6. Roll out the pastry to the thickness of a penny. Cut a long strip just wider than the rim of the pie dish, brush the dish with water and press down the strip.
7. Brush the strip with water and lay over the sheet of pastry. Press it down firmly. Cut away any excess pastry.
8. Cut a 1cm/½in hole in the centre of the pie top and cover loosely with a leaf-shaped piece of pastry (the hole is to allow the escape of steam).
9. Decorate the top with more pastry leaves. Brush all over with egg. Leave in the refrigerator to relax for 10 minutes.

10. Bake in the oven for 30 minutes or until the pastry is well risen and golden brown.

11. Lower the heat to 180°C/350°F, gas mark 4. Wrap the whole pie in wet brown or greaseproof paper and continue to cook for a further 2 hours. (The wrapping is to prevent the pastry burning while the meat cooks.)

12. Before serving remove the decoration over the hole in the pastry, test that the meat is tender with a skewer, and carefully fill the pie with the beef stock, heated to boiling point. Return the pastry leaf and serve.

Serves 4

Steak and Kidney Pie (II)
(with pre-cooked filling)

675g/1½ lb chuck steak
225g/½lb ox kidney
Oil *or* dripping
1 onion, finely chopped
30g/1oz flour
425ml/¾ pint beef stock

Salt and pepper
1 tablespoon chopped fresh parsley
225g/½lb flour-quantity rough-puff pastry (page 371)
Beaten egg

1. Trim away the excess fat from the steak and cut the meat into cubes about 2·5cm/1in square. Slice the kidneys finely, discarding any sinew.

2. Heat the oil or dripping in a frying pan and brown a few pieces of meat at a time until well browned all over, putting them on to a plate as they are done. Fry the onion in the same fat until soft and brown.

3. Stir in the flour and cook for 1 minute. Gradually add the stock, stirring continuously and scraping any sediment from the bottom of the pan. Bring to the boil and simmer for 1 minute. Return the meat to the pan, season with salt and pepper and simmer slowly until the meat is tender (about 2 hours). Add the chopped parsley.

4. If the sauce is greasy skim off the fat; if it is too thin remove the meat to a pie dish and boil the sauce rapidly until syrupy.

Pour the sauce over the meat and leave to get completely cold.

5. Set the oven to 200°C/400°F, gas mark 6.

6. Roll out the pastry to the thickness of a penny. Cut a long strip just wider than the rim of the pie dish, brush the lip of the dish with water and press down the strip.

7. Brush the strip with water and lay over the sheet of pastry. Press it down firmly. Cut away any excess pastry.

8. Cut a 1cm/½in hole in the centre of the pie-top and cover loosely with a leaf-shaped piece of pastry (the hole is to allow the escape of steam).

9. Decorate the top with more pastry leaves. Brush all over with egg. Leave in the refrigerator to relax for 10 minutes.

10. Bake in the oven for 30 minutes, or until the pastry is well risen and golden brown.

Serves 4

Pancake Pie

8 French pancakes (page 384)
2 teaspoons beef dripping
450g/1lb minced beef
1 large onion, chopped
Stick of celery, chopped
3 rashers rindless streaky
  bacon, diced
1 garlic clove, crushed
2 teaspoons flour
150ml/¼ pint stock
1 tablespoon madeira
2 teaspoons tomato purée
Pinch of thyme
1 tablespoon chopped fresh
  parsley
Salt and freshly ground black
  pepper
Soured cream sauce (page 310)

1. Make the pancake batter first and allow it to stand while preparing the meat sauce. (While the sauce simmers fry the pancakes. Keep them warm in the folds of a tea-towel in a low oven while finishing off the sauce.)

2. Melt half the dripping in a pan and when hot add some of the mince and brown thoroughly.

3. Lift out with a perforated spoon and place in a saucepan.

4. Fry the remaining mince, adding more fat if and when necessary, and transfer this to the saucepan too.

5. When all the mince has been fried, fry the onion, celery, bacon and garlic until just turning brown.

6. Add the flour and cook gently, stirring, for 1 minute.

7. Stir in the stock and madeira and bring to the boil, stirring continuously. Pour this into the saucepan.

8. Add the tomato purée, thyme, half the parsley and season with salt and pepper. Simmer gently for about 45 minutes (or until thick and syrupy).

9. When the meat sauce is cooked, reduce by rapid boiling if it is too runny. Season well.

10. Place one pancake on the serving dish, spoon over some meat sauce and cover with a second pancake.

11. Continue to layer the meat sauce and pancakes, finishing with a layer of meat sauce.

12. Sprinkle with the remaining parsley and serve immediately, with soured cream sauce offered separately.

Serves 4

Soured Cream Sauce

½ carton yoghurt
½ carton soured cream

Salt and pepper
½ garlic clove, crushed

Mix all ingredients together.

Shepherd's Pie or Cottage Pie

1 onion
1 carrot
Stick of celery
2 teaspoons beef dripping
675/1½lb minced beef
2 teaspoons flour

290ml/½ pint beef stock
1 bay leaf
1 teaspoon Worcestershire
 sauce (optional)
1 teaspoon tomato purée
Salt and pepper

For the top:
340g/¾lb mashed potato
 (page 228) made from
 675g/1½lb freshly cooked
 potatoes

Butter

1. Finely chop the onion, carrot and celery.
2. Heat the dripping in a large frying pan and when hot add half the mince. Brown well all over.
3. Remove with a draining spoon and place in a saucepan.
4. Add the remaining mince to the frying pan and fry until well browned. Lift out and add to the first batch.
5. Lower the heat and add the onion, carrot and celery.
6. When the vegetables are lightly browned stir in the flour and cook for a further minute.
7. Add the beef stock and slowly bring to the boil, stirring continuously. Add this to the saucepan.
8. Now add the bay leaf, Worcestershire sauce, tomato purée and seasoning.
9. Set the saucepan on a medium heat to simmer. Cover and leave to cook for 45–50 minutes.
10. Heat the oven to 200°C/400°F, gas mark 6.
11. Remove the bay leaf from the mince and tip the meat into a pie dish, reserving some of the liquid if the mixture is very runny.
12. When slightly cooled spread the potato on top.
13. Fork it up to leave the surface rough, or draw the fork over the surface to mark with a pattern.

14.   Dot the top with butter. Place in the oven for 20–30 minutes or until the potato is brown and crusty.

Note I: The confusion over Cottage Pie and Shepherd's Pie is complete. Cottage pie used to denote the use of leftover cooked meat, either beef or mutton. 'Shepherd's', naturally enough, meant that mutton was the meat used, usually pre-cooked. But to-day either name seems to mean either beef or lamb, made with leftover or fresh meat, the only certainty being the mashed potato top.

Note II: To make a cottage pie with leftover meat, simply mince the meat, season well with salt, pepper and Worcestershire sauce, add tomato purée and some fried onions, with any leftover gravy to moisten. Top with mashed potato, brush with butter and reheat.

Serves 4–5

Boiled Silverside

900g/2lb piece of salt silverside	4 medium onions
4 pieces of marrow bone	4 large carrots, quartered
Bouquet garni of 1 bay leaf, 2 parsley stalks, 6 peppercorns, 1 small onion, tied in muslin	2 turnips, quartered
	8 dumplings (page 313)
	Chopped fresh parsley

1.   Soak the beef in cold unsalted water for about 3 hours.
2.   Put the bones and beef in a large pan of fresh unsalted water and bring slowly to the boil, skimming as the scum rises to the surface.
3.   When simmering add the bouquet garni and half cover the pan. Simmer for 30 minutes to the pound. Remove the bouquet garni and skim off any fat.
4.   Now add the vegetables and simmer for an hour or until the meat and vegetables are tender.
5.   Meanwhile cook the dumplings: if there is room in the pot,

sink them in the liquid 20 minutes before the end of the cooking time. If not, take some of the stock (topping up with boiling water if necessary) and boil them in a separate saucepan.

6. Place the beef on a large serving dish. Surround it with the vegetables, dumplings, and marrow bones. Cover and keep warm.
7. Taste the stock. If weak-flavoured reduce by rapid boiling. Skim if necessary.
8. Ladle a cupful or so of hot liquid over the meat and vegetables, sprinkle with chopped parsley and serve at once. Hand more liquid separately in a sauceboat.

Serves 4

Dumplings

225g/½lb self-raising flour
Pinch of salt
110g/¼lb suet

About 5 tablespoons cold water
570ml/1 pint beef stock

1. Sift the flour and salt into a bowl. Mix in the suet.
2. Make a dip or 'well' in the flour. Add a little water to the well and using a palette knife mix in the surrounding flour. Draw the mixture together with your hands and knead gently to a soft dough.
3. With floured hands shape the mixture into dumplings about the size of a ping-pong ball.
4. Drop the dumplings into a pan of simmering beef stock, cover and cook for 20–25 minutes.
5. Remove with a perforated spoon. They should be light, not too doughy.

Serves 4

Beef Curry

1 tablespoon oil	1 tablespoon flour
900g/2lb chuck steak, cut in 5cm/2in cubes	425ml/¾ pint stock
1 large onion, finely chopped	2 tablespoons tomato purée
1 dessert apple, peeled and chopped	Salt and freshly ground black pepper
3 tablespoons curry powder	Squeeze of lemon
	1 tablespoon mango chutney

1. Heat the oil and fry the steak chunks, a few at a time, until well browned all over, putting them on to a plate as they are done.
2. Fry the onion in the same oil (adding a little more if necessary) until just turning colour, then add the apple.
3. Mix the curry powder and flour together, add it to the pan, and stir for 1–2 minutes.
4. Gradually add the stock and tomato purée and bring slowly to the boil, stirring all the time.
5. Add salt, pepper, a squeeze of lemon juice and the chutney.
6. Put back the meat, cover with the lid and simmer very slowly until the meat is tender – about 2 hours. Curry is best cooked so slowly that the sauce scarcely moves, or done in a slow oven (150 C/300 F, gas mark 2) for 3 hours or so.

Note: Curries are said to better eaten on the day after cooking when the meat has had time to absorb the sauce flavour.

Serves 4

ACCOMPANIMENTS FOR CURRIES

Banana and Coconut

Chop 2 bananas and squeeze the juice of 1 lemon over them.
Mix in 2 tablespoons of desiccated coconut.

Tomato and Onion

Chop 1 large onion and 3 peeled tomatoes finely. Mix them
together with salt and pepper, 1 tablespoon of olive oil and a
squeeze of lemon.

Chutney and Cucumber

Mix 1 cupful of chopped cucumber into the same amount of sweet
chutney (such as mango or apple).

Green Pepper, Apple and Raisin

Chop equal quantities of apple and green pepper finely, or mince
them. Add 1 tablespoon of raisins *or* sultanas and salt, pepper,
lemon juice, cayenne and sugar to taste.

Poppadums

These are large flat wafers, generally bought in boxes. They are
heated in the oven or under the grill, or fried in hot fat until crisp.
They can be bought spiced or plain.

Family Beef Stew

900g/2lb stewing beef
2 large mild onions, peeled
6 medium carrots, peeled
2 medium turnips, peeled
55g/2oz dripping
570ml/1 pint beef stock

Salt and pepper
1 bay leaf
2 parsley stalks
Pinch of fresh thyme
30g/1oz pearl barley

1. Set the oven to 200°C/400°F, gas mark 6.
2. Remove gristle and excess fat from the meat and cut it into 2·5cm/1in cubes.
3. Thinly slice the onions and carrots and cut the turnip into small cubes.
4. Melt half of the dripping in a sauté pan. Brown the beef cubes well on all sides, a few at a time, and transfer to an ovenproof casserole. If the bottom of the pan becomes too brown and sticky pour in a little stock and swish it about, scraping the sediment from the bottom of the pan. Pour this into the casserole, and then melt a little more fat and continue browning the meat until all is transferred to the casserole.
5. Fry the onion slices until golden brown and add them to the casserole. Lightly fry the carrot and turnip and place them in the casserole.
6. Pour the stock into the pan and bring to the boil, scraping any remaining sediment from the bottom. Stir in the seasoning, bay leaf, parsley stalks, thyme and barley and pour on to the meat.
7. Cover the casserole and place in the oven. After 20 minutes reduce the heat to 170°C/325°F, gas mark 3, and cook for another 2 hours. Skim off any excess fat.

Note: This stew is even better if kept for a day before eating – the barley swells up even more and the flavour improves.

Serves 4

Fried Steak

Sirloin steak cut in 2·5cm/1in slices

Freshly ground black pepper
Oil *or* dripping

For the herb butter:
Butter
Lemon juice
Chopped fresh parsley

Chopped fresh tarragon (optional)
Salt and pepper

1. Season the steak with pepper. Leave to warm to room temperature if it has been chilled. Do not be tempted to salt it, as this will draw out the juices.
2. Brush a frying pan out with a little oil or dripping and place over good heat until it is beginning to smoke.
3. Brown the steak quickly on both sides. For a blue or rare steak keep the heat fierce for the whole cooking time. For better done steaks lower the temperature to moderate after the initial good browning. Length of cooking time varies according to the thickness of the meat, the type of steak, the degree of heat, the weight of the frying pan etc. With experience it is possible to tell from the feel of the steak how well cooked it is – it feels very soft when blue, very firm, almost tough, when well done. But, if you want to be certain, there is nothing for it but to cut a tiny slit in the fattest part of the meat, and take a look. Don't do this until you are fairly sure the steak is ready – too many cuts will mean loss of juices. Cooking times, assuming a 2·5cm/1in steak and a good hot pan, would be about:

blue steak	2 minutes per side
rare steak	2½ minutes per side
medium rare	3 minutes per side
medium steak	3½ minutes per side
well done steak	4½ minutes per side

4. For the herb butter: simply cream about 15g/½oz butter per person and flavour it with lemon juice, chopped herbs, salt

and pepper. Shape into a block or roll and wrap in wet greaseproof paper or foil. Chill well.

5. Serve the steaks topped with a slice of herb butter.

Note: Steaks are sometimes lightly beaten with a rolling pin or mallet to tenderize them. But as this breaks the flesh, allowing the juices to run out during cooking, it is not advisable unless the steak is likely to be very tough.

Hamburgers

450g/1lb minced lean beef steak
1 small onion, grated
2 tablespoons parsley *or* mixed herbs

1 teaspoon Worcestershire sauce (optional)
Seasoning

1. Heat the grill.
2. Mix all the ingredients together with a fork. Taste for seasoning.
3. With floured hands shape the meat into flattish rounds, making sure that they are equal in size.
4. Grill steadily, turning once. Allow 3 minutes each side for rare burgers, 5 for well done.
5. Serve on a hot dish, or between heated halves of soft buns.

Note: See below for pickles and relishes to serve with the burgers.

Serves 4

RELISHES FOR HAMBURGERS

Hamburgers are usually served with a selection of mustard, chopped raw onion, bottled dill pickles and tomato ketchup. But these alternatives are good too.

Cucumber and Dill Relish

½ cucumber
1 small onion

Sprig of fresh dill
Salt and pepper

1. Finely dice the cucumber and onion.
2. Coarsely chop the dill.
3. Mix together and season with salt and pepper.

Corn and Pepper Relish

2 sweetcorn cobs *or* 1 small
   packet frozen corn
1 red pepper

½ chilli pepper, mashed to a
   paste
Salt and pepper

1. If using fresh corn cook for 10 minutes in boiling water and
   scrape the kernels from the cob. If using frozen corn place
   in boiling water for 5 minutes and drain.
2. Finely chop the red pepper.
3. Mix everything together and add salt and pepper.

Fresh Peach and Ginger Pickle

2 fresh peaches
2 teaspoons grated fresh ginger
4 tablespoons tarragon vinegar
2 tablespoons water

1 teaspoon cinnamon
4 cloves
55g/2oz sugar

1. Dip the peaches into boiling water for 6 seconds.
2. Peel the peaches, cut them in half and remove the stones.
   Chop finely.
3. Place in a pan with the rest of the ingredients and cover.
   Slowly bring to the boil and simmer gently for 10 minutes.

4. Remove the lid and continue to cook until the liquid becomes syrupy.
5. Remove the cloves and allow to cool before serving.

Mixed Grill

Grilling times depend on the thickness of the foods, and the temperature of the grill. The suggestions below should be regarded as guidelines only.

110g/¼lb rump *or* sirloin steak
55g/2oz lambs' *or* calves' liver
1 chipolata sausage
1 lamb's kidney
1 rasher back bacon
1 whole tomato
2 large flat mushrooms
Salt and freshly ground black pepper
Watercress to garnish

When preparing a mixed grill, begin grilling the meat that will take the longest time to cook and then gradually add the other ingredients so that everything is done at the same time.

Steak: Flatten the steak slightly, brush it with oil and season with pepper. Do not use salt as this drains out the juices and makes the meat tough and dry.

Liver: Remove the membrane that surrounds the liver, cut into thin pieces, brush with oil and season with pepper.

Chipolata sausages: Prick with a fork to allow the fat to escape during cooking. Do not add any extra fat.

Kidney: Skin and halve the kidney, snipping out the 'core'. Brush with oil and season with pepper.

Bacon: Cut off the rind. Put the bacon on a board and, using the back of a knife, stretch it. This helps to prevent shrinking and curling during grilling.

Tomato: Cut in half, brush with a little oil and season with salt and pepper.

Mushrooms: Wipe but do not peel the mushrooms, cut the stalk to ·5cm/¼in, brush with oil and season with salt and pepper.

1. Heat the grill.
2. When very hot, place the chipolata sausage under it.
3. After 1 minute add the liver and the kidney.
4. After a further minute add the steak and bacon. Cook for 1 minute.
5. Turn the sausage and steak over and cook for a further minute.
6. Add the tomatoes and mushrooms and grill for a further 2 minutes or so, turning the tomatoes over and turning the sausage if necessary.
7. As the items are ready put them on a heated platter, draining the fat from the sausage and bacon carefully. Just before serving season with salt and garnish with a sprig of watercress.

Note: Mixed grill is traditionally served with potato chips or straw potatoes.

Serves 1

Grilled Steak

Cooking times for different kinds of grilled steak are given on pages 117–18.

Steaks	Salt
Coarsely ground black pepper	Maître d'hôtel butter (see
Butter	below)

1. Have the steaks at room temperature. Press coarsely ground pepper into the surface.
2. Heat the grill. Do not start cooking until it is at maximum temperature.
3. Brush the grill rack with melted butter, and the steak too if

liked (this is not strictly necessary, and it adds calories for the diet-conscious, but improves the flavour).

4. Grill to the required degree, keeping the pan close to the heat.
5. Serve each steak sprinkled with salt and topped with a 15g/½oz pat of maître d'hôtel butter.

Maître d'Hôtel Butter

Butter
Chopped fresh parsley
Chopped fresh tarragon
  (optional)

Salt and pepper
Squeeze of lemon

1. Flavour the butter with the other ingredients, beating to a soft paste.
2. Spoon the mixture on to a piece of foil or greaseproof paper and shape into a block or long sausage.
3. Wrap up and chill, or freeze, until needed.

English Roast Beef

2·5 kilos/5½lb sirloin or rib
  roast of beef
4 tablespoons dripping
A little dry mustard

Salt and freshly ground black
  pepper
Horseradish cream (page 269)

1. Set the oven to 220°C/425°F, gas mark 7.
2. Place the beef on a rack and smear with the dripping. Sprinkle over a little mustard and plenty of pepper, but no salt.
3. Place the rack and beef over a roasting pan and roast for 20 minutes.
4. Turn the oven down to 165°C/325°F, gas mark 3 and cook slowly for 20 minutes per 0·5 kilo/1lb for medium-rare meat or 15 minutes for very rare.

5.   Sprinkle the beef with salt just before serving.

Note I: If allowed to cool for 20 minutes before serving, the meat is easier to carve, but, naturally, not so hot. Serve the horseradish cream separately.

Note II: If thickened gravy is required in addition to 'God's gravy' – the juices that will run from the meat before and during carving – roast the joint directly in the pan, not on a rack over it. Then pour off most of the dripping, taking care not to lose any brown juices. Add enough flour (usually about 2 teaspoons) to the remaining fat and juices and stir over the heat until the flour has browned, and any sediment from the bottom of the pan is loosened. Add up to 290ml/$\frac{1}{2}$ pint of stock and stir or whisk until boiling. Add salt and pepper to taste.

Serves 10

Yorkshire Pudding

125g/4$\frac{1}{2}$oz plain flour
Good pinch of salt
2 eggs

290ml/$\frac{1}{2}$ pint milk *or* milk and
    water mixed
4 tablespoons good beef
    dripping

1.   Sift the flour and salt into a bowl. Make a well in the centre and break the eggs into it.
2.   With a wooden spoon beat the eggs, gradually drawing in more flour to the centre.
3.   Beat in the milk little by little until the batter is smooth. Leave for 30 minutes before use.
4.   Heat the oven to 200°C/400°F, gas mark 6.
5.   Heat the dripping until smoking hot in a roasting tin, oven-proof dish or Yorkshire-pudding tin.
6.   Pour in the batter. Bake for 30 minutes or until the pudding is risen and golden.

Note I: If the pudding is to be served with roast beef it is a good idea to place the pudding between the open rack holding the beef, and the dripping pan below. In this way any dripping juices from the beef will fall on to the pudding and improve its flavour. Alternatively the batter can be poured directly into the hot dripping pan. The oven temperature must be turned up to 200°C/400°F, gas mark 6 when the pudding is put in. The pudding should go in half an hour before the beef will be ready if it is to be cooked in a single tin or dish, and 15 minutes before if individual patty moulds are used.

Note II: If making the pudding as a sweet course use flavourless oil instead of dripping and serve with honey, treacle or maple syrup.

Serves 4

LAMB

Moussaka

340g/¾lb aubergines
225g/½lb can tomatoes
1 onion, finely chopped
1 garlic clove, crushed
Oil for frying
450g/1lb cooked, minced lamb
2 teaspoons chopped fresh marjoram

2 teaspoons chopped fresh parsley
1 bay leaf
Pinch of ground nutmeg
2 teaspoons flour
Salt and freshly ground black pepper
340g/¾lb courgettes

For the topping:
20g/¾oz butter
20g/¾oz flour
290ml/½ pint milk
1 bay leaf

1 egg yolk
1 tablespoon cream
55g/2oz grated Gruyère *or* strong Cheddar cheese

1. Slice the aubergines into 1cm/½in slices, score the flesh with a sharp knife and sprinkle with salt. Leave for half an hour.

2. Roughly chop or cut up the tinned tomatoes. Keep the juice.

3. Meanwhile, in a heavy saucepan over gentle heat, soften the onions and garlic in one tablespoon of oil.

4. Add the meat, herbs, bay leaf and nutmeg to the onions. Stir in the flour and pour in the tomatoes and their juice. Bring to the boil, stirring, and simmer for 2–3 minutes. Season well.

5. Rinse and wipe the aubergines dry. Slice the courgettes.

6. Heat 2 tablespoons of oil in a frying pan. Fry first the courgettes, then the aubergines on both sides until brown, heating up more oil as necessary. As the courgettes are done put them into the bottom of a shallow casserole.

7. Tip the meat mixture on to the courgettes, then lay the fried aubergine on top of that. See that the top is as flat as possible.

8. Set the oven to 190°C/375°F, gas mark 5.

9. Melt the butter in a saucepan. Stir in the flour. Cook, stirring, for 1 minute, then draw the pan off the heat and add the milk slowly, beating out the lumps as you go. Add the bay leaf.

10. Return the pan to the heat and stir until boiling. Season with salt and pepper and simmer for 2 minutes.

11. Mix the egg yolk with the cream in a large bowl. Pour the sauce on to this mixture, stirring all the time. Add half the cheese and pour over the casserole.

12. Sprinkle the rest of the cheese on top and bake for 30–35 minutes until completely reheated and well browned.

Note: Moussaka can be made with fresh, as opposed to ready-cooked, meat but this *réchauffé* is very good, and is an excellent way of using up leftover roast lamb.

Serves 4

Babotie

1 slice white bread
290ml/½ pint milk
450g/1lb cooked lamb
1 onion
1 small apple
30g/1oz butter
1 tablespoon curry powder

1 tablespoon chutney
15g/½oz almonds, chopped
A few raisins
1 tablespoon vinegar *or* lemon
  juice
Salt and freshly ground black
  pepper

For the top:
2 eggs
Salt and pepper

2 lemon leaves

1. Soak the bread in the milk.
2. Grease a fireproof dish and set the oven to 180°C/350°F, gas mark 4.
3. Mince the lamb.
4. Chop the onion and apple and cook slowly in the butter until soft but not coloured. Add the curry powder and cook for a further minute.
5. Mix the apple and onion with the meat, chutney, almonds, raisins and vinegar or lemon juice. Squeeze the milk from the bread (but keep the milk) and fork the bread into the meat. Season with salt and pepper and pile into the dish.
6. Place in a warm oven until a slight crust has formed (about 10 minutes).
7. Meanwhile mix the eggs with the milk in which the bread has been soaked. Season with salt and pepper.
8. Pour this over the meat mixture, place on the lemon leaves and bake until the custard has set and browned (about 30–35 minutes).

Note: Bay leaves will do instead of lemon leaves but the flavour is not the same, though good.

Serves 4

Lancashire Hot-Pot

900g/2lb middle neck of
  mutton *or* lamb
3 lambs' kidneys (optional)
2 large onions
900g/2lb potatoes
2 carrots
Salt and freshly ground black
  pepper

Pinch of dried thyme *or* $\frac{1}{2}$
  teaspoon chopped fresh
  thyme
1 bay leaf
290ml/$\frac{1}{2}$ pint good stock
55g/2oz butter

1. Set the oven to 180°C/350°F, gas mark 4.
2. Cut the meat into chops, trimming away most of the fat.
3. Skin, split, core and quarter the kidneys.
4. Slice the onions finely.
5. Wash and peel the potatoes, discard any eyes and cut into slices about 0·5cm/$\frac{1}{4}$in thick.
6. Peel the carrots and slice them.
7. Butter a casserole dish and line it with a layer of potatoes. Season well with salt, pepper and thyme.
8. Layer the cutlets, sliced onions, carrots and kidneys on top of the potatoes, seasoning well with salt, pepper and thyme and adding the bay leaf when the pot is half full. Finish with a neat layer of potatoes overlapping each other.
9. Pour in enough stock to come to the bottom of the top layer of potatoes.
10. Brush the top with plenty of melted butter and season well with salt and pepper.
11. Cover the casserole and bake in the oven for about 2 hours.
12. Remove the lid and continue to cook for a further 30–40 minutes until the potatoes are brown and crisp and the meat is completely tender.

Serves 4

Lamb Cutlets Grilled with Herbs

12 French trimmed lamb
  cutlets
30g/1oz butter, melted
1 tablespoon oil

Fresh herbs: thyme, basil,
  parsley, marjoram and
  rosemary
Freshly ground black pepper

1. Heat the grill.
2. Brush the cutlets with melted butter and oil, sprinkle over half the herbs and season with pepper.
3. Place the cutlets under the grill, about 8cm/3in away from the heat, and cook for 4–6 minutes.
4. Turn them over, baste with the fat from the bottom of the pan and sprinkle over the remaining herbs.
5. Grill for 4–6 minutes. (4 minutes each side should give a succulent pink cutlet, 6 minutes a well-done cutlet.)
6. Dish the cutlets on a warmed serving dish and pour over the pan juices. Serve at once.

Note: See pages 130–1 for information about French trimmed cutlets.

Serves 4

Stuffed Breast of Lamb

2 boned breasts of lamb
1 small onion
Stick of celery
30g/1oz butter
1 tablespoon white
  breadcrumbs
110g/$\frac{1}{4}$lb sausage-meat
Grated rind and juice of $\frac{1}{2}$ large
  orange

2 teaspoons chopped fresh mint
1 tablespoon chopped fresh
  parsley
$\frac{1}{2}$ beaten egg
Salt and freshly ground black
  pepper
30g/1oz dripping
Watercress to garnish

For the gravy:

2 teaspoons flour

150ml/¼ pint stock

Juice of ½ small orange

1 teaspoon redcurrant jelly

Salt and pepper

1. Set the oven to 200°C/400°F, gas mark 6.
2. Weigh the lamb.
3. Chop the onion and celery very finely. Sweat them in the butter (melt the butter, add the vegetables, cover with a piece of greased paper or a lid and cook very slowly until soft but not coloured).
4. With a fork mix together the breadcrumbs, onion, celery, sausage-meat, orange juice and rind, mint and parsley.
5. Bind together with beaten egg until the mixture just holds its shape (too much egg will result in a heavy, doughy stuffing). Season well with salt and pepper.
6. Lay the breasts on a board, fatty side down. Spread the stuffing on one breast and sandwich the two together. Tie neatly with thin string.
7. Melt the dripping in a roasting pan and when hot add the lamb. Grind over some pepper.
8. Roast in the oven for 20–25 minutes to the pound. Baste every 45 minutes and turn over at half-time. If the lamb begins to brown too much cover with tin foil, but remove it for the last 10 minutes of cooking.
9. Place the lamb on a warmed serving dish and put it in the turned-off oven, leaving the door ajar if it is still very hot.
10. Tip all but a scant tablespoon of fat from the roasting pan, reserving as much of the meat juices as possible.
11. Add the flour and mix over the heat until browned.
12. Draw off the heat, add the stock and mix well with a wire whisk or wooden spoon. Return to the heat. Bring slowly up to the boil, whisking all the time.
13. Add the orange juice and redcurrant jelly, and season well.
14. Simmer for a few minutes until the gravy is shiny, and strain it into a gravy boat.
15. Remove the string from the lamb and garnish with a bunch of watercress.

Note: Breasts of lamb can be rolled up individually rather than sandwiched together but this means rather a lot of fat on the inside. If the meat is sandwiched, the fat, being outside, will be browned and crisp and more appetising.

Serves 4

Arabian Roast Shoulder of Lamb

30g/1oz butter
1 large onion, finely chopped
55g/2oz chicken livers, trimmed and diced
55g/2oz mushrooms, sliced
1 garlic clove, crushed
1 tablespoon mixed fresh chopped herbs (mint, thyme, parsley and rosemary)

Squeeze of orange juice
Salt and freshly ground black pepper
$\frac{1}{2}$ cup cooked rice
2 tablespoons sultanas
1 shoulder of lamb, boned

For the gravy:
1 teaspoon tomato purée
2 teaspoons flour

290ml/$\frac{1}{2}$ pint stock

1. Set the oven to 190 C/375 F, gas mark 5.
2. Melt half the butter in a frying pan and put in the onion. Fry gently until soft.
3. Add the liver and turn the heat up. Fry fairly fast to brown the liver on all sides.
4. Add the mushrooms, garlic, herbs and orange juice. Cook gently until the mushrooms are soft. Season with salt and pepper.
5. Remove from the heat and mix into the cooked rice. Add the sultanas.
6. Push this stuffing into the shoulder of lamb, sewing up the edges with thin string. Use a darning needle if you do not have a kitchen larding needle. Spread the remaining butter over the lamb.

7. Roast for about 2 hours, basting occasionally.
8. Lift the meat from the roasting pan and keep warm on a serving platter in the switched-off oven.
9. Pour off most of the fat from the roasting pan, and then stir in first the flour and then the tomato purée.
10. Add the stock, and stir over the heat until the sauce boils, scraping the brown bits from the bottom of the pan as you go. Taste and add salt and pepper if necessary.

Serves 4

PORK AND BACON

Pork Puff Pie

225g/½lb flour-quantity rough-puff pastry (page 371)
450g/1lb belly of pork, minced
½ teaspoon dried sage

½ teaspoon salt
½ teaspoon freshly ground black pepper
2 eggs

1. Roll out the pastry to an oblong 25cm × 10cm (10in × 4in).
2. Mix the minced pork, sage, salt and pepper with one whole egg and one yolk, reserving one egg white. Taste and add more seasoning if necessary.
3. Form the mixture into a roll and place down the centre of the pastry.
4. Fold one side of the pastry over the meat, brush the edge with lightly beaten egg-white and fold the other side over, pressing the join lightly to seal it.
5. Put the pastry roll, centre join underneath, on to a baking sheet and brush with the rest of the egg white. Make three small parallel cuts through the top of the pastry to allow the steam to escape.

331

6. Bake in a moderately hot oven (200 C/400 F, gas mark 6) for 40 minutes.

Note I: The pastry may, of course, be decorated with pastry leaves or shapes, or a fine lattice of pastry strips.

Note II: Tasting raw meat is not as nasty as you may think and it is vital to get the seasoning right.

Serves 4

Juniper Pork Chops

4 juniper berries
4 pork chops at least 2cm/¾in thick
Salt and freshly ground black pepper

A little flour
15g/½oz butter
4 tablespoons single cream
Watercress *or* spring cabbage to garnish

1. Lightly crush the juniper berries with a rolling pin or in a mortar.
2. Cut off the excess fat from the chops leaving only 0·5cm/¼in all the way round. Sprinkle with pepper and dust lightly with flour.
3. Heat the fat cut from the chops in a frying pan and cook until the liquid fat has run out and the pieces are crisp. Remove the pieces with a perforated spoon and throw away.
4. Put the chops in the hot pan. Fry fairly briskly for 5-7 minutes on each side until well browned. Take out the chops and keep warm in a low oven.
5. Pour off the pork fat from the pan and melt the butter in it. Toss the juniper berries in this for 3 minutes. Add the salt and cream and boil up. Pour over the chops.
6. Garnish with watercress or shreds of blanched (briefly boiled) and buttered spring cabbage.

Serves 4

Forcemeat Balls

450g/1lb pork sausage-meat
1 medium onion, finely
  chopped
1 tablespoon finely chopped
  fresh parsley
1 tablespoon finely chopped
  fresh sage *or* ½ teaspoon
  dried sage

Grated rind of ¼ lemon
30g/1oz fresh breadcrumbs
Salt and pepper
Plain flour for rolling
55g/2oz butter

1. Mix together the sausage-meat, onion, parsley, sage, lemon rind and breadcrumbs. Season with salt and pepper. Taste and add more seasoning if necessary.
2. Shape into balls the size of a ping-pong ball. Roll in flour.
3. Melt the butter in a frying pan and toss the balls over the heat until cooked and well browned—approximately 8–10 minutes.

Note: Tasting raw meat is not as nasty as you may think and it is vital to get the seasoning right.

Makes 24

Simple Sausages

This sausage meat mixture can be filled into sausage skins or simply made into skinless sausages as described below.

450g/1lb minced fatty pork
  (e.g. from the belly)
1 medium onion (optional)
4 slices white bread, crusts
  removed

1 egg
3 leaves of fresh sage *or* 1
  teaspoon rubbed dried sage
Salt and pepper
Fat for frying

1. Mix the belly of pork and onion (if used) together.

2. Make breadcrumbs out of the bread slices, and stir into the meat with the egg and the chopped sage.
3. Add plenty of salt and pepper and mix thoroughly. Taste and season further if necessary.
4. Flour your hands, and form the mixture into sausage shapes. Rolling the mixture on a floured table-top gives good results.
5. Fry the sausages in hot fat, turning them frequently. They should cook slowly, and will take about 12 minutes if 2·5cm/1in diameter. If grilling the sausages, brush them lightly with melted fat before doing so.

Note I: These sausages (especially if the onion is omitted) freeze well uncooked, they can then be slowly fried without prior thawing.

Note II: Tasting raw meat is not as nasty as you may think and it is vital to get the seasoning correct.

Serves 4

Spare Ribs

1¼ kilos/2½lb skinned belly of
   pork pieces (American spare
   ribs)

For the marinade:

2 tablespoons runny honey
2 tablespoons soy sauce
½ garlic clove, crushed

½ teaspoon dried basil
Juice of 1 lemon
Salt and pepper

1. Mix together the ingredients for the marinade and soak the spare ribs in it for 5 hours.
2. Heat the grill.
3. When really hot, grill the ribs, basting with the marinade until brown and crisp.
4. Lower the heat and continue grilling and turning the ribs for a further 20 minutes or until tender.

Note: Alternatively the ribs can be roasted in the oven; they are done when *very* dark brown, and tender.

Serves 4

Glazed Bacon Joint

1·35 kilos/3lb forehock of
   bacon
1 onion
1 carrot
1 bay leaf
Fresh parsley stalks

Peppercorns
2 tablespoons demerara sugar
1 teaspoon dry English
   mustard
Handful of cloves

1. Soak the bacon overnight in cold water. This removes excess salt.
2. Place it in a large pan of cold water and add the onion, carrot, bay leaf, parsley stalks and peppercorns. Bring slowly to the boil, cover and simmer for 75 minutes.
3. Leave the joint to cool slightly in the stock. Then lift out and carefully pull off the skin without removing any of the fat.
4. Mix the sugar and mustard together and press it all over the joint to form an even coating.
5. Using a sharp knife, cut a lattice pattern across the bacon through the sugar and fat. Press any sugar that falls off on again. Stick a clove into each diamond segment, or into the cuts where the lines cross.
6. Heat the oven to 220°C/425°F, gas mark 7 and bake the joint for about 20 minutes, or until brown and slightly caramelized.

Note I: If you haven't time to soak salty bacon overnight, cook it for 30 minutes in plain water and then transfer into a simmering pan ready prepared with the bay leaf, etc.

Note II: The cooking stock is useful for soups (especially pea or lentil soup).

Note III: The bacon joint can be decorated with a ham frill: to make one, cut a piece of greaseproof paper to about 20cm × 44cm/ 8in × 18in. Fold it loosely in half lengthwise, without pressing down the fold. Make 5cm/2in-long cuts, 1cm/½in apart, parallel

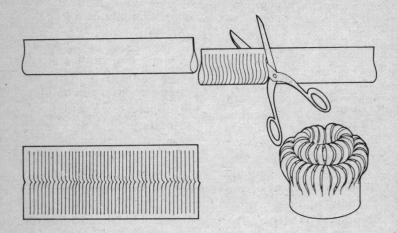

to the end of the paper, cutting through both thicknesses from the folded side towards the open sides. Make the cuts all along the strip. Now open out the paper and re-fold it lengthwise, in the opposite direction from the first time. Wrap the frill round the ham bone and secure with a paper clip.

Serves 4

Roast Pork

1·35 kilos/3lb loin of pork,   Salt
  with skin intact   Flour
Oil

For the gravy:
2 teaspoons flour   290ml/½ pint well flavoured
         stock

To serve:
Small bunch of watercress   Apple sauce (page 269)

1. Set the oven at 200°C/400°F, gas mark 6.
2. Score the rind (crackling skin) with a sharp knife in cuts about ½cm/¼in apart cutting through the skin but not right through the fat.
3. Brush the skin with oil and sprinkle with salt and flour to help give a crisp crackling.
4. Place in roasting pan and roast for 1 hour 40 minutes (25 minutes to the pound, plus 25 minutes extra).
5. Once the pork is cooked turn off the oven, put the pork on a serving dish and put it back into the oven leaving the door ajar if it is still very hot.
6. Tip all but a dessertspoonful of fat from the roasting pan, reserving as much of the meat juices as possible.
7. Add the flour and mix over the heat until well browned.
8. Draw off the heat, add the stock and mix well with a wire whisk or wooden spoon. Return to the heat and bring slowly up to the boil, whisking all the time. Simmer for a few minutes until the gravy is shiny. Season with salt and freshly ground black pepper to taste. Strain into a warmed gravy boat.
9. Garnish the pork with a bunch of watercress and serve with gravy and apple sauce.

Note: Remove the crackling before carving, then cut it with scissors into thin strips.

Serves 4

OFFAL

Kidneys Turbigo

9 lambs' kidneys
Butter for frying
225g/½lb small pork sausages
12 baby onions *or* shallots,
  peeled
225g/½lb button mushrooms
2 tablespoons sherry
425ml/¾ pint stock

Bouquet garni (1 stick of celery,
  1 bay leaf, sprigs of parsley
  and thyme, tied together with
  string)
Salt and pepper
30g/1oz butter
30g/1oz flour
1 carton soured cream (about
  150ml/5fl.oz)

1. Skin the kidneys, halve them and remove the core.
2. Heat the butter in a frying pan. Brown the kidneys quickly (a few at a time) on both sides. They should cook fast enough to go brown rather than grey. Remove them into a bowl as you go.
3. Now fry the sausages, then the onions, and finally the mushrooms in the same way. Put them on to a plate – not with the kidneys.
4. Pour off the blood that will have run from the kidneys (it can be very bitter).
5. Put everything back into the pan. Pour over the sherry and stock and sink the bouquet garni in the liquid. Add salt and pepper and cover with the saucepan lid.
6. Cook very gently for about 45 minutes or until the kidneys and onions are tender.
7. Lift the meat and vegetables on to a serving dish and discard the bouquet garni.
8. Work the butter and flour together to a paste (beurre manie). Drop about half of it into the sauce and whisk or stir briskly

while bringing slowly to the boil. If the sauce is still on the thin side add the rest of the butter and flour mixture in the same way, whisking out the lumps. Boil for 1 minute.

10.   Add the soured cream, stir (but do not boil) and pour over the dish. Alternatively, serve the cream separately.

Note: Classic turbigo does not have the soured cream but the addition is delicious.

Serves 4

Beef Marrow on Toast

Beef marrow bones   Butter
Beef stock   4 slices bread, toasted

Boil the bones in beef stock until the marrow is tender (about 40 minutes). Scoop out all the marrow from the bones on to the buttered toast. Serve at once.

Note: Marrow bones may be served loosely wrapped in a napkin, on a dish, with the toast handed separately.

Oxtail Stew

2 oxtails   Salt and freshly ground black
340g/¾lb carrots   pepper
225g/½lb onions   ½ teaspoon sugar
30g/1 oz beef dripping   1 teaspoon tomato purée
40g/1¼oz flour   Juice of ½ lemon
150ml/¼ pint red wine   2 slices white bread
570ml/1 pint water *or* stock   3 tablespoons oil
1 teaspoon chopped fresh   2 tablespoons chopped fresh
  thyme   parsley

1.   Wash and dry the tails. Chop them into 5cm/2in lengths.
2.   Peel the carrots and slice them thickly. Slice the onions.

3. Melt the dripping in a heavy saucepan and add the oxtail, browning the sides evenly and well. Remove.

4. Brown the carrots and onions in the same pan.

5. Replace the oxtail. Sprinkle on the flour and blend it in well. Pour over the wine and water or stock, add the thyme, salt and pepper and the sugar. Bring to the boil and simmer for 2 hours.

6. Set the oven to 150 C/300 F, gas mark 2.

7. Take out the pieces of meat and vegetables and place in a casserole.

8. With a small ladle or spoon, skim off the fat which will rise to the top of the remaining liquid. Add the tomato purée and lemon juice and bring quickly to the boil.

9. Pour this over the oxtail, cover with a lid, and place in the pre-heated oven for approximately 3 hours, or until the meat is almost falling off the bone.

10. Remove the crusts from the bread and cut the slices into 4 triangles. Heat the oil in a heavy frying pan and gently fry the triangles in the fat, one side after the other until crisp right through and evenly brown. Drain on absorbent paper.

11. When the oxtail is tender take it out of the oven, place the croutes around the edge of the dish and sprinkle over the chopped parsley. If the sauce is too thin remove the meat and vegetables to a serving dish and boil the sauce rapidly until reduced to the desired consistency.

Note: When buying oxtail choose short fat tails with a good proportion of meat on them. Long stringy thin tails are poor value – pale in flavour and short on meat.

Serves 4

Pressed Tongue

1 ox tongue, fresh *or* salted
Salt
6 peppercorns
Bouquet garni (stick of celery, bay leaf, sprigs of parsley and thyme, tied together with string)

2 onions
2 carrots
1 stick celery
425ml/¾ pint aspic made from beef stock and gelatine *or* from a packet of aspic mix

1. If the tongue is salted soak it in fresh water for four hours. If the tongue is fresh soak it in brine (salty water) for 1–2 hours.
2. Place it in a saucepan, cover and pour in enough water to cover completely.
3. Add salt if the tongue is fresh. Add the peppercorns, bouquet garni, onions, carrots and celery.
4. Bring gently to the boil, skimming off any scum. Cover tightly and simmer for 2–3 hours, or until tender when pierced with a skewer. Leave to cool for 1 hour in the liquid.
5. Take out and remove the bones from the root of the tongue and peel off the skin.
6. Curl the tongue tightly and fit it into a deep round cake tin or tongue press.
7. Pour a little cool jellied stock or aspic into the tin.
8. Place a plate which just fits inside the tin on top of the tongue. Stand a heavy weight (about 4 kilos/8lb) on the plate and leave overnight in the refrigerator.

To carve: slice thinly across the top of the round.

Note: The stock in which the tongue is cooked is suitable for use in making the jellied stock if it is not too salty.

Serves 4

Brains with Brown Butter (cervelles beurre noisette)

4 calves' brains
Court bouillon (page 260)
Salt and pepper
About 3 gherkins

About 10 capers
Chopped fresh parsley
55g/2oz butter
3 tablespoons lemon juice

1. Wash the brains well and soak in cold water for 2–3 hours. Drain them.
2. Bring the court bouillon to the boil, add the brains and poach for 15 minutes. Remove and drain thoroughly.
3. Cut the brains into slices, removing any membranes. Lay on a heated serving dish and season with salt and pepper.
4. Chop the gherkins, capers and parsley.
5. Heat the butter in a pan until just turning brown. Immediately add the gherkins, capers, parsley and lemon juice. Boil up, pour over the brains and serve immediately.

Serves 4

Liver and Bacon

450g/1lb calves' *or* lambs' liver
Seasoned flour
6 rashers rindless bacon
55g/2oz butter
1 onion thinly sliced
About 2 teaspoons flour

290ml/½ pint beef stock *or* a stock cube and 290ml/½ pint water
Small glass sherry (optional)
Watercress to garnish

1. Remove the film of membrane from the liver and cut the meat into 0.5cm/¼in slices. Dip the slices in seasoned flour and keep well separated on a plate.
2. Heat the grill. Cook the bacon under it until crisp and brown but not brittle. Turn off the grill and leave the bacon under it to keep warm.

3. Heat half the butter in a frying pan and fry the onion slowly in it until soft and brown. Tip the onion into a saucer.
4. Heat the rest of the butter in the frying pan and fry the liver slices, a few pieces at a time, adding more butter if necessary. Fry briskly for the first minute or two, and turn over when browned. Fry briskly on the second side at first, then more gently for a further 2 minutes (only about 6 minutes in all: liver is easily spoiled by overcooking). Dish on a shallow platter and keep warm.
5. Put the onion, and any of its fat, back into the pan and add a sprinkling of flour – just enough to absorb the fat. Pour in the stock and stir well as it comes to the boil. Add the sherry if using.
6. Boil the sauce rapidly to reduce in quantity and thicken the gravy. This will also give a richer appearance and concentrate the flavour.
7. Pour the sauce over the liver, top with the bacon and garnish with watercress. Serve at once as liver toughens on standing.

Serves 4

Kidney Kebabs

8 lambs' kidneys	Oil
4 rashers rindless fatty bacon	Pinch of thyme (fresh *or* dried)
8 firm tomatoes	Freshly ground black pepper

1. Heat the grill.
2. Skin, halve and core the kidneys.
3. Skewer them alternately with small pieces of fatty bacon and tomatoes cut in half.
4. Brush with oil and sprinkle with thyme and pepper.
5. Place under the hot grill and cook for about 8 minutes, turning the skewers as the kidneys brown.
6. Serve immediately as kidneys toughen on standing.

Serves 4

MEALS WITH VEGETABLES, PASTA AND RICE

Baked Stuffed Aubergines

2 medium-sized aubergines
15g/½oz beef dripping
285g/10oz minced beef
1 onion, finely chopped
½ green pepper, chopped
55g/2oz mushrooms, chopped
1 garlic clove, crushed
1 teaspoon flour
290ml/½ pint beef stock
1 bay leaf
2 teaspoons tomato purée

1 teaspoon chopped fresh
   parsley
Salt and pepper
Lemon juice
290ml/½ pint tomato sauce
   (page 271)
15g/½oz butter
Grated Gruyère *or*
   strong Cheddar cheese
Dried crumbs.

1. Cut the aubergines in half lengthwise and scoop out the
   centre leaving the shell with about 0·5cm/¼in of flesh attached.
   Sprinkle lightly with salt and leave upside down to drain.
2. Chop up the aubergine flesh and sprinkle with salt. Leave
   to drain on a tilted board or in a sieve for 20 minutes.
3. Melt the beef dripping in a sauté pan. Add the mince and
   brown thoroughly all over.
4. Rinse and dry the aubergine flesh. Add to the mince with
   the onion, green pepper, mushroom and garlic and cook for
   a further 3–4 minutes.
5. Stir in the flour. Cook for 1 minute, then add the beef stock,
   bay leaf, tomato purée, parsley, pepper and lemon juice.
6. Bring to the boil, stirring continuously, cover and simmer
   for 20–25 minutes.

7. Remove the bay leaf.
8. While the stuffing is cooking make the tomato sauce.
9. Set the oven to 200 C/400 F, gas mark 6.
10. Wash and dry the aubergine shells, brush with the butter (melted) and fill with the mince mixture.
11. Sprinkle over the grated cheese and crumbs. Bake in the pre-heated oven for 30 minutes, or until the shells are tender and the cheese well browned and crusty.
12. Serve with the tomato sauce.

Serves 4

Bubble and Squeak

450g/1lb mashed potatoes (page 228)

450g/1lb cooked vegetables, such as cabbage *or* onion *or* leek

55g/2oz good dripping

1. Mix the potato with the other vegetables. Season to taste.
2. Melt the dripping in a heavy-based pan.
3. Put in the vegetable mixture, pressing it down flat on the hot dripping. Cook slowly to heat through and allow a crust to form on the bottom of the mixture.
4. Now flip the cake over on to a plate and return it to the pan to brown the second side.
5. Slide on to a warm serving dish and serve immediately.

Note: Bubble and squeak is really a left-over fry-up and it does not matter if the cake is neat and even or crumbly and broken. But if you prefer it to be round and neat so that you can cut it into slices, a beaten egg added to the mixture will ensure that the ingredients hold together.

Serves 4

Stuffed Green Peppers

4 green peppers
30g/1oz butter
1 medium onion, finely diced
1 garlic clove, crushed
110g/¼lb mushrooms, sliced
30g/1oz split blanched almonds
140g/5oz long-grain rice
290ml/½ pint chicken stock
  (page 285)

1 teaspoon chopped fresh
  rosemary
30g/1oz raisins
1 tablespoon chopped fresh
  parsley
Salt and pepper
290ml/½ pint tomato sauce
  (page 271)

1. Cut off the tops of the peppers and remove core and seeds.
2. Drop the peppers into boiling water for 2 minutes. Plunge immediately into cold water to cool.
3. Set the oven to 190°C/375°F, gas mark 5.
4. Melt the butter and cook the finely diced onion in it until transparent. Add the garlic, mushrooms and almonds.
5. Sauté (fry briskly, while tossing the contents of the pan in the butter) for a further 2 minutes.
6. Stir in the rice and fry for a further minute.
7. Pour on the stock and bring to the boil. Add the rosemary, raisins, parsley and seasoning. Cover and bake in the oven for 20 minutes.
8. When the rice is cooked fill the peppers with it and place them in a deep fireproof dish.
9. Pour on the tomato sauce. Cover and put back into the oven for 40 minutes.

Serves 4

Macaroni Cheese

170g/6oz macaroni
Oil
30g/1oz butter

Salt, pepper and
  English mustard
110g/6oz grated cheese

30g/1oz flour   ½ tablespoon breadcrumbs
425ml/¾ pint milk

Optional additional ingredients:
1–2 fried bacon   1 hardboiled egg
1 small onion   2 tomatoes

1. Lightly butter the sides of a shallow ovenproof dish large
    enough to hold ½ litre/1 pint.
2. Boil the macaroni in plenty of salted water with a tablespoon
    of oil. The water must boil steadily to keep the macaroni
    moving freely and prevent it sticking to the pan; the lid is
    left off to prevent boiling over. Cook the macaroni for 10–15
    minutes or until it is just tender.
3. Meanwhile chop and fry the bacon (if used) and put it in
    the bottom of the dish; or chop the onion finely and cook
    it till quite soft in the butter; or chop the hardboiled egg
    to be added to the sauce later; or scald, skin and slice
    the tomatoes.
4. Drain the macaroni.
5. Melt the butter (with the cooked onion if used). Add the
    flour and cook for ½ a minute. Pour on the milk and bring
    gradually to the boil, stirring continually. Simmer for 1
    minute. Add a pinch of mustard.
6. Stir the macaroni into the sauce and reheat if necessary.
7. Season the sauce to taste and add tomatoes or hardboiled
    egg if using.
8. Stir in all but one level tablespoon of cheese and turn the
    mixture into the dish.
9. Heat the grill.
10. Mix the reserved cheese with the crumbs and sprinkle evenly
    over the sauce; make sure that all the sauce is covered or
    it will form brown blisters under the grill.
11. Grill fairly quickly until the top is browned and crisp.

Serves 4

Risotto

55g/2oz butter
110g/¼lb streaky bacon, diced
1 large onion, diced
2 large garlic cloves, crushed
1 green pepper, sliced
3 sticks celery, diced
110g/¼lb mushrooms, sliced
2 tablespoons tomato purée
½ teaspoon dried *or* 1 teaspoon fresh basil (optional)
½ teaspoon dried *or* 1 teaspoon fresh thyme
Salt and freshly ground black pepper
170g/6oz piece of ham, diced
225g/½lb cooked rice
4 medium tomatoes
30g/1oz Parmesan cheese
Chopped fresh parsley

1. Melt the butter in a large sauté pan. Gently fry the bacon in it.
2. Add the onion and garlic and cook until the onion is transparent.
3. Add the green pepper, celery and mushrooms. Sweat (cook gently) for 10 minutes.
4. Stir in the tomato purée. If the mixture looks dry, add a tablespoon or two of water.
5. Add the herbs, salt and pepper.
6. Stir in the ham and rice and gently heat for 5 minutes.
7. Plunge the tomatoes into boiling water for 5 seconds. Skin them, remove the seeds and cut into eighths.
8. Add to the rice mixture with the Parmesan. Correct the seasoning.
9. Pile into a warm serving dish and garnish with plenty of chopped parsley.

Note: Good risottos can be made with almost any leftover meat, and/or vegetables. Sliced fried onion always helps to improve the flavour.

Serves 4–6

6
Puddings and Sweets

SWEET SAUCES

Creme Chantilly

150ml/¼ pint double cream
2 tablespoons iced water

1 teaspoon icing sugar
2 drops vanilla essence

1. Put all the ingredients into a chilled bowl and whisk with a balloon whisk, steadily but not too fast, for about 2 minutes or until the cream has thickened and doubled in volume.
2. Whisk faster for 30–40 seconds until the mixture is very fluffy and will form soft peaks.

Note: Chilling the ingredients and the bowl gives a lighter, whiter result.

Crème Pâtissière

290ml/½ pint milk
2 egg yolks
55g/2oz caster sugar

20g/¾oz flour
20g/¾oz cornflour
Vanilla essence

1. Scald the milk.

2. Cream the egg yolks with the sugar and when pale mix in the flours. Pour on the milk and mix well.
3. Return the mixture to the pan and bring slowly up to the boil, stirring continuously. (It will go alarmingly lumpy, but don't worry, keep stirring and it will get smooth.) Allow to cool slightly and add the vanilla essence.

Crème Anglaise (*English Egg Custard*)

290ml/½ pint milk
1 tablespoon sugar

½ vanilla pod *or* few drops of
   vanilla essence
2 egg yolks

1. Heat the milk with the sugar and vanilla pod (if available) and bring slowly to the boil.
2. Beat the yolks in a bowl. Remove the vanilla pod and pour the milk on to the egg yolks, stirring steadily. Mix well and return to the pan.
3. Stir over gentle heat until the mixture thickens so that it will coat the back of a spoon; do not boil. Pour into a cold bowl.
4. Add the vanilla essence if using.

Sugar Syrup

285g/10oz granulated sugar
570ml/1 pint water

Pared rind of 1 lemon

1. Put the sugar, water and lemon rind in a pan and heat slowly until the sugar has completely dissolved.
2. Bring to the boil and cook until the syrup feels tacky between finger and thumb. Allow to cool.
3. Strain. Keep covered in a cool place until needed.

Note: Sugar syrup will keep unrefrigerated for about five days, and for several weeks if kept cold.

Apricot Sauce with Kernels

85g/3oz granulated sugar   225g/½lb apricots
290ml/½ pint water   Juice of ½ lemon

1. Dissolve the sugar in the water over a gentle heat. Do not allow to boil until the sugar has completely dissolved (this will prevent the syrup from crystallizing).
2. Wash and halve the apricots and add to the pan with the stones and lemon juice.
3. Bring to the boil and cook until the apricots are soft (about 15 minutes).
4. Remove the stones, but keep them.
5. Boil the apricots rapidly for a further 5–10 minutes, or until the pulp is reduced to a syrupy consistency. Push the apricot sauce through a nylon or stainless steel sieve. Taste and add extra sugar if necessary.
6. Crack the stones and remove the kernels. Chop the kernels roughly and add to the sauce. Serve hot or cold.

Raspberry Jam Sauce

3 tablespoons raspberry   90g/3oz sugar
 jam   125ml/¼ pint water

1. Put the sugar and water in a saucepan and heat slowly until the sugar has dissolved. Then boil rapidly until the syrup feels tacky between finger and thumb.
2. Add the jam, stir until smooth, then sieve to remove the pips.

Hot Chocolate Sauce

170g/6oz unsweetened chocolate
2 tablespoons water

1 teaspoon instant coffee powder
15g/½oz butter

1. Melt the chocolate slowly with the water, stirring frequently.
2. Add the coffee and butter, and heat, without boiling, until the butter has melted and the sauce is thin and shiny.

Caramel Sauce

170g/6oz granulated sugar
425ml/¾ pint water

1. In a heavy saucepan melt two-thirds of the sugar slowly. When it is bubbly and brown, pour on the water. (It will fizz dangerously, so take care.)
2. Add the rest of the sugar. Reboil, stirring, and then boil the sauce until it is of a syrupy consistency.

Hard Brandy Sauce

Cream equal quantities of unsalted butter and caster sugar together until very light. Add finely grated orange rind and brandy to flavour fairly strongly.

MOUSSES, FOOLS AND CUSTARDS

Orange Fool

2 small oranges
290ml/½ pint double cream

2 tablespoons icing sugar

1. With a potato peeler, pare about half the rind off 1 orange. The strips should have no white pith on the underside. Using a very sharp fruit knife, cut into tiny thin strips about 2·5cm/1in long.
2. Place these needleshreds in a pan of boiling water for 5 minutes. Rinse in cold water until completely cool. Drain.
3. Grate the remaining orange rind and squeeze the juice.
4. Whip the cream. When stiff, stir in the orange juice, grated rind and sugar.
5. Spoon into small glasses or little china pots or coffee cups. Scatter over the needleshreds of orange rind to decorate.

Serves 4

Simple Apricot Mousse

For the apricot purée:
425g/15oz can apricots *or*
   450g/1lb stoned apricots
   cooked in 150ml/¼ pint water
   and 85g/3oz sugar
1 tablespoon caster sugar

2 teaspoons kirsch (optional)
8g/¼oz gelatine
290ml/¼ pint double cream,
   lightly whipped

For the decoration:
Whipped cream
Apricot pieces
Browned nibbed almonds

1. To make the apricot purée liquidize or sieve the apricots with their syrup.
2. Mix the caster sugar and kirsch with the apricot purée. Taste and add more sugar if necessary to bring out the flavour.
3. Put 3 tablespoons of water in a small saucepan, sprinkle on the gelatine and set aside to 'sponge' for 5 minutes.
3. Dissolve the gelatine over a gentle heat and when clear and warm stir it into the purée. Leave to set slightly, then fold in the lightly whipped cream.
4. Pour the mixture into a dish and leave to set in the refrigerator for 2–3 hours. When set, decorate with rosettes of cream, apricot pieces and browned nuts.

Serves 4

Chocolate Mousse

3 eggs   170/6oz dark sweetened (e.g.
30g/1oz caster sugar   Bourneville) chocolate

1. Separate the eggs and beat the yolks with the sugar until you have a pale creamy mousse.
2. Put the chocolate in a saucepan with 3 tablespoons of water and melt slowly. (Alternatively, melt the chocolate in a double saucepan or in a saucer over boiling water, but do not melt it on direct heat without any water, as it will go lumpy and hard.)
3. While the chocolate is still warm, add to the yolks and sugar mixture. Whip the whites stiffly and fold them into the chocolate mixture.
4. Turn immediately into a soufflé dish or into individual pots or glasses.
5. Chill until set, preferably overnight, but for at least 4 hours.

Note: Brandy, chopped preserved ginger, rum, grated orange rind and strong coffee flavours are all delicious additions. They should be stirred into the basic mousse mixture before the whites are folded in.

Serves 4

Stripey Fool

For the raspberry purée
285g/10oz fresh raspberries   1 tablespoon water
110g/¼lb sugar

For the custard:
290ml/½ pint creamy milk   55g/2oz caster sugar
20g/¾oz cornflour   150ml/¼ pint double *or*
2 egg yolks   whipping cream, lightly
3 drops vanilla essence   whipped

1. Put raspberries, sugar and water in a saucepan. Crush the fruit and stew gently until soft.
2. Push the fruit and juice through a nylon sieve and allow to cool.
3. Mix a little of the milk with the cornflour and egg yolks and put the rest into a thick pan to heat. When boiling add the hot milk to the cornflour mixture and then pour this mixture back into the pan.
4. Stir continuously over a heat until the sauce thickens. Boil for 1 minute. Remove from the heat, add all but a teaspoonful of the sugar and mix thoroughly.
5. Sprinkle over the remaining sugar (this will prevent a skin forming) and set aside to cool.
6. Fold in the whipped cream.
7. Serve in a glass bowl or in individual glasses: spoon a thin layer of raspberry purée into the bottom of the glasses or serving bowl then add a layer of the custard. Continue the raspberry/custard layers, finishing with raspberry, but

reserving a little custard to swirl into the top layer of raspberry for decoration.

Note: There are many pretty variations on this theme. The fool can be made with several purées used at once: layers of cherry, strawberry, raspberry and rhubarb for example, or apricot, peach, passion fruit and greengage. But using red and yellow fruits together looks a bit lurid.

Semolina Cream Mould with Blackcurrant Sauce

Few drops oil
570ml/1 pint milk
85g/3oz semolina
2 eggs

85g/3oz caster sugar
Juice of 1 lemon
Few drops vanilla essence
4–5 tablespoons double cream

For the blackcurrant sauce:
450g/1lb blackcurrants
150ml/$\frac{1}{4}$ pint sugar syrup
   (page 350)

1. Oil a $1\frac{1}{2}$ litre/$2\frac{1}{2}$ pint smooth jelly mould or pudding basin.
2. Heat the milk in a heavy saucepan and when boiling gradually stir in the semolina.
3. Reduce the heat and simmer for 10 minutes or until the semolina is cooked. Remove from heat and allow to cool slightly.
4. Separate the eggs. Whisk the yolks and sugar until light and fluffy and stir into the semolina mixture.
5. Beat in the lemon juice, vanilla essence and cream. Cool to lukewarm.
6. Whisk the egg whites until stiff and fold into the semolina mixture with a metal spoon. Pour into the mould and leave in the refrigerator overnight to set.

7. Meanwhile prepare the blackcurrant sauce. Remove the stalks from the blackcurrants. Wash thoroughly and drain.
8. Liquidize the blackcurrants with the sugar syrup and push the purée through a nylon sieve. Taste and if not sweet enough beat in a little sifted icing sugar.
9. To dish, run a knife round the edge of the mould to detach the sides. Put a serving plate over the top of the mould, making sure that it is dead centre, then quickly invert both plate and mould. Give a sharp shake to dislodge the mould.
10. Pour the sauce over the top and serve immediately.

Note I: Semolina is finely ground processed hard wheat.

Note II: If the mould cannot be left overnight to set increase the semolina quantity to 110g/¼lb.

Serves 4–6

Butterscotch Tapioca Custard

85g/3oz quick-cooking tapioca   425ml/¾ pint milk
Pinch of salt   55g/2oz butter
2 eggs beaten   85g/3oz brown sugar

1. Mix the tapioca, salt, eggs and milk in a pudding basin and set over a saucepan of boiling water. Cook for 7 minutes without stirring.
3. Stir, and then cook for a further 5 minutes.
4. Remove from the heat and allow the tapioca to thicken as it cools.
5. Melt the butter. When it is foaming add the brown sugar and cook for 30 seconds. It will separate alarmingly at this stage but don't worry. Stir into the tapioca cream.

Note: Tapioca is a farinaceous food processed from the Brazilian cassava root.

Serves 4

Honeycomb Mould

570ml/1 pint cold but not set
  lemon jelly (*see below*)

For the custard:
290ml/½ pint milk   2 eggs, separated
1 tablespoon sugar

1. First make the custard: heat the milk with the sugar until
    near boiling.
2. Beat the egg yolks and pour on the hot milk, mixing well.
    If the custard does not immediately thicken return it to the
    pan and stir over gentle heat until it will coat the back of
    a spoon, but take care not to let it boil. Allow to cool.
3. Whisk the jelly (which should be on the point of setting)
    lightly. Whisk it into the cold custard.
4. Whisk the egg whites until stiff but not dry-looking. Stir one
    tablespoon into the jelly and custard to loosen the mixture
    and then carefully fold in the rest.
5. Wet a jelly mould and pour in the mixture. Leave in the
    refrigerator until set.
6. To turn out: loosen the top edge all around with a finger
    and dip the mould briefly in hot water. Place a dish over the
    mould and invert the two together. Give a good sharp shake
    and remove the mould.

Serves 4

Lemon Jelly

4 large lemons   125g/4½oz sugar
425ml/¾ pint water   Green *or* yellow colouring
30g/1oz gelatine   (optional)

1. With a sharp knife or potato peeler carefully remove the rind (without any pith) from the lemons. Squeeze the fruit and measure the juice. You need 225ml/8fl.oz.
2. Put 3 tablespoons of the water into a small pan and sprinkle on the gelatine. Do not stir, but set aside to soak and 'sponge'.
3. Put the remaining water, lemon rind and sugar together in a pan, cover and place over gentle heat. Do not boil. Remove from the heat and keep the liquid hot for 15 minutes in order to extract all the flavour from the lemon rind. Make sure that all the sugar has dissolved and then strain it; allow to cool until lukewarm.
4. Slowly dissolve the gelatine over gentle heat, without boiling. When clear add it to the water and sugar.
5. Add the lemon juice. Taste the mixture and add extra sugar, if necessary, stirring until it is dissolved. At this stage a few drops of green or yellow colouring may be added if desired.
6. Wet a jelly mould. Pour in the liquid jelly, and leave refrigerated until set (at least 4 hours), but preferably overnight.
6. Turn out the jelly: loosen the top edge all round with a finger. Dip the mould briefly into hot water. Place a dish over the mould and invert the two together. Give a good sharp shake and remove the mould.

Serves 4

Junket

570ml/1 pint fresh milk   1 teaspoon rennet
2 teaspoons sugar

1. Heat the milk with the sugar to blood temperature (lukewarm).
2. Stir well and pour into a serving bowl.
3. Stir in the rennet and leave to set at room temperature. Once set the dish may be refrigerated.

Variations on plain junket:
Spoon over a little whipped cream and sprinkle with crumbled ratafia biscuits.
Sprinkle the surface with grated nutmeg.
Flavour with coffee essence, orange rind or grated chocolate.

Serves 4

Orange Jelly and Caramel Chips

For the orange jelly:
70g/2½oz caster sugar
150ml/¼ pint water
20g/¾oz gelatine

570ml/1 pint orange juice, just tepid
290ml/½ pint double cream, whipped lightly

For the caramel:
55g/2oz granulated sugar

1. Start with the jelly: put the caster sugar and water in a small saucepan. Sprinkle on the gelatine and allow to stand for 10 minutes. Dissolve over a very gentle heat without allowing the gelatine to boil. Do not stir.
2. When the gelatine is clear and liquid mix with the orange juice and pour into a wet plain jelly mould or pudding basin.
3. Chill in the refrigerator 2–4 hours, or until set.
4. Meanwhile start the caramel. Put the sugar in a heavy pan and set over a gentle heat.
5. Lightly oil a baking sheet.
6. When the sugar has dissolved boil rapidly to a golden caramel. Immediately pour on to the baking sheet. Leave to harden and cool completely.
7. Break up the caramel into chips.
8. Loosen the jelly round the edges with a finger. Invert a serving plate over the jelly mould, turn the mould and plate over together, give a sharp shake and remove the mould. If the jelly won't budge dip the outside of the mould briefly in hot water to loosen it.

9. Spread over the cream to completely mask the jelly.
10. Just before serving, scatter the caramel over the jelly (do not do this in advance as the caramel softens quickly).

Serves 4

FRIED AND DEEP-FRIED PUDDINGS

Fried Milk

This recipe is best started a day in advance.

290ml/½ pint milk
1 tablespoon granulated sugar
2 drops vanilla essence
4 eggs
7g/¼oz butter

Dried white breadcrumbs
Butter for frying
Caster sugar
Cinnamon

1. Set the oven to 170°C/325°F, gas mark 3.
2. Heat the milk and sugar together. Allow to cool slightly and add the vanilla essence.
3. Lightly beat 3 of the eggs with a fork.
4. Pour on the hot milk and mix well. Strain this custard into a lightly buttered ovenproof dish with straight sides, preferably rectangular.
5. Stand the dish in a roasting tin full of boiling water and place in the oven. Bake for 25 minutes or until the custard is set. Allow to cool, then refrigerate until very cold, preferably overnight.
6. When the baked custard is chilled and very solidly set, cut it into 5cm/2in cubes or pieces.
7. Beat the remaining egg with a fork.
8. Roll the blocks of baked custard carefully in the egg. Now coat them evenly with breadcrumbs.

9. Heat a good ounce of butter in a thick-bottomed frying pan, and when foaming put in the custard squares. Fry them gently, turning to brown all sides.
10. Serve sprinkled with caster sugar and cinnamon.

Note: This is delicious served with apricot sauce (page 351).

Serves 4

Sweet Soufflé Omelette

2 eggs
2 tablespoons jam
1 tablespoon lemon juice

30g/1oz caster sugar
15g/½oz butter
Icing sugar to decorate

1. Separate the eggs.
2. Set the oven to 180°C/350°F, gas mark 4. Heat the grill set at the highest temperature.
3. Warm the jam with the lemon juice.
4. Beat the yolks with the caster sugar until light and frothy.
5. Whisk the egg whites until stiff but not too dry. (The mixture should form a 'medium' peak when the whisk is lifted from it, not too floppy, not too rigid.)
6. Heat a 15cm/6in frying pan and melt the butter in it.
7. Fold the egg whites into the yolks and when the butter is foaming, but not coloured, pour in the omelette mixture.
8. Lower the heat and cook for 1 minute until the underside has just set.
9. Place in the oven for 10 minutes until the omelette top is just set – do not overcook.
10. Get a long skewer red hot under the grill. Leave it there while dishing the omelette.
11. Spread the warmed jam over half the omelette and fold in two with a spatula.
12. Slip on to a heated flat serving dish. Sprinkle the surface with icing sugar.
13. Brand a criss-cross pattern in the sugar with the red hot skewer. Serve immediately.

Note I: It is not strictly necessary to finish the cooking in the oven, but it avoids the risk of burning the bottom before the top is set.

Note II: The branding with the hot skewer is not essential either, but the omelette should be sprinkled with icing sugar before serving.

Serves 4

Banana Fritters

8 bananas
150ml/¼ pint fritter batter (see below)

Oil for shallow frying
Icing sugar

1. Peel the bananas and cut in half lengthwise.
2. Dip immediately into the prepared batter.
3. Heat 6mm/¼in of oil in a frying pan and when hot fry the fritters for about 2 minutes on each side until golden brown. Drain well and dust with icing sugar.

Serves 8

Sweet Fritter Batter

125g/4½oz plain flour
Pinch of salt
2 eggs

1 tablespoon oil
50g/1¾oz sugar
150ml/¼ pint milk

1. Sift the flour with the salt into a bowl.
2. Make a well in the centre, exposing the bottom of the bowl.
3. Put one whole egg and one yolk into the well and mix with a wooden spoon or whisk until smooth, gradually incorporating the surrounding flour and the milk. A thick cream consistency should be reached.
4. Add the oil and sugar. Allow to rest for 30 minutes.

5. Whisk the egg white and fold into the batter with a metal spoon just before using.

Note: This batter can be speedily made in a blender. Simply put all the ingredients, except the egg white, into the machine and whizz briefly.

COMPOSITE PUDDINGS

Nice Biscuit Refrigerator Cake

190ml/⅓ pint double cream
3 tablespoons milk
2 tablespoons sherry
15 Nice *or* 'morning coffee' biscuits

225g/½lb sweetened chestnut purée (tinned)
110g/¼lb chocolate
30g/1oz butter
A few walnut halves

1. Whip the cream until thick.
2. Mix the milk and sherry together.
3. Soak 3 biscuits in the milk and sherry and place them side by side on the serving dish.
4. Spread half the cream over this.
5. Soak the next 3 biscuits and place them on top of the cream.
6. Spread this with half the chestnut purée.
7. Repeat these two layers.
8. Top with 3 biscuits.
9. Place the chocolate in a pan with a very little water and heat gently until smooth and thick. Beat in the butter.
10. Pour over the biscuits and when nearly set decorate with the walnuts. Refrigerate.

Serves 4

Coffee Rum Tipsy Cake

2 plain sponge cakes *or* 2 boxes small bought sponge cakes
150ml/¼ pint boiling water
3 heaped tablespoons instant coffee
4 tablespoons sugar
1 tablespoon rum

140g/5oz icing sugar
85g/3oz butter
290ml/½ pint double cream
55g/2oz whole blanched almonds

1. Break up the cakes roughly and put them in a large bowl.
2. Boil the water, pour on to the coffee and sugar, and stir until the sugar has dissolved.
3. Add the rum and pour over the cake. Do not mix it in too much (the cake should retain a 'marbled' look, half white, half brown) but turn with a metal spoon.
4. Press the cake into a mixing bowl, and leave it with a weight on top (a 1 kilo/2lb can of fruit standing on a side plate will do) while you make the icing.
5. Beat the icing sugar and butter together until very light and creamy.
6. Whip the cream until just firm enough to hold its shape.
7. Brown the nuts under the grill.
8. Unmould the cake on to a plate. Using a palette knife dipped in hot water, spread the butter icing over the cake.
9. Then spread a layer of whipped cream over the icing and stud with the almonds.

Serves 4

Trifle

1 sponge cake, preferably stale
Raspberry jam
4 tablespoons sherry
2 tablespoons brandy
425ml/¾ pint milk
2 tablespoons sugar
5 egg yolks
2 drops vanilla essence

290ml/½ pint double
  cream
30g/1oz split blanched
  almonds
6 glacé cherries
Angelica (optional)
A few ratafia biscuits
  (optional)

1. Cut the sponge cake into thick pieces. Spread each piece sparingly with jam. Pile them into a glass dish.
2. Pour over the sherry and brandy and leave to soak while you prepare the custard.
3. Put the milk and sugar into a saucepan and bring to the point of boiling.
4. In a large bowl, lightly beat the yolks with a fork. Pour the scalding milk on to them, stirring with a wooden spoon.
5. Return the mixture to the saucepan and reheat carefully, stirring all the time, until it thickens enough to coat the back of the spoon. Care must be taken not to boil the custard, lest it curdle. Add the vanilla.
6. Strain on to the cake and leave to get quite cold.
7. Whip the cream until fairly stiff and spread or pipe over the trifle.
8. Decorate with the almonds, glacé cherries, angelica cut into diamond-shapes, and ratafia biscuits.

Note I: A perfectly acceptable quick custard can be made more simply by first making a very thin custard with custard powder, and then pouring this boiling custard from a height on to the egg yolks, stirring continuously. Alternatively the milk can be thickened with a level tablespoon of cornflour, and then poured on to the egg yolks. The inclusion of the egg yolks is desirable, however.

Note II: A fruit trifle is made by adding cooked or raw fruits before pouring on the custard. The use of jelly is abominable.

Serves 4

Chocolate Crumble Cake

85g/3oz dark chocolate
85g/3oz butter
45g/1½oz caster sugar
2 tablespoons golden syrup

340g/¾lb broken biscuits
85g/3oz glacé cherries
85g/3oz flaked almonds

1. Chop the chocolate and melt it slowly with the butter, sugar and syrup, stirring all the time.
2. Add the crushed biscuits, cherries and almonds.
3. Grease a sheet of greaseproof paper and the inside of a 20cm/8in flan ring.
4. Press the mixture on to the paper and flatten it, using the flan ring to get a round shape.
5. Allow to cool until set hard.
6. Cut into small slices.

Serves 4

Cannon-Ball Christmas Pudding

1 dessert apple
110g/¼lb self-raising flour
Pinch of salt
1 level teaspoon mixed spice
½ level teaspoon ground cinnamon
¼ level teaspoon ground nutmeg
225g/½lb shredded beef suet
225g/½lb fresh white breadcrumbs
340g/¾lb soft brown sugar
55g/2oz flaked almonds

225g/½lb seedless raisins
225g/½lb currants
225g/½lb sultanas
110g/¼lb chopped mixed peel
110g/¼lb prunes, soaked
2 tablespoons black treacle
3 eggs
290ml/½ pint stout *or* brown ale *or* milk
2 tablespoons rum (optional)
Grated rind and juice of 1 lemon

To serve:

1 sprig of holly   Hard brandy sauce
Brandy *or* rum

1. Grate the apple, skin and all.
2. Sieve the flour, salt and spices into a large bowl. Add the suet, apple, and the other dry ingredients.
3. Heat the treacle until warm and runny. Mix all the liquids together (treacle, eggs, beer or milk, rum and lemon juice). Then add to the dry ingredients. Mix well – the mixture should fall off the spoon in large blobs.
4. Fill the mixture into a buttered 'freezing quality' polythene bag and tie the top. Put into a muslin cloth. Using strong string, tie up like Dick Whittington's bag.
5. Suspend this bag in a large pan of boiling water so that the whole pudding is submerged but not touching the bottom. (Use a really large saucepan with a wooden spoon laid across the top to tie the pudding strings to.)
6. Boil gently but steadily for 10 hours, topping the pan up with more boiling water as necessary.
7. Cool the pudding in the suspended position, with the water poured away (cooling it on a plate would spoil its cannon-ball shape).
8. Hang in a cool place until needed.
9. To reheat: replace the buttered polythene bag with a fresh one, wrap in a cloth again, suspend in the saucepan as before and repeat the boiling process for 3 hours.
10. Unwrap with care. Dish the pudding, best and smoothest side up. Stick in a sprig of fresh holly.
11. Slightly warm a small ladle of brandy or rum, set it alight and pour it flaming over the pudding. The holly will crackle and splutter, drawing the attention of the diners to the burning pudding.

Note: This pudding may be steamed or boiled in the usual way in two 1 litre/2 pint basins or one 2 litre/4 pint. Two smaller basins will require 6 hours' cooking and 2 hours' re-heating, the larger one 10 hours' cooking and 3 hours' reheating.

Serves 12

PASTRIES AND CRUMBLES

Shortcrust Pastry

170g/6oz plain flour
Pinch of salt
30g/1oz lard

55g/2oz butter
Very cold water

1. Sift the flour with the salt.
2. Rub in the fats until the mixture looks like breadcrumbs.
3. Add 2 tablespoons of water to the mixture. Mix to a firm dough – first with a knife, and finally with one hand. It may be necessary to add more water, but the pastry should not be too damp. (Though crumbly pastry is more difficult to handle, it produces a shorter, less tough result.)
4. Chill, wrapped, for 30 minutes before using. Or allow to relax after rolling out but before baking.

Rich Shortcrust Pastry

170g/6oz plain flour
Pinch of salt
100g/3½oz butter

1 egg yolk
Very cold water

1. Sift the flour with the salt.
2. Rub in the butter until the mixture looks like breadcrumbs.
3. Mix the yolk with 2 tablespoons of water and add to the mixture.
4. Mix to a firm dough – first with a knife, and finally with one hand. It may be necessary to add more water, but the pastry should not be too damp. (Though crumbly pastry is

more difficult to handle, it produces a shorter, less tough result.)

5. Chill, wrapped, for 30 minutes before using, or allow to relax after rolling out but before baking.

Wholemeal Pastry

140g/5oz butter
110g/¼lb wholemeal flour
110g/¼lb plain flour

Pinch of salt
1 egg yolk
Water

1. Rub the butter into the flours and salt until the mixture looks like coarse breadcrumbs.
2. Mix the yolk with 2 tablespoons of water and add to the mixture.
3. Mix to a firm dough – first with a knife and then with one hand. It may be necessary to add more water, but the pastry should not be too damp. (Although crumbly pastry is more difficult to handle, it produces a shorter, less tough result.)
4. Chill in the refrigerator for at least 30 minutes before using, or allow the rolled-out pastry to relax before baking.

Note I: To make sweet wholemeal pastry mix in two level tablespoons of sugar once the fat has been rubbed into the flour.

Note II: All wholemeal flour may be used if preferred.

Suet Pastry

(And how to line a pudding basin)

Butter for greasing
340g/¾lb self-raising flour
Salt

170g/6oz shredded beef suet
Water to mix

1. Grease a pudding basin.
2. Sift the flour with a good pinch of salt into a bowl. Rub in

the shredded suet and add enough water to mix, first with a knife, and then with one hand, to a soft dough.

3. On a floured surface roll out two-thirds of the pastry into a round about 1cm/½in thick. Sprinkle the pastry evenly with flour.

4. Fold the round in half and place the open curved sides towards you.

5. Shape the pastry by rolling the straight edge away from you and gently pushing the middle and pulling the sides to form a bag that, when spread out, will fit the pudding basin.

6. With a dry pastry brush remove all excess flour and place the bag in the well-greased basin.

7. Fill the pastry bag with the desired mixture.

8. Roll out the remaining piece of pastry and use it as a lid, damping the edges and pressing them firmly together.

9. Cover the basin with buttered greaseproof paper, pleated in the centre and a layer of pleated tin foil. (Pleating the paper and foil allows the pastry to expand slightly without bursting the wrappings.) Tie down firmly to prevent water or steam getting in during cooking.

Note: Occasionally suet pastry is used for other purposes than steamed puddings, in which case it should be mixed as above and then handled like any other pastry, except that it does not need to relax before cooking.

Rough-Puff Pastry

225g/½lb plain flour
Pinch of salt

140g/5oz butter
Very cold water

1. Sift the flour and salt into a cold bowl. Cut the butter into knobs about the size of a sugar lump and add to the flour. Do not rub in but add enough water to just bind the paste together. Mix first with a knife, then with one hand.

2. Wrap the pastry up and leave to relax for 10 minutes in the refrigerator.

3. On a floured board, roll the pastry into a strip about 15cm × 10cm (6in × 4in). This must be done carefully: with a heavy rolling pin press firmly on the pastry and give short sharp rolls until the pastry has reached the required size. The surface of the pastry should not be over-stretched and broken.
4. Fold the strip into three and turn so that the folded edge is to your left, like a closed book.
5. Again roll out into a strip 1cm/½in thick. Fold in three again and leave, wrapped, in the refrigerator for 15 minutes.
6. Roll and fold the pastry as before then chill again for 15 minutes.
7. Roll and fold again, by which time the pastry should be ready for use, with no signs of streakiness.
8. Roll into the required shape.
9. Chill again before baking.

Choux Pastry

85g/3oz butter
220ml/7½fl.oz water
105g/3¾oz plain flour, well sifted

Pinch of salt
3 eggs

1. Put the butter and water together in a heavy saucepan. Bring slowly to the boil so that by the time the water boils the butter is completely melted.
2. *Immediately* the mixture is really boiling fast, tip in all the flour and draw the pan off the heat.
3. Working as fast as you can, beat the mixture hard with a wooden spoon: it will soon become thick and smooth and leave the sides of the pan. Beat in the salt.
4. Stand the bottom of the saucepan in a basin or sink of cold water to speed up the cooling process.
5. When the mixture is cool, beat in the eggs a little at a time until it is soft, shiny and smooth. If the eggs are large it may not be necessary to add all of them. The mixture should be of dropping consistency – not too runny. ('Dropping con-

sistency' means that the mixture will fall off a spoon rather reluctantly and all in a blob – if it runs off it is too wet, if it will not fall off even when the spoon is slightly jerked, it is too thick.)

6. Use as required.

Apple and Orange Crumble

1 kilo/2lb cooking apples
3 tablespoons demerara sugar

Pinch of cinnamon
3 oranges

For the crumble:
110g/¼lb butter
170g/6oz plain flour

Pinch of salt
55g/2oz sugar

1. Peel and core the apples. Cut into chunks and place in a saucepan with the demerara sugar and cinnamon.
2. Add enough water to come 0·5cm/¼in up the pan. Stew gently until the apples are just beginning to soften.
3. Peel the oranges as you would an apple, with a sharp knife, removing all the pith.
4. Cut out the orange segments leaving behind the membranes. Add to the apple mixture.
5. Allow to cool, then tip off any excess juice.
6. Set the oven to 200°C/400°F, gas mark 6.
7. Rub the fat into the flour, add salt and when the mixture resembles coarse breadcrumbs mix in the sugar.
8. Pour the apple and orange mixture into an ovenproof dish and sprinkle over the crumble mixture.
9. Bake for 25–30 minutes or until hot and slightly browned on top.

Note: If using wholemeal flour for the crumble top use 140g/5oz of *melted* butter. Instead of rubbing it into the flour mix briskly with a knife.

Serves 4

Plum Pie

225g/½lb plain flour
Pinch of salt
55g/2oz lard

85g/3oz butter
2–3 tablespoons cold water

For the filling:
675g/1½lb plums
3 tablespoons demerara sugar

½ level teaspoon ground cinnamon

Caster sugar to dredge

1. Preheat the oven to 220°C/425°F, gas mark 7.
2. Sift the flour with the salt into a bowl. Rub in the fats until the mixture resembles breadcrumbs.
3. Stir in enough water to bind the paste together. Push together into a lump, wrap up and chill in the refrigerator while you prepare the filling.
4. Wash the plums and place them in a pan with just enough water to cover the bottom of the pan. Add the demerara sugar and cinnamon. Stir gently until the sugar dissolves and the plums are half cooked.
5. Put the plums and a cupful of the juice into a 1 litre/1½ pint pie dish. Allow to cool.
6. Roll out the pastry on a floured board. Cut a band of pastry wider than the rim of the dish. Wet the rim and press the band on all the way round. Brush with water and lay over the rolled out pastry. Trim the edges, press them down firmly and mark with a fork or press into a frilly edge with fingers and thumb.
7. Shape the pastry trimmings into leaves. Brush the top of the pie with water and decorate with the leaves. Brush the leaves with water and dredge the whole pie with caster sugar.
8. Cut one or two small slits in the pastry top to allow the steam to escape. Bake for 25–35 minutes.

Note I: Classically, sweet pastry pies are not decorated with leaves etc., but why ever not?

Note II: If the liquid in which the plums have been poached is very thin, reduce it rapidly until slightly thickened.

Serves 6

Treacle Tart

110g/¼lb plain flour
Pinch of salt
70g/2½oz butter

1 level tablespoon caster sugar
1 egg yolk
Very cold water

For the filling:

4 heaped tablespoons fresh
   white breadcrumbs
8 tablespoons golden syrup

Grated rind of ½ lemon and
   2 teaspoons of the juice
Pinch of ginger (optional)

1. Set the oven to 190 C/375 F, gas mark 5.
2. Sift the flour with the salt. Rub in the butter until the mixture looks like breadcrumbs. Add the sugar.
3. Mix the yolk with 2 tablespoons of water, and add to the mixture.
4. Mix to a firm dough – first with a knife, and finally with one hand. It may be necessary to add water but the pastry should not be too wet. (Though crumbly pastry is more difficult to handle, it produces a shorter, less tough result.)
5. Roll the pastry out to 0·5cm/¼in thick, and line a pie plate or flan ring with it. Prick the bottom with a fork.
6. Heat the syrup with the lemon juice and rind to make it a little runny. Add the ginger if using.
7. Pour half the syrup into the pastry case.
8. Sprinkle with crumbs until they are soaked. Pour in the remaining syrup and sprinkle in the remaining crumbs.
9. Bake for about 30 minutes or until the filling is almost set and the edge of the pastry is brown. The filling should be a little on the soft side if the tart is to be eaten cold, because it hardens as it cools. Ideally, serve lukewarm.

Serves 4

Lemon Meringue Pie

170g/6oz plain flour
Pinch of salt
100g/3½oz butter

1 teaspoon caster sugar
1 egg yolk
Very cold water

For the filling:
30g/1oz cornflour
290ml/½ pint milk
30g/1oz sugar

2 egg yolks
Grated rind and juice of 1
    lemon

For the meringue:
110g/¼lb caster sugar
Little extra caster sugar

1. First make the pastry: sift the flour with the salt. Rub in the butter until the mixture looks like breadcrumbs. Add the sugar.
2. Mix the yolk with 2 tablespoons of water. Add this to the mixture.
3. Mix to a firm dough – first with a knife, and finally with one hand. It may be necessary to add more water, but the pastry should not be too wet. (Though crumbly pastry is more difficult to handle, it produces a shorter, less tough result.)
4. Roll out the pastry and use it to line a 20cm/8in flan ring. Leave it in the refrigerator for about 30 minutes to relax (this prevents shrinkage during cooking).
5. Heat the oven to 190°C/375°C, gas mark 5.
6. Bake the pastry blind.
7. Meanwhile, make the filling: mix the cornflour with a tablespoon of the milk.
8. Heat the remaining milk. Pour this on to the cornflour paste, stir well and return the mixture to the pan. Boil for 3–4 minutes, stirring continuously. Add the sugar.
9. Allow to cool slightly, then beat in the egg yolks, lemon rind and juice.
10. Pour this mixture into the pastry case. Return to the oven

for 2 minutes to set. Whisk the egg whites until stiff. Add half the caster sugar and whisk again until very stiff and solid.

11. Fold in the remaining sugar. Pile the meringue on to the pie. It is essential to cover the filling completely or the pie will weep. Dust with a little extra caster sugar.

12. Place in the oven for 5 minutes or until the meringue is a pale biscuit colour.

Note: Lemon curd (page 451) makes a good alternative to the lemon custard filling.

Baking blind: See page 211, *note*.

Serves 4

Raisin and Yoghurt Tartlets

170g/6oz flour-quantity sweet
  wholemeal pastry (page 370)
1 large egg
55g/2oz caster sugar
1 tablespoon plain flour
Pinch of nutmeg

Pinch of cinnamon
2 teaspoons lemon juice
Rind of ½ lemon
150ml/5 fl. oz yoghurt
55g/2oz raisins

1. Set the oven to 200°C/400°F, gas mark 6.
2. Roll out the pastry thinly and cut into rounds a size larger than the patty tins.
3. Turn the patty tins upside down and press the pastry firmly over the outside of the tin moulds. Prick them lightly. Bake for 10 minutes. Reduce the oven to 180°C/350°F, gas mark 4.
4. Remove the pastry cases from the outside of the tins and turn them right side up on a baking sheet. Return to the oven until the pastry is crisp and cooked.
5. Put the egg and the sugar into a pudding bowl. Stand this over a pan of boiling water. Whisk until the mixture thickens sufficiently to leave a 'ribbon' trail.

6. Fold in the flour, spices, lemon juice, rind, yoghurt and raisins.
7. Fill the mixture into the tartlet cases and bake for 20–25 minutes or until the mixture is firm. Leave to cool on a wire rack.

Makes 18

Cherry Tartlets

110g/¼lb flour-quantity rich
   shortcrust pastry (page 369)
Two 450g/15oz tins morello
   cherries, pitted

45g/1½oz arrowroot
4 tablespoons water
225g/½lb cream cheese
2 tablespoons caster sugar

1. Set the oven to 190 C/375 F, gas mark 5.
2. Line 16 tartlet moulds with pastry and bake blind.
3. Drain the cherries well and heat the juice in a saucepan.
4. Mix the arrowroot with the water.
5. When the cherry juice is nearly boiling add a little to the arrowroot and then return the mixture to the pan. Bring gradually up to the boil, stirring continuously, and boil for 2 minutes. Keep warm.
6. Mix the cream cheese with the sugar and place a little in each tartlet.
7. Arrange the cherries in the tartlet cases, making sure that they are well filled.
8. Brush the warm cherry sauce over the cherries (each cherry must be individually glazed) and leave to cool.

Note: A layer of crème chantilly or crème pâtissière (page 349) under the cherries is good too.

Baking blind: See page 211, *note*.

Makes 16

Apple Florentine

1 kilo/2lb cooking apples
55g/2oz butter
50g/2oz demerara *or*
  barbados sugar

1 teaspoon ground cinnamon
Grated rind of 1 lemon
225g/½lb flour-quantity rough-
  puff pastry (page 371)

Spiced cider:
150ml/¼ pint cider
Pinch of ground nutmeg and
  ginger

1 stick cinnamon
Pared rind of ½ lemon
55g/2oz sugar

To serve:
Icing sugar

Ice cream *or* whipped cream

1. Set the oven to 200°C/400°F, gas mark 6.
2. Peel, core and quarter the apples.
3. Melt the butter in a frying pan and when foaming add the apples. Fry until delicately browned.
4. Tip into a pie dish and mix in the sugar, cinnamon and lemon rind. Allow to cool.
5. Roll out the pastry on a floured board to ½cm/¼in thickness.
6. Cut a strip of pastry very slightly wider than the edge of the dish. Brush the rim with water and press the strip down all round it.
7. Lift the pastry with the aid of the rolling pin and lay it on the pie. Press down the edge and trim the sides.
8. Mark round the edge with the prongs of a folk or the tip of a knife. Brush with cold water and dust with caster sugar.
9. Bake the pie for 25–30 minutes until golden brown.
10. Prepare the spiced cider: heat all the ingredients together in a pan over a gentle heat for 10 minutes without boiling. Strain.
11. Remove the pie from the oven and with a sharp knife lift off the crust in one piece. Pour in the spiced cider.
12. Return the crust on to the pie and dust with icing sugar. Serve hot with ice cream or whipped cream.

Note: 'Florentine' is an obsolete word for pie.

Serves 4

Tarte Française

110g/¼lb flour-quantity rough
  puff pastry (page 371)
3 tablespoons warm apricot
  glaze (page 399)
Squeeze of lemon

Fruit as for a fruit salad: say 1
pear, 1 orange, small bunch
black grapes, small bunch
white grapes, 6 strawberries,
2 bananas etc.

1. Roll out the pastry into as neat a rectangle as you can. It should
   be the thickness of a penny. Prick it well all over.
2. Bake in a hot oven (230 C/450 F, gas mark 8) for 12 minutes
   or until crisp and brown.
3. Remove from the oven and turn over on to a flat serving
   plate. Trim the edges neatly and allow to cool.
4. Use a little of the glaze to brush the surface of the pastry.
5. Cut the fruit up as you would for a fruit salad, and lay the
   pieces in rows on the pastry as neatly and closely together
   as possible. Be careful about colour (do not put two rows
   of white fruit next to each other, or tangerine segments next
   to orange segments etc.). As each row goes down, paint it
   carefully with the glaze. This is most important especially
   with fruit that discolours, like bananas, apples and pears.
6. Serve with crème chantilly (page 349).

Serves 4

Chocolate Profiteroles

For the profiteroles:
3 egg quantity choux pastry
  (page 372)

For the filling and topping:
170g/6oz chocolate
4 tablespoons water
15g/½oz butter

570ml/1 pint whipped cream,
sweetened with 1 tablespoon
icing sugar

1. Set the oven to 200 C/400 F, gas mark 6.
2. Put small teaspoons of the choux mixture on a wet baking sheet, about 8cm/3in apart.
3. Bake for 20–30 minutes. The profiteroles should swell, and become fairly brown. If they are taken out when only slightly brown they will be soggy when cool.
4. Make a hole the size of a pea in the side of each profiterole and return to the oven for 5 minutes to allow the insides to dry out. Cool on a wire rack.
5. When cold fill each profiterole with cream, using a forcing bag fitted with a small plain nozzle.
6. Melt the chocolate with the water and butter and stir, without boiling, until smooth and shiny.
7. Dip the tops of the profiteroles in the chocolate and allow to cool.

Note: If no piping bag for filling the profiteroles is available they can be split, allowed to dry out, and filled with cream or crème pâtissière when cold, and the icing can be spooned over the top. They are then messier to eat in the fingers, however.

Serves 4

Coffee Éclairs

3 egg quantity choux pastry
  (page 372)

For the filling and topping:
425ml/$\frac{3}{4}$ pint double cream *or*   2 tablespoons very strong hot
  crème pâtissière (page 349)   black coffee
225g/$\frac{1}{2}$lb icing sugar

1. Heat the oven to 200 C/400°F, gas mark 6. Wet two baking sheets.
2. Make up the choux pastry.
3. Using a forcing bag with a 1cm/$\frac{1}{2}$in plain nozzle, pipe 5cm/2in lengths of choux pastry on to the baking sheets (keep them

well separated as choux pastry swells during cooking). Bake for 25–30 minutes until hard and pale brown.

4. Make a pea-sized hole in each one with a skewer to allow the steam to escape and return to the oven for 5 minutes to dry the insides out. Place on a wire rack to cool.

5. Whip the cream and put it (or the crème pâtissière) into a forcing bag fitted with a medium nozzle. Pipe cream into the éclairs through the hole made by the skewer, until well filled.

6. Mix the icing sugar and coffee together and beat with a wooden spoon until smooth. The mixture should be just runny.

7. Dip each éclair upside down into the icing so that the top becomes neatly coated.

8. Set aside to dry. Alternatively, the icing can be carefully spooned along the top ridge of each éclair.

Note: The éclairs may be split lengthwise when cooked, allowed to dry out, and filled with cream or crème pâtissière when cold. The tops are then replaced and the icing spooned over. They are then messier to eat in the fingers, however.

Serves 4

Choux á la Crème (Cream Puffs)

3-egg quantity choux pastry   Icing sugar
  (page 372)
290ml/½ pint crème chantilly
  (page 349)

1. Set the oven to 200 C/400 F, gas mark 6. Wet a baking sheet.
2. Put spoonfuls of the choux paste, about the size of a golf ball, on to the wet baking sheet 8cm/3in apart.
3. With a fork lift the paste into peaks all over the balls so that they have a spiky appearance.
4. Bake for 30 minutes. They should swell and become a good brown.
5. Remove the buns from the oven and loosen from the baking

sheet. Split them in half horizontally and return to the oven for 5 minutes to dry out, or scoop out dry uncooked pastry and discard. Allow to cool.

6. Fill the bases with the crème chantilly and press the lids back on gently. Dust with icing sugar.

Serves 4

Apricot Ring

110g/¼lb apricots
150ml/¼ pint sugar syrup (page 350)
3 egg quantity choux pastry (page 372)

2 tablespoons apricot jam
140g/5oz icing sugar
290ml/½ pint double cream, whipped
30g/1oz browned almonds.

1. Set the oven to 200 C/400 F, gas mark 6.
2. Wash and halve the apricots and remove the stones. Poach in the sugar syrup until just tender (about 15 minutes). Drain well and leave to cool.
3. Pipe the choux paste mixture into a circle about 15cm/6in in diameter on a wet baking tray. Cook for about 30 minutes until brown and crisp.
4. Split horizontally with a bread knife. Scoop out any uncooked paste and discard; leave on a wire rack to cool.
5. Heat the jam and spread it on to the base of the choux ring.
6. Mix 30g/1oz of the icing sugar with the whipped cream and fold in the apricots.
7. Spoon the mixture on to the base and press the lid on firmly.
8. Mix the rest of the icing sugar with a little boiling water until just runny. Coat the top of the choux ring with the icing, and while still wet sprinkle with browned almonds.

Serves 6

PANCAKES

French Pancakes (Crêpes)

110g/¼lb plain flour
Pinch of salt
1 egg
1 egg yolk

290ml/½ pint milk *or* milk and
    water mixed
1 tablespoon oil
Oil for frying

1. Sift the flour and salt into a bowl and make a well in the centre exposing the bottom of the bowl.
2. Into this well place the egg and egg yolk with a little of the milk.
3. Using a wooden spoon or whisk mix the egg and milk and then gradually draw in the flour from the sides as you mix.
4. When the mixture reaches the consistency of thick cream beat well and stir in the oil.
5. Add the rest of the milk—the consistency should now be that of thin cream. (Batter can also be made by placing all the ingredients together in a liquidizer for a few seconds, but take care not to over-whizz or the mixture will be bubbly.)
6. Cover the bowl and refrigerate for about 30 minutes. This is done so that the starch cells will swell, giving a lighter result.
7. Prepare a pancake pan or frying pan by heating well and wiping out with oil. Pancakes are not fried in fat like most foods – the purpose of the oil is simply to prevent sticking.
8. When the pan is ready, pour in about 1 tablespoon of batter and swirl about the pan until evenly spread across the bottom.
9. Place over heat and, after 1 minute, using a palette knife and your fingers, turn the pancake over and cook again until brown. (Pancakes should be extremely thin, so if the first

one is too thick, add a little extra milk to the batter. The first pancake is unlikely to be perfect, and is often discarded.)
10. Make up all the pancakes, turning them out on to a tea-towel or plate.

Note I: Pancakes can be kept warm in a folded tea-towel, on a plate over a saucepan of simmering water, in the oven, or in a warmer. If allowed to cool, they may be reheated by being briefly returned to the frying pan or by warming in an oven.

Note II: Pancakes freeze well, but should be separated by pieces of greaseproof paper. They may also be refrigerated for a day or two.

Makes about 12

Orange and Grand Marnier Pancakes

8 French pancakes (page 384)
Grated rind of 1 large orange
290ml/½ pint crème pâtissière
  (page 349)

2 tablespoons Grand Marnier
Icing sugar

1. Heat the grill.
2. Mix the orange rind with the crème pâtissière and the Grand Marnier.
3. Divide the mixture between the pancakes.
4. Fold each pancake in half and dust heavily with icing sugar.
5. Place under a hot grill until the icing sugar begins to caramelize.

Note: May be served with more Grand Marnier poured over and flamed, if liked.

Serves 4

Apricot Pancake Pie

12 French pancakes (page 384)

For the filling:
140g/5oz sugar
290ml/½ pint water

450g/1lb apricots, halved and
  stoned

For the decoration:
150ml/¼ pint double cream

30g/1oz toasted almonds

1. Dissolve the sugar in the water and when clear add the apricots and poach gently for 6–8 minutes. Lift out the fruit and drain well. Cut into thin slices.
2. Boil the sugar syrup rapidly until thick. Allow to cool and put back the apricots.
3. Layer the cold pancakes and the apricots (with the sugar syrup) alternately, finishing with a pancake. Make sure the pie is flat-topped.
4. Half-whip the cream, and spread it evenly on the top and sides of the pile and sprinkle with toasted almonds.
5. Serve cut in wedges.

Note: As the pancakes are to be served cold it is vital that they are paper-thin. Thick cold pancake is very doughy.

Serves 4

FRUIT

Stewed Apples

170g/6oz sugar
570ml/1 pint water
450g/1lb dessert apples

Stick of cinnamon
Squeeze of lemon juice

To serve:
Cream (optional)

1. Dissolve the sugar in the water. When completely dissolved, boil rapidly until you have a thin syrup (3–4 minutes).
2. Peel, core and quarter the apples. Place them in the sugar syrup with the cinnamon.
3. Bring slowly to the boil, then reduce the heat and poach gently until the apples are tender.
4. Remove the apples with a draining spoon and arrange in a shallow dish.
5. Reduce the syrup rapidly by further boiling until it is tacky, then add the lemon juice. Pour over the fruit.
6. Serve hot with cream, or chilled with or without cream.

Serves 4

Blackcurrant Kissel

450g/1lb blackcurrants
Caster sugar to taste (about
  170g/6oz)

2 teaspoons arrowroot

1. Wash the blackcurrants and remove the stalks.
2. Barely cover with water and add the sugar. Stew gently for about 20 minutes.
3. Mix a little cold water with the arrowroot and mix to a smooth paste.
4. To the arrowroot add a cupful of the boiling juice and mix thoroughly. Add the arrowroot mixture to the fruit, stirring, and allow to thicken. Simmer for 2–3 minutes.
5. Push the mixture through a nylon or stainless steel sieve. Stir and then pour into a serving bowl. Sprinkle evenly with caster sugar to prevent a skin forming.

Serves 4

Baked Apples

Smallish cooking apples   Sultanas
Brown sugar

1. Wash the apples and remove the cores with an apple corer. With a sharp knife cut a ring just through the apple skin round the fattest part of each apple.
2. Put the apples in a fireproof dish and stuff the centres with a mixture of brown sugar and sultanas.
3. In addition to this scatter a dozen or so sultanas for each apple over the top, and sprinkle 2 teaspoons of brown sugar over each apple. Then pour ½cm/¼in of water into the bottom of the dish.
4. Bake in a moderate oven (200°C/400°F, gas mark 6) for about 1 hour or until the apples are soft right through when tested with a skewer.

Melon with Ginger Wine

Small melons
Ginger wine

1. Buy Ogen melons, either tiny individual ones or slightly bigger ones that can be split between two people.
2. Scoop out the seeds of the melons and pour 1 tablespoon of ginger wine into each. Chill well before serving.

Note: This is much nicer than melon with port.

Red Fruit Salad

675g/1½lb assorted raspberries, strawberries, redcurrants, watermelon, plums *or* any fresh red fruit

425ml/¾ pint sugar syrup (page 350)
2 tablespoons kirsch (optional)

1. Check over the raspberries, discarding any bad ones.
2. Hull and halve the strawberries.
3. Wash, top and tail the redcurrants.
4. Cut the melon flesh into cubes, discarding the seeds.
5. Halve and stone the plums.
6. Put the fruit into a glass dish and add the syrup, and kirsch if required.

Serves 4

Green Fruit Salad

225g/½lb granulated sugar
570ml/1 pint water
Pared rind of 1 lemon
Green-coloured fresh fruit, e.g.:
  1 green dessert apple
  225g/½lb Chinese
    gooseberries

225g/½lb greengages
225g/½lb white grapes
  1 small ripe melon with green
    flesh
Juice of ½ lemon
2 tablespoons kirsch (optional)

1. Put the sugar and water on together to boil and add the lemon rind. Boil until the syrup feels tacky. Remove from the heat and allow to cool.
2. Do not peel the apple, but core it and cut into thin slivers. Put immediately into the syrup.
3. Peel and slice the gooseberries. Stone and quarter the greengages and halve and seed the grapes.
4. Using a melon baller, scoop the melon flesh into balls, or simply cut into even-sized cubes.
5. Put all this into the syrup and add the lemon juice, and kirsch if required. Chill well.

Serves 6–8

Pineapple Fruit Salad Basket

4 small pineapples   110g/¼lb black grapes
1 apple   110g/¼lb green grapes
3 oranges   110g/¼lb melon
1 banana   6 strawberries

1. Cut the pineapples in half lengthwise, making sure that each half has an equal amount of green leaves.
2. With a grapefruit knife carefully remove the flesh around the edge of the shell; reserve the juice.
3. With a stainless steel knife core and cut the apple into slivers. Put them immediately into the pineapple juice.
4. Peel the oranges with a knife as you would an apple, making sure that all the pith is removed with the skin. With a sharp knife cut into neat segments, discarding all the skin and membrane.
5. Cut the banana into chunks and place immediately into the pineapple juice.
6. Halve and pip the grapes.
7. Scoop the melon into balls with a melon baller.
8. Toss the fruit in pineapple juice and pile into the pineapple shells.
9. Hull and halve the strawberries and scatter over the top.

Serves 8

Pineapple in the Shell

1 large pineapple

1. Cut the top and bottom off the pineapple so that you are left with a cylinder of fruit. Do not throw away the leafy top. With a sharp knife cut round inside the skin, working first from one end and then from the other, so that you can push the fruit out in one piece. Try not to pierce or tear the skin.

2. Slice the pineapple very finely. Stand the pineapple skin in a shallow bowl, put the fruit back in it and replace the top. If the fruit is very sour, sprinkle sugar between the slices as you replace them. Kirsch can be sprinkled in too if liked.

Oranges in Caramel

$1\frac{1}{2}$ oranges per person
Caramel sauce (page 352)

1. With a potato peeler pare the rind of 1 or 2 oranges very finely, making sure that there is no pith on the back of the strips. Cut into very fine shreds.
2. Simmer these needleshreds in caramel sauce or sugar syrup until soft and almost candied. They should be very sticky and quite dark.
3. Peel the remaining oranges with a knife as you would an apple, making sure that all the pith is removed.
4. Slice each orange.
5. Place the oranges in a glass bowl and pour over the cold caramel sauce. Chill well.
6. Scatter with needleshreds of orange before serving.

ICES

Detailed instructions on ice cream making are on pages 163–6.

Rich Vanilla Ice Cream

570ml/1 pint milk	8 egg yolks
290ml/$\frac{1}{2}$ pint single cream	Few drops vanilla essence
225g/$\frac{1}{2}$lb caster sugar	

1. Set the freezer or ice compartment to coldest. Put the milk, cream and sugar into a heavy saucepan and bring slowly to the boil. Beat the yolks with the vanilla in a large bowl.
2. Pour the boiling milky mixture on to the yolks, whisking as you do so. Strain into a roasting pan or into two ice trays. Cool.
3. Freeze until solid but still soft enough to give when pressed with a finger.
4. Tip the ice cream into a cold bowl, break it up, then whisk with a rotary beater until smooth, pale and creamy. If you have a Magimix, all the better. Refreeze.

Note: If the ice cream is made more than six hours in advance it will be too hard to scoop. Put it in the refrigerator for 40–60 minutes before serving to allow it to soften.

Serves 6–8

Damson Ice Cream

450g/1lb damsons
340g/¾lb caster sugar
150ml/¼ pint water
2 large egg whites

Juice and finely grated rind of
  1 small orange
290ml/½ pint double cream

1. Wash the damsons and put them, still wet, with 110g/¼lb of the sugar in a thick-bottomed saucepan. Stew gently, covered, over very gentle heat or bake in the oven until soft and pulpy.
2. Push through a sieve removing the stones.
3. Dissolve the remaining 225g/½lb sugar in the water and bring to the boil.
4. Boil steadily for 5 minutes.
5. While the syrup is boiling beat the egg whites in an electric mixer or by hand until stiff. Pour the boiling syrup on to the egg whites, whisking as you do so. The mixture will go rather liquid at this stage but keep whisking until you have a thick meringue.

6. Stir in the orange rind and juice and the purée.
7. Whip the cream until thick but not solid and fold it into the mixture.
8. Freeze. It is not necessary to re-whisk the ice cream during freezing.

Note: The damson purée can be replaced by a purée of cooked plums, greengages, rhubarb, dried apricots or prunes, or a raw purée of soft fruit, apricots or peaches.

Serves 6–8

Redcurrant Water Ice

450g/1lb sugar
425ml/¾ pint water

7g/¼oz gelatine
425ml/¾ pint redcurrant juice

1. Dissolve the sugar in the water over a low heat and when completely dissolved boil to the thread (i.e. when a little syrup is put between finger and thumb and the fingers opened, it should form a sticky thread 2·5cm/1in long).
2. In a small saucepan soak the gelatine in 2 tablespoons of redcurrant juice.
3. Add the rest of the juice to the sugar syrup.
4. Dissolve the gelatine over a low heat and when clear stir into the redcurrant mixture.
5. Allow to get quite cold.
6. Chill, then freeze. (See freezing notes.)

Serves 4

Lemon Sorbet

Pared rind and juice of 3
  lemons
170g/6oz granulated sugar

570ml/1 pint water
½ egg white

1. Place the lemon rind, sugar and water together in a thick-bottomed saucepan. Dissolve the sugar over a gentle heat and when completely clear boil rapidly until you have a thick syrup (i.e. sufficiently thick for a thread to form between finger and thumb when the fingers are dipped in the syrup and then moved apart).
2. Allow to cool. When the syrup is cold add the lemon juice and strain.
3. Freeze for 30 minutes or until the syrup is beginning to solidify.
4. Whisk the egg white until stiff and fold into the lemon syrup mixture.
5. Freeze until solid.

Serves 4

Strawberry Sorbet

170g/6oz caster sugar
560ml/½ pint water
Juice of ½ lemon *or* ½ small
  orange

340g/¾lb fresh or frozen
  strawberries
2 egg whites

1. Place the sugar and water together in a thick-bottomed saucepan. Dissolve over a gentle heat and when clear boil gently for 5 minutes. Add the lemon or orange juice and cool.
2. Liquidize or mash the strawberries to a pulp and add the syrup. Put in a bowl in the freezer for 30 minutes or until the syrup is beginning to solidify.
3. Whisk the egg whites until stiff and fold into the half frozen mixture. Return to the freezer until solid.

Serves 4

Black Coffee Granita

570ml/1 pint black coffee (four
  times normal strength)
2 teaspoons rum
225g/½lb brown sugar

To serve:
Whipped cream, sweetened
Toasted almonds

1. While the coffee is still hot stir in the rum and sugar until the sugar has completely dissolved. Taste and add more sugar if necessary.
2. When cold pour the mixture into an ice-tray and freeze until just solid.
3. Take the half-frozen coffee out, turn into a bowl and beat with a rotary beater until broken up, slushy and without large lumps, but not yet quite liquid.
4. Pour back into the ice-tray and pack down well, pressing the crystals with the back of a large spoon. Re-freeze.
5. Serve in tall chilled glasses with a swirl of sweetened whipped cream and a scattering of toasted almonds on top.

Note: This water ice should be slightly gritty in texture, not smooth and creamy like a sorbet.

Serves 4

BAKED AND STEAMED PUDDINGS

Baked Custard

3 whole eggs plus 1 egg yolk
3 drops vanilla essence

425ml/¾ pint very creamy milk
  or milk plus single cream
55g/2oz caster sugar

395

1. Set the oven to 170°C/325°F, gas mark 3.
2. Lightly mix the eggs, extra yolk and vanilla essence together; don't get them frothy.
3. Heat the milk to boiling point with the sugar, stirring as you do so.
4. Remove from the heat, cool for a second or two, and then pour on to the eggs, stirring all the time with a wooden spoon, not a whisk (you are trying to avoid creating bubbles).
5. Strain the mixture into an ovenproof dish (straining removes any egg 'threads' which would spoil the smooth texture of the finished custard).
6. Stand the custard dish in a roasting tin of hot water and bake in the oven for 40 minutes. It is set when there is a definite skin on the top and when the middle of the custard is no longer liquid (although it will still wobble).
7. Serve hot, warm or chilled.

Note: A good variation of this custard has a thickish layer of real lemon curd (page 451) spread on top when the custard is just warm. Serve with dollops of cream. Or sprinkle ground nutmeg on the surface before baking, or flavour with grated orange rind.

Serves 4

Rice Pudding

A nut of butter

1 level tablespoon sugar

55g/scant 2oz round (pudding) rice

570ml/1 pint milk

Vanilla essence

Ground nutmeg

1. Set the oven to 150°C/300°F, gas mark 2.
2. Rub the butter round a pie dish. Put the sugar, rice, milk and vanilla essence into the dish. Sprinkle with nutmeg.
3. Stir, and bake in the oven for 3–4 hours, by which time it should be soft and creamy with an evenly coloured brown skin.

Note: If the milk has not all been absorbed when you are ready to serve the pudding, here is a good trick. Mix a large egg in a teacup, carefully lift the pudding skin and spoon out some of the hot milk. Mix this with the egg in the teacup and then stir this milky egg into the rice. Replace skin and leave for 10 minutes in the oven. The milk should now set as in a custard.

Serves 4

Bread and Butter Pudding

1½ slices of plain bread	2 eggs and 1 yolk
30g/1oz butter	1 tablespoon sugar
2 level tablespoons currants	290ml/½ pint creamy milk
and sultanas, mixed	Vanilla essence
2 teaspoons candied peel	Ground cinnamon

1. Cut the crusts off the bread and spread with butter. Cut into fingers. Layer in a shallow ovenproof dish, butter side up, and sprinkle with currants, sultanas and candied peel as you proceed.
2. Make the custard: mix the eggs and yolk with the sugar and stir in the milk and vanilla essence.
3. Pour the custard carefully over the bread and leave to soak for 30 minutes. Sprinkle with ground cinnamon.
4. Heat the oven to 180°C/350°F, gas mark 4.
5. Place the pudding in a roasting tin of hot water and cook in the middle of the oven for about 45 minutes or until the custard is set and the top brown and crusty.

Note: The pudding may be baked without the bain-marie (hot water bath) quite successfully, but if used it will ensure a smooth, not bubbly custard.

Serves 4

Queen's Pudding

290ml/½ pint milk
15g/½oz butter
30g/1oz caster sugar for the custard
2 tablespoons fresh white breadcrumbs

Rind of 1 lemon
2 eggs
2 tablespoons raspberry jam, warm
110g/¼lb caster sugar for the meringue

1. Butter a fireproof pie dish. Set the oven to 190°C/375°F, gas mark 5.
2. Heat the milk and add the butter and sugar. Stir until the sugar dissolves, then add the breadcrumbs and lemon rind.
3. Separate the eggs. When the breadcrumb mixture has cooled slightly, mix in the egg yolks. Pour into the pie dish and leave to stand for 30 minutes.
4. Bake for 25 minutes or until the custard mixture is set. Remove and allow to cool slightly.
5. Reduce the oven to 170°C/325°F, gas mark 3.
6. Carefully spread the jam over the top of the custard. (This is easier if you melt the jam first.)
7. Whip the egg whites until stiff. Whisk in half the meringue sugar. Whisk again until very stiff and shiny and fold in all but half a teaspoon of the remaining sugar.
8. Pile the meringue on top of the custard and dust the top with the reserved sugar.
9. Bake until the meringue is set and straw coloured (about 10 minutes).

Note: This is particularly good served hot with cold whipped cream.

Serves 4

Apple Charlotte

1·125 kilos/2½lb apples
85g/3oz sugar
2 tablespoons apricot jam

15g/½oz butter
8 slices stale crustless bread
110g/4oz melted butter

Apricot glaze:
3 tablespoons apricot jam
4 tablespoons water

1. Peel, core and slice the apples and put them into a heavy pan. Add the sugar and cook, without water, until very soft. Boil away any extra liquid and push through a sieve. Whisk in the apricot jam.
2. Butter a charlotte mould or deep cake tin.
3. With a pastry cutter stamp one piece of bread into a circle to fit the bottom of your mould or tin and cut it into six equal sized triangles. Cut the remaining bread into strips.
4. Set the oven to 200°C/400°F, gas mark 6.
5. Dip the pieces of bread into the melted butter. Arrange the triangles to fit the bottom of the mould and arrange all but four of the strips in overlapping slices around the sides.
6. Spoon in the apple purée and arrange the four remaining strips of buttery bread on top.
7. Bake for 40 minutes. Allow to cool for 10 minutes.
8. Meanwhile, make the apricot glaze. Put the jam and water into a small heavy pan and heat, stirring occasionally, until warm and completely melted.
9. Turn out the pudding: invert a plate over the mould and turn the mould and plate over together. Give a sharp shake and remove the mould.
10. Brush the charlotte with the apricot glaze and serve with cream or custard.

Serves 5

Annabel's Cheesecake

For the crust:
1 packet babies' rusks *or*
   digestive biscuits, crushed
   (about 16 biscuits)
85g/3oz caster sugar
110g/¼lb butter, melted

For the topping:
½ carton soured cream
1 teaspoon caster sugar

For the filling:
225g/½lb best-quality soft
   cream cheese
5 tablespoons double cream
1 whole egg and 1 yolk
1 teaspoon vanilla essence
Sugar to taste (about 1
   tablespoon)

1. Set the oven to 190°C/375°F, gas mark 5.
2. Mix the crust ingredients together and line a shallow pie dish
   or flan ring with the mixture, pressing firmly against the sides
   and base. Be careful not to get the corners too thick.
3. Bake for 10 minutes or until hard to the touch.
4. Mix all the filling ingredients together until smooth and pour
   into the case.
5. Return to the oven until the filling has set (about 20 minutes).
6. Take out and allow to cool.
7. Spread with the soured cream mixed with the sugar.

Note: The top can be decorated with nuts, sultanas or fresh fruit
such as redcurrants or halved seeded grapes, but it is very good
as it is.

Serves 6

Eve's Pudding

675g/1½lb cooking apples
150ml/¼ pint water
110g/¼lb sugar
Grated rind of ½ lemon
Butter for greasing

For the crust:
55g/2oz butter

55g/2oz sugar
1 egg, beaten
85g/3oz self-raising flour
Pinch of salt
Grated rind of ½ lemon
2 tablespoons milk

1. Set the oven to 200°C/400°F, gas mark 6. Butter a pie dish.
2. Peel, core and slice the apples and place them in a heavy saucepan with the water, sugar and lemon. Stew gently until just soft, then tip into the pie dish.
3. Cream the butter until soft and beat in the sugar. When light and fluffy, add the beaten egg by degrees and mix until completely incorporated.
4. Sift the flour with the salt and fold it into the butter and egg mixture.
5. Add the lemon rind and enough milk to bring the mixture to dropping consistency. Spread this over the apple.
6. Bake in the oven for about 25 minutes or until the sponge mixture is firm to the touch and slightly shrunk at the edges.

Serves 4

Meringues

4 egg whites
225g/½lb caster sugar

For the filling:
Whipped cream

1. Set the oven to 110°C/225°F, gas mark ½.
2. Place greaseproof paper on two baking sheets, brush with oil and dust lightly with sugar.
3. Whisk the egg whites until stiff but not dry.
4. Add half the sugar and whisk again until very stiff and shiny.
5. Fold in the rest of the sugar.
6. Put the meringue mixture out on the paper-covered baking sheets in spoonfuls set fairly far apart. Use a teaspoon for tiny meringues, a dessertspoon for large ones.
7. Bake in the oven for about 2 hours until the meringues are dry right through and will lift easily off the paper.
8. When cold sandwich the meringues together in pairs with whipped cream.

Makes 50 *miniature or* 12 *large meringues*

Italian Meringue Pie

1 whisked sponge cake about 15cm/6in in diameter (page 413)
1 small can stoned black cherries
1 tablespoon marsala *or* rum

75ml/3fl.oz double cream, stiffly whipped
4 egg whites
255g/9oz icing sugar
Few drops vanilla essence

1. Cut the sponge cake in half. Lay the top half, crust down, next to the bottom one and pour enough of the warmed black cherry juice, and all the marsala or rum, over the cake to soak it in patches.
2. Mix the whipped cream and cherries together and spread on the bottom layer. Sandwich the cake together again.
3. Heat the oven to 220°C/425°F, gas mark 7.
4. Place the egg whites, sugar and vanilla essence in a bowl. Fit the bowl over a saucepan of simmering water and whisk until very thick.
5. Using a palette knife entirely coat the sponge with this meringue.
6. Bake in the oven for 3–4 minutes or until the meringue is lightly coloured.

Serves 4

Pavlova

2 egg whites
110g/¼lb caster sugar
1 teaspoon cornflour
1 teaspoon vanilla essence
½ teaspoon vinegar

290ml/½ pint double cream
30g/1oz broken walnuts
450g/1lb fresh pineapple, cored and cut into cubes, *or* one can tinned pineapple pieces

1. Set the oven to 140°C/275°F, gas mark 1.
2. Put a sheet of foil on a baking sheet, brush with oil and dust with caster sugar.

3. Whisk the egg whites until stiff. Add half the sugar and whisk again until thick, shiny, smooth and very stiff.
4. Whisk in the remaining sugar, the cornflour, the vanilla and the vinegar.
5. With a palette knife or spatula spread the meringue mixture on to the baking sheet in a large round or oval shape.
6. Place in the oven for 50 minutes. The meringue should look pale brown and dry but should be soft in the middle.
7. Immediately it is ready, turn it over on to a flat dish or platter, and peel away the paper. (If you allow the meringue to cool it will stick like the devil.) The middle may sink slightly.
8. Whip the cream and incorporate half the nuts and pineapple. Spoon into the hollow.
9. Decorate with the rest of the nuts and pineapple.

Note: Any fruits in season can be substituted for nuts and pineapple.

Serves 4

Walnut and Lemon Meringue Cake

A little oil *or* melted lard
  for greasing
4 egg whites
255g/9oz caster sugar

140g/5oz walnuts
290ml/½ pint thick cream
4 heaped tablespoons lemon
  curd (page 451)

1. Set the oven to 190°C/375°F, gas mark 5.
2. Line the bottom of two sandwich tins with rounds of grease-proof paper. Brush the paper and sides of the tins with a very little oil or melted lard.
3. Whisk the egg whites until stiff, then add half the sugar. Beat again until stiff.
4. Beat in the rest of the sugar and whisk until the meringue holds its shape.
5. Chop the nuts roughly, reserving a handful, and stir into the mixture.

6. Divide the mixture between the two pans, smoothing the tops slightly.
7. Bake the cakes for 40 minutes. Turn them out on a wire rack and peel off the paper.
8. Whip the cream and mix half of it with the lemon curd. Sandwich the cakes with this.
9. Use the rest of the whipped cream and nuts for the top.

Serves 4

Cabinet Pudding

½ Swiss roll (page 414), sliced
6 glacé cherries
290ml/½ pint milk
1 tablespoon sugar

2 eggs
Few drops vanilla essence
Raspberry jam sauce (page 351)

1. Grease a 425ml/¾ pint pudding basin. Wash and halve the cherries and arrange them on the bottom.
2. Arrange the Swiss roll slices to line the basin, putting any trimmings or leftover cake in the middle.
3. Heat the milk with the sugar and pour it on to the eggs, stirring well. Add the vanilla essence. Strain into the basin. Cover with greased greaseproof paper with a folded pleat in it (to allow for expansion when the pudding rises) and tie down. Leave to soak for 30 minutes.
4. To cook: steam in a double steamer, with the water just simmering, for 40 minutes; or bake in a roasting pan half-filled with hot water for 40–60 minutes. It should be just firm in the centre.
5. Turn the pudding out and serve with hot jam or fruit sauce.

Serves 4

Treacle Sponge

2½ tablespoons golden syrup
2 teaspoons fine white
   breadcrumbs
110g/¼lb butter
Grated rind of 1 lemon
110g/¼lb caster sugar

2 eggs, beaten
110g/¼lb self-raising flour
Pinch of salt
1 teaspoon ground ginger
75ml/3fl.oz milk

To serve:
Custard *or* cream

1. Grease a pudding basin with a knob of butter.
2. Mix together the syrup and breadcrumbs at the bottom of the basin.
3. Cream the butter and when very soft add the lemon rind and sugar. Beat until light and fluffy.
4. Gradually add the eggs, beating well between each addition.
5. Sift and fold in the flour with the salt and ginger.
6. Add enough milk to make the mixture just loose enough to drop from a spoon.
7. Turn into the pudding basin, cover and steam for 2½ hours.
8. Turn out and serve with custard or cream.

Serves 4–6

7
Baking

CAKES

Lemon Victoria Sponge

Oil *or* melted lard for preparing the cake tins
170g/6oz butter
170g/6oz sugar

Grated rind and juice of 1 lemon
3 large eggs
170g/6oz self-raising flour

For the filling and topping:
Lemon curd (page 451)
Feather icing (page 436)

1. Set the oven to 190°C/375°F, gas mark 5.
2. Prepare two 18cm/7in cake tins (see page 42, creaming method).
3. Cream the butter and sugar together and add the lemon rind. Beat until light and fluffy.
4. Beat in one egg at a time, each time with a tablespoon of flour.
5. Beat very well, adding the lemon juice gradually. Then fold in the remaining flour.
6. Divide the mixture between the tins and bake for 20–25 minutes or until the cakes are well risen, golden and feel spongy to the finger tips.
7. Allow the cakes to cool for a few minutes in the tins, then turn out on to a wire rack to cool completely.

8. Sandwich the cakes with lemon curd.
9. Ice the top and 'feather' it as described in the recipe.

Madeira Cake

Melted lard for greasing	4 eggs
170g/6oz unsalted butter	285g/10oz plain flour
Grated rind of 1 lemon	1 teaspoon baking powder
Pinch of ground cinnamon	75ml/2½fl.oz milk
225g/½lb caster sugar	4 slices candied citron peel

1. Prepare a 20cm/8in cake tin (see page 42, creaming method).
2. Set the oven to 180°C/350°F, gas mark 4.
3. Cream the butter and gradually beat in the lemon, cinnamon and sugar until light and fluffy.
4. Beat in the eggs one at a time, adding a little flour as you beat, to prevent the mixture from curdling.
5. Sift the remaining flour with the baking powder. Fold it in with a metal spoon.
6. Add enough milk to bring the mixture to dropping consistency (it will drop rather than run off a spoon).
7. Spoon the mixture into the cake tin and spread with a palette knife or spatula. Decorate with peel.
8. Bake for 1½ hours, turning the temperature down to 165°C/325°F, gas mark 3 after 45 minutes.
9. Cool the cake for 10 minutes in the tin before gently easing out on to a wire rack.

Christmas Cake
(With rough icing)

This cake is for a 20cm/8in cake tin, 8cm/3in deep.

170g/6oz butter
170g/6oz soft dark brown sugar
4 eggs
225g/½lb plain flour
Pinch of salt
½ teaspoon mixed spice
2 tablespoons black treacle
225g/½lb currants, washed and dried
225g/½lb sultanas
55g/2oz chopped candied peel
110g/¼lb glacé cherries, cut in half

110g/¼lb chopped almonds
3 tablespoons brandy *or* stout
1 small apple grated

For the covering and icing:
450g/1lb marzipan (page 437)
450g/1lb icing sugar
1–2 egg whites
½ teaspoon glycerine
Few drops blue colouring

For the decoration:
Red ribbon
2 sprigs holly

1. Set the oven to 180°C/350°F, gas mark 4. Grease and line the cake tin as instructed on page 42.
2. Cream the butter and sugar until light and fluffy.
3. Beat the eggs in one by one, then fold in the flour, salt and spice.
4. Stir in the remaining ingredients in the order in which they are listed. Beat very well.
5. Put the mixture into the greased and lined tin and bake for 1 hour. Turn the oven down to 170°C/325°F, gas mark 3 and bake for a further 1½ hours, covering the top of the cake with thick brown paper for the last hour if it seems to be browning too fast.
6. The cake is cooked when a skewer will emerge dry after being stuck into the middle.
7. Cool the cake before turning it out. Remove the paper.
8. When the cake is quite cold wrap it up in greaseproof paper and put into an air-tight container.
9. If the cake is to be iced it should be covered in marzipan

at least two weeks before Christmas: follow the instructions on pages 438–9.

10. About a week before Christmas ice the cake. Sift the icing sugar into a bowl.

11. Whisk the egg white until frothy and beat enough of it, little by little, into the sugar to get the icing absolutely smooth but stiff enough to stand up in peaks.

12. Beat in half a teaspoon of glycerine (to prevent the icing setting like concrete) and a drop or two of colouring (to make it look less yellow and more pure-white).

13. Using a large knife or spatula spread the icing all over the cake: dip the knife in hot water to get the sides smooth, and use a fork to lift the top into spiky peaks all over.

14. Next day, when the icing is dry, wrap the ribbon round it and cover the join with one of the holly sprigs, secured with a long pin. Put the other holly sprig on top.

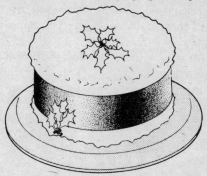

Upside-down Pineapple Cake

For the topping:
70g/2½oz butter

70g/2½oz light brown sugar
1 small can pineapple, drained

For the cake:
225g/8oz plain flour
½ teaspoon salt
4 level teaspoons baking
  powder

55g/2oz butter
140g/5oz caster sugar
1 egg, beaten
150ml/¼ pint milk

To serve hot:
Custard *or* cream

1. First make the topping. Cream the butter with the sugar and spread thickly over the bottom and sides of a 23cm/9in cake tin. Arrange the drained pineapple over the bottom.
2. Set the oven to 180°C/350°F, gas mark 4.
3. Now make the cake. Stir the flour with the salt and baking powder and set aside.
4. Cream the butter, add the sugar and beat until light and fluffy.
5. Gradually add the egg, beating well all the time.
6. Add the flour alternately with the milk, using a large spoon to mix and fold them in. Spoon the mixture into the tin.
7. Bake for 50–60 minutes. When the cake is cooked (it will have slightly crinkled edges and a skewer pressed into the centre will come out clean), invert it immediately on to a serving plate.
8. Leave it for a few minutes to allow the brown sugar mixture to run over the cake.
9. Remove the tin and scrape any toffee mixture sticking to the bottom on to the cake.
10. Serve hot with custard or cream, or allow to cool and serve plain for tea.

Chocolate Fudge Cake

225g/½lb plain flour
1 teaspoon salt
2 tablespoons cocoa powder
1 teaspoon baking powder
½ teaspoon bicarbonate of soda
55g/2oz plain chocolate, grated
110g/¼lb butter

170g/6oz caster sugar
1 egg, beaten
1 carton soured cream
Vanilla essence
Chocolate butter icing (page 436)

1. Grease a 5cm/2in deep rectangular cake tin. Set the oven to 190°C/375°F, gas mark 5.
2. Sift the flour, salt, cocoa powder, baking powder and bicarbonate of soda together.
3. Melt the chocolate with about two tablespoons of water. Allow to cool slightly.
4. Cream the butter and beat in the sugar until light and fluffy.
5. Beat in the egg gradually until thoroughly incorporated.
6. Add half the flour mixture and mix.
7. Add half the chocolate and half the soured cream and mix again.
8. Add the remaining flour.
9. Add the rest of the chocolate and soured cream. Finally stir in the vanilla essence.
10. Pour the mixture into the prepared tin and spread flat.
11. With a sharp knife mark out 4cm/1½in squares.
12. Bake in oven for 1 hour, then allow to cool in the tin.
13. When cold cut the cake into squares and spread with chocolate butter icing.

Squashy Rhubarb Cake

For the cake:
85g/3oz butter
85g/3oz sugar
2 small eggs
85g/3oz self-raising flour, sifted
  with a pinch of salt
Milk

Icing sugar to finish

For the filling:
675g/1½lb rhubarb, cut into
  2·5cm/1in pieces
1 tablespoon sugar

For the crumble top:
85g/3oz plain flour
55g/2oz butter
30g/1oz sugar

1. Prepare a deep 20cm/8in cake tin (see page 42, creaming method). Set the oven to 190°C/375°F, gas mark 5.
2. First make the crumble mixture: rub the butter into the flour and add the sugar. Set aside.

3. Now make the cake: cream the butter until soft and well-beaten. Add the sugar and beat until very pale, light and fluffy.

4. Lightly beat the eggs and add them to the sugar mixture, beating in a little at a time, and folding in a spoon of flour if the mixture curdles.

5. Fold in the rest of the flour and add a few dribbles of milk if the mixture is now too stiff. It should be of 'dropping' consistency – it will fall off a spoon rather reluctantly.

6. Turn the cake mixture into the prepared cake tin and spread it flat.

7. Cover carefully with the raw rhubarb pieces and sugar. Sprinkle with the crumble mixture.

8. Bake for about 45 minutes or until the cake feels firm on top. Leave to cool in the tin.

9. Just before serving remove from the tin and sift over a thin layer of icing sugar.

Note: If using canned rhubarb you will need a 450g/1lb can.

Sticky Ginger Cake

110g/¼lb preserved ginger
110g/¼lb butter
110g/¼lb treacle
110g/¼lb soft brown sugar
½ teaspoon bicarbonate of soda

4 tablespoons milk
225g/½lb plain flour
Pinch of salt
1 teaspoon ground ginger
1 egg

1. Prepare a shallow rectangular cake tin (see page 42, melting method). Set the oven to 170°C/325°F, gas mark 3.

2. Chop the preserved ginger finely.

3. Melt the butter, treacle and sugar together without boiling.

4. When the sugar has dissolved add the chopped ginger and allow to cool.

5. Mix the bicarbonate of soda with a tablespoon of the milk.

6. Sift the flour into a bowl with the salt and the ground ginger and make a well in the centre.
7. Add the milk and the slightly beaten egg to the treacle mixture.
8. Slowly beat the treacle mixture into the flour, pouring a little at a time into the well, and drawing the flour in from the sides as you mix.
9. When all the flour is incorporated in the treacle mixture stir in the bicarbonate of soda.
10. Turn the mixture into the prepared tin and bake for about 1 hour. The gingerbread should feel moist and slightly tacky, but firm.
11. Let it cool before turning it out. It will keep for about 2 weeks in an airtight container, and freezes perfectly.

Whisked Sponge

3 eggs
85g/3oz caster sugar

85g/3oz plain flour
Pinch of salt

1. Set the oven to 180°C/350°F, gas mark 4. Prepare a cake tin (see page 42, whisking method).
2. Place the eggs and sugar in a bowl and fit it over (not in) a saucepan of simmering water. Whisk the mixture until light, thick and fluffy. (If using an electric mixer no heat is required.)
3. Remove the bowl from the heat and continue whisking until cool.
4. Sift the flour and salt and, with a large metal spoon, fold into the mixture, being careful not to beat out any of the air.
5. Turn the mixture into the prepared tin and bake in the middle of the oven for about 30 minutes.
6. Test to see if it is cooked. (When the cake is done it will shrink slightly and the edges will look crinkled. When pressed gently it will feel firm but spongy and will sound 'creaky'.)
7. Turn out on to a wire rack to cool.

Swiss Roll

55g/2oz plain flour
Pinch of salt
2 eggs
55g/2oz caster sugar

1 tablespoon warm water
2–3 drops vanilla essence
3 tablespoons warmed jam
Caster sugar

1. Heat the oven to 190°C/375°F, gas mark 5. Prepare a Swiss roll tin by brushing a little melted lard or oil on the bottom and sides. Place in it a piece of greaseproof paper cut to fit the bottom of the tin exactly and brush again with melted fat. Dust with flour and sugar. (If no Swiss roll tin is available a baking sheet fitted with a tray of doubled greaseproof paper will do.

2. Sift the flour with the salt.

3. Put the eggs and sugar in a bowl and fit it over (not in) a saucepan of simmering water. Whisk the mixture until light, thick and fluffy. (If using an electric mixer no heat is required.) Continue beating until the mixture is cool again.

4. Using a large metal spoon fold the water, essence and flour into the egg mixture.

5. Pour the mixture into the tin.

6. Bake for 12–15 minutes. It is cooked when, if touched with a finger gently, no impression remains. The edges will also look very slightly shrunk.

7. Lay a piece of greaseproof paper on the work top and sprinkle it evenly with caster sugar. Using a knife, loosen the the edges of the cooked cake, then turn it over on to the sugared greaseproof paper. Remove the rectangle of greaseproof paper from the bottom of the cake.

8. While the cake is still warm spread it with the jam.

9. Using the paper under the cake to help you, roll the cake up firmly from one end.

10. Dredge the cake with caster sugar. To serve, cut in slices.

Note: If the cake is to be filled with cream this cannot be done while it is hot. Roll the cake up, unfilled, and keep it wrapped in greaseproof paper until cool. Unravel carefully, spread with whipped cream, and roll up again.

Chocolate Swiss Roll

Follow the above recipe but add a good teaspoon of cocoa powder to the flour in the cake mixture. Spread the cake with a mixture of raspberry jam and melted chocolate.

BREADS

White Bread

You will need a 1 kilo/2lb bread tin. If it is old and used you may not need to grease or flour it, but if it is new and not non-stick brush it out very lightly with flavourless oil and dust with flour.

15g/½oz fresh yeast (see *note*)
290ml/½ pint lukewarm milk
1 teaspoon caster sugar
30g/1oz butter

450g/1lb plain flour
½ teaspoon salt
1 egg, lightly beaten

1. Dissolve the yeast with a little of the milk and the sugar in a teacup.
2. Rub the butter into the sifted flour and salt as you would for pastry.
3. Pour in the yeast mixture, the milk and the beaten egg and mix to a stiffish dough.
4. Add a small amount of flour if the dough is too sticky. When the dough will leave the sides of the bowl press it into a ball and tip it out on to a floured board.
5. Knead until it is elastic, smooth and shiny (about 15 minutes).
6. Put the dough back in the bowl and cover it with a piece of lightly greased polythene.
7. Put it somewhere warm and draught-free and leave it to rise until it has doubled in size. This should take at least 1 hour.

Bread that rises too quickly has a yeasty, unpleasant taste; the slower the rising the better – overnight in a cool larder is better than half an hour over the boiler!

8. Knead for a further 10 minutes or so.
9. Shape the dough into an oblong and put it into the loaf tin.
10. Cover with the polythene again and allow to rise again until it is the size and shape of a loaf.
11. Set the oven to 220 C/425 F, gas mark 7. Bake the loaf for 10 minutes, then turn the oven down to 190 C/375 F, gas mark 5 and bake for a further 25 minutes or until it is golden and firm.
12. Turn the loaf out on to a wire rack to cool. It should sound hollow when tapped on the underside. If it does not, or feels squashy and heavy, return it to the oven, without the tin, for a further 10 minutes.

Note: If using dried yeast use half the amount called for, mix it with three tablespoons of the liquid (warmed to blood temperature) and a teaspoon of sugar. Leave until frothy, about 15 minutes, then proceed. If yeast does not go frothy it is dead and unusable.

Brown Soda Bread

900g/2lb wholemeal flour *or* 675g/1½lb wholemeal flour and 225g/½lb plain white flour
2 teaspoons salt
2 teaspoons bicarbonate of soda
4 level teaspoons cream of tartar
2 level teaspoons sugar
45g/1½oz butter
570–860ml/1–1½ pints milk (if using all wholemeal flour the recipe will need more liquid than with a mixture of two flours)

1. Set the oven to 190 C/375 F, gas mark 5.
2. Sift the dry ingredients into a warm dry bowl.
3. Rub in the butter and mix to a soft dough with the milk.

4. Shape into a large round about 5cm/2in thick. With the handle of a wooden spoon make a cross on the top of the loaf. The dent should be 1·5cm/¾in deep.
5. Bake on a greased baking sheet for 25–30 minutes. Allow to cool on a wire rack.

Wholemeal Baps

20g/¾oz fresh yeast (see *note*, page 416)
290ml/½ pint lukewarm milk
1 teaspoon caster sugar
225g/½lb wholemeal flour
225g/½lb plain white flour
1 teaspoon salt
55g/2oz butter
1 egg, lightly beaten

1. Dissolve the yeast with a little of the milk and the sugar in a teacup.
2. Warm a large mixing bowl and sift the flours and salt into it. Rub in the butter as you would for pastry.
3. Pour in the yeast mixture, the milk and the beaten egg and mix to a fairly slack dough.
4. When the dough will leave the sides of the bowl press it into a ball and tip it out on to a floured board. Knead it until it is elastic, smooth and shiny (about 15 minutes).
5. Put the dough back in the bowl and cover it with a piece of lightly greased polythene. Put it somewhere warm (on a shelf above a radiator, on the grill rack over a pan of very gently simmering water on the cooker, in the airing cupboard or just a draught-proof corner of the kitchen). Leave it there until the dough has doubled in size. This should take at least 1 hour, the longer the better.
6. Take the dough out of the bowl, punch it down and knead it again for 10 minutes.
7. Set the oven to 200°C/400°F, gas mark 6.
8. Divide the dough into eight pieces and shape them into flattish ovals (using a rolling pin if you like). Put on a floured baking sheet and prove (allow to rise again) for 15 minutes.
9. Bake for 20 minutes or until firm.

Gugelhopf

340g/¾lb plain flour
1 teaspoon salt
25g/scant 1oz fresh yeast
 (see *note*, page 416)
225ml/7½fl.oz lukewarm milk
30g/1oz caster sugar

2 small eggs, beaten
110g/¼lb butter, softened
110g/¼lb raisins and currants
 mixed
30g/1oz flaked almonds

1. Sift the flour and salt into a warmed bowl.
2. Dissolve the yeast in the warm milk with the sugar. Mix with the beaten eggs and the softened butter.
3. Mix the liquid into the flour. Now add the fruit and nuts.
4. Butter a gugelhopf tin (fluted round shape) and dust it out with sugar.
5. Put in the mixture, which should three-quarters fill it. Put in a warm place to rise until the mixture reaches the top of the tin.
6. Stand the tin on a baking sheet.
7. Set the oven to 190°C/375°F, gas mark 5.
8. Bake for 45 minutes or until golden and firm. Remove from the tin and cool on a wire rack.

Selkirk Bannock

This is a round flat yeasted fruit loaf.

290ml/½ pint milk
30g/1oz fresh yeast (see *note*,
 page 416)
225g/½lb sugar
110g/¼lb butter
110g/¼lb lard
900g/2lb flour

Pinch of salt
225g/½lb sultanas
225g/½lb raisins
110/¼lb candied peel
A little warm milk mixed with
 sugar for glazing

1. Warm the milk to blood heat.
2. Cream the yeast with a teaspoon of the sugar.
3. Soften the butter and the lard until almost liquid but not hot.

4. Add the fats to the milk with the yeast mixture.

5. Sift the flour with a pinch of salt into a large warmed bowl. Make a well in the centre to expose the bottom of the bowl. Into this hollow slowly pour the milky mixture, stirring with a wooden spoon and gradually drawing in the surrounding flour until you have a smooth, stiffish batter.

6. Cover the bowl with a piece of greased polythene or with a cloth and put in a warm place until doubled in bulk. This should take about 1 hour.

7. Tip the dough on to a well-floured board and, with floured hand, knead well. Work in the dried fruits and the sugar, kneading until the fruits are evenly distributed. Shape into four rounds and place on a floured baking sheet.

8. Cover the dough once again with the polythene or cloth and return to the warm place to prove.

9. Set the oven to 200°C/400°F, gas mark 6. After 15 minutes or so the bannocks should be well risen and ready for baking, and the oven hot.

10. Brush the bannocks with milk. Bake for 35–40 minutes, or until firm and brown.

Cornish Splits

15g/½oz fresh yeast (see *note*, page 416)
1 teaspoon sugar
2 level teaspoons salt
450g/1lb plain flour
45g/1½oz lard
290ml/½ pint milk
15g/½oz margarine *or* butter

For the filling:
290ml/½ pint whipped cream
Fresh raspberries *or* raspberry jam

To finish:
Icing sugar

1. Set the oven to 220°C/425°F, gas mark 7. Grease two baking sheets and dredge them lightly with flour.

2. Cream the yeast with the sugar and salt and leave for 10 minutes.

3. Sift the flour into a warmed bowl and rub in the lard until the mixture resembles breadcrumbs.

4. Heat the milk to blood temperature and add it to the yeast mixture.

5. Make a well in the centre of the flour and pour in the yeast mixture. Mix the liquid and gradually draw in the surrounding flour. Mix to a soft dough.

6. Knead until the mixture is smooth and shiny and leaves the fingers.

7. Put the dough in a greased mixing bowl, cover with a greased piece of polythene and leave to rise in a warm place until it has doubled in bulk (about 1 hour).

8. Turn the risen dough on to a floured surface and knead for 10 minutes. Shape into 18–20 balls, flattening them slightly. Leave to prove on the greased baking sheets for 15–20 minutes.

9. Bake for 20–25 minutes. Then brush with a little melted butter or margarine and leave on a wire rack to cool.

10. Cut the Cornish splits diagonally across from the top. Fill with whipped cream and raspberries or raspberry jam and dust with icing sugar.

Makes 18

Chelsea Buns

15g/½oz fresh yeast (see *note*, page 416)
85g/3oz caster sugar
450g/1lb plain flour
1 teaspoon salt
85g/3oz butter

1 egg
225ml/7½fl.oz tepid milk
½ teaspoon mixed spice
55g/2oz sultanas
55g/2oz currants

1. Cream the yeast with a teaspoon of the sugar.

2. Sift the flour into a warm dry bowl with the salt. Rub in half the butter and stir in half the sugar.

3. Beat the egg and add to the yeast mixture with the tepid milk.

4. Make a well in the centre of the flour and pour in the liquid. Using first a knife and then your hand gradually draw the flour in from the sides of the bowl and knead until smooth.

5. Cover the bowl and leave to rise in a warm place until doubled in bulk (about 1 hour).
6. Punch the dough down again and knead again on a floured board. Roll into a square about 23cm/9in across.
7. Mix the remaining butter with half the remaining sugar and dot it over the bun mixture.
8. Fold the dough in half and roll it out again to form a second square.
9. Set the oven to 220°C/425°F, gas mark 7. Grease a baking sheet.
10. Sprinkle the remaining sugar, the spice, sultanas and currants over the yeast mixture.
11. Roll it up like a Swiss roll and cut into 3·5cm/1½in slices.
12. Arrange the buns cut side up on the baking sheet and leave to prove for 15 minutes.
13. Sprinkle with sugar. Bake for 20–25 minutes.
14. Leave the buns to cool on a wire rack before separating.

Makes 8

Tea Ring

Scant 150ml/¼ pint milk
15g/½oz fresh yeast (see *note*, page 416)
30g/1oz sugar
1 egg
225g/½lb plain flour
½ teaspoon salt

½ teaspoon mixed spice
30g/1oz butter
30g/1oz currants *or* sultanas
30g/1oz mixed peel
Grated rind of ½ lemon
Milk for glazing

Glacé icing:
110g/¼lb icing sugar

Boiling water to mix

1. Warm the milk to blood temperature.
2. Cream the yeast with the sugar and a little of the warmed milk.
3. Mix the egg with the remaining milk.
4. Sift the flour, salt and spice into a warmed mixing bowl.

Rub the butter into the flour until the mixture resembles coarse breadcrumbs.

5. Add the dried fruit, peel and lemon rind.

6. Make a well in the centre so that the bottom of the bowl is exposed. Gradually pour in the liquid, mixing to a soft dough. Knead for 10 minutes.

7. Cover the bowl with a piece of greased polythene and leave to rise in a warm place for 1 hour or until doubled in bulk.

8. Set the oven to 200°C/400°F, gas mark 6. Grease a savarin tin or metal ring mould.

9. Knock the dough back (i.e. punch it down). Divide into five pieces and shape each one into a smooth ball.

10. Fit the balls of dough into the prepared tin (they will barely touch each other) and leave to rise again (prove) for 15 minutes. By now they should be tightly stuck together. Brush with milk.

11. Bake for 30–40 minutes or until firm and brown. Cool on a wire rack.

12. Mix the icing sugar with a very little boiling water to a just-runny consistency. Dribble the icing in ribbons all over the tea ring while it is still warm.

Rum Baba

For the sugar syrup:
170g/6oz loaf sugar
225ml/8 fl.oz water

2 tablespoons rum

Yeast mixture:
110g/¼lb plain flour
15g/½oz fresh yeast (see *note*, page 416)
15g/½oz caster sugar

3 tablespoons warm milk
2 egg yolks
Grated rind of ½ lemon
55g/2oz butter

For the decoration (optional):
Fresh fruit such as grapes and raspberries

150ml/¼ pint double *or* whipping cream

1. First make the sugar syrup: dissolve the sugar in the water and boil rapidly for 3 minutes. The syrup should be boiled to the 'thread' (when a little syrup is put between finger and thumb and the fingers are opened the syrup should form a short thread). Add the rum.

2. Now make the yeast mixture: sift the flour into a warmed bowl.

3. Mix the yeast with half a teaspoon of the sugar, 1 teaspoon of the flour and enough milk to make a batter-like consistency.

4. Whisk the egg yolks, remaining sugar and lemon rind until fluffy.

5. Clarify the butter: melt it slowly in a saucepan and strain through a folded J-cloth or muslin, leaving the sediment behind.

6. Make a well in the centre of the flour and add the yeast and beaten eggs. With your fingers mix together and gradually draw in the flour from the sides, adding more milk as you take in more flour. When all the flour has been incorporated beat with your hand until smooth.

7. Gradually add the clarified butter, kneading and slapping the dough until it looks like a very thick batter and no longer sticks to the palm of your hand.

8. Cover and leave to rise in a warm place (e.g. the airing cupboard) for about 45 minutes. It should double in size.

9. Set the oven to 190°C/375°F, gas mark 5. Grease a 1 litre/ 1½ pint savarin (ring) mould with plenty of butter.

10. When the dough has risen beat it down again and fill into the mould. It should half fill the tin.

11. Cover and leave to prove (rise again) for 10–15 minutes in a warm place.

12. Bake in the oven for 30–35 minutes until golden brown.

13. Turn out on to a wire rack and while still warm prick with a toothpick and brush with plenty of rum syrup until the baba is really soaked and shiny. Put on a serving dish.

14. Serve plain or surround with fresh fruit and pile the whipped cream into the centre.

Serves 4

Doughnuts

225g/½lb plain flour
Pinch of salt
2 egg yolks
7g/¼oz fresh yeast (see *note*, page 416)
45g/1½oz sugar

30g/1oz butter
150ml/¼ pint warm milk
Caster sugar flavoured with cinnamon
Fat for deep frying

1. Sift the flour with the salt and warm it in a low oven.
2. Cream the yeast with a teaspoon of the sugar.
3. In a warm bowl, rub the butter into the flour. Make a well in the centre.
4. Mix together the egg yolks, yeast mixture, remaining sugar and warm milk. Pour this into the well in the flour.
5. Using the fingertips of one hand mix the central ingredients together, gradually drawing in the surrounding flour. Mix until smooth.
6. Cover the bowl with a piece of greased polythene and leave to rise in a warm place for 45 minutes.
7. Knead the dough well for at least 10 minutes.
8. Roll out on a floured board to 1cm/½in thick. With a plain cutter press into small rounds.
9. Place on a greased tray and leave to prove until doubled in size.
10. Heat the fat until a crumb will sizzle vigorously in it.
11. Put the doughnuts into the fryer basket and lower into the fat.
12. Fry until golden brown, then drain on absorbent paper.
13. Toss in caster sugar and cinnamon.

Note I: To make a hole in the centre of the doughnuts, stamp out a 2·5cm/1in round from the flattened balls before proving.

Makes 10

BUNS AND SCONES

Rock Buns

225g/½lb self-raising flour
Pinch of salt
110g/¼lb butter
85g/3oz caster sugar
110g/¼lb sultanas and currants,
  mixed

30g/1oz chopped candied peel
2 eggs, lightly beaten
A little milk if necessary

1. Set the oven to 190°C/375°F, gas mark 5. Grease a large baking sheet.
2. Sift the flour into a bowl with the salt. Rub in the butter until the mixture resembles breadcrumbs.
3. Stir in the sugar, fruit and peel.
4. Mix in the eggs, adding a little milk if necessary, but the mixture should be very stiff.
5. Using two forks put the mixture out on the baking sheet, each rocky-looking bun being the size of a small egg.
6. Bake for 15–20 minutes until pale brown. Leave to cool on a wire rack.

Makes 10

Scones

225g/½lb plain flour
3 level teaspoons baking
  powder
½ level teaspoon salt

55g/2oz butter
55g/2oz sugar (optional)
150ml/¼ pint milk

For glazing:
1 egg, beaten

1. Set the oven to 220°C/425°F, gas mark 7. Lightly grease a baking sheet.
2. Sift the flour with the other powder ingredients.
3. Rub in the butter until the mixture resembles breadcrumbs. Stir in the sugar if required.
4. Make a deep well in the flour, pour in all the liquid and mix to a soft, spongy dough with a palette knife.
5. On a floured surface, knead the dough very lightly until it is smooth. Roll or press out to about 1cm/½in thick and stamp into small rounds.
6. Heat the baking sheet in the oven.
7. Brush the scones with beaten egg for a glossy crust or sprinkle with flour for a soft one.
8. Bake the scones at the top of the hot oven until well risen and brown. Leave to cool on a wire rack, or serve hot from the oven.

Note: 30g/1oz sultanas or other dried fruit may be added to the dried ingredients.

For cheese scones substitute 30g/1oz grated strong cheese for half the butter, and omit the sugar.

Makes 12

Mocha Buns

340g/¾lb self-raising flour
Pinch of salt
85g/3oz lard
140g/5oz soft brown sugar

1 egg
1 tablespoon coffee essence to flavour
Scant 150ml/¼ pint milk

For the filling:
110g/¼lb chocolate butter icing (page 436)

For the topping:
Icing sugar

1. Set the oven to 220°C/425°F, gas mark 7. Grease 2 baking sheets.
2. Sift the flour with the salt into a mixing bowl. Add the fat and rub it in finely. Stir in the sugar.
3. Beat the egg with the coffee essence and add enough milk to give 150ml/¼ pint liquid in all. Add to the flour, lard and sugar and mix until smooth.
4. Divide the dough into 14 even-sized pieces. Place on the baking sheet and bake for about 15 minutes.
5. When the buns are cool split them and sandwich with coffee butter icing. Dust with icing sugar.

Makes 14

Welsh Scones

225g/½lb self-raising flour
Small pinch of salt
55g/2oz butter
30g/1oz caster sugar

55g/2oz sultanas *or* currants
About 150ml/¼ pint sour milk
   or buttermilk (if not
   available use fresh milk)

1. Sift the flour with the salt. Rub in the butter. Add the sugar and sultanas.
2. Using first a knife and then your hand work in enough of the milk to make a soft dough.
3. Knead lightly on a floured surface. Pat or roll out into a round about 2cm/¾in thick. Using a biscuit cutter stamp into discs; otherwise cut into wedges.
4. Heat a lightly greased girdle iron or thick-bottomed frying pan over gentle heat.
5. Cook the scones on both sides until firm to the touch and browned. They will take about 7 minutes on each side.
6. Serve hot with butter or butter and jam.

Makes about 12

English Madeleines

110g/¼lb butter
110g/¼lb caster sugar
2 eggs

110g/¼lb self-raising flour
2 tablespoons redcurrant jelly
55g/2oz desiccated coconut

1. Set the oven to 180°C/350°F, gas mark 4. Grease and flour about 12 dariole moulds.
2. Cream the butter and sugar until light and fluffy.
3. Beat in the eggs a little at a time.
4. Fold in the flour. Add a little water, if necessary, to make a soft dropping consistency.
5. Fill the tins half full and bake for 15–20 minutes.
6. Cool upside down on a wire rack.
7. Brush with warm redcurrant jelly and roll in desiccated coconut.

Makes 12

Coffee Buns

110g/¼lb butter
110g/¼lb caster sugar
2 eggs
110g/¼lb self-raising flour
2 teaspoons instant coffee
   powder

¼ teaspoon vanilla essence
55g/2oz chopped walnuts
55g/2oz chocolate

1. Set the oven to 180°C/350°F, gas mark 4. Grease and flour 12 bun tins or paper moulds.
2. Cream the butter and sugar until light and fluffy.
3. Beat in the eggs a little at a time.
4. Fold in the flour, coffee, vanilla essence and chopped nuts. Add a little water if necessary to make a soft dropping consistency.

5. Fill the tins or paper moulds two-thirds full and bake for 15–20 minutes. Leave to cool on a wire rack.
6. Grate the chocolate. Melt it on a plate over a pan of boiling water.
7. Spread each bun with a little melted chocolate and leave to cool and harden.

Makes 12

Eccles Cakes

225g/½lb flour-quantity rough-puff pastry (page 371)

For the filling:

15g/½oz butter	¼ teaspoon nutmeg
55g/2oz brown sugar	¼ teaspoon ground ginger
110g/¼lb currants	Grated rind of ½ lemon
30g/1oz chopped mixed peel	1 teaspoon lemon juice
½ teaspoon cinnamon	

For the glazing:

1 egg white	Caster sugar

1. Set the oven to 220°C/425°F, gas mark 7.
2. Roll the pastry to 0·5cm/¼in thick. Cut out rounds 7·5cm/3in across. Put aside to relax.
2. Melt the butter in a pan and stir in all the other filling ingredients.
3. Place a good teaspoon of filling in the centre of each pastry round.
4. Damp the edge of the pastry and press together in the centre, forming a small ball. Turn the balls over and lightly roll them until the fruit begins to show through the pastry.
5. With a sharp knife make 3 small parallel cuts on the top.
6. Lightly beat the egg white with a fork. Brush the top of the Eccles cakes with this and sprinkle with caster sugar.
7. Place on a wet baking sheet and bake for 20 minutes or until lightly browned.

Makes 12

BISCUITS AND BATTERS

Shortbread Fingers

110g/¼lb butter
55g/2oz caster sugar

170g/6oz plain flour
30g/1oz split almonds

1. Set the oven to 190°C/375°F, gas mark 5.
2. Beat the butter and sugar together until soft and creamy.
3. Work in the flour by degrees, with a minimum of beating.
4. Pat the paste into a smooth ball, then into a square about 1cm/½in thick.
5. Slide a floured baking sheet under the paste.
6. Prick with a fork and cut into fingers. Sprinkle with caster sugar. Decorate with split almonds, pressing them in gently.
7. Bake to a pale biscuit colour (about 20 minutes).

Makes about 18

Gingernuts

30g/1oz brown sugar
55g/2oz butter
85g/3oz golden syrup
110g/¼lb flour

½ teaspoon bicarbonate soda
1 heaped teaspoon ground ginger

1. Set the oven to 170 C/325 F, gas mark 3. Grease a baking sheet.
2. Melt the brown sugar, butter and syrup together slowly, without boiling. Make sure the sugar has dissolved. Allow to cool.

3. Sift the flour, bicarbonate of soda and ground ginger into a mixing bowl. Make a well in the centre.
4. Pour the melted mixture into the well, beat it with a wooden spoon, gradually drawing in the flour from the sides as you mix.
5. Place the mixture in teaspoonfuls 8cm/3in apart on the prepared baking sheet. Bake for 15–20 minutes. The ginger-nuts will not be crisp until they cool and set.

Makes 16

Macaroons

110g/¼lb ground almonds
170g/6oz caster sugar
1 teaspoon plain flour
2 egg whites

2 drops vanilla essence
Rice paper for baking
Split almonds for decoration

1. Set the oven to 180°C/350°F, gas mark 4.
2. Mix the almonds, sugar and flour together.
3. Add the egg whites and vanilla. Beat very well.
4. Lay a sheet of rice paper or vegetable parchment on a baking sheet and with a teaspoon put on small heaps of the mixture, well apart.
5. Place a split almond on each macaroon and bake for 20 minutes. Allow to cool.

Note I: To use this recipe for petits fours the mixture must be put out in very tiny blobs on the rice paper. Two macaroons can then be sandwiched together with a little stiff apricot jam and served in petits fours paper cases.

Note II: Ratafia biscuits are tiny macaroons with added almond essence.

Makes 25

Brandy Snap Cups

110g/¼lb sugar   Juice of ½ a lemon
110g/¼lb butter   110g/¼lb flour
110g/¼lb *or* 4 tablespoons   Large pinch of ground ginger
   golden syrup

To serve:
Whipped cream *or* ice cream

1. Set the oven to 190°C/375°F, gas mark 5. Grease a baking sheet, palette knife and one end of a wide rolling pin or a narrow jam jar or bottle.
2. Melt the sugar, butter and syrup together. Remove from heat.
3. Sift in the flour, stirring well. Add the lemon juice and ginger.
4. Put the mixture on the baking sheet in small teaspoonfuls about 15cm/6in apart. Bake for 5–7 minutes. They should go golden brown but still be soft. Watch carefully – they burn easily. Remove from the oven.
5. When cool enough to handle, lever each biscuit off the baking sheet with a greased palette knife.
6. Working quickly, shape them around the end of the rolling pin or greased jam jar to form a cup-shaped mould.
7. When the biscuits have taken shape remove them and leave to cool on a wire rack.
8. Serve filled with whipped cream or ice cream.

Note I: If the brandy snaps are not to be served immediately they must, once cool, be put into an airtight container for storage. They become soggy if left out.

Similarly, brandy snaps should not be filled with wettish mixtures like whipped cream or ice cream until shortly before serving, or the biscuit will quickly lose its crispness.

Note II: Do not bake too many snaps at a time as once they are cold they will be too brittle to shape – though they can be made pliable again if briefly returned to the oven.

Makes 8

Brandy Snaps

The mixture for these is exactly the same as for brandy snap cups (above) but the biscuits are shaped round a thick wooden spoon handle and not over the end of a rolling pin or jam jar. They are filled with whipped cream. This is done with a piping bag fitted with a medium nozzle.

Miniature brandy snaps (served as petits fours after dinner) are shaped over a skewer. These are not generally filled.

Waffles

2 eggs
170g/6oz plain flour
Pinch of salt
3 level teaspoons baking
  powder

30g/1oz caster sugar
290ml/½ pint milk
55g/2oz butter, melted
Vanilla essence
Extra melted butter

To serve:
Butter
Honey, maple syrup *or* jam

1. Separate the eggs.
2. Sift the flour, salt, baking powder and sugar together. Make a well in the centre and drop in the egg yolks.
3. Stir the yolks, gradually drawing in the flour from the edges and adding the milk and melted butter until you have a thin batter. Add the vanilla essence.
4. Grease a waffle iron and heat it up.
5. Whisk the egg whites until stiff but not dry and fold into the batter.
6. Add a little melted butter to the hot waffle iron, pour in about 4 tablespoons of the mixture, close and cook for 1 minute per side.

7. Serve hot with butter and honey, maple syrup or jam.

Note: The first waffle always sticks to the iron.

Makes 10

Scotch Pancakes or Drop Scones

225g/½lb plain flour
½ teaspoon salt
½ teaspoon bicarbonate of soda
½ teaspoon cream of tartar

2 tablespoons golden syrup
½ a beaten egg
290ml/½ pint milk

To serve:
Butter
Jam

1. Sift together the flour, salt, bicarbonate of soda and cream of tartar.
2. Make a well in the centre of the mixture and into it pour the syrup and half the milk.
3. Beat the syrup and milk, gradually drawing in the flour from the sides of the bowl.
4. Add the egg and beat well.
5. Stir in more milk until the batter is the consistency of thick cream and will just run from a spoon. Cover and leave to stand for 10 minutes.
6. Meanwhile grease a heavy frying pan or girdle iron and heat it. When really hot, drop 2 or 3 spoonfuls of batter on to the surface, keeping them well separated.
7. Cook for 2–3 minutes. When the undersides of the pancakes are brown, bubbles have risen to the surface and the pancakes can be lifted with a fish-slice, turn over and brown the other side.
8. Serve hot or cold with butter and jam.

Makes 20

Sponge Fingers

3 eggs	85g/3oz plain flour sifted with a
85g/3oz caster sugar	pinch of salt
Vanilla essence	Extra caster sugar for glazing

1. Set the oven to 190°C/375°F, gas mark 5. Grease and flour a baking sheet and have ready a piping bag fitted with a medium-sized plain nozzle.
2. Whisk the egg yolks with the sugar until light and fluffy.
3. Add a few drops of vanilla essence.
4. Whisk the whites until stiff and fold a third of them into the yolk mixture.
5. Fold in the flour. Fold in the remaining whites very lightly with a large metal spoon.
6. Pile the mixture into a piping bag and pipe on to the baking sheet in 5cm/2in lengths.
7. Dust each finger with plenty of caster sugar. Bake for 5–6 minutes and cool on a wire rack.

Makes 12

ICINGS AND MARZIPAN

Apricot Glaze

3 tablespoons apricot jam	Juice of $\frac{1}{2}$ lemon
2 tablespoons water	

1. Place all the ingredients together in a thick-bottomed pan.
2. Bring slowly up to the boil, stirring gently (avoid beating in bubbles) until syrupy in consistency. Strain.

Note: When using this to glaze food, use when still warm, as it becomes too stiff to manage when cold. It will keep warm standing over a saucepan of very hot water.

Chocolate Butter Icing

110g/¼lb plain chocolate, chopped
55g/2oz unsalted butter

110g/¼lb icing sugar, sifted
1 egg yolk

1. Melt the chocolate in a heavy saucepan with a tablespoon of water, stirring continuously.
2. Beat the butter and sugar until light and fluffy.
3. Beat in the egg yolk followed by the melted chocolate.

Feather Icing

Icing sugar
Boiling water

Colouring *or* chocolate

1. Sift the icing sugar into a bowl (225g/½lb will be sufficient for an 18cm/7in sponge).
2. Add enough boiling water to mix to a fairly stiff coating consistency. The icing should hold a trail when dropped from a spoon but gradually find its own level.
3. Take 2 tablespoons of the icing and colour it with food colouring or chocolate.
4. Place in a piping bag fitted with a fine writing nozzle.
5. Spread the remaining icing smoothly and evenly over the top of the cake, using a warm palette knife.
6. While it is still wet quickly pipe lines, about 2·5cm/1in apart, across the top of the cake.
7. Now draw lines at right angles to the coloured lines with a pin or a sharp knife, dragging the tip through the coloured lines which will be pulled into points.

If the pin is dragged in one direction through the coloured icing lines this pattern will result:

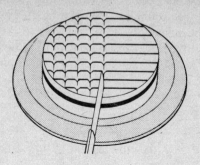

If the pin is dragged alternately in opposite directions through the coloured icing lines this pattern will result:

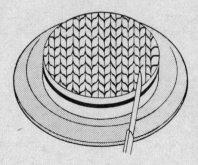

Note: Smooth melted jam can be used instead of coloured icing for the feathering.

Marzipan or Almond Paste

225g/½lb caster sugar

225g/½lb icing sugar

450g/1lb ground almonds

2 egg yolks

2 whole eggs

2 teaspoons lemon juice

6 drops vanilla essence

1. Sift the sugars together into a bowl and mix with the ground almonds.
2. Mix together the egg yolks, whole eggs, lemon juice and vanilla essence. Add this to the sugar mixture and beat briefly with a wooden spoon.
3. Lightly dust the working surface with icing sugar. Knead the paste until just smooth (overworking will draw the oil out of the almonds, giving a too greasy paste).
4. Wrap well and store in a cool place.

Cooked Marzipan

This recipe gives a softer, easier-to-handle paste than the more usual, uncooked marzipan.

2 eggs
170g/6oz caster sugar
170g/6oz icing sugar

340g/¾lb ground almonds
4 drops vanilla essence
1 teaspoon lemon juice

1. Lightly beat the eggs.
2. Sift the sugars together and mix with the eggs.
3. Place the bowl over a pan of boiling water and whisk until light and creamy. Remove from the heat.
4. Add the ground almonds, vanilla and lemon juice, and beat briefly with a wooden spoon. The marzipan should be a soft paste.
5. Lightly dust the working surface with icing sugar. Carefully knead the paste until just smooth. (Overworking will draw out the oil from the almonds giving a too greasy paste.) Wrap well and store in a cool place.

To Cover a Cake with Marzipan

675g/1½lb marzipan (this will amply cover a 23cm/9in diameter cake)

Icing sugar
Apricot jam

If using uncooked marzipan or almond paste:

1. Take one-third of the marzipan and roll it into a circle a little larger than the cake top, using a rolling pin and board dusted with icing sugar to prevent the paste sticking.

2. Roll the remaining two-thirds to a strip as long as the circumference of the cake and just a little wider than the height of the cake.

3. Melt and sieve the jam. Bring to the boil and use it to paint the sides of the cake.

4. Turn the cake on its side and roll it on to the long strip of marzipan, keeping the top edge of the cake level with the edge of the marzipan, and sticking the marzipan to the cake as you go.

5. Turn the cake right side up again and brush the top with boiling jam.

6. Place the cake upside down on top of the circle of marzipan.

7. Using a palette knife and your fingers work the joins together, making sure that the edge meets the table-top (i.e. it is square, not rounded).

8. Turn the cake right side up and brush off any excess icing sugar.

9. Leave the cake to stand uncovered to dry for at least 2 days before icing.

If using cooked marzipan:

1. Melt and sieve the jam. Bring to the boil and brush over the top and sides of the cake.

2. Lightly dust the table-top with icing sugar and roll the marzipan to a large circle, about 10cm/4in bigger than the diameter of the cake.

3. Turn the cake upside down on to the marzipan.

4. Using the side of your hand work the marzipan evenly up the sides of the cake.

5. Take a jam jar and roll it around the sides of the cake to make sure that the sides are quite straight, and the edges square.

8
Preserving

The word 'preserves' should cover all food that has been treated to keep for longer than it would if fresh. Frozen food, dried food, salted food and smoked food are all preserves. But the word in household language means jams, jellies, marmalades, pickles, and sometimes bottled food; in short, the sort of preserves found on a good countrywoman's larder shelf.

To be precise: *Jellies* are clear preserves, made from strained fruit juice. They should be neither runny nor too solid. *Jams* are made from crushed fruit. They should almost hold their shape, but be runnier than jelly. *Conserves* are jams containing a mixture of fruits, generally including citrus fruit, and sometimes raisins or nuts. *Marmalade* is jam made exclusively from citrus fruit. *Fruit butters* are made from smooth fruit purées, cooked with sugar until the consistency of thick cream. *Fruit cheeses* are made in the same way but cooked until very thick. Butters and cheeses, because they are not set solidly and generally contain less sugar than jams, should be potted in sterilized jars. *Curds* generally contain butter and eggs, are best kept refrigerated, and will not keep more than a month or two.

To add to the confusion the word 'preserve' is sometimes used to mean whole fruit jams, or whole fruits suspended in thick syrup.

JAMS, JELLIES AND MARMALADES

These preserves depend on four main factors to make them keep:

a. The presence of pectin. This is a substance, converted from the gum-like pectose found to some degree in all fruit, which acts with the acids of the fruit and with the sugar to form a jelly-like set. Slightly under-ripe fruit is higher in pectin than over-ripe fruit, and some fruit, notably apples, quinces, damsons, sour plums, lemons and redcurrants are high in pectin so that jam from them will set easily. Jam from low-pectin fruit such as strawberries, rhubarb, mulberries and pears may need added commercial pectin or lemon juice (or a little high-pectin fruit) to obtain a set.

To test for pectin: take a teaspoon of the simmered fruit juice (before adding the sugar) and put it into a glass. When it is cold add three tablespoons of methylated spirit. After a minute a jelly will have formed. If it is in one or more firm clots there is adequate pectin in the fruit. If the jelly clots are numerous and soft the jam will not set without the addition of more pectin.

b. A high concentration of sugar, which is itself a preservative. Without sufficient sugar the pectin will not act to form the set.

c. The presence of acid which, like sugar, acts with the pectin to form a gel or set. Acid also prevents the growth of bacteria, and it helps to prevent the crystallization of the sugar in the jam during storage. If the fruit is low in acid, tartaric acid, citric acid or lemon juice may be added.

d. The elimination and exclusion of micro-organisms. The jam itself is sterilized by rapid boiling. Jam jars need not normally be sterilized since the heat of the jam should be sufficient to sterilize them. However, harmless moulds do sometimes form round the

441

rim and on the surface of jams potted in this way, and sterilizing the jars does help to prevent this. Jam jars to be sterilized should be put, clean, into a large saucepan, covered with hot but not boiling water and brought to the boil. 20 minutes' boiling will sterilize jars in an open saucepan, 2 minutes' in a pressure cooker. Alternatively they may be soaked in solutions bought at chemists for sterilizing babies' bottles etc. Ordinary household bleach will do too, but the bottles should be rinsed in boiling water afterwards. The jam funnel should be sterilized with the jars. It is not necessary to sterilize ladles or spoons except by leaving them in the bubbling jam for a minute or two. Jelly cloths or bags need not be sterilized as the juice is dripped through them before being boiled.

The jam, once put into the clean jars, is sealed to prevent the infiltration of mildew spores etc. Melted paraffin wax (melted white candles will do) poured over the surface of the jam, or used to stick down the edges of the paper covers, makes a good old-fashioned and most effective seal, but most cooks rely on ordinary paper jam covers and a bit of luck.

Ideally sealing should be done while the jam is boiling hot – i.e. before any fresh mildew spores can enter. However, if liquid wax is used on hot jam it may disturb the flat surface. So the slightly cooled but still clear wax is poured on once the jam is set. Two applications of wax are necessary if the first covering shrinks away from the sides of the jar, leaving a gap.

Perhaps the best method of sealing is to use screw-tops. They should be sterilized and checked for a tight fit. The jam should be poured up to the shoulder of the jars, leaving a good 1cm/$\frac{1}{2}$in. The caps are screwed on tightly as soon as the jars are filled. The cooling air in the neck will form a partial vacuum, tightly sealing the jar. (A word of warning: if the screw-tops are rusty or are of metal not coated in plastic they should not be used.)

If, in spite of all precautions, mould appears on the top of the jams, it can be scraped off and the jam beneath will be perfectly good. But it should be eaten fairly soon as mould spores in the air of the larder could affect other preserves. Scraping off visible mould will not prevent the invisible spores from multiplying.

YIELD

The amount of finished jam obtained varies according to type, jellies giving comparatively little, marmalades and whole fruit jams much more. But, as a general rule, the mixture will yield between 1½ times and double the weight of sugar used. It is wise to over-estimate the amount of jars needed, rather than have to prepare more at the last minute.

EQUIPMENT

Making jam is easy enough, but it requires a little organization. First the equipment should be assembled:

> Accurate scales
> Preserving pan *or* a large heavy pan with a solid base
> Sharp knives
> Grater
> Mincer
> Long-handled wooden spoons
> Perforated spoon
> Metal jug with a large lip *or* a jam funnel
> Jam jars
> Jam covers, labels and rubber bands (available from chemists and stationers) *or* screw-top lids with enamelled *or* plasticized inner rims
> Sugar thermometer (not essential but useful)
> Perforated skimmer (not essential but useful)

POINTS TO REMEMBER

a. Make sure all equipment is absolutely clean.
b. Use dry, unblemished, barely ripe fruit.
c. Use preserving, lump, granulated or caster sugar. Modern white sugars are highly refined and therefore suitable. They need little skimming and give a clear preserve. Using preserving sugar has a slight advantage, because the crystals are larger and

the boiling liquid circulates freely round them, dissolving them rapidly. Caster sugar is inclined to set in a solid mass at the bottom of the pan and take longer to dissolve. Brown sugar gives an unattractive colour to preserves.

d. Covering lukewarm jam could lead to mildew. If the jam is covered immediately any bacteria or mildew spores present in the atmosphere are trapped between jam and seal and will be killed by the heat. If the atmosphere is lukewarm and steamy, perfect incubating conditions are created.

BASIC PROCEDURE

1. Wash and dry the jam jars and warm them in the oven.
2. Pick over the fruit and wash or wipe if necessary.
3. Put the fruit and water in the pan and set to simmer.
4. Warm the sugar in a cool oven. (When it is added to the fruit it will then not lower the temperature too much, and cause prolonged cooking which could impair the colour of the jam.)
5. Bring the fruit to a good boil. Tip in the sugar and stir, without reboiling, until the sugar has dissolved.
6. Once the sugar has dissolved boil rapidly, stirring gently but frequently.
7. When the mixture begins to look like jam (usually about 10 minutes) test for setting. It is important not to overboil since this can make the colour too dark and the texture too solid. It will also ruin the flavour. Overboiling can sometimes even prevent a set by destroying the pectin. If using a thermometer, setting point is 105°C/220°F for jam and 106°C/222°F for marmalade. *To test for setting* put a teaspoon of the jam on to an ice-cold saucer and return it to the ice compartment or freezer to cool rapidly. When cold, push it gently with a finger. The jam will have a slight skin, which will wrinkle if setting point is reached. If a finger is drawn through the jam, it should remain separated, not run together. Also, clear jam or jelly should fall from a spatula, not in a single stream but forming a wavy curtain or 'sheet'. (See the drawings.)

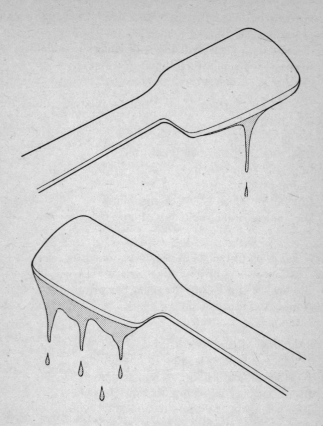

8. As soon as a setting test proves positive draw the jam off the heat. Skim carefully then, if the jam contains whole fruit or large pieces of fruit, allow to cool for 15 minutes. This will prevent the fruit rising to the top of the jam jars.

9. Put the hot jars close together on a wooden board or tray. Fill them with hot jam with the aid of a jug or jam funnel.

10. Seal at once with screw-tops or put waxed paper-discs, waxed-side down, on the surface of the jam, and cover the tops of the jars with cellophane covers, securing them with a rubber band. Brush the cellophane tops with water which will slightly stretch them. Carefully pull them tight. As they dry they will shrink tightly around the jars.

11. Wipe the sides of the jars with a hot, clean, damp cloth to remove any drips of jam.
12. Label each jar with the type of jam and the date.
13. Leave undisturbed overnight.
14. Store in a cool, airy, dark place.

Mildew on the surface of the jam is probably caused by one of the following:

a. Using wet jars
b. Covering the jam when lukewarm
c. Imperfect sealing
d. Damp or warm storage place
e. Equipment which is less-than-spotless

The mildew should be removed, and the jam consumed fairly quickly.

Crystallization of the sugar in jam is caused by:

a. Insufficient acid in the fruit
b. Boiling the jam before the sugar has dissolved
c. Adding too much sugar
d. Leaving jam uncovered

Fermentation of jam is caused by:

a. Insufficient boiling leading to non-setting
b. Insufficient acid leading to non-setting
c. Insufficient pectin leading to non-setting
d. Insufficient sugar leading to non-setting
e. A storage place which is too warm
f. Jars which are less than spotless

Gooseberry and Orange Jam

450g/1lb gooseberries
Grated rind and juice of 2
  oranges

900g/2lb warm sugar
150ml/¼ pint water

1. Top and tail the gooseberries.
2. Put them with the rind and juice of the oranges and the water into the pan. Simmer until soft and yellowish.

3. Add the warmed sugar, allow it to dissove, then boil rapidly until setting point is reached.
4. Pour into dry, warm jars.
5. Cover and label the jars.
6. Leave undisturbed overnight. Store in a cool, dark, airy place.

Blackcurrant and Rhubarb Jam

450g/1lb blackcurrants   150ml/¼ pint water
55g/2oz rhubarb   450g/1lb sugar

1. Wash the blackcurrants and remove the stalks.
2. Cut the rhubarb into 0·5cm/¼in chunks.
3. Put the rhubarb, blackcurrants and water together in a pan and boil for 30 minutes.
4. Warm the sugar and add it to the pan.
5. When the sugar has dissolved boil rapidly until the jam reaches setting point (about 10–15 minutes).
6. Pour into dry, warm jars.
7. Cover and label the jars.
8. Leave undisturbed overnight. Store in a cool, dark, airy place.

Plum Jam

900g/2lb barely ripe plums   900g/2lb sugar

1. Halve and stone the plums. Crack half the stones and remove the kernels.
2. Put the fruit and sugar together in a bowl and leave to stand overnight. (Do not use a metal container.)
3. Next day transfer to a large saucepan or preserving pan and heat slowly until the sugar has dissolved. Then boil fast until the jam reaches setting point (about 7–10 minutes). Add the kernels while the jam is still bubbling.

4. Pour into dry, warm, clean jars.
5. Cover and label the jars.
6. Leave undisturbed overnight. Store in a cool dark, airy place.

Note I: If the plums are difficult to stone, or damsons or greengages are used, simply slit the flesh of each fruit before mixing with the sugar. During boiling the stones will float to the top and can be removed with a perforated spoon.

Note II: As no water is added to this recipe the flavour is very concentrated. But the basic method described on pages 444–6 works well too.

Strawberry Jam

900g/2lb barely ripe
   strawberries
675g/1½lb sugar, warmed

Juice of 2 lemons
15g/½oz unsalted butter

1. Hull the strawberries.
2. Crush a handful in the bottom of a preserving pan with 2 tablespoons of the sugar. Add the lemon juice and stir over a gentle heat until the sugar dissolves.
3. Add the remaining fruit and bring to the boil.
4. Add the warmed sugar and when dissolved boil rapidly for 10–12 minutes until the jam reaches setting point.
5. Stir in the butter and allow to cool for 15 minutes. This will help prevent the berries rising in the jars.
6. Pour into warm, dry, clean jars.
7. Cover, and label the jars. Leave undisturbed overnight.
8. Store in a cool, dark, airy place.

Note: The making of a little syrup with fruit, sugar and lemon juice before adding the bulk of the fruit is done to provide some liquid in which to cook the fruit. Stirring it in a dry pan would lead to crushing and mashing. If possible the fruit should remain whole, suspended in the jam.

Orange Marmalade

900g/2lb Seville oranges	2·85 litres/5 pints water
2 lemons	1·8 kilos/4lb sugar

1. Cut the oranges and lemons in half and roughly squeeze them into a large bowl. (Do not bother to extract all the juice: squeezing is simply done to make removing the pips easier.)
2. Remove the pips and tie them up in a piece of muslin or a clean J-cloth.
3. Slice the fruit skins, finely or in chunks as required, and add them to the juice with the bag of pips and the water. Leave to soak for 24 hours.
4. Transfer to a preserving pan or large saucepan and simmer gently until the orange rind is soft and transparent looking – about 2 hours.
5. Warm the sugar in a slow oven for 20 minutes or so, then tip into the orange pulp. Stir while bringing the mixture slowly to the boil.
6. Once the sugar has dissolved boil rapidly until setting point is reached (106°C/222°F). This may take as much as 20 minutes, but is usually less. Test after 5 minutes and then again at 3-minute intervals.
7. Allow to cool for 10 minutes then fill into warm dry jars. Cover with jam covers and leave for 24 hours.
8. Label and store in a cool, dark, airy place.

Clear Grapefruit Marmalade

2 grapefruit	2·28 litres/4 pints water
4 lemons	1·5 kilos/3lb sugar

1. Wash the grapefruit and lemons. Cut in half and squeeze out the juice.
2. Strain the juice into a bowl with the water.

3. Shred or chop the peel and pith of both lemons and grapefruit. Put them in a loose muslin bag with the pips of the lemons only.
4. Put the bag in the pan of juice and water. Allow to soak overnight.
5. Transfer the juice and muslin bag to a preserving pan or saucepan and boil until the skins in the bag are tender ($1\frac{1}{2}$–2 hours) and the liquid in the pan has reduced by half.
6. Warm the sugar.
7. Remove the muslin bag, squeezing it to extract all the juice before discarding.
8. Add the warmed sugar, stir and bring to the boil.
9. Boil rapidly for 8–10 minutes and test for setting.
10. Pour the marmalade into warm, dry jars and cover. Leave undisturbed for 24 hours. Store in a dark, dry place.

Note: If shreds of rind are wanted in the jelly pare the rind from the pith and shred it separately. Add to the boiling liquid.

Redcurrant Jelly

Redcurrants   450g/1lb sugar to each 570ml/
                                1 pint of juice extracted

1. Place the washed fruit in a stone or earthenware pot, cover and place in a moderate oven, 180°C/350°F, gas mark 4. If your jar or pot is glass rather than pottery stand it in a bain-marie before placing in the oven.
2. Cook until the fruit is tender and the juice has run from it (about 1 hour). Mash the fruit with a fork 3 or 4 times during the cooking process.
3. Turn into a scalded muslin or jelly bag and allow to drain overnight.
4. Measure the juice and mix with 450g/1lb sugar to each 570ml/1 pint of juice.

5. Dissolve over a gentle heat and then boil rapidly until setting point is reached (about 5 minutes).
6. Pour into warm, dry jars.
7. Cover and tie down. Label and store.

Note: This jelly, made without the addition of water, gives a strong concentrated fruit flavour, but yields comparatively little jelly. It is not worth doing with less than 1·35 kilos/3lb fruit. The more usual method is to simmer the fruit in water, then proceed from 3.

Lemon Curd

2 large lemons	225g/½lb granulated sugar
85g/3oz butter	3 eggs

1. Grate the rind of the lemons on the finest gauge on the grater, taking care to grate rind only, not pith.
2. Squeeze the juice from the lemons.
3. Put the rind, juice, butter, sugar and lightly beaten eggs into a heavy saucepan or double-boiler and heat gently, stirring all the time until the mixture is thick.
4. Strain into a bowl and allow to cool.

Note: This curd will keep in the refrigerator for about three weeks.

BOTTLING FRUIT

(See also *Lemonade Bottling*, page 494)

The preservation of food by bottling works on the principle of destruction (by heat) of all micro-organisms present in the fruit or syrup. Because a partial vacuum is created in the jar (by expelling air during processing) a tight seal is formed between lid and jar, keeping the sterilized contents uncontaminated.

The principle of canning is similar. But cans need a special machine to seal them.

The procedure described here applies to the bottling of fruit only. Vegetables and meat (because they contain little or no acid, and therefore are likely to harbour bacteria) need considerably longer processing at higher temperatures to become safe. This lengthy heating tends to spoil the texture and flavour of the vegetables or meat. In general, bottling meat and vegetables is not worth the effort, time and risks involved. But fruit and tomatoes, because they are fairly acid, will not contain bacteria; and the relatively harmless yeasts and moulds are more easily destroyed.

PREPARING THE FRUIT

Fruit can be bottled raw or cooked. If the fruit is cooked the processing time need only be long enough for sterilization, not for tenderizing the fruit. If raw, the fruit is cooked and sterilized at the same time, and may need longer processing. Some fruits, which cook to a pulp easily, such as berries and cooking apples, are generally processed from raw as the minimum time at great heat is the objective. Other fruits such as pears and peaches, which require an uncertain time to soften, are frequently pre-cooked as it is then possible to tell if they are tender. Pre-cooking has a further advantage. Once the fruit is cooked and softened, more of it can be packed into the jars. Also, it will not rise up in the jar when sterilized. Fruit bottled from raw frequently rises. This does not matter but means the expensive jars contain more syrup and less fruit. The only certain way to prevent fruit rising is to bottle it in a very light syrup, which is not always desirable. Once the jars are sealed testing is of course impossible. A few points are worth remembering:

a. Make sure the bottling jars are not cracked and the tops are in good condition. Kilner jars must have new lids each year, and Parfait jars new washers. Screw bands or metal clips should work properly and jars should be clean.
b. Make the sugar syrup before peeling the fruit.

c. Choose perfect, not over-ripe fruit.

d. If fruit needs cutting or peeling use a stainless steel knife.

e. If it is likely to discolour (apples or pears) drop the pieces into cold water containing a teaspoon of ascorbic acid (vitamin C powder or a fizzy Redoxon tablet will do) until you are ready to process them.

f. Pack the fruit (cooked or raw) up to the necks of the jars.

JARS

Kilner jars come with a metal lid with a rubber band incorporated in it. The lid is kept in place by a metal screw-band. The lid must not be re-used as it will not give a good seal twice, and the rubber is perishable. Kilner jars are closed loosely before processing, and only tightened fully when they come *out* of the sterilizer or saucepan, while still hot. As the hot air inside cools it will contract, pulling the lid on tightly as it does so. The pressure of the partial vacuum will cause the lid (which starts off convex in shape) to 'pop' into a concave position. The sound of this can be alarming but it simply means that a vacuum seal has been achieved.

Parfait jars are similar to Kilner jars but have glass lids with rubber washers round them. The lid is held in place by a metal gimp or clip. It is clipped shut *before* processing. There is sufficient spring in the gimp to allow the escape of steam during heating. The lid tightens automatically as the jar cools after processing.

PROCESSING THE FRUIT

Processing (or sterilizing) of the fruit can be done in the following ways:

a. In a sterilizer (sometimes called a pressure canner). This is a purpose-made machine like a large pressure cooker. It is reliable and easy to use, but by no means essential. Follow the manufacturer's instructions.

b. *In a pressure cooker*, which works like a sterilizer but holds fewer jars and will not hold tall ones. About 2·5cm/1in of water in the bottom is sufficient as no evaporation will take place: the process is very quick, and the jars and fruit sterilize in the steam. Wedge the jars with cloths to stop them rattling. Allow the pressure to fall before opening the cooker. Consult the maker's manual.

c. *In a deep saucepan or bath of boiling water*. Stand the jars in the container and wedge them with cloths to stop them rattling or cracking. Fill with hot water right over the tops of the jars, or at least up to their necks. Cover as best you can with lid or foil and tea-towels to keep in the steam. (See table on pages 455–9.)

Note I: Processing in the oven is not recommended. The temperatures cannot be reliably checked and the jars sometimes crack or explode, or boil over.

Note II: If the fruit has been cooked in an open pan with its syrup, it is possible to get a good seal by closing the jar as soon as the hot fruit and boiling syrup are in it, without further sterilization, but the method is less reliable.

TESTING FOR SEALING

After processing, the jars should be lifted on to a board. Kilner jars should be screwed up tight. Jars should be left undisturbed for 24 hours. They must then be tested for sealing. Remove the metal bands on the Kilner jars, or loosen the clips on the Parfait jars. It should be possible to lift the jars by the lids, without breaking the seal. If the lid of a jar comes off the jar must be reprocessed with a new washer (Parfait jars) or lid (Kilner jars) or the contents must be eaten within a day or two.

STORING

Wipe the jars with a damp clean cloth, label them with the date of bottling, and store in a dark place. They will keep for at least 18 months, probably for many years.

BOTTLING FRUITS AND TOMATOES

Fruits are usually bottled in sugar syrup, made by dissolving sugar in water. The more sugar the heavier the syrup. Equal measures (using a cup, a jug, or any container) of sugar and water heated together will give a very thick syrup suitable for peaches or sour plums, half as much sugar as water will give a light thin syrup. Use whatever kind of syrup you like, or you think the fruit calls for. The sugar is not necessary as a preservative but for flavour. Tomatoes are bottled in salted water.

PROCESSING

Fruit	Preparation	Pre-cook or pack raw?	Syrup	Length of time in deep saucepan or boiling water bath (at rolling boil)	Length of time in pressure cooker or canner (at 5lb pressure)
Whole dessert apples	Peel, core, quarter. Keep in water containing a teaspoon of vitamin C powder to prevent discoloration until ready.	Poach in thin syrup until tender.	Pack in hot jars with hot syrup.	1 kilo/2lb jars for 10 minutes. 2 kilos/4lb jars for 15 minutes.	1 kilo/2lb jars for 1 minute. 2 kilos/4lb jars for 2 minutes. Leave undisturbed until pressure is reduced to normal.

Fruit	Preparation	Pre-cook or pack raw?	Syrup	Length of time in deep saucepan or boiling water bath (at rolling boil)	Length of time in pressure cooker or canner (at 5lb pressure)
Slices of cooking apple	Peel and slice. Keep in water containing a teaspoon of vitamin C powder to prevent discoloration until ready.	Pack raw slices tightly in jars. Fill up to neck of jars.	Cover with hot thin syrup.	1 kilo/2lb jars for 20 minutes. 2 kilos/4lb jars for 30 minutes.	1 kilo/2lb jars for 1 minute. 2 kilos/4lb jars for 2 minutes. Leave undisturbed until pressure is reduced to normal.
Soft berries and currants	Wash only if sandy or muddy. Pick over carefully.	Pack raw, to neck of jars, liberally sprinkle with sugar and leave to stand overnight.	Do not add any more liquid. The juice will be enough.	1 kilo/2lb jars for 10 minutes. 2 kilos/4lb jars for 15 minutes.	1 kilo/2lb jars for 1 minute. 2 kilos/4lb jars for 2 minutes. Leave undisturbed until pressure is reduced to normal.

Cherries	Wash, de-stalk and prick each cherry with a needle (to prevent bursting).	Pack raw, shaking down firmly, to neck of jars.	Cover with hot heavy syrup for sour cherries; hot medium syrup for sweet ones.	1 kilo/2lb jars for 20 minutes. 2 kilos/4lb jars for 30 minutes.	1 kilo/2lb jars for 1 minute. 2 kilos/4lb jars for 2 minutes. Leave undisturbed until pressure is reduced to normal.
Gooseberries Rhubarb	Wash and prepare as for stewing.	Pack raw, filling jars to neck.	Cover with hot thick syrup.	1 kilo/2lb jars for 10 minutes. 2 kilos/4lb jars for 15 minutes.	1 kilo/2lb jars for 1 minute. 2 kilos/4lb jars for 2 minutes. Leave undisturbed until pressure is reduced to normal.
Peaches (halved)	Boil in water for 10 seconds, or until the skin will come off easily. Peel, halve and stone.	Pack raw, filling jars to neck.	Cover with hot medium or heavy syrup.	1 kilo/2lb jars for 25 minutes. 2 kilos/4lb jars for 30 minutes.	1 kilo/2lb jars for 2 minutes. 2 kilos/4lb jars for 3 minutes. Leave undisturbed until pressure is reduced to normal.

Fruit	Preparation	Pre-cook or pack raw?	Syrup	Length of time in deep saucepan or boiling water bath (at rolling boil)	Length of time in pressure cooker or canner (at 5lb pressure)
Peaches (sliced)	Peel as above and slice.			1 kilo/2lb jars for 20 minutes. 2 kilos/4lb jars for 25 minutes.	1 kilo/2lb jars for 1 minute. 2 kilos/4lb jars for 2 minutes. Leave undisturbed until pressure is reduced to normal.
Ripe pears	Peel, half and core.	Pack raw, filling jars to neck.	Cover with hot medium syrup.	1 kilo/2lb jars for 30 minutes. 2 kilos/4lb jars for 40 minutes.	1 kilo/2lb jars for 3 minutes. 2 kilos/4lb jars for 4 minutes. Leave undisturbed until pressure is reduced to normal.

Whole hard pears	Peel. Keep in water containing a teaspoon of vitamin C powder to prevent discoloration until ready.	Poach in medium syrup until tender.	Pack in hot jars with hot syrup.	1 kilo/2lb jars for 10 minutes. 2 kilos/4lb jars for 15 minutes.	1 kilo/2lb jars for 1 minute. 2 kilos/4lb jars for 2 minutes. Leave undisturbed until pressure is reduced to normal.
Plums	Wash, de-stalk and prick with large needle. Halve and remove stones if of the 'free stone' type.	Pack raw, filling jars to neck.	Cover with hot medium syrup.	1 kilo/2lb jars for 20 minutes. 2 kilos/4lb jars for 25 minutes.	1 kilo/2lb jars for 1 minute. 2 kilos/4lb jars for 2 minutes. Leave undisturbed until pressure is reduced to normal.
Tomatoes	Dip into boiling water for 5 seconds. Skin and quarter or slice.	Pack raw, with a sprinkling of salt and sugar between layers, filling jars to neck.	Do not add any more liquid. The juice will be enough.	1 kilo/2lb jars for 35 minutes. 2 kilos/4lb jars for 40 minutes.	1 kilo/2lb jars for 3 minutes. 2 kilos/4lb jars for 4 minutes. Leave undisturbed until pressure is reduced to normal.

Bottled Apples

340g/¾lb sugar   12 apples
1 litre/2 pints water

1. Prepare the sugar syrup: dissolve the sugar in 1 litre/2 pints of water over a gentle heat and when completely dissolved boil rapidly for 2–3 minutes.
2. Peel and slice the apples.
3. Pack tightly into 1 kilo/2lb jars.
4. Pour over the hot syrup.
5. Cover with the lids (not screwed too tight if Kilner jars) and place in the hot water bath. Cover with boiling water.
6. Boil steadily for 20 minutes.
7. Remove the jars and (if Kilner jars) seal firmly.
8. Leave for 24 hours and test for sealing.

Spiced Pears

560g/1¼lb sugar   15g/½oz stick cinnamon
0·5 litre/¾ pint white malt   5 cloves
  vinegar *or* white wine   2 dried chillies (optional)
6 small whole pears, peeled   2 pieces stem ginger, diced

1. Heat the sugar with the vinegar over gentle heat and when completely dissolved, bring to the boil.
2. Add the prepared pears, the spices and the ginger.
3. Simmer gently until the pears are tender but not broken (about 35 minutes).
4. Remove the pears with a draining spoon and pack into a preserving jar.
5. If the syrup is rather thin boil it rapidly until fairly thick and tacky.
6. Pour over the pears, and add the spices and ginger.
7. Put on the lid (if using a Kilner jar do not tighten). Process in a boiling water bath for 10 minutes.

8. Lift out and (if using a Kilner jar) tighten the lid.
9. Leave for 24 hours, then test for sealing.

Bottled Raspberries

900g/2lb raspberries   340g/¾lb granulated sugar

1. Pick over the fruit but do not wash it.
2. Pack into 1 kilo/2lb jars, sprinkling with dry sugar between the layers. Shake the jars to settle the fruit. Leave overnight.
3. Top up to absolutely full with more fruit and sugar.
4. Cover with the lids (not screwed too tightly if Kilner jars). Process in a boiling water bath for 10 minutes.
5. Lift out of the water and tighten the lids if using Kilner jars.
6. Leave for 24 hours, then test for sealing.

PICKLES

Note: Brass, old-fashioned iron or copper preserving pans or saucepans should not be used in the preparation of foods containing vinegar. The acid reacts with the metal, spoiling both colour and flavour of the food, and sometimes rendering it mildly poisonous.

Pickles are foods, usually vegetables or fruit, preserved in vinegar. Fruit for pickles is generally cooked in sugared vinegar, and stored in this sweetened vinegar syrup. Vegetables are usually, but not always, pickled raw, and are generally salted in dry salt, or steeped in brine before being immersed in the vinegar. This salting is done to draw moisture out of the food. If the salting is omitted the juices from the vegetables would leak into the vinegar during storage and so dilute it and impair its keeping quality.

Salt also has preservative powers, and its penetration into the food must help to prevent it 'going bad', but the main preservative in pickles is vinegar, which prevents the growth of bacteria.

The best salt is pure rock salt or crushed block salt. Pure sea salt is good too, but very expensive. Table salt has additives which make it conveniently free-flowing, but which may cause the pickle to go cloudy.

Brining

Brine is a solution of salt in water, and is suitable for the steeping of most vegetables for pickling.

450g/½lb pure salt (not table salt)   3 litres/4 pints water

1. Heat the salt and water slowly together until the salt has dissolved.
2. Allow to cool.
3. Prepare (peel, cut up etc.) the vegetables to be pickled, put them into a bowl and pour over the cold brine. Put a plate on top to keep the food submerged.
4. After 24 hours (usually, but check individual recipes) drain well, pat dry and pack into clean jars ready for pickling.

Dry-Salting

This is suitable for 'wet' vegetables such as marrow and cucumber.

110g/¼lb dry pure salt (not table salt) is needed for each 1 kilo/2lb prepared vegetables

1. Prepare (peel, cut up etc.) the vegetables. If they are tough (like onions or shallots) pierce them deeply with a needle.
2. Put them in a bowl, sprinkling each layer liberally with salt. Cover and keep cool for 24 hours.

3. Tip off all the liquid, rinse the vegetables in cold water and pat dry in a clean cloth.
4. Pack into clean jars ready for pickling.

THE VINEGAR

Pickling vinegar should be strong, containing at least 5 per cent acetic acid. Most brand vinegars contain sufficient acid, but home-made vinegars or draught vinegars will not do. Brown malt vinegar is the best vinegar for flavour, especially if the pickle is to be highly spiced, or is made from strong-tasting foods. White vinegar has less flavour, but obviously gives a clearer pickle. Wine vinegar is suitable for delicate mild-tasting foods. Commercial cider vinegar is good too. The vinegar may be spiced and flavoured according to taste by the addition of hot spices such as cayenne, ginger or chillies, or aromatic spices such as cardamon seeds, cloves or nutmeg. Whole spices are best as they can be easily removed, and will not leave the vinegar murky. Ready-spiced pickling vinegar may also be bought.

Basic Spiced Vinegar for Pickles

1·14 litres/2 pints malt vinegar
8g/¼oz blades of mace
8g/¼oz cinnamon stick
8g/¼oz allspice berries
8g/¼oz black peppercorns

8g/¼oz mustard seed
4 whole cloves
1 chilli
15g/½oz sliced root ginger

1. Put everything into a large saucepan (not an unlined copper or brass or iron one) and heat gently, covered tightly, until on the point of simmering. Remove from heat.
2. Leave for 3 hours, then strain through muslin, a jelly bag or J-cloth. The vinegar is now ready for use.

THE JARS AND LIDS

Any wide-necked jar is suitable for pickles provided it has a good air-tight lid. This is not so much to keep bacteria out (the vinegar will see to that) but to prevent the vinegar evaporating. Cork stoppers, glass stoppers, or stone lids are suitable. Raw metal corrodes if allowed in contact with vinegar, so metal screw-tops must be protected by waxed cardboard, plastic film, or thick greaseproof paper. Many jars from commercial products are suitable as their lids are sprayed with a coat of paint or a thin film of plastic. Preserving jars with sealing lids are suitable but not necessary. Paper jam covers do not make sturdy enough seals. They are unsuitable for liquids and anyway might allow the evaporation of the vinegar.

Stoppers that do not fit perfectly can be sealed tight with a little melted paraffin wax.

Sterilization of the jars for pickles is not normally considered necessary as the vinegar will prevent the growth of micro-organisms.

PACKING THE JARS

1. Pack the vegetables or fruit, tightly but without bruising, in the clean jars.
2. Top up with the vinegar (hot or cold according to the recipe). Cover the food by at least 1cm/$\frac{1}{2}$in to allow for evaporation. If the jars have metal lids (even protected as described above) leave a little headroom. Otherwise fill to the brim.
3. Cover the jar (and seal it with paraffin wax if necessary) at once.
4. Store for six months, if possible, before using.

Pickled Shallots or Small Onions

An example of a raw pickle, salted in brine.

Small, even-sized onions, *or*   Brine (page 462)
   shallots   Pickling vinegar (page 463)

1. Scald the onions to make peeling them easier. Peel them. Prick deeply all over with a needle or skewer.
2. Put the onions or shallots in a bowl and cover with brine. Leave for 48 hours.
3. Drain thoroughly and pat dry with a clean cloth.
4. Pack tightly, but without bruising, into clean jars.
5. Cover well with the cold pickling vinegar.
6. Seal and store for six months before eating.

Pickled Beetroot

An example of a cooked pickle, not given preliminary salting.

Small, even-sized beetroots   Pickling vinegar (page 463)
Pure salt

1. Cook the beetroots, unpeeled, in boiling, heavily salted water (1 tablespoon to 1·1 litres/2 pints) until tender ($1\frac{1}{2}$–2 hours).
2. Drain and allow to cool. Skin them.
3. Pack, without bruising, into jars.
4. Cover well with cold pickling vinegar.
5. Add a level teaspoon pure salt to each 1 kilo/2lb jar.
6. Seal and store.

Note: If a milder pickle is wanted the vinegar may be diluted by an equal amount of water. But if this is done the beetroot must be packed in a preserving (Kilner or Parfait) jar, and must be given a sterilization treatment in a boiling water bath for 30 minutes, or in a pressure cooker or canner for 2 minutes (see page 464).

Gooseberry Pickle

A pickle in which the fruit is cooked in vinegar and sugar, and stored packed in the cooking liquid.

450g/1lb barely ripe gooseberries
110g/¼lb demerara sugar
¼ teaspoon salt
570ml/1 pint white wine vinegar

8g/¼oz mustard seed, bruised
3 garlic cloves, crushed
170g/6oz stoned raisins
pinch of cayenne

1. Top and tail the gooseberries.
2. Place in a pan with the sugar, salt and half the vinegar. Stir over a gentle heat until the sugar dissolves.
3. Bring to the boil and simmer until the gooseberries are tender.
4. Pour the hot gooseberries over the mustard seed, garlic, raisins and cayenne. Add the remaining vinegar and stir.
5. Pour into hot, dry jars.
6. Seal and store.

Dill Cucumber Pickle

An example of a pickle dry-salted and packed in sweet spiced vinegar.

900g/2lb cucumbers
Pure salt
Pickling vinegar (page 463)
1 fresh dill head, *or* 1 tablespoon dill seeds

2 teaspoons mustard seed
2 garlic cloves, sliced
170g/6oz granulated *or* preserving sugar

1. If the cucumbers are small enough to leave whole, prick them all over with a needle. If large cut them into chunks, without peeling, and put into a bowl, sprinkling each layer liberally with salt. Leave for 24 hours.
2. Put the spiced vinegar (about 1 litre/1¾ pints) into a saucepan

and add the dill, mustard seed, garlic and sugar. Bring slowly to the boil, then cool.

3. Rinse the cucumber and pat dry with a clean cloth.
4. Pack the cucumber into jars. Cover with the cooled vinegar, adding the flavourings if liked.
5. Seal and store.

CHUTNEYS

Chutneys are the easiest preserves to make. They are mixtures, always sweet and sour, somewhere between a pickle and a jam. They are generally made of fruit (or sometimes soft vegetables such as tomato or marrow), with vinegar, onion and spices.

Both sugar and salt, themselves preservatives, are present in chutneys, but they are there for flavour more than for their keeping powers. As with jams, the boiling of the ingredients destroys micro-organisms, but with chutneys obtaining a set is not necessary – like pickles, they depend on vinegar for their keeping qualities.

Fruit and vegetables for chutneys should be sliced or cut small enough to be lifted with a teaspoon, but not so small as to be unidentifiable in the chutney.

As the ingredients are seldom used whole, damaged or bruised fruit, with the imperfect bits removed, can be used.

Chutneys improve with keeping. They can generally be eaten after two months (before this their taste is harsh) but are at their best between six months and two years.

If the chutney is to be kept for more than six months a more certain seal than a jam cover is advisable. See the notes for jars and lids for pickles on page 464.

BASIC PROCEDURE FOR CHUTNEY

1. Prepare the ingredients: wash fruit and vegetables, peel where necessary, cut up etc. Wash dried fruit if bought loose. Chop or mince onions. Use a stainless steel fruit knife for fruit or vegetables liable to discolour.
2. Put all ingredients, except sugar and vinegar, into a saucepan (*not an unlined copper, brass or old-fashioned iron one:* see note on page 461). The spices should be tied in a muslin bag if they are to be removed later.
3. Add enough to the vinegar to easily cover the other ingredients.
4. Cook slowly, covered or not, until the fruit or vegetables are soft, and most of the liquid has evaporated.
5. Add the sugar and the rest of the vinegar and stir until the sugar has dissolved.
6. Boil to the consistency of jam, thick and syrupy.
7. Put into clean, hot jars. Cover as for jam if to be eaten within six months. Use non-metal lids or stoppers if to be kept longer.

Note: In recipes for chutneys that do not require prolonged cooking to soften the ingredients (e.g. apricot and orange chutney, page 469) the sugar and vinegar may be added with the other ingredients – the whole being boiled together.

Green Tomato and Apple Chutney

1·35 kilos/3lb green tomatoes
900g/2lb apples (any kind)
2 large onions, chopped
110g/¼lb sultanas
1 teaspoon salt
1 teaspoon ground ginger
½ teaspoon ground nutmeg
½ teaspoon white pepper
Pinch of allspice
860ml/1½ pints vinegar
340g/¾lb granulated *or* preserving sugar

1. Chop the tomatoes. Peel and chop the apples.
2. Put everything except the sugar and a cup of the vinegar into a saucepan and simmer gently, giving an occasional stir, for 1½ hours or until the ingredients are soft and the liquid almost gone.
3. Add the rest of the vinegar and the sugar, and stir slowly until the sugar has dissolved.
4. Boil fast, stirring, until thick.
5. Pour into hot, dry jars. If to be eaten within six months, cover as for jam. If to be kept longer use non-metal lids or stoppers.

Apricot and Orange Chutney

4 oranges
900g/2lb apricots (weight when stoned)
1 onion, thinly sliced
225g/½lb sultanas
450g/1lb demerara sugar
170g/6oz preserving sugar, chopped
2 teaspoons rock salt
570ml/1 pint cider vinegar
1 tablespoon mustard seed
1 teaspoon turmeric

1. Boil the oranges whole for 5 minutes. Pare the skin with a sharp knife, removing all pith left on the back.
2. Shred the rind into thin needleshreds.
3. Peel the oranges and discard all the pith. Chop up the flesh.
4. Place the orange rind and flesh together with all the other ingredients in a large pan and simmer until the fruit is soft and pulpy and the mixture thick and syrupy.
5. Pour immediately into warm, dry jars and cover with jam covers if to be eaten within a few months, or more securely with non-metal lids or stoppers if to be kept longer.

9
Breakfast

Framed Eggs

4 large slices of white bread   Butter
Oil for frying   2 large tomatoes
4 large flat mushrooms   4 eggs

1. With a large round biscuit cutter remove the middle from the bread slices. Do not throw away the rest of the bread.
2. Fry the rounds in oil until brown on both sides.
3. Dot the mushrooms with butter and grill them.
4. Cut the tomatoes in half; grill them until just cooked.
5. Set each mushroom on a round of fried bread and put half a tomato on top. Keep warm.
6. Now fry the bread frames (the pieces left after the middle was removed from the bread slices) on one side.
7. Turn them over and break an egg into the middle of each.
8. Fry until the whites are set, spooning over some of the hot fat to help the process.
9. Serve each framed egg with the mushroom and tomato on fried bread.

Serves 4

Poached Eggs on Toast

Salt and vinegar   4 very fresh cold eggs
4 slices fresh toast, buttered

1. Fill a large saucepan with water until 7·5cm/3in deep. Add salt and 1 tablespoon vinegar and bring to simmering point.
2. Crack an egg on the side of the pan and, holding the shell as near to the water as possible, drop the egg in.
3. Raise the temperature so that the water bubbles gently.
4. With a perforated spoon, draw the egg white close to the yolk.
5. Poach each egg for 2 or 3 minutes.
6. Lift out with the perforated spoon, drain on absorbent paper and, if the egg whites are very ragged at the edges, trim them.
7. Place each egg on a piece of toast and sprinkle with salt and pepper. Serve immediately.

Serves 4

Jugged Kippers

4 kippers   Freshly ground black pepper
Butter

1. Place the kippers, tail up, in a tall stoneware jug. Pour over enough boiling water to cover the kippers and leave to stand for 5–10 minutes.
2. Serve immediately on a warm dish with a knob of butter and plenty of pepper.

Note: This is a simple labour-saving method of cooking kippers.

Serves 4

Kedgeree

55g/2oz butter
140g/5oz long-grain rice, boiled
  (weighed before cooking)
340g/¾lb smoked haddock
  fillet, cooked, skinned and
  boned *or* cooked fresh
  salmon if preferred

3 hardboiled eggs, coarsely
  chopped
Salt, pepper and cayenne

1. Melt the butter in a large shallow pan and add everything else.
2. Stir gently until very hot.

Note: If making large quantities, heat in the oven instead of on the top. Kedgeree will not spoil in a low oven (130°C/250°F, gas mark 1). Stir occasionally to prevent the sides getting hot before the middle.

Serves 4

Muesli

Named after Bircher Muesli, a Swiss doctor and health fanatic, this should contain nothing but natural ingredients, and no refined cereals. It usually consists of flaked oats, crushed or flaked wheat (including the bran and wheatgerm) and can include other cereals too. If cracked wheat or maize is included it needs to be soaked overnight before eating. Instant porridge oats or flaked oats can be eaten without soaking. Almost any fresh fruit can be added to muesli and it is served with yoghurt, milk or cream (or mixture of any or all of these). If muesli is sweetened this should be done with raw unrefined brown sugar or honey.

To make a family supply of Muesli mix together:

450g/1lb instant porridge oats
55g/2oz dried apricots, chopped
55g/2oz sultanas
110g/¼lb dried apple flakes
55g/2oz hazelnuts, chopped
55g/2oz bran
30g/1oz flaked almonds
110g/¼lb 'honey crunch' *or* 'granola' *or* other toasted cereal (optional, but improves the texture)
30g/1oz unrefined brown sugar

Porridge

1·14 litres/2 pints water
110g/¼lb medium oatmeal
1 good teaspoon salt

1. Boil the water in a saucepan and add the salt.
2. Sprinkle in the oatmeal, keeping the water on the boil and stirring all the time.
3. Simmer for 30 minutes, stirring occasionally. If necessary add a little more water.

Note: Porridge keeps for an hour or so in a cool oven if covered with a lid, but should not be made too far in advance. Traditionall it is served with salt in Scotland, but in the south milk and sugar are added. Brown sugar and cream are wonderful.

Serves 4

10
Party Savouries,
Petits Fours and Drinks

PARTY SAVOURIES

Pumpernickel with Salami

450g/1lb salami, skinned and   Butter
   thinly sliced
About 30 slices of pumpernickel
   bread

1. Get the delicatessen to skin and slice the salami on their machine as thinly as they can.
2. Cut each slice of pumpernickel into two, or cut two rounds out of it with a pastry cutter.
3. Butter and cover with slices of salami.

Makes 60 *canapés*

Curried Eggs

10 hardboiled eggs   1 tablespoon thick mayonnaise
1 tablespoon butter   (page 266)
1 teaspoon mild curry powder   Sliced gherkin *or* sultanas for
                                     garnish

1. Trim the pointed end from each egg and cut in half across the middle parallel to the trimmed end.
2. Remove and sieve the yolks.
3. Melt the butter and add the curry powder; cook for 1 minute and add to the egg yolks. Stir in the mayonnaise.
4. Stand the egg whites on the flat ends and fill the egg mixture into them using a forcing bag or spoon.
5. Decorate with a piece of sliced gherkin or a sultana.

Note: Each egg will yield three curried eggs if the instructions for cutting and filling them, given in the next recipe, are followed.

Makes 20

Caviar Eggs

10 hardboiled eggs
1 tablespoon soured cream
Pepper

1 tablespoon mock caviar
(Danish lumpfish roe)

1. Trim the pointed end from each egg. Cut the eggs across in three (see diagram).

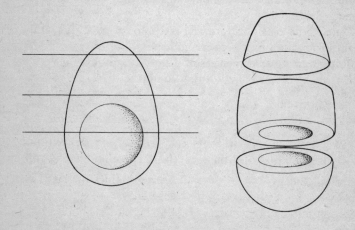

2. Remove the yolks and mash or sieve them until smooth. Add enough sour cream to make a soft but not sloppy paste. Season with pepper.
3. Fill the egg white 'cups' with the mixture, using a forcing bag or spoon, and, treating the slices of egg white as a base, simply pipe a small round of mixture on to them.
4. Decorate the top of the stuffed eggs with the caviar.

Makes 30

Smoked Salmon Catherine Wheels

1 very large square-edged loaf of brown bread
Butter, well softened

450g/1lb thinly sliced smoked salmon
Freshly ground black pepper
Lemon juice

1. Put the loaf of bread on a board and carefully cut off the top crust all along the length of the loaf.
2. Butter the top of the bread, being careful not to crumble it.
3. Now cut as thin a horizontal slice as you can.
4. Again butter the loaf and cut off the next slice and so on through the loaf. You should end up with about 10 or 12 long slices.
5. Cut off the crusts and lay smoked salmon on all the slices. Sprinkle with black pepper and lemon juice.
6. Now, starting at one end, roll them up carefully.
7. Cut each roll into about 8 thin rounds.

Note I: Unravelling can be prevented if the rolls are wrapped in foil and refrigerated for a few hours before slicing.

Note II: For larger rolls or 'Catherine wheels' two slices of bread may be used: roll up one, then roll the next round the first roll.

Makes about 80

Smoked Salmon Triangles

Butter   Pepper
20 slices brown bread   450g/1lb smoked salmon

1. Butter the bread, sprinkle with pepper and lay the smoked
    salmon slices carefully on top.
2. Cut off the crusts and cut each slice into four triangles.

Makes 80

Stuffed Dates

110g/¼lb nibbed almonds   340g/¾lb cream cheese
60 dates (about 2 boxes)

1. Brown the almonds under the grill or in a hot oven and allow
    to cool.
2. Cut the dates open lengthwise. Replace each stone with a
    teaspoon of cream cheese.
3. Slightly close the dates, leaving the cream cheese showing.
    Dip the cheese into the nuts.

Note: Dried dates are good. Fresh ones are wonderful.

Makes 60

Prawn Ritz

450g/1lb frozen peeled prawns   4 tablespoons very thick
Butter   mayonnaise (page 266)
60 Ritz crackers (about 1   Paprika
   packet) *or* small savoury
   biscuits

1. Thaw the prawns.
2. Butter the crackers well.
3. Squeeze out any moisture from the prawns – they should be quite dry.
4. Mix the prawns with the mayonnaise and spoon a blob on to each biscuit. Sprinkle with paprika.

Makes 60

Celery and Cream Cheese

10 sticks celery	Chives, finely chopped
340g/¾lb cream cheese	Pepper and salt

1. Wash and scrub the celery, and cut into 5cm/2in lengths. If the sticks are very wide they should be split into two.
2. Cream the cheese and add the chives, pepper and salt.
3. Using a forcing bag fitted with a fluted nozzle pipe the cheese into the hollow of the celery sticks. It may be necessary to trim the underside of each celery stick to prevent it rolling over when on a plate.

Makes about 50

Pâté on Baked Bread

15 large slices white bread	Slices of black olive for
Butter	decoration
450g/1lb smooth pâté (fish *or* meat) beaten until soft	

1. With a small round cutter cut four rounds out of each slice of bread.
2. Bake these in a cool oven until crisp and dry like rusks.

3. When cool spread well with butter and pipe a swirl of pâté on to each.
4. Decorate with a slice of olive.

Makes about 60

Chicken Livers Wrapped in Bacon

450g/1lb chicken livers   (Wooden cocktail sticks)
60 small slices streaky bacon

1. Set the oven to 220°C/425°F, gas mark 7.
2. Trim and discard the discoloured part from the livers.
3. Roll small pieces of liver in bacon and lay them side by side in a roasting pan, fairly tightly packed to prevent unravelling.
4. Bake for about 15 minutes or until they are just beginning to go brown on top. Drain well.
5. Stick a cocktail stick into each roll. They are now ready to serve, but if they are to be reheated, remove them from the roasting pan and keep in a cool place until needed. If the cocktail sticks are stuck in before reheating, make sure they are wood and not plastic. Reheat for 10 minutes.

Makes about 60

Prawn Bouchées

60 bouchée cases, cooked *or*   Beaten egg
   450g/1lb flour-quantity puff
   pastry (frozen is fine)

For the filling:
55g/2oz butter
½ onion, finely chopped   560ml/1 pint creamy milk
55g/2oz flour   Salt and pepper
340g/¾lb frozen peeled prawns,
   thawed and well drained

1. Set the oven to 200°C/400°F, gas mark 6.
2. Roll out the pastry to about the thickness of a penny.
3. With a small round pastry cutter stamp it out in rounds.
4. With a slightly smaller cutter or the end of a large piping nozzle mark a circle in the centre of each round, but be careful not to stamp the pastry through.
5. With the beaten egg brush the top of the outer rings only.
6. Bake until very brown and crisp (about 12 minutes). Cool.
7. Melt the butter, add the onion and cook slowly until pale and transparent.
8. Add the flour and cook for a further minute.
9. Stir the milk to make a thick paste. Season with salt and pepper. Simmer for 2 minutes.
10. Add the prawns and bring to the boil, stirring.
11. Fill the hot bouchées with the mixture.

Makes 60

Cocktail Sausages with Mustard Dip

60 chipolata *or* 120 cocktail   (Cocktail sticks)
  sausages (450g/1lb)

For the dip:
Mustard mayonnaise
  (page 481)

1. Set the oven to 200°C/400°F, gas mark 6.
2. Make the chipolata sausages into cocktail size by twisting each sausage into two. After twisting, cut them apart.
3. Put them into a greased roasting pan and bake for 20 minutes or until beginning to brown. The roasting pan should be shaken at intervals to prevent the sausages sticking. They should be stirred around to prevent those in the edge getting browner than those in the middle.

4. Drain well and stick in the cocktail sticks. Serve the dip separately.

Makes 120

Mustard Mayonnaise

French mustard
Mayonnaise (page 266)
Finely chopped onion

Crushed garlic
Chopped mint

Mix together French mustard and mayonnaise in equal quantities and add finely chopped onion, crushed garlic and freshly chopped mint to taste.

Stuffed Artichokes

50 artichoke bottoms (about 6 cans)
450g/1lb crab meat (frozen *or* canned)

290ml/$\frac{1}{2}$ pint thick mayonnaise (page 266)
2 teaspoons lemon juice
Salt, pepper and cayenne

1. Drain the artichoke bottoms and lay them hollow-side-up on a tray.
2. Pick over the crab meat, removing any pieces of hard cartilage. Drain well and mix with the mayonnaise, lemon juice, salt, pepper and cayenne to taste.
3. Fill each artichoke bottom with a spoonful of crab mixture.

Note: Canned artichoke hearts may be more easily available than bottoms. Drain very well and remove a few inside leaves to make room for the filling.

Makes 50

Anchovy Puff Pastry Fingers

225g/½lb flour-quantity rough-
puff pastry (page 371)
40 anchovy fillets (about 1
can)

6 tablespoons milk
Beaten egg

1. Divide the pastry into two and roll each piece thinly to a
   rectangle 30cm × 10cm/12in × 4in. Slide on to baking sheets
   and put in the refrigerator to relax.
2. Soak the anchovies in milk for 15 minutes to remove oil and
   and excess salt. Drain and trim the fillets neatly.
3. Heat the oven to 200°C/400°F, gas mark 6.
4. Brush one piece of pastry with beaten egg, prick with a fork
   and place the anchovy fillets neatly on it. You should be able
   to lay out two neat rows of twenty fillets in each row.
5. Cover with the second piece of pastry and brush again with
   egg wash. Press well together and prick all over with a fork.
6. Bake in the oven for 10–12 minutes until a golden brown.
   Leave to cool on a wire rack.
7. When cold cut the pastry into neat fingers of 5cm × 1cm/
   2in × ½in in such a way that each finger has an anchovy fillet
   sandwiched between it.
8. Warm through before serving.

Makes 40

Asparagus Rolls

15 pieces canned asparagus
Butter

15 slices very fresh brown bread
Pepper and salt

1. Drain the asparagus well on absorbent paper. It should be
   as dry as possible.
2. Butter the bread, season and cut off the crusts.

3. Lay a piece of asparagus along the edge of a slice of bread and roll up.
4. Trim the edges neatly and cut in half. If the slice of bread is very large it will have to be trimmed or the roll will be too thick.

Note: If the bread is not fresh enough to roll easily without cracking, the slices (crusts cut off) can be lightly rolled with a rolling pin before buttering: this makes them easier to roll up. If the rolls are inclined to unravel lay them tightly packed in a covered box in the refrigerator for a few hours (or overnight).

Makes 30

Twisted Cheese Straws

170g/6oz plain flour
Pinch of salt
100g/3½oz butter
45g/1½oz grated Parmesan *or*
  mixed Parmesan and
  Gruyère *or* Cheddar cheese

Salt and pepper
Pinch of cayenne pepper
Pinch of dry English mustard
Beaten egg

1. Set the oven to 190°C/375°F, gas mark 5.
2. Sift the flour into a basin with a pinch of salt. Rub the butter into the flour with your fingertips until the mixture resembles breadcrumbs. Add the grated cheese and seasonings.
3. Bind the mixture together with enough egg to make a stiff dough. Refrigerate for 10 minutes.
4. Line a baking sheet with greaseproof paper. Roll the paste into a rectangle and cut into strips 9cm × 2cm/3½in × ¾in. Twist each strip two to three times like a barley sugar stick. Bake for 8–10 minutes. They should be a biscuit brown.

Makes 50

MISCELLANEOUS

Clarified Butter

Method 1: Put butter in a pan with a cupful of water and heat until the butter is melted and frothy. Allow to cool and set solid, then lift the butter, now clarified, off the top of the liquid.

Method 2: Heat the butter until foaming without allowing it to burn. Pour it through a fine muslin or a double layer of J-cloth

Method 3: Melt butter in a heavy pan and skim off the froth with a perforated spoon.

Note: Clarified butter will act as a 'seal' on pâtés or potted meats, and is useful for frying as it will stand great heat before burning.

Croutons

2 slices bread from an unsliced   Oil for frying
  slightly stale white loaf   Salt

1. Cut the crusts off the bread and cut into small 0·5cm/¼in cubes.
2. Heat the oil until a crumb will sizzle vigorously in it. Fry the bread for about 1 minute or until golden brown.
3. Drain on absorbent paper and sprinkle with salt.

Melba Toast

6 slices white bread

1. Light the grill and set the oven to 150°C/300°F, gas mark 2.
2. Grill the bread on both sides until well browned.
3. While still hot, quickly cut off the crusts and split the bread in half horizontally.
4. Put the toast in the oven and leave until dry and brittle.

Note: Melba toast can be kept for a day or two in an airtight tin but it will lose its flavour if kept longer, and is undoubtedly best straight from the oven.

Walnut Bread

1½ slices brown bread per person

Butter
Chopped walnuts

1. Place a whole loaf in the deep freeze for half an hour. This will stiffen the loaf and make it easier to cut accurately.
2. Using a sharp knife cut off the crust and spread the exposed bread with softened butter.
3. Cut a thin slice and repeat until you have enough slices. Cut off the crusts.
4. Place each slice, butter side down, in a flat dish containing the walnuts, and press down slightly so that the walnuts stick to the butter.
5. Cut each slice in half diagonally.

SNACKS AND SAVOURIES

Welsh Rarebit

110g/¼lb Cheddar cheese
1 teaspoon French mustard
Salt, pepper and cayenne
1 egg, beaten

1 tablespoon beer
2 slices bread
Butter for spreading

1. Heat the grill.
2. Grate the cheese and mix all but one level tablespoonful with the mustard, seasoning, beaten egg and beer.
3. Toast the bread and spread with butter.
4. Spoon the cheese mixture on to the toast and spread it neatly, making sure that all the edges are covered.
5. Sprinkle over the remaining cheese and grill until nicely browned.

Serves 2

Roquefort Toasts

2 slices streaky rindless
    bacon
110g/¼lb Roquefort cheese
1 level tablespoon tomato
    chutney

1 teaspoon Worcestershire
    sauce
1 teaspoon grated onion
4 slices bread, cut into 4
squares

1. Set the oven to 200°C/400°F, gas mark 6.
2. Dice the bacon finely. Fry in a heavy pan until crisp but not brittle. Drain well on absorbent paper and break up into small pieces.

3. Mix the Roquefort, tomato chutney, Worcestershire sauce and onion into a smooth paste.
4. Divide the mixture between the squares of bread and spread it evenly, being sure to cover all the edges.
5. Bake for 5 minutes until crisp and brown.
6. Sprinkle with the fried bacon and serve immediately.

Makes 16

Croque Monsieur

85g/3oz butter
8 slices thin white bread
4 slices ham
4 slices Edam *or* Gruyère
  cheese

Freshly ground black pepper
Fat *or* oil for frying

1. Butter the bread.
2. Make four sandwiches, each with a slice of ham and a slice of cheese inside, seasoned with pepper but not salt. Press well together.
3. Fry in 0·5cm/¼in hot fat until golden brown on both sides, turning the sandwiches over as necessary. Drain well, cut in half, and serve immediately.

Serves 4

Mozzarella in Carozza

Oil for deep frying
Butter
8 slices soft white bread
4 large slices Mozzarella cheese

Salt and pepper
Milk
Beaten egg
Breadcrumbs

1. Heat the deep fat until a crumb will sizzle vigorously in it.
2. Butter the bread and make four rounds of cheese sandwiches,

seasoning well with salt and pepper, and making sure that there is plenty of filling, mostly in the centre of the sandwich.

3. Trim off the crusts and press the edges together firmly. Lay each sandwich for 1–2 minutes each side in a dish of milk. They should be wet but not thoroughly soggy.

4. Pat the bread dry with a piece of absorbent paper or a cloth, then dip each sandwich in beaten egg, covering them well. Dip the edges in the breadcrumbs, then again in more egg, to seal them well.

5. Fry until crisp and brown and serve at once.

Note: The carozzas ('carriages' for the cheese) can also be shallow-fried, turning once to brown the second side.

Sausage Rolls

400g/14oz sausage-meat	225g/½lb flour-quantity
30g/1oz chopped parsley	shortcrust pastry (page 369)
30g/1oz chopped onion	1 egg, beaten
Salt and pepper	

1. Set the oven to 200 C/400 F, gas mark 6.
2. Mix together sausage-meat, parsley, onion and seasonings.
3. Roll out the pastry to a large rectangle about 0·25cm/⅛in thick and cut in half lengthwise.
4. With floured hands roll the meat mixture into two long sausages the same length as the pastry and place one down the centre of each piece.
5. Damp one edge of each strip and bring the pastry over the sausage-meat, pressing the edges together and making sure that the join is underneath the roll.
6. Brush with beaten egg. Cut into 5cm/2in lengths. Using a pair of scissors snip a small V in the top of each sausage roll. (This is to allow steam to escape during cooking. A couple of small diagonal slashes made with a sharp knife will do as well.)
7. Place on a baking sheet and bake for 25–30 minutes.

Makes 12

PETITS FOURS

Marzipan Dates

About 20 dates (fresh *or* dried)
225g/½lb marzipan (page 437)
Green colouring (optional)

1. Split the dates lengthwise almost in half. Take out the stones carefully, making sure that the dates stay whole.
2. Form the marzipan into a long sausage about 0·5cm/¼in diameter. Cut it into lengths about the size of the dates.
3. Place a piece of marzipan in each date and half-close the opening. Place in tiny paper cases.

Note: The marzipan can be coloured pale green by the addition of a few drops of green colouring. Work the colour into the marzipan by kneading with one hand.

Makes 20

Tommies

70g/2½oz caster sugar   140g/5oz plain flour
110g/¼lb butter   Honey
85g/3oz ground hazelnuts   225g/½lb dark chocolate

1. Set the oven to 180°C/350°F, gas mark 4.
2. Cream the sugar and butter together until white.
3. Stir in the hazelnuts and flour.
4. As soon as the mixture becomes a paste wrap and leave it in the refrigerator for 30 minutes.

5. Roll out thinly and cut into 2·5cm/1in rounds with a biscuit cutter or an upturned glass.
6. Place on a baking sheet and bake for 12 minutes. Put on a wire rack to cool.
7. Spread honey on half the biscuits, then sandwich them with the others. Return to the cooling rack.
8. Warm the chocolate on a plate over a pan of hot water until it has melted and there are no lumps.
9. Spoon over the chocolate to cover the biscuits completely.
10. When set (and if there is enough chocolate) fill a small piping bag fitted with a writing nozzle with melted chocolate and pipe a design over the set chocolate. Store in an airtight container.

Makes 20

Marzipan Logs

110g/¼lb caster sugar	1 egg yolk
110g/¼lb icing sugar	2 drops peppermint essence
225g/½lb ground almonds	Few drops green colouring
1 egg	170g/6oz plain chocolate

1. First make the marzipan: sift the icing sugar and caster sugar together in a bowl. Mix with the ground almonds.
2. Mix together the egg, egg yolk, peppermint essence and green colouring.
3. Add the sugar mixture and beat briefly with a wooden spoon. Knead with the hands just enough to give smoothness (overworking will draw the oil out of the almonds, giving too greasy a paste).
4. Shape the paste into thin sausages 1cm/½in in diameter and leave to dry slightly on a wire rack. Meanwhile break the chocolate into a pudding basin, put the basin in a pan of simmering water and melt the chocolate, stirring occasionally. Remove the basin and allow the chocolate to cool until runny but fairly thick.
5. Put the wire rack over a tray to catch any drips of chocolate,

then spoon the melted chocolate over the top and sides of the marzipan and leave to set.

6. When the chocolate has set turn the log over and spoon chocolate (you may have to melt it again slightly) on to the other side.

7. When the chocolate is on the point of setting take a fork and mark lines on the chocolate with the prongs to represent the bark of a log. Cut into 2½cm/1in pieces.

Makes about 30

Coconut Ice

450g/1lb granulated sugar
190ml/⅓ pint milk
170g/6oz desiccated coconut
Peppermint *or* vanilla
  flavouring

2 tablespoons sweetened
  condensed milk
Pink colouring

1. Put the sugar and milk into a pan and place over a low heat until the sugar has melted.

2. Let it boil for about 10 minutes (or until it reaches 125 C/ 240 F) when the mixture will form a soft ball if dropped into cold water.

3. Remove from the heat, add the coconut and a few drops of peppermint or vanilla flavouring. Mix well and pour half of the mixture into a greased tin.

4. Add a few drops of pink colouring to the other half of the mixture and stir well. Pour this over the white half of the mixture in the tin. Leave until it is cold and firm. Cut into small oblong pieces.

Makes 24

Chocolate Fudge

450g/1lb caster sugar
290ml/½ pint water
1 large can condensed milk

30g/1oz butter
110g/¼lb chocolate
Vanilla essence

1. Lightly oil two shallow baking tins.
2. Dissolve the sugar slowly in the water, bring to the boil and add the condensed milk and butter.
3. Boil for a further 30 minutes, stirring occasionally to prevent sticking, or until the mixture leaves the side of the pan.
4. Melt the chocolate and add it to the mixture with a few drops of vanilla essence.
5. Pour into the oiled tins, cut into small squares and leave to set.
6. Cut again and put into an airtight tin or jar for storage.

Makes 16

Truffles

110g/¼lb cake crumbs
55g/2oz caster sugar
55g/2oz cocoa powder
55g/2oz unsalted butter, melted

2 tablespoons rum
225g/½lb plain chocolate
2 tablespoons water
Extra cocoa to finish

1. Place the crumbs, caster sugar and cocoa and stir well together in a mixing bowl.
2. Stir in the butter and rum and mix to a soft but firm paste, shape into balls and leave in the refrigerator until firm.
3. Meanwhile melt the chocolate with the water. Dip the truffles in the melted chocolate and leave on a piece of greaseproof paper.
4. When the truffles are nearly dry, roll them in cocoa powder.

Note: These are best made a few days in advance.

Makes 20

DRINKS

Real Lemonade

2 lemons
55g/2oz lump sugar
570ml/1 pint boiling water

To serve:
Ice cubes
Mint leaves

1. Rub the sugar lumps all over the lemons to extract and absorb the aromatic oils in the rind.
2. Slice the lemons and put them with the sugar in a bowl.
3. Pour over the boiling water and steep for 12 hours. Strain.
4. Serve with ice cubes and mint leaves.

Elderberry Lemonade Concentrate

8 lemons
4·5 litres/8 pints water
4 elderflowers

1·35 kilos/3lb granulated sugar
1 wine glass vinegar (optional)
30g/1oz tartaric acid

To serve:
Water *or* soda water
Ice

Mint leaves

1. Slice the lemons into a spotlessly clean bucket. Boil the water and pour it on to the lemons. Add the elderflowers and stir. Leave until cool enough to put your hand in.

2. Squeeze the lemon slices with your hand to release any remaining juice. Strain the liquid through a jelly bag or cloth into a large saucepan.

3. Add the sugar and bring slowly to the boil, stirring occasionally. Once the sugar has dissolved and the liquid has boiled remove from the heat and stir in the vinegar, if using, and tartaric acid. Pour into clean warm bottles. Keep in a cool place. (It will keep for months in the refrigerator, and for a month in a cool larder. But at room temperature it might ferment in a week or so.) If you have no cool place to keep it, sterilize the bottles as below.

4. To serve, dilute the concentrate with water or soda water to taste and add ice and mint leaves.

Note: Lemonade can be made similarly but without boiling the water. This gives a fresher-tasting drink but does not keep as long and cannot be bottled for long storage as described below. It is advisable to add a preservative such as a Campden tablet or pecto-enzyme powder (both available from shops selling home wine-making equipment) if the drink is to be stored at all.

TO BOTTLE FOR LONG STORAGE

a. First sterilize the lids (screw top lids will do) by submerging in boiling water for 20 minutes.

b. Fill the bottles with lemonade concentrate to within 2·5cm/1in of the rim. Put on the lids, but do not screw them too tight – just turn them until they are no longer loose.

c. Stand the bottles on a folded tea-towel or cloth in the bottom of a deep saucepan, and pack another cloth between them to prevent them rattling against each other or the side of the pan.

d. Fill the saucepan with boiling water, ideally to come to the bottle necks. Cover the whole saucepan and bottles as best you can with a tea-towel and folded foil to keep as much steam in as possible. Simmer for 20 minutes.

e. Remove the coverings and lift the bottles on to a wooden board or table top. Tighten the screw-caps and leave to get stone cold before storing. The lemonade will now keep a year, after which the flavour deteriorates.

INDEX